The Essential Legal Guide to Events

A practical handbook
for event professionals
and their advisors

by David Becker

Dynamic Publishing, 2006

Published by Dynamic Publishing Limited

Copyright © David Becker, 2006

Front cover photographs courtesy of Action Images

Cover design by Nick Castle
Typesetting and design by Mckore Graphics, Cape Town
Printed and bound by Mega Digital, Cape Town

10-digit ISBN 0-9550570-0-0
13-digit ISBN 978-0-9550570-0-7

For more information, contact www.legalguidetoevents.com or www.davidbecker.co.uk

NOTICE TO THE READER
The reader is notified that this text is an educational tool, not a practice book. Since the law is in constant change, no rule or statement of law in this book should be relied upon for any service to any client. The reader should always refer to standard legal sources for the current rule or law. Neither the publisher nor the author accept any responsibility for the information provided in this book and readers are advised to take independent legal advice before acting on any of the information contained herein.

Neither the publisher nor the author make any representation or warranty of any kind, including but not limited to, the warranties of fitness for particular purpose or merchantability, nor are any such representations implied with respect to the material set forth herein. Neither the publisher nor the author shall be liable for any special, consequential, or exemplary damages resulting, in whole or part, from the readers' use of, or reliance upon, this material.

Contents

About the Author

David Becker, BA LLB, is an internationally qualified lawyer specialising in the entertainment industry. He has extensive experience advising on a cross-selection of events ranging from high profile events – such as the Rugby World Cup 2003, the Clipper Round the World Yacht Race, Nike Run London, the MOBO Music Awards, the Sports Industry Awards, the Laureus World Sports Awards and the Paralympic World Cup – to exhibitions, conferences and weddings.

David is ranked as a leader in the field of sports law in the 2005 Chambers Legal Directory and is listed in the 2005 edition of the *Legal 500's Who's Who in the Law*. He has lectured on sports law and contributed chapters to the sports law textbook *Sport: Law and Practice*, by Lewis and Taylor (Butterworths, 2003).

David has appeared regularly on BBC radio and TV as an expert in the field of sports law, commenting on high profile matters involving Chelsea Football Club, the UEFA Cup, the English Football Association, tennis player Greg Rusedski and Olympic sprinter Dwain Chambers to name a few.

In his spare time David enjoys competing in endurance events. He has represented his native Western Province in squash, run the 7-day Marathon des Sables (Sahara Ultra-marathon), competed in the World Memory Championships and obtained a bronze medal in the Mind Sports Olympiad.

Born in South Africa, David trained with Sonnenberg, Hoffman & Galombik before joining leading international law firm Freshfields in London. Now based in London, David is currently a partner with the law firm Collyer-Bristow.

Preface

The events industry has become a lucrative industry. It has also become increasingly complex. Understanding the legal issues in and around an event is now a vital part of successful event planning and management.

Whilst event professionals will almost always require legal advice of some kind in relation to an event, my experience is that they are usually unable or unwilling to dedicate a part of an event budget to paying legal fees. Books on event management generally do have a chapter on the legal issues surrounding an event. However, they do not deal with the issues in sufficient detail (usually because they are not written by lawyers).

The aim of this book is to assist event professionals (such as event organisers, venue owners and suppliers) and their advisors by providing an accessible, easy-to-read guide setting out the most important legal issues surrounding an event. It also describes key deal terms for a range of different event contracts and provides a valuable collection of sample contracts that can be used as a basis for a specific event.

It should be noted that this book sets out basic legal principles relevant for events, with particular reference to the law in the United Kingdom, United States and South Africa (as at 1 October 2005). However, local advice is always recommended, particularly for complex legal issues that may arise in relation to applicable legislation in a given country or territory.

The events industry has a number of different terms for the parties involved in the industry, many of which vary from country to country. In this book I have referred to the party who either owns the rights in the event, or controls those rights, as the 'event organiser', and any third party contracting with the event organiser, broadly, as the 'vendor'. The term 'event owner' will be avoided, for the reason that in many jurisdictions there is no such thing as a 'proprietary right' in an event and therefore it is incorrect to speak of 'owning' the rights in or to an event.

Finally, I would like to thank the following people without whom the production of the book itself would not have been possible:

My extremely patient and supportive partner Siobhan Gallagher, Mark Anastasi, Atilla Czinke, Tim Ivison, Lewis Pugh, Aaron Wise, George van Niekerk, Thekla Davids, Willem van der Colff, Steve Cornelius, Michelle Dite, Penny Snowden, Alan Pascoe, Fearga McEvoy, Kanya King, Howard Stupp, Ardi Kolah, Richard Dorfman, Julian Topham, Kelly Smith, Susan Parker, Alan Burdon-Cooper, Jane Lindop and Jessica Medling.

This book is dedicated to my grandmother, Helen Becker, who recently celebrated her 90th birthday – an event in itself.

CHAPTER ONE

The Event

1.1   Introduction

The events industry is a massive and fast-growing industry. It generates billions of dollars each year in revenue around the world. According to a European Commission report the sports events industry alone accounts for in excess of 2.5% of world trade.

As the industry has grown, so has the need for sound event planning and management.

First, event goers have never had such an array of events from which to choose. As a result of increasing competition in the events industry, events need to be better organised and more memorable than ever before.

In addition, the staging of events has become an inherently risky endeavour. Event management has been likened to a hire-wire performance without safety nets. Once the event has started, there are no second chances. It is done in one take, and there are no dress rehearsals. One cannot predict how attendees, participants and suppliers will interact when they are brought together. However, one can plan and prepare carefully in order to maximise the chances of the event being a success.

As mentioned, understanding the legal consequences and relationships around an event is an *essential* part of successful event planning and management.

Despite the fact that events companies and event professionals will almost always require legal advice of some kind in relation to an event, they are usually unable to dedicate part of the event budget to legal fees. Or they do not wish to reduce their profits from the event by paying legal fees.

This book is a solution to that problem. It aims to provide event professionals (and their advisors) with a basic guide setting out the key legal issues surrounding events. It also describes the types of legal contracts that may be required for an event, explains key deal terms for these contracts and provides simple precedent documents for use and reference by those in the events industry.

1.2   The Nature of an Event

There is no strict legal definition of the word 'event'. It is primarily a descriptive word to describe an occasion.

An 'event' may be loosely defined as a significant gathering of people for cultural, educational, charitable, sporting, business, political or recreational purposes. An event usually has an objective and theme of some kind. In almost all cases an event has an element of formality to it.

1.3   The Need for Legal Contracts

As a result of this element of formality, contracts are often required to record the rights and obligations of the various parties involved in the event. Not all events will require contracts of course. A school fête will not usually require legal contracts, nor will a monthly kite-flying contest in the park. However, in this day and age, as events become more and more complex and the commercial value of events has grown, so the rights and obligations of the parties involved in the event have become more complex and the need to record arrangements in writing has increased.

The most fundamental reason for having a written contract is to set out the exact terms of the arrangement between the parties so that the rights and obligations of the parties are clearly defined. This not only brings a level of certainty to the arrangement, but sets out the consequences if the obligations of one party are not fulfilled.

We all have horror stories to share about disputes with event organisers, sponsors, caterers, promoters and the like. Parties would be well-advised to sit down before an event and consider potential issues which could arise. This very often saves a great deal of money and time in the long run. Indeed, it is a vital part of sound planning and preparation for the event.

In addition, contracts help to deal with risk. Firstly, as mentioned above, events are inherently risky. If the terms of an arrangement are also vague and undefined, this increases the risk for the parties involved. Secondly, we live in an increasingly litigious world, where event professionals not only face potential claims from attendees and participants at the event but also from commercial partners. Finally, the risks of cancellation of an event as a result of political activity, economic instability and natural phenomena have increased.

The result of the above is that the existence of written contracts for events has largely become a necessity.

Small, relatively simple events such as parties, functions or receptions may only require a basic venue hire contract. Events such as weddings, competitions and exhibitions may require additional contracts, such as catering and corporate hospitality contracts, supplier contracts, participation contracts and performers' contracts. Large-scale events will usually require further contracts, such as broadcasting contracts, sponsorship contracts, ticketing contracts and merchandising contracts. In addition, all of these events will carry risk and will have legal implications.

Examples of the types of contracts (or legal expertise) that may be required for an event are set out in the diagram below.

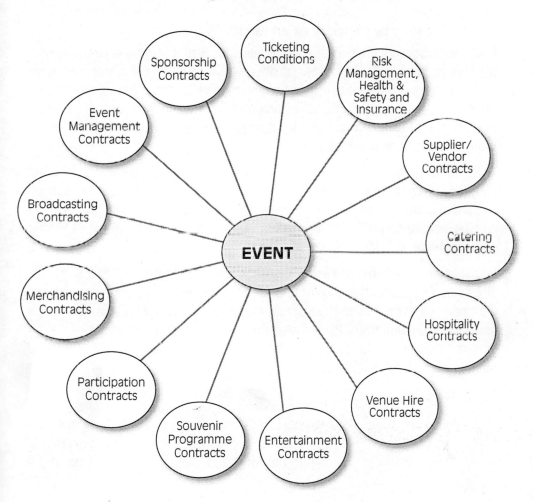

1.4   'Rights' in an Event

Event professionals often speak about 'owning' the rights in an event. Indeed, one often sees a statement at the beginning of a contract that one party 'owns' the rights in an event.

'Ownership' of an event or the rights in an event is a relatively complex and important topic and requires further discussion. It becomes particularly important when a third party, without license or authorisation, attempts to derive commercial benefit from an event without paying for it.

1.4.1   The Idea or Concept of an Event

Event organisers are often astounded to find that even if they have come up with the idea or concept for the event, it does not necessarily mean that the event organiser 'owns' the event. It is important to note that the idea or concept for the event is not usually protectable under law[1]. That is why in practice we see a number of similar events taking place throughout the world, such as fêtes, balls, sports competitions and exhibitions.

This can be frustrating for an event organiser who has come up with a fantastic idea for an event and wishes or needs to share this idea with third parties. Generally, it will not be possible to protect the idea of that event in law, nor will it be possible to prevent a third party from taking that idea and running a similar event based on that idea.

It is recommended that in such a case, the event organiser enters into a non-disclosure or confidentiality contract with the third party in terms of which the third party agrees not to disclose the information (the idea) with anyone else nor use the information itself. In this way, the event organiser will at the very least have a contractual remedy against the third party and can take legal action if there is a breach of that contract.

1.4.2   The Format of an Event

In general, format rights do not exist as distinct and separate rights capable of protection. In other words, the format of an event is not usually protectable in its own right. By way of example, the format of the game-show 'Opportunity

---

[1] Copyright legislation will usually only extend to the *expression* of an idea, and not the idea itself (even if that idea is original). In the United Kingdom, the United States and South Africa, for example, an event is not a protected copyright work within the definitions of the relevant copyright acts (the Copyright, Design and Patents Act 1988, the Copyright Act of 1976 and the Copyright Act 98 of 1978 respectively).

Knocks', which consisted of the use of a 'clapometer' and various catchphrases, was held not to amount to a work capable of protection under law[2].

However, the fact remains that each year large amounts are paid to license format rights of shows around the world. In addition, two recent cases in Holland and Brazil indicate a shift in the movement towards recognising protectable format rights[3].

In the same way that the idea of the event is not protectable, but the expression of that idea may well be, an expression of the proposed format may be protectable, however. For instance, if the format of an event is recorded in writing in a document, that document would usually be capable of protection as a literary work by the law of copyright, provided that the work is not copied and originates from the author[4].

1.4.3 A 'Proprietary' Right in an Event

Apart from the fact that the idea or format for an event is not usually protectable in law, in many countries there is also no recognised 'proprietary' right in an event itself. In other words, one cannot rely on a distinct and separately enforceable right to protect an event.

Whilst there is no generally accepted proprietary right in an event in the United States, in some states the courts have been prepared to accept that there is such a thing as a proprietary right in an event, more particularly in the information arising from the event. This right is intricately tied to the doctrine of commercial

---

[2] See *Green v Broadcasting Corporation of New Zealand* [1989] 2 All ER 1056, where the Privy Council held that the features which constituted the 'format' of the television show, which were accessories used in the presentation of, and additional to, other dramatic or musical performances, did not attract protection as a dramatic work under copyright law. More recently, both in the UK and the United States, this principle has been supported. In the UK, see the case of *Miles v ITV Network Limited* (2004) where the claimant failed to successfully argue that the show *Dream Street* was a copy of *Trusty and Friends*. In the United States, the broadcaster CBC attempted to obtain an injunction against competitor ABC in 2003 on the basis that the show *I'm A Celebrity Get Me Out of Here* was a copy of their show *Survivor*. However ABC successfully argued that their show was an original format and that injunctive relief was an inappropriate remedy.

[3] In the case of *Castaway Television Productions Ltd & Planet 24 Productions Limited v Endemol* (2004), although the Dutch Supreme Court found that the *Big Brother* format was not an infringing copy of the *Survivor* format on the facts, it was prepared to find that such a format right may exist, saying that "A format consists of a combination of unprotectable elements...An infringement can only be involved if a similar selection of several of these elements have been copied in an identifiable way. If all have been copied, there is no doubt. In that case copyright infringement is involved. If only one (unprotected) element has been copied, the situation is also clear: in that case no infringement is involved. A general answer to the question of how many elements must have been copied for infringement to be involved cannot be given; this depends on the circumstances of the case."

In Brazil, the Court found in 2004 that SBT's show *Casa Dos Artistas* was a 'badly disguised and rude copy' of the format of Endemol's *Big Brother*. The Court found that the *Big Brother* format enjoyed copyright protection under the Brazilian law of copyright. It found that the format was extensive and much more than a mere idea.

[4] See 1.5.3(a) below for further explanation on the law of copyright.

misappropriation i.e. that no one should be permitted to 'rip off' the fruits of the labour, skill and expense of the creator of the event[5]. However, thirty-six states in the United States do not currently recognise this doctrine. Moreover, recent cases involving the NBA appear to have restricted the use of the doctrine as a basis for protecting a property right in an event[6].

Event organisers in those states that do recognise the doctrine may have a greater chance of success in establishing a claim for misappropriation if they can show that the information they wish to protect is so-called 'hot news'. The essence of 'hot news' is that the event organiser invests significant resources to collect information about an event (or produce an event) and then puts the information into some useful format, which it then sells to the public. If the public will be deprived of access to the useful information by virtue of the fact that the event organiser loses its incentive to gather it (or produce the event) because someone else is simply 'free-riding' on the event organiser's efforts, such information may be protectable under the doctrine of 'hot news'[7].

It is interesting to note that in a recent case involving the PGA golf tour, a Florida court was prepared to recognise that the PGA had a 'property right' in the 'real-time' scores produced through the PGA's on-site tracking system, despite Florida not recognising a state tort law of misappropriation[8].

---

[5] The misappropriation branch of the tort of unfair competition goes back to the U.S. Supreme Court decision in *International News Service v Associated Press*, 248 U.S. 215, 63 L.Ed. 211, 39 S.Ct 68 (1918). In this case, the Supreme Court upheld a decision enjoining INS from copying AP's news bulletins and then selling the data in competition with AP. AP had gathered the data at considerable expense and effort.

[6] See the Southern District Court of New York *SportsTrax* case (*National Basketball Association and NBA Properties, Inc v Sports Team Analysis and Tracking Systems, Inc d/b/a Stats, Inc and Motorola, Inc d/b/a SportsTrax* 1996 U.S. Dist. LEXIS 10262 (S.D.N.Y. 1996). In this case, the defendants Motorola and Stats developed and marketed portable electronic pagers, called 'SportsTrax', which provided NBA game information on a 'real-time' basis to consumers. The NBA were initially successful in claiming that the defendants had engaged in unfair competition in violation of New York common law through their commercial misappropriation of the NBA's proprietary rights in the NBA's games. However, in 1997 the Second Circuit Court of Appeal overturned that decision, holding that the defendants were entitled to transmit information the 'real-time' game over the pagers sold commercially. The Court of Appeal held that federal copyright law, which did not protect the information, pre-empted a claim of misappropriation in this area. It found that misappropriation cannot be a form of de facto copyright protection for what would otherwise be 'uncopyrightable' material.

[7] This doctrine emerges from the case *International News Service v Associated Press*, 248 U.S. 215 (1918), where the Supreme Court found that the Associated Press had a property right in news stories, in particular 'hot-news', that it was the first to acquire.

[8] See the cases of *Morris Communications Corp Inc v PGA Tour Inc*, 117 F. Supp. 2d 1322 (M.D. Fla. 2000), *Morris Communications Corp Inc v PGA Tour Inc*, 235 F.Supp. 2d 1269 (M.D. Fla 2002) and *Morris Communications Corp Inc v PGA Tour Inc*, 364 F.Supp. 3d 1288 (11th Cir. 2004). The resolution of this issue turned on the nature of the PGA's proprietary 'Real Time Scoring System' for compiling golf scores, as well as the nature of golf tournaments, in which athletes compete with one another simultaneously but on different parts of the course. In the 2002 case the Florida court held that '...the PGA Tour does have a property right in the scores compiled by the use of the RTSS, but that property right vanishes when the scores are in the public domain' (at 1281). In 2004 the Eleventh Circuit were prepared to find that the PGA had a 'property interest' in the scores but unfortunately failed to identify the source of that interest.

British Commonwealth countries (such as the United Kingdom, Australia, New Zealand, Canada, South Africa and others) do not recognise independent proprietary rights in an event per se[9]. In Germany, Switzerland, Sweden and Japan, the consensus appears to be the same[10].

This is not to say that commercially such rights do not exist. The large amounts paid in the form of rights fees every year in the events industry indicates that they do. It means that in these countries the organiser of an event has to find some element of the event that is protected by law, rather than rely on a general proprietary right in the event itself. In other words, the event organiser must identify breaches of existing and recognised legal rights to provide indirect protection for the commercial interests in the event per se.

Through a combination of real property law, sound contractual provisions, intellectual property law and tort law, the event organiser can usually protect the event and its constituent elements from commercial misappropriation by third parties. It does this though control over the event, rather than distinct rights of ownership in the event. This is dealt with further below.

1.5   Protection of an Event and the Commercial Rights Relating to an Event

Even though an event organiser may not be able to protect the idea or format of an event, or have a proprietary right in the event itself, the event organiser may be able to protect 'ownership' of that event through the following avenues:

Moreover, it should be noted that the purpose for which the 2002 court found a property right was merely as a defence to an antitrust claim where taking action to protect 'private property' (for federal anti-trust purposes) constitutes a valid business justification to what would otherwise be considered unlawful anti-competitive or monopolising conduct.

[9] The leading authority for this proposition is an Australian case, *Victoria Park Racing and Recreation Grounds Co Ltd v Taylor* (1937) 58 CLR 479, HC of A. The plaintiff operated a racecourse in Sydney. One of the defendants owned residential property alongside the racecourse and permitted the other defendants to erect a scaffolding tower on his front lawn that overlooked the boundary fence around the racecourse and enabled them to produce a commentary of the races that they then broadcast live on radio. The plaintiff maintained that, having invested money and other resources into staging the races, it had a 'quasi-property' right in them with which the defendants had unjustly interfered. The Australian High Court rejected this argument as a matter of law on the basis that the defendants had not infringed any right belonging to the plaintiff. Chief Justice Latham stated: "The court has not been referred to any authority in English law which gives credence to such a right...the mere fact that damage results to the plaintiff from such a description cannot be relied upon as a cause of action...A 'spectacle' cannot be 'owned' in any ordinary sense of the word". This decision was recently affirmed by the Australian case of *Moorgate Tobacco Ltd v Philip Morris Ltd* 156 C.L.R 414 (1984). In Canada, the most recent decision in this regard is the British Columbia Court of Appeal's decision in *NHL et al v Pepsi-Cola Canada* 122 D.L.R 4th 412 (B.C.C.A 1995). In this case the National Hockey League claimed that it had (as the court phrased it) "some form of exclusive quasi-property right in the schedules, scores and popularity of the Stanley Cup Playoffs". Carrothers, J.A. rejected this argument, concluding: "I have not been shown that such a right exists..."

[10] See Wise *A "Property Right" in a Sports Event: Views of Different Jurisdictions* [1996] 4(3) SATLJ 63 and Wise and Meyer *International Sports Law and Business* (Kluwer Law International, Cambridge, Mass, 1996), Part IV, sections 4 and 5.9 in particular.

1.5.1 Access Rights

The event organiser must try to control access to the venue. It does this by ensuring that it has access rights to the venue in which the event is going to be held. It must also be able in practice to control third party access to the venue and ensure that the attendees, participants and the media admitted to the event are not entitled to benefit commercially from their attendance[11].

Control over the venue is itself based on the law of real property, contract and tort. Real property law provides the ownership, leasehold or licensed interest in the land that allows the event organiser to enforce the right of exclusive possession and control of the venue. Contract law provides the event organiser with the ability and the right to make entry to the venue subject to certain terms and conditions that can protect the commercial value of the event, and to exclude those who do not abide by such terms and conditions. Tort law generally makes a trespasser of anyone who enters onto the land without permission, or enters with permission but then violates the terms and conditions of that permission.

Of course where an event takes place in a public place, it may not be possible for an event organiser to control access to the event. Examples would include events such as the Oxford-Cambridge Boat Race, the Tour de France or the Cape Town Peninsula Marathon. In this case, the event organiser may be able to obtain assistance from the government (special legislation may be enacted for the event) or local authorities (ordinances may be implemented). A local authority may also be able to assist in restricting access to certain areas in order to prevent third parties from exploiting the event for commercial purposes e.g. recording or broadcasting footage of the event.

1.5.2 Contractual Restrictions on Commercial Partners, Participants and Attendees

The event organiser may be in a position to exploit various rights in the event commercially. For instance, it may wish to offer sponsorship rights to one party, broadcasting rights to another party and catering and hospitality rights to another party.

These are loosely referred to as the 'commercial rights' in an event, in that the exploitation of these rights has commercial value. The parties who take up these rights are usually referred to as the 'commercial partners'. They will pay money to the event organiser for these rights.

If an event organiser has granted exclusive sponsorship rights to one party,

---

[11] See the Chapter 5 on Ticketing Contracts, Chapter 11 on Participation Contracts and Chapter 13 on Broadcasting Contracts for mechanisms to control third party access.

which includes the right to place branding at the event, the event organiser will want to ensure that its other commercial partners do not take advantage of their presence at the event to interfere with, or diminish the value of, the sponsorship rights that have been granted. Similarly, if an event organiser has granted the exclusive right to sell hospitality packages to a hospitality provider, it will want to ensure that neither the event sponsor nor a third party caterer attempts to sell their own hospitality packages for commercial gain. These assurances can be given in the contracts entered into with the various commercial partners. They will assist in protecting the value of the commercial rights that arise by virtue of the event.

Similarly, if the event organiser has entered into sponsorship contracts with sponsors in relation to the event, it will not want any participants in the event to promote competing brands, either directly or indirectly, at the event. This is likely to upset the sponsors and also reduce the value of their sponsorship. For the same reason, the event organiser will also not want participants to record or broadcast footage of the event for commercial gain if exclusive broadcasting rights have been granted to another party. Accordingly, the event organiser will want to include terms in its contract with the participants to the effect that the above activities are not permitted.

Finally, the event organiser can protect the commercial rights by imposing conditions of entry on the attendees at an event. The most obvious way of doing this is to include such conditions of entry in ticket terms and conditions. The purchase of the ticket will be deemed to be an acceptance of these terms and conditions, so that a contract will exist between the event organiser and the purchaser of the ticket. This is dealt with in more detail in Chapter 5 on ticketing.

1.5.3   Intellectual Property Rights Relating to an Event

Intellectual property is the product of the intellect or mind. The event organiser may be able to protect its 'ownership' of the event through a variety of intellectual property rights listed below. This will essentially depend on the law of the country or region in which the event takes place. Accordingly, event organisers are advised to seek specialist advice from local lawyers in order to ascertain the exact nature and scope of such protection in their respective countries.

a)   Copyright

Copyright is a property right. It is a right which prevents others from copying works without permission. Although there is no particular form of copyright which covers events specifically, the law of copyright can be successfully applied to the events industry.

The source of copyright law will usually be a piece of legislation. In the United Kingdom, this is the Copyright Designs and Patents Act 1988 (CDPA 1988). In the United States, this is the Copyright Act of 1976, and in South Africa, the Copyright Act 98 of 1978 is the relevant piece of legislation. Most countries tend to have similar pieces of legislation[12].

This legislation will set out what is protectable. As a general principle, organised events are not subject to copyright protection, as mentioned above. Copyright law protects the expression of an original work. These may be literary, dramatic, musical or artistic works[13]. The work should not be copied and should originate from the author. An author usually needs to show that he or she has expended his or her own skill and effort in order to justify protection.

The law contains an exception for cases known as "work made for hire". In circumstances where the author created the work as part of his or her employment, copyright will usually vest in the employer. However, if the author was hired as an independent contractor to create the work, copyright will usually vest in the independent contractor, unless otherwise provided in the contract.

Within the context of the events industry, whilst the format of an event is not generally protectable, the expression of that format may well be. So any plans that an event organiser has drawn up in the process of organising the event may be protectable as a literary work under the relevant legislation. Likewise, any stage designs, floor designs, table plans, menus, scripts, project plans, syntax, schedule of events, trade catalogues, brochures, event programmes, team sheets, notes on the opposition and written schedules of plays or moves that are produced in the course of organising an event may be protectable. It is important to remember that it is the author of those works who will be entitled to claim copyright protection in those works. Whilst the event organiser may commission a caterer to draw up a menu, the menu itself will belong to the caterer under copyright law (unless the parties have agreed otherwise by way of contract).

---

[12] It is worth noting that copyright protection also extends internationally through a network of reciprocal agreements governed by membership of one or other (or both) of the international copyright conventions. The Berne Convention and the Universal Copyright Convention lay down minimum standards of protection for copyright owners between those countries that have ratified those conventions. Both conventions have many members and some countries have ratified both conventions.

[13] The exact categories vary slightly from country to country. For example, the US Copyright Act of 1976 protects 'original works of authorship fixed in any tangible medium of expression' including literary works, musical works, dramatic works, pantomimes and choreographic works, pictorial, graphic or sculptural works, motion picture and other audio-visual works, sound recordings and architectural work. In the UK, the CDPA 1988 protects original literary, dramatic, musical or artistic works, sound recordings, films, broadcasts or cable programmes, and the typographical arrangement of published editions. In South Africa, the Copyright Act 98 of 1978 protects literary, musical and artistic works, cinematographic films, sound recordings, broadcasts, programme-carrying signals, computer programmes and published editions.

The name of an event will not usually qualify for protection as a literary work under copyright legislation.

In Europe, the compilation and use of sports databases for commercial reasons has led to the development of the law in this area. In the United Kingdom, a database may be protectable as a 'literary work' under the CDPA 1988, but only if, by reason of a selection or arrangement of its contents, the database constitutes the author's own intellectual creation[14]. Under the CDPA 1988, while the creator of a database may have copyright in the way he or she has selected and arranged the data, that copyright may not be infringed by someone who takes the information from the database and simply arranges it in a different way. The European Union's Database Directive, adopted in 1996, and the Copyright and Rights in Databases Regulations 1997, created a new 'database right', which avoids this problem[15]. Now the position is that, whilst copyright may subsist in the database as a literary work, in addition, if there has been (either qualitively or quantitively) substantial investment in the obtaining, verifying or presentation of the contents of the database, the person who makes that investment thereby obtains a 'database right'[16].

The question of whether or not a performance at an event is protectable is dealt with at paragraph 10.4 below. The general position is that the performance of a dancer, singer or actor would be protectable as a dramatic work under copyright law, but a performance during a sports event would not be protectable.

Whilst a performance at an event will not generally be protectable under copyright law, any recording and broadcast of that performance will be protectable under copyright law. Recordings will generally include any sound recordings (such as interviews and commentaries), visual recordings and audio-visual recordings. Accordingly, footage of the event will be protectable under copyright. Ownership under copyright will usually vest in the person who creates the recording and not the event organiser (again, unless agreed otherwise by way of contract). This subject is dealt with more fully in Chapter 13 on Broadcasting Contracts.

In the United Kingdom, the United States and South Africa, there is no registration requirement for copyright to subsist in a work. It will arise automatically on the expression of the work[17].

---

[14] Section 3A of the CDPA 1988.

[15] Regulation 6 of these Regulations define a 'database' as a 'collection of independent works, data or other materials arranged in a systematic or methodical way and individually accessible by electronic or other means'.

[16] See *Sport: Law and Practice* by Jonathan Taylor and Adam Lewis, Butterworths (2003), section D1.63 to D1.75 for a detailed explanation of the law in this area, as well as the 2004 European Court of Justice ruling in *British Horseracing Board Ltd & Others v William Hill Organisation Limited* and the 2005 English Court of Appeal ruling, which appears to limit the extent of that database right.

[17] In the United States, registration may be a prerequisite for certain remedies for infringement. In South Africa, registration is required for cinematographic films.

b) Trade Marks

A trade mark is, broadly speaking, a mark that denotes the nature or origin of goods or services. It is a sign which is capable of being represented graphically and which is capable of distinguishing the goods or services of one undertaking from those of another. For example, the trade mark 'Nike', along with the Nike 'swoosh', identify the shoes made by Nike and distinguish them from shoes made by other companies e.g. Reebok.

In general, a trade mark may consist of words, signatures, symbols, emblems, designs, letters, numerals, patterns or the shape of goods or their packaging. As in the case of copyright, the law of trade marks is usually governed by legislation enacted in a particular country or region. As such, it may differ from country to country[18].

Registration of a trade mark in the relevant national or regional register may offer protection over the use of the marks. The owner of the mark can bring an action against anyone making unauthorised use of the mark.

An event organiser may be able to register the name of the event as a trade mark, provided that the words are sufficiently distinctive[19]. For example, word marks such as 'World Cup' would be difficult to register as trade marks on the basis that the words are not sufficiently distinctive. However, filing a trade mark for the distinctive name of a trade show, such as "WidgetExpo" would probably be acceptable.

The event organiser may also be able to register an event logo. The registration of the name and logo of the event will create goodwill in the event and help to create a public recognition of its status and unique nature.

Trade mark registration is territorial in nature. In other words, a trade mark registered with the United Kingdom Trade Mark Registry is enforceable in the UK and may be infringed by conduct that takes place in the UK, but it will not be infringed by conduct that takes place in a foreign jurisdiction, unless it has also been registered in that jurisdiction's trade mark registry (or, within the European Community, if it has been registered as a Community Trade Mark). Accordingly, an event organiser with an established international brand, such as the FIA Formula One World Championship) should consider a registration programme including all commercially valuable territories throughout the world.

---

[18] In the United Kingdom, the Trade Marks Act 1994 largely governs the law of trade marks. In the United States, the primary pieces of legislation are the Lanham Act of 1946 (commonly referred to as the 'Trademark Act') and the U.S. Trademark Regulations, which are those parts of Title 37 of the Code of Federal Regulations which pertain to trade marks (state law also complements these pieces of legislation). In South Africa, the Trade Mark Act 194 of 1993 governs the law of trade marks.

[19] The words should not be generic or descriptive, unless they have acquired a secondary meaning.

c) Unregistered Marks/Passing Off

In some countries, even though a mark may not be registered, an event organiser may be able to protect that mark through an action for 'passing off'[20]. This is a tort (sometimes known as a 'delict') and based on the basic premise that no one has any right to represent his or her goods as the goods of someone else.

In order to rely on such a protection, the event organiser will generally need to show that it has developed sufficient goodwill in, or association with, the mark (usually through use of the mark), that the offending party has misrepresented that he or she owns the mark and this has led to confusion amongst customers, and that the event organiser has suffered financial loss as a result of this misrepresentation.

d) Patents

Patent law essentially protects new inventions or processes that are capable of industrial application and are an advancement in the industry. Patent legislation usually allows the owner of the patent to register it in a particular territory and thereby secure the exclusive right to make, use and exploit the product or process in that territory[21].

Most event organisers will not usually be in a position to use patent law to protect an event. However, event organisers who are in the business of manufacturing specific goods or equipment for their events may find this form of protection useful. An example might be an event organiser who manufactures rides for funfairs.

1.5.4 Sanction

An event organiser may be able to secure greater protection for the event by obtaining some form of sanction from a governing body, if possible. Event organisers are not usually required to obtain such a sanction in order to run an event. However, the event organiser may want the event to be officially recognised by that governing body or want the results of the event to count towards a central points scoring system e.g. a leg of the World Surfing Tour. Irrespective of this, if an event organiser can obtain a sanction which is exclusive to a particular territory, it may be able to protect its position as against third party event organisers, who may be able to stage a similar event but will not have the benefit of the official sanction (i.e. recognition) from the governing body.

---

[20] The United Kingdom and South Africa have such an action available under common law. In the United States an action for passing off can be brought under state law of unfair competition or under federal unfair competition law under the Lanham Act.

[21] In the United Kingdom, the CDPA 1988 is the primary piece of legislation governing patent law. In the United States, the main body of law concerning patents is found in Title 35 of the United States Code and Title 37 of the Code of Federal Regulations. In South Africa, the Patents Act of 1978 applies.

1.5.5　Ambush Marketing

Ambush marketing (sometimes known as 'parasitic' marketing) is any kind of unauthorised association by a business of its name, brand, products or services, via any one of a range of marketing activities, with an event. The word 'ambush' is used because the marketers are competitors of the official commercial partners of the event, who pounce in the lead-up to or during the event to generate commercial impact. An example is the draping of a gigantic Nike banner over the front of the car park opposite the Millenium Stadium in Cardiff on the opening day of the 1999 Rugby World Cup. Ambush marketing may be carried out as a one-off stunt or may be part of a dedicated marketing campaign around an event.

Whilst ambush marketing does not generally affect the staging of the event in itself, it can have a significant impact on the value of the commercial rights relating to the event. Commercial partners may pay significant fees for exclusive rights of association and exploitation in relation to an event. If the event organiser does not protect the value of the rights granted to its commercial partners, such commercial partners may be reluctant to continue their association with the event in future years, and may simply decide to join the ambush marketer in exploiting the event without paying for the event organiser's authorisation to do so.

In those countries where there is no 'proprietary' right in an event in itself, the ability of the event organiser to protect an event from ambush marketing will depend largely on the following:

- The extent to which the ambushers make use of features or elements of the event (such as trade marks, logos, photographs and audio-visual footage) in which the event organiser owns or controls intellectual property rights;
- The extent to which additional laws (outside the scope of intellectual property rights) provide remedies to deal with ambush marketing activities, such as unfair competition, misleading advertising, false trade descriptions, street vending regulations, ticket touting regulations etc[22]; and
- The extent of protection and control the event organiser has obtained over the venue, surrounding spaces (including airspace), attendees at the event, public watching the event, the media reporting on the event, participants in the event and commercial partners of the event organiser[23].

---

[22] This will depend on the laws of the country in which the ambush marketing activities take place.

[23] For example, the event organiser can ensure that provision is made for a 'clean' venue in its venue hire contract with the venue owner. It can also try to ensure that the definition of the venue is comprehensive and extends to the surrounding environment, where possible. The event organiser may be able to persuade the local government to pass by-laws that might prevent ambush marketing. For example, in the lead up to the Atlanta Olympic Games in 1996, the local organising committee asked the Federal Aviation Authority to ban all unauthorised flights within the city limits for the duration of the Games to prevent

It should be noted that, owing to the fact that ambush marketing has become more prevalent, many countries bidding to host major events are now expected to commit in their bidding documentation to passing legislation to combat ambush marketing in that country. When hosting the Cricket World Cup in 2003, the South African government amended existing legislation to prohibit ambush marketing 'by association' (where ambushers attempt to associate themselves to the event in some way) and ambush marketing 'by intrusion' (where ambushers attempt to piggy-back on spectator and media exposure in relation to the event). Many other countries have followed suit in passing similar legislation for big sporting events. Also in South Africa, the draft Safety at Sports and Recreational Events Bill makes it a requirement for an anti-ambush marketing strategy to be implemented for events taking place in all stadiums and venues with a capacity of over 2000 people[24].

1.6 Conclusion

As the events industry has grown, so has the need for sound contracts between the relevant stakeholders. The diagram on page 3 sets out some of the key contracts that may be necessary for an event. Whether or not there is a proprietary right in the event itself, the steps in paragraph 1.5 above are a valuable means of protecting the both the event and the commercial rights arising from the event.

---

aerial ambush marketing, and in the Euro 2004 football (soccer) competition, event organisers UEFA obtained the assistance of the Portuguese government in enacting specific legislation relating to ambush marketing (similar legislation will be provided in the Olympic Bill for the Games to be held in London in 2012). In addition, the event organiser can impose restrictive terms and conditions on entry to the event through its ticket conditions and through any contracts with participants (See Chapters 5, 11 and 13). For further reading on ambush marketing, refer to Bitel 'Ambush marketing' [1997] 5(1) SATLJ 12; Roper-Drimie *Sydney 2000 Olympic Games – A Case Study on How To Combat Ambush Marketing* (2001) 7(7) Sports Law Administration & Practice 1 (2000 Olympic Games); Wall *The Game Behind the Games* (2002) 12 Marquette Law Review 557 and Elliot *Tackling Ambush Marketing* (2002) Sportbusiness.com, 16 July.

[24] See section 39 of the draft Safety at Sports and Recreational Events Bill 2005 proposed by the Department of Sports and Recreation South Africa.

CHAPTER TWO

Contracts

2.1   Introduction

In Chapter 1, we discussed why contracts are becoming a necessity in the events industry. Before one can understand the nuances of specific event contracts, it is important to understand the basic elements of contract law. Let us now look at the nature and basic terms of a legal contract.

2.2   What Constitutes a Contract?

In its simplest form, a contract consists of an offer, an acceptance of that offer, and consideration which passes between the parties. This is the case in the UK, many European countries and the United States. In some countries, such as South Africa, an offer and acceptance will suffice and consideration is not a legal requirement[1].

2.2.1   Offer

An offer is a proposal to do or give something of value in exchange for something else. The offer must be sufficiently certain or definite. There must also be an intention on the part of the offeror to create legal relations. For example it is not sufficient for the offeror to merely state, "I think I may wish to enter into a contract to hold an event." Furthermore, it is a generally accepted legal principle that the offer must be communicated to the other party involved. It is not enough to want to enter into a contract but not communicate that to the other party.

An offer can be terminated if it is revoked by the offeror before acceptance. It can also be terminated before acceptance on the expiration of a determined period of time. If the offeree comes back with a counter-offer, this is considered a rejection of the offer and also terminates the offer (although a simple request for information on the offer would not amount to rejection).

---

[1]   Consideration still commonly forms part of many contracts in South Africa, however.

2.2.2　Acceptance

The acceptance of the offer must be unequivocal and in the same terms as the offer. Any deviation from the terms of the offer will be regarded as a counter-offer, which will then need to be accepted by the original offeror in order for a valid contract to exist.

In general, there must also be sufficient specificity with regards to the terms of the contract so that each party has a reasonable understanding of what each is getting[2]. This understanding should constitute what is sometimes referred to as a 'meeting of the minds' or, as it is known in the United States, 'mutuality'.

Acceptance must be communicated to the offeror. Mere silence on the part of the offeree cannot be construed as acceptance, and the offeror cannot impose a contract on the other party by stating that the contract will be assumed if a response is not provided by a certain date.

2.2.3　Consideration

The word 'consideration' in a legal sense means something altogether different from the definition of the word in everyday language. In relation to contracts, consideration means something of value exchanged for something else of value[3].

Consideration generally involves the payment of money for the other party's promise to perform certain functions. For example, an event organiser pays a performer money in exchange for which the performer agrees to perform at the event. Whilst consideration is usually expressed in monetary terms, it need not be however. For example, mutual promises can be construed as consideration in a valid contract. Consideration must be of benefit to the recipient of the consideration or a detriment to the party providing the consideration. The degree of fairness of the exchange is irrelevant – the law does not concern itself as to whether or not one party paid too much for what they received.

2.2.4　Contractual Capacity

For a contract to be valid, the respective parties must have legal capacity to contract. They must have the capacity in particular to understand the terms and conditions of the contract and appreciate that failure to abide by the contract may give rise to legal liability. For example, in many countries a person who is a minor or mentally incompetent does not have independent legal capacity to enter into a contract[4].

2　If the terms of the contract are too vague, the contract may not be enforceable.

3　This is different from a gift, for example, which is one-sided: one person gives something to another and receives nothing in return.

4　This is the case in the UK, United States, South Africa and most of the countries in Western Europe.

2.2.5 Legality

In order for a contract to be enforceable, it must have a legal objective. If what the parties promise to do is actually illegal, the contract is void and will not be enforceable. For example, if a person contracts with another to kill someone else, this contract will be illegal and void. Another example in the events industry is where a number of parties, such as a group of hotels or convention centres, enter into a price-fixing arrangement. This will generally violate antitrust or anti-competition laws in many countries, so that if one party in the group attempted to enforce that contract, they will not be entitled to do so.

2.2.6 Are Oral Contracts Binding?

Oral or verbal contracts are also legally binding if they meet the above requirements. However, for obvious reasons, they are much harder to prove. For this reason, it is advisable to record a contract in writing. Note that in some countries certain contracts must be in writing to be valid and enforceable. For example, contracts for the sale or lease of land usually have to be in writing. This will depend on the laws in that particular country.

It is also worth noting, for the avoidance of doubt, that a contract can be partly written and partly oral. For instance, if a supplier makes an offer to provide certain services in relation to an event and the event organiser verbally accepts this offer, a valid contract will exist.

2.2.7 Negotiations

Parties should be careful in negotiations that an exchange of correspondence does not give rise to a contract before important issues have been satisfactorily agreed. For this reason, parties often record the notation 'subject to contract' in such correspondence. Similarly, parties should note that 'heads of agreement' may not be legally binding unless it is clear from the document that they are intended to be so.

In Chapters 3 to 15 I have described the nature and terms of a number of contracts relating to the production of an event. In general, these contracts should all contain certain key clauses, such as the parties, the term or duration of the contract, payment provisions and termination provisions. Rather than repeat these key clauses in each chapter, I have included a brief outline of these key clauses, and their purpose, in the section below. These can also be gleaned from the sample documents contained in the appendices.

2.3 Key Terms for All Contracts

When concluding a contract between an event organiser and a third party in relation to the event, the following general clauses should be considered:

2.3.1   Parties

This may appear somewhat obvious, but it is very important to ensure that the contract not only contains the correct parties, but that it refers to those parties correctly. The basic legal principle is that the parties whose names and signature appear on the contract are the ones with legal responsibility. It is very difficult to enforce rights against a party who is not a party to the contract.

The nature of the parties to the contract should also be considered. Is the other contracting party a limited company, an association, an individual, or a governing body? Is it a 'man of straw'? Whether you are the event organiser or a third party contracting with the event organiser, you should undertake some level of due diligence in respect of the other contracting party, primarily to ensure that the other party is not merely a 'shell' and can in fact deliver up the rights and fulfil the necessary obligations under the contract.

The parties to the contract must have legal capacity to enter into the contract. A party entering into a contract on behalf of a company, such as a hotel or sponsor, must have authority to bind that company.

In this book, for ease of reference, I will refer to the party who either owns the rights in the event, or controls those rights, as the 'event organiser', and any third party contracting with the event organiser, broadly, as the 'vendor'. The term 'event owner' will be avoided, having regard to the reasons stated in paragraph 1.4 above.

2.3.2   Recitals

Most contracts include a brief section setting out the background, nature and objectives of the contract. This is not strictly necessary, but is used to set the scene for those who may, at a later point, have to assess the proper intention of the parties. Be aware that recitals are not necessarily operative and may be overridden by an inconsistent provision in the body of the contract.

2.3.3   Definitions

Drafting convention dictates that certain terms throughout the contract will begin with a capital letter[5]. This refers the reader back to the definitions section of the contract, since a word so used will have the meaning ascribed to it in the definitions section. Care should be taken when defining terms such as 'Brand Sector', 'Venue' and 'Rights' as the exact definition of terms such as these will have a significant impact on the contract as a whole.

---

[5]   In some countries, there is a move towards doing away with this approach. For instance, in the UK, see the Plain English Society and their website www.plainenglish.co.uk.

2.3.4   Term/Duration

a)   When Does the Contract Begin?

The general principle is that contracts become operative once they are signed by both parties, unless otherwise agreed. The parties may choose to perform obligations prior to the date of signature of the contract, although strictly speaking these will fall under the ambit of a verbal contract, unless they are brought within the ambit of the terms of the contract by reference to an earlier commencement date. For example, the contract may refer to a 'commencement date' which is earlier than the date of signature and which will be deemed to be the starting date for the observation of obligations under the contract.

b)   When Does the Contract End?

Contracts may finish immediately upon completion of an event. However, there may be certain rights (such as merchandising rights) or obligations (such as confidentiality obligations) which may run beyond the date of the event itself. A termination date should always be specified, unless the contract runs for an indefinite period, in which case a notice period should be specified and termination may be exercised by either party on written notice.

c)   Renewals or Extensions

The parties should consider whether or not they wish to include provisions in relation to the renewal or extension of the contract. There are a number of variations set out below which may be considered.

i)   Unilateral Option

A clause can be drafted heavily in favour of either party (usually the vendor) giving that party the right to renew the contract for a further period on the same terms and conditions. In such circumstances, terms setting out the mechanism and consideration paid for exercising that option should also be included. The party in whose favour the option is granted then has the opportunity to assess the commercial viability of a renewed deal upon the approaching termination of the initial term of the contract. An option which is contingent upon terms of the subsequent contract being agreed or negotiated in good faith may not constitute a binding contract at all, but may simply be an agreement to agree or negotiate, both of which are unenforceable.

ii)   First Negotiation

This allows a party to have the first opportunity to negotiate a new contract once the current contract period draws to a close, but if there is no consensus or 'meeting of the minds', that party is able to look elsewhere after an appropriate negotiation period has expired. It is important to define the term of the negotiation period. This is also sometimes called a 'right of first refusal'. As indicated above, however, an agreement simply to negotiate may be unenforceable because it is too uncertain. As a result, such clauses are often included alongside a 'right to match'.

iii) Right to Match

This allows a vendor, such as a sponsor, who has failed in the first negotiation stage (described above) to have a right to match any offer capable of legal acceptance which a third party may wish to conclude with the event organiser. In such circumstances, if the vendor matches that offer, the event organiser is then obliged to enter into a further contract with that vendor.

iv) Break Clauses

For various reasons the parties may wish to sign a long-term contract that permits one or other of the parties to terminate the contract in certain circumstances or after a certain period of time. Those circumstances or periods will need to be carefully defined. Termination may be at the absolute discretion of one or other of the parties, or triggered by a failure to meet certain performance targets specified in the contract.

2.3.5   Consideration/Remuneration

As discussed at paragraph 2.2 above, one of the legal requirements, in the UK and USA at least, is an exchange of consideration. The value of that consideration need not necessarily be 'fair'. Each party simply has to provide something to the other under the contract. Usually this will be cash, in exchange for rights. However, it does not have to be cash. 'Benefits in kind' or 'value in kind' or 'contra deals' will be sufficient.

a)   Cash

In general, the event organiser will be granting various rights under contracts with vendors in exchange for payment of cash from the vendors. The event organiser will usually want up-front payments upon signature of the contract, or, at the very least, at the commencement of the event for cash-flow purposes. Vendors will usually be looking to spread payments over the period of the contract, or link such payments to performance targets under the contract. Accordingly, the payment provisions in a contract can be contentious and a matter of negotiation.

Clauses relating to repayment, rights of reduction of fees paid, and performance-related payments are discussed further in Chapter 3 relating to sponsorship.

b) Benefits in Kind

In some contracts, such as sponsorship contracts or supply contracts, payment will be in the form of 'benefits in kind'. A key issue arising in this regard is how the benefits in kind will be valued. Will this be the saving the event organiser makes in relation to the price of the goods on the open market, or the cost of manufacture of the goods to the vendor? The value of the goods, or the mechanism for valuation should be stated in the contract. Alternatively, a price list with agreed values for the goods can be agreed and attached to the contract as an appendix.

Bear in mind that where benefits in kind are being provided by the vendor, the vendor should provide a warranty that any goods supplied will be of sufficient quality, fit for purpose, and manufactured to the highest standards[6]. Such a clause would no doubt have been included in the supply and sponsorship contract concluded between Swatch and the International Olympic Committee for the Athens Olympic Games in 2004, in terms of which Swatch would have been asked to warrant the suitability and quality of the timekeeping instruments used in the Olympics, for example.

This is discussed in more detail in Chapter 7 on Supplier/Vendor Contracts.

2.3.6 Obligations on the Event Organiser

Vendors should be looking to include in the contract a number of obligations on the part of the event organiser. Some of these may be in the form of warranties. A warranty is basically a promise that something is the case. The expectation is that the promisee is entitled to rely on the warranty and that a breach of that warranty will give rise to legal liability on the part of the promisor or warrantor.

a) Organise and Stage the Event

This would be the most basic obligation on the part of the event organiser. Vendors could also insist on including obligations to stage the event in accordance with an agreed format set out in an appendix to the contract, procure that the venue has all the necessary facilities to support the performance of the event organiser's obligations to the vendor and procure that participants of an appropriately high quality will participate in the event. For example, sponsors of the Rugby World Cup may well have included an obligation on the part of the event organiser to conclude a participation agreement with the different national governing bodies to ensure the participation of the leading nations in the competition.

---

[6] Warranties are discussed further at paragraph 2.3.6 below.

b) 'Owns' or Controls the Rights in the Event

It is common to see a warranty in a contract as to the ownership of the rights to the event. As a matter of law, this may not be correct. The reason for this is that, as discussed above, in many countries there is no such thing as a proprietary right in a sports event[7].

In those countries where a 'proprietary' right in an event does not exist, the vendor should, at the very least, obtain a warranty from the event organiser that it is entitled to hold the event at the venue, that it controls access to the event, and that it owns the trade marks and other relevant intellectual property rights relating to the event. The vendor can go further and insist that the event organiser takes specific steps to combat unauthorised commercial exploitation of the event by virtue of attendance e.g. inserting restrictive provisions in the ticket terms and conditions and participation contracts.

c) Other Parties

A vendor may insist that the event organiser undertakes not to grant any rights to any other third party in respect of the event which may interfere with the ability of the vendor to exercise its rights.

d) Format and Scheduling

An event organiser may be asked to include obligations in respect of format and scheduling of the event. For example, the event organiser may be obliged not to alter either without the consent of the vendor as this may affect the value of the rights granted to the vendor.

e) Good Conduct Clauses

These types of clauses are also sometimes called 'morality clauses'. The event organiser should be obliged to support the vendor's initiatives, and undertake not to take any action, or make any statement, which is defamatory of the vendor or is detrimental to the vendor's reputation. The event organiser may also look to impose a similar term on the vendor, as suggested below.

f) Trade Marks

It is fairly common for the event organiser to be asked to provide those warranties set out in paragraph 3.5.3 below in respect of the trade marks relating to the event.

---

[7] See paragraph 1.4 above.

g) Ambush Marketing

An event organiser may be asked to use its best endeavours to counter any 'ambush marketing' in relation to the event that may impact adversely on the rights granted to the vendor.

2.3.7   The Vendor's Obligations

The event organiser would be looking to include the following obligations on the part of the vendor:

a) Pay the Consideration

The most fundamental obligation on the part of the vendor is to provide payment of the fees or the benefits in kind. This obligation will usually extend to providing such payment or benefits in kind by the dates set out in the contract.

b) Comply with Regulations

Should the event be subject to any regulations, rules or codes of conduct imposed by any body, such as a governing body, the event organiser should be looking to include an obligation to comply with such regulations, rules or codes of conduct.

c) Authority to Enter into Contract

It is common for the vendor to be asked to warrant that it has the requisite authority to enter into the contract.

d) Other Commercial Rights

Similarly, it is common for the vendor to undertake that it will not exercise any other commercial rights in the event other than those granted to it or do anything that might affect the value of the commercial rights in the event.

e) Good Conduct Clause

The vendor should undertake not to take any action, or make any statement, which is defamatory of the event organiser or the event or is detrimental to the event organiser's reputation.

f) Directions

The vendor may be asked to observe and comply with all reasonable directions, instructions and guidelines issued by the event organiser in respect of the event.

g) Trade Marks

As in the case of the event organiser, the vendor may be asked to give warranties of the kind described in paragraph 3.5.3 below.

2.3.8 Termination

Termination clauses deal with the termination of the contract before the contract is due to expire. Parties will generally envisage that if a certain event happens, it is so fundamental that it will entitle the other contracting party to bring the contract to an end. If the terminating party has suffered financial losses as a result, that party may also have a claim for such losses against the other party. The parties may also choose to expressly provide for a return of any fees paid by a vendor under the contract prior to termination.

The usual events giving rise to a right to terminate the contract are the following:

a) Insolvency/Liquidation of the Other Party

If a party is liquidated, becomes insolvent, enters into administration or ceases to do business during the term of the contract, the other party is usually provided with the right to terminate the contract.

b) Material Breach

It is common to include a clause to the effect that if a party commits a material breach of the contract and fails to remedy that breach within a specified period, the innocent party is entitled to terminate the contract. For example, if a caterer fails to provide food for an event as planned, this would amount to a material breach of the catering contract. Exactly what will be deemed to be material will inevitably depend on the nature of the contract and the nature of the breach. Failure to perform by a promised date does not automatically amount to a material breach, except where "time is of the essence"[8].

c) Change of Control

It is also common to include a clause giving rise to termination of the contract in the event that there is a change of control of either party e.g. a party is bought out by another party.

---

[8] See paragraph 2.3.8(e)(iv). For example, a catering company's failure to provide food for the event as contracted would amount to a material breach, but the event organiser's failure to pay a catering company's bill within the time specified in the contract would not generally be regarded as a material breach, unless the parties express that "time is of the essence" in the contract.

d) Disrepute

If either party's image or reputation is brought into serious disrepute, the other party may wish to have the right to terminate the contract. This may create public relations difficulties for sponsors who are associated with an event, for example.

e) Other

Other less common terms may also be included in the contract, such as the following:

i) Partial Performance

Where in a series of events there is a failure to stage a proportion of the events, or where in an international sports event major countries do not participate, the vendor may be provided with the right to terminate the contract. Similarly, where the standards of participants participating in the event are not what is expected (e.g. where junior teams are sent to an event instead of leading athletes) a vendor (such as a sponsor) may wish to have the right to terminate the contract.

ii) Broadcasting

Where rights have been sold to a vendor on the basis of a specified and guaranteed level of television coverage and that coverage is not provided, a vendor may be provided with the right to terminate the contract.

iii) Termination on Notice

If the contractual relationship is of an experimental nature, and the parties are unsure of whether they wish to enter into a long-term agreement, they may wish to include a clause providing termination on notice. In such circumstances, a party may be entitled to terminate by providing one month's written notice, for example.

iv) Time of the Essence

Where time is made an express condition of the contract (e.g. "time is of the essence") then the failure of a party to perform in accordance with the time stipulated generally gives rise to a right to terminate the contract, on the grounds that failure to perform in time is a material breach of the contract. For example, in a catering contract where the performance of the catering services is material to the contract, time will usually be made of the essence by the recipient of the catering services.

2.3.9 Force Majeure

Although the term 'force majeure' (sometimes referred to as an 'Act of God') is well-known in the commercial world, particularly in the events industry, the term has no recognised meaning in English law, USA law or South African law. Accordingly, it should only be used in contracts where the term is properly defined.

The underlying principle of a force majeure clause is that no party to an agreement should be held to performance of its obligations where, by reason of circumstances outside its control, it is prevented from doing so. A force majeure clause usually suspends the contract while the unexpected event continues, and any party affected by it is not required to perform or be liable for failure to perform its obligations.

Force majeure clauses have received some attention in the last few years in particular, as a number of events had to be cancelled because of acts of terrorism, or the threat of terrorism. The 1997 Grand National horse race in England was cancelled due to a bomb scare. The 2001 Ryder Cup golf tournament had to be cancelled shortly after the September 11 terrorist attacks in the United States. In 2004, the England Cricket Board argued that political disorder in Zimbabwe entitled it not to honour various cricketing obligations in Zimbabwe.

In the case of the Ryder Cup, several companies entered into contracts relating to these events, but failed to include force majeure clauses in their contracts, to their detriment.

Force majeure clauses are defined by references to circumstances beyond the control of the party concerned. If there is doubt as to whether any particular important occurrence is included, then this should be expressly referred to in the force majeure clause. This will also depend to a certain extent on the event concerned. In some sports events, for instance, rain, snow, hail or extreme heat are considered as elements which challenge competitors and not therefore a reason for cancelling the event. It is often a question of degree. Events or circumstances which are usually included are lightening, storms, fire, explosion, earthquake, epidemic, war, acts of terrorism, satellite failure, electrical power cuts, riot or civil disturbances, strikes or government orders.

A vendor, such as a sponsor, may wish to specify that player strikes, labour disputes, participants prevented from attending an event for political reasons, or the failure of the broadcast of the event, are not force majeure events per se, but rather events immediately giving rise to a right of termination and/or repayment of sponsorship fees.

Usually a force majeure clause will suspend the liability of the party concerned until the event giving rise to the non-performance or delay is removed. A comprehensive clause would provide that a party hindered by an event of force majeure would be required to provide notice of the occurrence of the event to the other party, and to use all reasonable endeavours to remove the event of force majeure and resume their obligations under the contract. Such a clause would also provide that if an event of force majeure continues unabated for an extended period, or there is no reasonable prospect of such occurrence discontinuing, the parties would be entitled to terminate the agreement, in which case neither party would have any liability to the other under the contract going forward[9]. Alternatively, the contract might provide for the parties being able to renegotiate within a certain time period and if that fails, they are to appoint a third party (such as an expert) to resolve the matter. This approach is sometimes used in sponsorship contracts providing for a reduction in sponsorship fees for postponement, cancellation or reduction in the nature or value of an event.

For examples of force majeure clauses, please refer to the relevant provisions contained in the sample contracts in the appendices.

Owing to the prevalence of unforeseen incidents in the events industry, and their potential impact on events themselves, it is advisable to include a comprehensive clause in event-related contracts.

It is also advisable for an event organiser to include similar force majeure clauses in all of its event-related contracts e.g. sponsors, suppliers, broadcasters etc. Otherwise, the event organiser may be left with a situation where some contracts are still in existence while others are terminated.

In conclusion, it is worth noting that in the absence of a force majeure clause, the contract may still be brought to an end automatically if performance under the contract becomes impossible (it is frustrated) or if performance becomes something so radically different from that contemplated by the parties at the time of entering into the contract that it could be said that the fundamental purpose of the contract has been removed. In such a case both parties are also released from the terms of the contract[10]. Owing to the drastic effect, however, exceptional circumstances will usually be required for a court to be satisfied that a contract has been frustrated.

---

[9] It is worth noting that in the United Kingdom, because a force majeure clause is essentially an exemption clause (it may relieve a party from liability), it may contravene the Unfair Contract Terms Act 1977 and be unenforceable. For instance, if dealing on standard terms of business or dealing with a consumer, such a clause may be unenforceable if the clause does not satisfy the test of reasonableness.

[10] In the United Kingdom, the Law Reform (Frustrated Contracts) Act provides that, upon frustration of the contract, any payments made before the frustrating event are to be returned, subject to the payee's right to deduct a 'just sum' (within the discretion of the Court) for expenses incurred in performance of the contract against that repayment. The level and range of expenses to be deducted can vary substantially from case to case.

2.3.10 Liability and Damages

When there is non-performance under a contract, the innocent party will have the right to terminate the contract and claim damages from the offending party. The measure of damages is calculated to place the injured party in the same position he or she would have been in had the contract been properly performed. These are sometimes referred to as 'compensatory damages'. Courts will generally not award punitive damages for breach of contract, as courts are reluctant to impose penalties on a party who fails to honour an obligation.

Another kind of damages is 'consequential damages'. These are indirect damages (damages which flow indirectly from the breach) and are usually not recoverable unless they are specifically provided for in the contract and they are quantifiable. Cancellation of a venue hire contract by the venue owner may result in the event organiser having to find another venue and print new pamphlets to promote the event. In such a case, the costs of printing the new pamphlets would generally be regarded as consequential damages. Loss of profits from a cancelled event will also usually be regarded as consequential damages.

It is fairly common in commercial contracts relating to events to include a clause excluding liability from indirect or consequential loss or damages or to cap liability at a certain amount (such as the total amount of the consideration paid to the event organiser).

Many contracts provide for 'liquidated damages' or 'fixed damages'. This is where the parties agree in advance on the amount of damages to be awarded in the event of a breach, because the actual calculation of damages may be difficult or uncertain or the parties simply do not wish to leave the determination of damages to a court's discretion. Liquidated damages should be a genuine pre-estimate of loss and not expressed as a penalty, as penalty clauses will generally be unenforceable.

When a contract is breached, the law imposes a duty on the injured party to mitigate their damages. For example, if the event organiser cancels a venue hire contract, the venue owner will be required to seek to re-hire the venue to a third party as soon as possible, so as to minimise its loss.

Parties may wish to include a limitation of liability clause in the contract, in terms of which liability is limited or excluded under the contract.

There may be restrictions on the ability of a party to limit or exclude their liability in a contract. In England, for instance, limitation of liability clauses are restricted by a statutory requirement of 'reasonableness'[11].

---

[11] See paragraph 6.4.2(b) and Chapter 6, n 9.

The parties may also wish to include indemnities for any loss or damage incurred by each party as a result of any breach by the other party of the warranties set out in the contract or as a result of the acts or omissions of the other party. An indemnity is essentially a promise to shield the other party from some risk, usually financial.

The indemnity will usually cover legal fees, so that if one party has to spend money defending a law suit caused by the acts or omissions of the other party, it will be able to recover those fees under the indemnity. In order to ensure that the party providing the indemnity has sufficient financial resources to back it up, it may be asked to carry insurance to cover claims under the indemnity.

2.3.11 General

Parties should seek to include a number of general clauses, such as those relating to service of notices under the contract, assignment, confidentiality and the governing law. These are sometimes referred to as 'boilerplate' clauses.

A governing law clause will set out the law which governs the contract and the interpretation thereof. In the United States, this will usually be the law of a specific state.

A dispute resolution clause should specify the manner in which any disputes in respect of the contract should be settled. Parties will wish to specify that any disputes are settled by the courts in the jurisdiction in which they are based.

Other means of dispute resolution may also be specified, such as arbitration or mediation. In relation to sports events in Europe, it has become common to refer disputes to the Court of Arbitration for Sport in Lausanne, Switzerland. Arbitration is often quicker, cheaper and more private than court proceedings. If arbitration is chosen by the parties as a means of dispute resolution, the contract should specify the location of the arbitration, how arbitrators will be decided and whether or not the decision of the arbitrator will be final and binding.

2.4   Conclusion

Whilst the above clauses are the kinds of clauses that should be considered for any contract with an event organiser or vendor in any jurisdiction, specific additional clauses should be considered for the types of contracts described in paragraph 1.3. These types of contracts have been dealt with in more detail in the chapters following. In addition, specialist advice should be taken from local attorneys or solicitors in your area in regard to the overall contract.

CHAPTER THREE

Sponsorship Contracts

The global sponsorship spend was valued at $28 billion in 2004, up from $26.2 billion in 2003[1]. Event sponsorship forms a big part of that market[2]. There is no doubt that sponsorship fees have become a key revenue stream for event organisers. Likewise, sponsors constantly seek to associate their brands with events as a means of increasing exposure and profile.

Sports events in particular have the advantage of delivering a large number of viewers and spectators. Well-established brands such as Coca-Cola have long used event sponsorship to maintain their public awareness. They have had a long-term relationship with events such as the Wimbledon Tennis Championships, the Olympics and the FIFA World Cup. In the UK, title sponsor Stella Artois has built up such a strong association with the Queen's tennis tournament (which occurs every year just prior to the Wimbledon Championships) that the event is now commonly referred to as 'The Stella Artois'. In the United States, event sponsorship is big business. Nextel recently agreed a 10-year deal to sponsor the popular NASCAR motor racing series for a reported figure of $750 million[3].

3.1   What is Sponsorship?

The term sponsorship has been described by the International Advertising Association as 'an investment, in cash or kind, in an activity, in return for access to the exploitable commercial potential associated with that activity'. 'Activity' covers events, individuals, teams, leagues, broadcast programmes and projects.

In this book we focus on event sponsorship. The object capable of being sponsored, in this case the event, is often referred to as the 'property', and the ability to associate oneself with a property is often referred to as a 'right'.

---

[1] Sports Marketing Surveys (2004). See also *Maximising the Value of Sponsorship* by Ardi Kolah (2003), SportsBusinessGroup, FMM International.

[2] Expenditure on sports sponsorship alone is expected to reach $16.8 billion by the end of 2005 (including $4.9 billion in Europe and $5.9 billion in North America), according to sponsorship consultancy Arksport (see www.arksport.com).

[3] As reported by www.forbes.com on 30/06/03.

3.2   Valuation of Sponsorship

There is no universally agreed measure for the valuation of sponsorship. The valuation will depend to a large extent on the sponsor's objectives and the degree of exposure which can be obtained for the sponsor's brand. Sponsors should also consider the extra leverage that can be obtained from related activities e.g. hospitality at an event. Sponsors should try to ensure that they have the rights to run promotions, competitions or advertisements that focus on the sponsorship. For example, Nescafé promoted its sponsorship of the *Friends* television series with parties in Central Park. It also secured advertising time directly before and after the different segments of the show. Telecommunications companies such Vodafone and Orange have used their sports sponsorships to acquire content rights for their platforms, the rights to which have become increasingly valuable.

3.3   Types of Event Sponsorship

3.3.1   Sole and Title Sponsorship

A sole sponsor will be the exclusive sponsor of the event. It may also secure title sponsorship, which is the right to have its name associated with the event itself (e.g. rugby union's Heineken Cup). As the exclusive sponsor, the sponsor will have the advantage of strong branding in relation to the event, which will not be diluted by the existence of other sponsorships. This exclusivity will need to be recorded in the contract.

3.3.2   Primary Sponsorship

A primary sponsor may not be the sole sponsor, but will have superior levels of rights compared to one or more secondary sponsors. A primary sponsor may also wish to secure title sponsorship of the event.

3.3.3   Secondary and Co-sponsorship

a) The Advantages of Secondary or Co-sponsors

Usually an event organiser will want to secure a number of secondary sponsors or co-sponsors, if possible. Securing a number of sponsors to an event can have certain advantages for the event organiser. First, the financial risk is spread, if for example any sponsor were to default. Second, the promotion of the event is increased as each sponsor will be promoting its association with the event separately. Finally, the individual rights packages are more saleable as each package can be offered at a more attractive price to sponsors, but the total sponsorship revenue will usually exceed that where a single primary sponsor is secured.

Sponsors, on the other hand, may try to include a term in the contract limiting the number of other sponsors, or at least ensuring that they have exclusivity in respect of their 'brand sector' or 'product category'.

b) Product Categories or Brand Sectors

A practice has developed to secure secondary or co-sponsors for different product categories or brand sectors, and offering exclusivity within that product category or brand sector. This was first used with great success in the 1984 Olympic Games in Los Angeles. It is now quite common in a large event to see sponsors representing a number of different brand sectors, such as the beverages brand sector, telecommunications brand sector, financial services brand sector, consumer goods brand sector, and food brand sector.

It is essential in this case to define the brand sector carefully. Do beverages include alcoholic beverages and fruit juices, for instance? Will a beer sponsor want exclusivity in cereal malt beverages only (such as lager, bitter, pilsners, ales, stouts and cider) or will it want to include hard alcohol such as vodka, gin and rum?

Precise contract drafting will be required. Typically, the event organiser will want the product category or brand sector definition to be as narrow as possible, so as not to potentially exclude the opportunity of attracting other similar sponsors (the All England Tennis Championships at Wimbledon, for example, has split the 'drinks' category into a number of distinct categories, concluding separate deals with manufacturers of mineral water, cordials, wines and champagne). On the other hand, a sponsor will want the definition to be as broad as possible, so as to exclude the possibility of a similar sponsor being secured.

c) Official Suppliers

Secondary sponsors often provide technical services or essential goods required in the running of the event in exchange for limited sponsorship rights. They may be granted 'official supplier' status e.g. Sixt car hire were an Official Supplier to the Laureus World Sport Awards.

Ultimately, the number of sponsors, and the packages offered to them, will depend on the size and status of the event.

3.4 The Nature of the Sponsorship Contract

The sponsorship contract should, at the outset, include those key terms described in Chapter 2.

Sponsorship contracts can be very short and simple, depending on the size of the event and the extent and value of the rights packages offered to a sponsor. However, where one is dealing with a large event and a complex collection of rights and obligations, the contract will need to be more detailed.

As a general point, it is advisable (and often necessary) to have a comprehensive sponsorship contract agreed and signed immediately after the parties have agreed terms. For one thing, event organisers will have deadlines in respect of the event. Secondly, the event organiser will want to secure sponsorship fees quickly so that they can fund the production of the event.

But the drafting and negotiation of a comprehensive sponsorship contract can take time, particularly if the sponsor is a large company, authorisation will need to be obtained at various management levels and the matter is thereafter referred to two sets of lawyers representing the two parties!

For this reason, a short form 'heads of agreement' for sponsorship has been included in Appendix 1A. This document can usually be agreed reasonably quickly. Parties should preferably state whether or not such a heads of agreement is intended to be binding. This heads of agreement can serve as an interim agreement whilst the long form, and more comprehensive, sponsorship contract is being drafted and agreed.

A comprehensive sponsorship contract for an event has also been included in Appendix 1B. As mentioned above, the finalisation of a document of this nature should remain the ultimate objective of the parties.

3.5 Key Legal Issues

The following are additional key legal issues in relation to sponsorship contracts:

3.5.1 Territory

In most cases, a sponsor will require that the sponsorship rights be exploited world-wide. If so, a clause to this effect should be included, for the avoidance of doubt. Whether or not the rights are in fact exploited world-wide or not will depend almost entirely on the coverage of the event.

On occasion, sponsorship rights can be split territorially. For instance, in a round-the-world yacht race, certain sponsors may wish to exploit sponsorship rights only in particular territories. In addition, new technology allowing manipulation of audio-visual footage of the event, such as the ability to digitally superimpose different advertisements electronically on advertising boards at an event, could enable the event organiser to sell sponsorship or advertising rights to sponsors in different countries, which may not be of interest to a sponsor if it does not wish to target those countries.

3.5.2 Sponsor's Rights

This is the key part of any sponsorship contract. It sets out the content of the rights offered to the sponsor, for which the sponsor is paying. Owing to the fact that it is such a fundamental part of the sponsorship contract, adequate attention needs to be given to negotiating, crystallising and recording the exact nature and scope of these rights in the contract. These are usually included in a schedule at the back of the contract. An example of such a schedule is set out in the sample long form sponsorship contract in Appendix 1B.

a) Naming/Title Rights

This is the right of the sponsor to have its name incorporated in the title of the event in all pre- and post-event publicity, such as posters, websites, and television and radio advertising. An example of this might be The Buick Invitational golf tournament.

As an alternative, the event organiser may wish to retain the current name of the event, but include the wording 'in association with' the sponsor. This is a more subtle form of title sponsorship. The latter is less attractive for a sponsor, as the event is unlikely to become synonymous with the sponsor's name.

The parties will also have to decide whether the title sponsor will be the exclusive sponsor.

Finally, designation rights are an inherent part of title sponsorship. These are the rights of a sponsor to refer to its relationship with the event e.g. 'Title Sponsor of XYZ event', or 'Official Sponsor of XYZ event'.

b) Official Supplier Rights

As mentioned in paragraph 3.3(c), included in the package of rights offered to a sponsor may be a right to supply exclusively certain key services or products required for the staging of the event. This may include technology, equipment, beverages, balls etc and may also include the right to the designation 'Official Supplier of ABC to XYZ event' or, simply, 'Official ABC Supplier'. An example of this is Gilbert who was the 'Official Supplier' of balls to the Lions Rugby Tour of Australia in 2001. More on this subject is discussed in Chapter 7 dealing with official supplier contracts.

c) Advertising and Branding Rights

Parties often describe this right in the contract merely as a 'right to branding' or 'branded presence' at the venue. However, this is vague, and generally leads to misunderstandings and failed expectations on the part of one of the parties. Advertising and branding may be minimal or extensive. Generally, a sponsor will want to try and procure as much advertising and branding at the venue as is reasonably possible.

Advertising may appear on static, fixed boards at and around the venue. The contract should stipulate exactly how many boards are permitted and their locations. Ideally, a site plan should be attached as a schedule to the contract indicating the location of the boards. If advertising is used on rotating boards, which is becoming more commonplace, then the sponsor will need to agree timing of the advertising in relation to performances at the event. In general, the timing and profile of the branding at a venue will affect the price paid for such rights.

A point which is often omitted from the sponsorship contract is the cost of such advertising or branding. This can become a contentious issue if it is not dealt with in the contract, due to the costs inherent in such an endeavour. Although essentially a matter for negotiation, usually the sponsor will be responsible for producing and providing the signage or branding. The costs of installing, maintaining and/or storing advertising boards can be borne by either party, but usually such costs are borne by the event organiser.

Do not forget to include rights of access to the venue for the purposes of installing advertising and branding, if necessary.

The extent of the branding at a venue will depend largely on the size and nature of the venue. Signage can be placed on scoreboards, on seats, on computerised or video display screens, on the playing surface itself, in goals nets, on corner flags or poles, on necessary equipment, on clocks, on stages, on riggings, on platforms, on podiums, on television backboards, at press conferences, at launches, at bars and fast food outlets inside the venue and on entry tickets, for example.

Regardless of the size or nature of the signage, a sponsor will want an undertaking from the event organiser that such branding is not obscured during the event.

Again, depending on the size and nature of the venue, a sponsor may wish to secure a 'clean' venue in order to maximize its advertising potential. This ensures that the sponsor can secure and control advertising at the event venue. For example, a football club hosting a UEFA Champions League fixture in Europe must provide a 'clean' stadium, which means that no advertising except that officially authorised by the governing body UEFA may be located within normal camera range. Somewhat controversially, New Zealand was denied the opportunity of co-hosting the 2003 Rugby World Cup because of the failure to guarantee 'clean' stadiums. Conversely, if an event organiser has a number of different sponsors, each with advertising and branding rights, it will resist the inclusion of such a clause in the contract.

Although it is possible for the event organiser to control 'unofficial' advertising inside a venue, it may be extremely difficult to do so outside the venue. This opens the door for 'ambush marketing', which can undermine the value of the sponsorship rights for the sponsor[4]. Who will forget NIKE's sponsorship of buildings in and around Atlanta during the 1996 Olympic Games, which created substantial exposure for them at the expense of rivals Adidas? In order to maximise the sponsorship, a sponsor may wish to secure the rights to advertise on billboards and streets in and around the venue. This may involve the event organiser having to secure such rights from the local authorities, the costs of which should be agreed between the parties.

With the development of the internet, the sponsor will also want to secure branding on the event organiser's website or any website established specifically for the event itself. In particular, the sponsor will want to ensure that there are reciprocal links to and from such websites. The event organiser may wish to specify that the sponsor is not entitled to establish and run a separate website in relation to the event.

Event organisers and sponsors should be aware that in some countries there are restrictions on certain types of advertising. For instance, in France a national law bans all alcohol advertising at French based events and restricts the appearance of alcohol brand-related signage for events held outside France but screened in France itself. In the UK, tobacco advertising is regulated by the Voluntary Tobacco Agreement and in 2001 the European Commission issued a directive severely restricting tobacco advertising. The directive looks set to be adopted in late 2005[5].

d) Hospitality Rights

There are a number of ancillary rights relating to the event which may be of importance to a sponsor. It may wish to have access to an office or hospitality suites at the venue. It may wish to secure a certain number of tickets to the event for the purposes of entertaining its own clients or customers, or for prizes in promotional competitions. In addition, it may wish to secure a right to other entitlements, such as food, beverages, entertainment and car park passes. The exact extent of the hospitality rights e.g. how many tickets, which part of the event, seating entitlements, quality of service etc should all be detailed in the schedule of rights.

e) Presentation Rights

The sponsor may wish to secure the right to present a trophy or awards at the event, as part of an official ceremony. This can create substantial additional

---

[4] This is dealt with further in Chapter 1 at paragraph 1.5.5.

[5] European Directive 2003/33/EC on Advertising and Sponsorship prohibits tobacco advertising in the press and other printed publications, in radio broadcasting and through tobacco-related sponsorship events or activities taking place in several member states or otherwise having cross-border effects. See www.dh.gov. uk.

exposure for a sponsor. For example, Vodacom secured the right for their Chief Executive Officer to present the trophy to the winning captain in the 2004 Tri-Nations rugby tournament in a ceremony which was watched by well over a million viewers in New Zealand, Australia and South Africa. This right may also include the right to make event or tournament awards e.g. The Barclays Man of the Match Award, or the Adidas Performance of the Year Award.

f) Merchandising Rights

The sponsor may also wish to secure the right to manufacture t-shirts (or other kinds of so-called 'premium items') branded with the event organiser's logo and the sponsor's logo. The sponsor will want to distribute such items at and around the venue to increase its profile at the event. Event organisers will seek to resist providing such a right, particularly if the event organiser believes that this might interfere with its own merchandising programme or licensing programme.

g) Associative Marketing Rights

This may include the right of a sponsor to use the event mark (and/or the event organiser's logo and/or any composite logo created using both the event organiser and sponsor's marks) on the sponsor's products, on its letterheads or on any of its marketing and promotional material despatched to third parties. For more on the use of the marks and logos of the respective parties, please see paragraph 3.5.3 below.

h) Broadcasting Delivery

Strictly speaking, broadcast coverage is not a contractual right in a sponsorship contract. It is more aptly described as an obligation on the event organiser, although very often it is included in the rights package.

Television and other media coverage in relation to an event are fundamental to the value of sponsorship. It enables the sponsor's brand or product message to be delivered to thousands, possibly millions, of viewers.

Usually the event organiser will secure a television producer and distributor, or a broadcaster, before sourcing sponsorship. A sponsor will want the event organiser to warrant that broadcasting has been secured. Where broadcasting has not been secured, and a sponsor deems broadcasting as fundamental to its sponsorship contract, it should seek to include an obligation on the event organiser that it will procure such rights prior to the event. It may wish to include this as a condition precedent to the sponsorship contract i.e. a condition that must be fulfilled prior to the coming into operation of the contract. The event organiser, on the other hand, would only agree to such an obligation or condition precedent if it feels confident that it will procure broadcasting. In general, the event organiser should take care not to oversell the potential for broadcasting to a sponsor where such broadcasting has not as yet been secured contractually.

A compromise position is often reached by linking consideration to media value obtained or by way of an agreed reduction mechanism, whereby a failure to secure the guaranteed broadcasting, or a viable alternative, results in the sponsor receiving a refund of part of the consideration. For more on rights of reduction, see paragraph 3.5.4 below.

If broadcasting has been secured, the sponsor will want to procure warranties from the event organiser as to the quality of the television coverage and the extent, quantity and scheduling of such coverage. As regards the former, obligations regarding transmission of the sponsor's branding (e.g. on backboards for television interviews) and on-screen credits when referring to the event should be included. As regards the latter, obligations regarding timing, frequency and duration of coverage should be included. In addition, details regarding coverage of other 'event-related matters', such as draws, winning parades and interviews should also be agreed.

Event organisers should be aware that in some countries, such as the UK, there may be laws or guidelines regulating broadcasting of events which might have an impact on sponsorship rights. These regulations or guidelines have usually been put in place to ensure that the integrity of the broadcasting is not compromised by the influence of a sponsor. This is dealt with more fully in Chapter 13 on Broadcasting Contracts.

i) Other Ancillary Rights

The sponsor may wish to consider a number of additional rights:

- The sponsor may wish to have access to, and license, certain intellectual property owned by the event organiser, such as fixture lists or designs;
- The sponsor may wish to gain access to the supporter lists or databases belonging to the event organiser for the purpose of sending out promotional materials to those parties. The event organiser needs to ensure that it is complying with any relevant data protection regulations that may be in force[6], such as the Data Protection Act 1998 (applicable in the UK);
- The sponsor should consider including the right to film, or obtain film footage of, the event. It may wish to use this footage for its own marketing and promotional purposes. The event organiser needs to ensure that the provision

---

[6] Examples are the Data Protection Act 1998 in the UK; the data protection measures contained in the Electronic Communications and Transactions Act 25 of 2002, The Promotion of Access to Information Act 2 of 2000 and the Constitution of the Republic of South Africa 108 of 1996 in South Africa; and the data protection principles contained in the US safe harbor laws.

of such rights does not amount to a breach of any contract it has with an event broadcaster or media partner;

- Certain other ancillary rights may be appropriate to particular kinds of sponsors. For instance, a beer sponsor will wish to obtain exclusive 'pouring rights' in certain areas inside the venue. A retail sponsor or kit supplier may wish to secure the right to establish promotional outlets or 'promo trucks' at various locations at the venue in order to sell its own merchandise. A telecommunications sponsor may wish to secure the rights to certain footage in order to make such footage available for downloading via its mobile telephone network;
- Rights in relation to players/performers may also be negotiated. These rights usually refer to the right to use certain players or performers for appearances, or the right to use their images for various promotions. It is unusual to include this right in the schedule of rights for a sponsor who is sponsoring an event. This is because the event organiser may not be in a position to grant these rights itself. However, an event organiser may have secured such rights via a participation agreement (in terms of which teams agree to participate in an event) or via a performer's agreement (in terms of which a performer agrees to perform at an event);
- Rights in relation to product or services displays and premium give-aways at the venue.

3.5.3 Trade Marks

Usually the event organiser and the sponsor will wish to use trade marks or logos belonging to the other as part of the sponsorship contract. For instance, the sponsor will want to use the event organiser's logo in conjunction with the designation it has acquired. The event organiser may wish to use the sponsor's logo on official promotional materials for the event, or on letterheads and invitations relating to the event.

The parties should consider including warranties or undertakings in the contract to the effect that: each party owns the trade marks that the other is entitled to use or has a right to grant a licence for its use; the trade marks do not infringe the intellectual property rights of any other third party; all trade marks to be used have been registered in the proper classes at the relevant trade mark registry for that country, and in other appropriate jurisdictions; the trade marks will be used in accordance with the form and guidelines as set out in an appendix to the contract; and both parties will co-operate in policing the use of the trade marks, inform the other of trade mark infringements and, if necessary, take action in respect of such infringement.

Often a sponsor may wish to combine its logo with that of the event organiser to form a composite or event logo. This may give rise to issues surrounding ownership of the composite logo. The usual practice is that such logo is registered and owned jointly by both parties, and once the sponsorship relationship has ended, the registration is allowed to die. The sponsor and event organiser will also want to prevent the use of the composite logo by the other party without their approval.

It is not unusual for a party to include right of approval over use of their trade marks on any materials being distributed by the other party, such as promotional materials. Although this right of approval seems sensible in theory, parties should decide whether this is necessary and desirable in practice, as it may be a laborious, time-consuming and expensive process to post materials back and forth for approval. If such a clause is included, the approval mechanisms should be set out in detail, including a clause to the effect that if a reply to a request for approval is not provided by the other party within a certain period of time, such approval will be deemed to have been given. This ensures that a party is not unnecessarily delayed in finalising and distributing the materials by the tardiness of the other party.

3.5.4 Reduction of Consideration

A sponsor may wish to include rights of reduction in the contract. This usually includes the right to a part refund of the sponsorship fees if the value of the sponsorship rights is reduced in any way.

For instance, a sponsor may feel that this is warranted if there is a change in circumstance which affects the sponsorship rights. Such changes in circumstances could include, for example, a change in the number and status of participating teams or performers in the event, a change in structure of the event, cancellation of a part of the event or less extensive broadcast coverage of the event.

Alternatively, a sponsor may wish to be compensated by way of a reduction in the event that its logos or advertising boards are altered, deleted or defaced in any way during the event.

The parties may feel that in such circumstances, it would not be necessary or appropriate to provide the sponsor with a right to terminate the contract. Some element of financial compensation, however, would be appropriate. In this way, the sponsor ends up paying an appropriate amount for the rights, and the event organiser can be assured that a possible termination of the contract by the sponsor is eliminated.

The obvious question which follows is this: how do the parties decide on what level of reduction is appropriate, and what if they cannot agree on this level?

To cater for this, it is important to include a mechanism in the contract referring this question to an independent third party expert, if the parties cannot agree on an appropriate level of reduction.

The event organiser may also wish to reserve the right to offer alternative sponsorship rights to the sponsor (to make up the value) prior to the right of reduction being exercised.

3.6 Conclusion

Sponsorship can be a major source of revenue for an event organiser. A variety of different sponsorship rights can be granted, ranging from sponsorship of kit or equipment to be used in the event to banner advertising in or around the venue. Some of these rights are set out in paragraph 3.5.2 above.

However, event organisers need to be aware that sponsors are becoming more educated and more sophisticated in the outlook towards event sponsorship. They are looking at ways to build partnerships with the owner of a property and create value on a number of different levels. Sponsors are also becoming more demanding about the protection of their rights as the threat of ambush marketing increases, particularly for those events that have a high profile.

CHAPTER FOUR

Venue Hire Contracts

In almost all cases in order for an event to take place a venue needs to be secured. This could be a small conference room or a large stadium. The nature and size of the venue will obviously depend on the nature and size of the event. In some cases, a number of separate venues will be required for the event e.g. the FIFA World Cup.

It is unusual for the event organiser to own the venue. Accordingly, an event organiser will need to enter into a contract in terms of which a venue is made available to the event organiser for the purposes of staging the event.

4.1   The Nature of the Venue Hire Contract

In a venue hire contract a party secures the right from the venue owner to use the venue for a certain limited period for the purposes of staging the event[1].

The venue hire contract should, at the outset, include those standard terms set out in Chapter 2, or terms similar thereto.

It should also include terms dealing with the key legal issues outlined below. A comprehensive venue hire contract is set out in Appendix 2.

4.2   Key Legal Issues

4.2.1   Grant of Rights/Licence to Use the Venue

The venue owner will need to make the venue available to the event organiser for the purpose of staging the event. It is important for the event organiser to stipulate not only that the venue will be available for its use during a determined period but that it will have rights of access for its employees, agents and sub-contractors for the purposes of preparing for and organising the event. It is in the interests of both parties to stipulate the period during which personnel will have such rights of access. The venue owner will want to ensure that the preparation for the event does not interfere with the termination of another event at the

---

[1]   In some countries the contract is in the form of a licence to use the venue.

same venue. At the same time the event organiser will want to ensure that it has sufficient time to prepare for the event so as to make it a success.

The event organiser will also want to ensure that the venue will be available for its sole and exclusive use during the determined period. In this way, the event organiser can control access to the venue and ensure that it is able to maximise its ability to generate commercial revenue from its use of the venue[2].

4.2.2   Definition of Venue

It is essential to define the term 'venue' in the contract. This is to avoid misunderstandings about the *extent* of the space being provided to the event organiser. For instance, does the venue include dressing rooms, stands, boxes, offices, hospitality areas, concourses, walkways, car parks, media and broadcasting facilities (including camera positions and TV, radio and internet facilities)?

Often it is beneficial to attach a diagram as a schedule to the contract identifying the exact nature and extent of the venue.

Parking deserves special mention, for a number of reasons. Firstly, lack of parking facilities can have a significant impact on the success of an event. Secondly, parking has become a major source of revenue (and hence disagreement) for venue owners and event organisers alike. Thirdly, the provision of parking carries security issues which need to be considered. Fourthly, parking is often provided as part of hospitality and VIP packages. Finally, parking places and loading bays may be required for the event organiser in preparing for the event.

For these reasons alone the parties should include provisions in the contract dealing with parking and the provision of parking facilities.

4.2.3   Consideration/Licence Fee

The amount of the fee paid by the event organiser to the venue owner will vary according to the size and extent of use of the venue. It will also vary according to which party will undertake the services described in paragraph 4.2.5 below. The fees are essentially a matter of commercial negotiation between the parties, as is the timing of any payments that make up the fee. Ideally, the event organiser will want to pay such fees after the event has taken place, or in instalments. The venue owner will, on the other hand, at least want part payment in advance of the event or some sort of security deposit.

In addition to payment of the fees referred to above, the venue owner will usually require payment of costs relating to the use of utilities at the venue during the hire period, such as electricity, gas, water, lighting, heat and telephone. This is

---

[2]   See paragraph 1.5.1 above.

more likely to be the case if the event is a large-scale event running over a period of several days or weeks.

The event organiser should establish whether the consideration paid includes the costs of cleaning the venue and the disposal of waste and litter, the costs of which can be substantial in some cases.

A venue owner may also require the payment of a nominal amount to the local community, particularly if they are likely to be inconvenienced as a result of the event. For instance, if a large and noisy concert is going to be held close to a residential area, this might be considered appropriate.

On occasion, a venue owner may demand a percentage of ticket or merchandising sales arising from an event. This usually occurs only in respect of very large events, and is once again a matter of negotiation between the parties. If a revenue sharing arrangement is agreed between the parties, provisions will need to be included as to accounting, collection of monies and remission of such monies.

It is common for a security deposit or 'damage deposit' to be required before taking occupation of the venue. Provisions should be included dealing with how and when this deposit will be returned to the event organiser.

Further clauses may also be included dealing with repayment of consideration in the event of cancellation or postponement of the event.

Taxes may be chargeable by the venue owner in some jurisdictions on the rental fees to be paid by the event organiser.

4.2.4   Warranties

The venue owner may be asked to provide warranties that:

- It has full rights and title to enter into the contract;
- It is not aware of anything which might prevent performance by the venue owner of its obligations under the contract;
- The venue meets and complies with all applicable laws, rules, regulations, health and safety requirements and that all licences, consents, clearances and approvals have been obtained from the necessary authorities (including all health and safety certificates and liquor licences) to enable the event to take place at the venue; or
- The venue is free from all advertising and other branding (unless otherwise agreed).

The venue owner should not be asked to provide a warranty as to the suitability of the venue for the staging of the event. It is up to the event organiser to satisfy itself as to the suitability of the venue for the staging of the event.

The event organiser may be asked in turn to provide warranties that:

- It shall not use the venue for any purpose other than to stage the event;
- It will not do anything which might invalidate any insurance maintained by the venue owner in respect of the venue;
- It will observe all applicable statutes, licences, by-laws and regulations relating to the use of the venue for the event;
- It will pay to the venue owner the costs of making good all damage to the venue suffered during the period of use which is not covered by insurance;
- It will not make any alterations or additions to the venue without the prior written consent of the venue owner;
- It will make all administrative arrangements to ensure that the maximum number of persons at the venue (including employees, sub-contractors, performers and attendees/spectators) does not exceed a specified amount; or
- It will not permit or facilitate the commercial operation of bookmakers in the venue other than licensed bookmakers.

4.2.5   Obligations on the Parties

In a contract to hire a venue, there are usually a number of practical considerations that will need to be clarified. Who will provide the security? Who will clean up the venue after the event? If there is a grass playing surface at the venue, will this need to be protected during the event? Will concession stands be available and who will run them?

The obligations of the parties need to be clearly established and recorded, either in the contract itself, or in a schedule attached to the contract, so that the performance of these obligations has legal implications and can be enforced if necessary. More than one function has been ruined because it was not clear which party was to provide toilet facilities!

In addition, provisions dealing with the costs of fulfilling the respective obligations need to be included within the contract.

a)   Obligations of the Venue Owner

These may include any number of the following:

- Providing access to the venue for particular time periods before and after the event for the personnel of the event organiser and the commercial partners of the event organiser;
- Providing use of certain specified rooms, including changing rooms, offices, boxes or hospitality areas;
- Providing media facilities;
- Providing electrical power supply, heating, refrigeration, gas, or water;

- Providing toilet facilities, including portable toilets, if necessary;
- Providing temporary phone, fax and internet lines;
- Providing, storing, testing, operating or dismantling equipment, such as tables, chairs, sound equipment, lighting equipment or sports equipment (including scoring equipment);
- Providing and operating video screens at the venue;
- Providing scoring or scoreboard facilities;
- Providing secure car and truck parking facilities and parking passes;
- Providing rigging equipment and facilities;
- Providing a forklift during the pre- and post-event periods;
- Cleaning of the venue, including all dressing rooms and catering facilities prior to the event;
- Providing personnel for all the abovementioned services;
- Providing first-aid facilities and a full first-aid service;
- Providing a certain number of stewards and security guards responsible for providing 24-hour security before, during and after the event, controlling access to certain areas at the venue, controlling spectator movement before, during and after the event, directing VIP's to certain areas at the venue, managing car parking, searching bags and manning turnstiles[3];
- Procuring the full co-operation and adequate levels of resource from the local police force to ensure that the event is staged safely, including securing necessary traffic control, re-routing and co-ordination;
- Providing the services of a fire and safety officer responsible for providing fire extinguishers and ensuring that the safety facilities in the venue comply with the appropriate regulatory requirements;
- Providing a ticket box office and on-site ticket sale operations;
- Providing screening, ropes and signage for blocking access to certain areas at the venue;
- Providing a detailed plan of the venue, and all suitable trade stand locations if necessary;
- Providing facilities for the sale of event programmes;
- Using reasonable or best endeavours to assist the event organiser in preventing ambush marketing around the venue (this may include ensuring that certain buildings or facilities around the venue are free from advertising);
- Using reasonable or best endeavours to assist the event organiser in preventing the sale of unauthorised sale of tickets at the venue (by ticket touts, for example).

---

[3] In the United Kingdom, this may be governed by the Safety of Sports Grounds Act 1975, which applies to large sports stadia. See paragraph 4.2.9(a)(iii) below.

b) Obligations of the Event Organiser

These may include any number of the following:

- Undertaking and managing all matters relating to the staging of the event at the venue;
- Undertaking and managing all matters relating to the design, printing, pricing, distribution, sale and checking of tickets and programmes for the event;
- Preparing and providing the venue owner with detailed reports on ticket sales and ticket allocations;
- Removing all litter and waste from the venue after the event and handing back the venue in a clean condition;
- Using reasonable or best endeavours to ensure that the attendees have left the venue by a particular time;
- Ensuring that any playing surface is protected during the event, if necessary;
- Making good or repair any damage caused to the venue during the event;
- Providing a certain number of complimentary tickets to the venue owner for the event;
- Procuring that none of the event organiser's commercial partners, or any performers taking part in the event, use images of the venue itself without the prior consent of the venue owner; or
- Ensuring that the noise levels from the event immediately outside the venue shall not exceed a certain level, and that the event organiser shall comply with any regulations or by-laws issued by local authorities in this regard.

Some of the obligations outlined above may be imposed on the other party in the contract. For instance, whilst it is more common for the venue owner to produce the tickets and manage the ticket sales, in some cases the parties will agree that it is more appropriate for the event organiser to control and manage these aspects.

4.2.6 Rights of Parties

In addition to the obligations, there may be a number of rights granted to the parties which should be recorded in the contract.

Rights granted to the venue owner may include the following:

- The right to operate concession stands at the venue;
- The right to prevent access to or remove from the venue any person acting in a way which in the reasonable opinion of the venue owner is regarded as offensive, harmful or undesirable, or who represents a security risk;
- The right at any time after the period of hire to remove from the venue, and dispose of, all structures, goods, equipment, waste and other materials

brought into the venue by the event organiser or its employees and left at the venue; and

- The right of free access at any time during the period of hire for certain representatives of the venue owner.

Rights granted to the event organiser may include the following:

- The right to place advertisements or branding of title/event sponsors of the event within and outside the venue but so that no such advertisement or branding shall be affixed to walls or other parts of the venue so as to cause damage to the venue;
- Rights of access to the venue during the period of hire[4];
- The right to exploit all the commercial rights in the event, including the right to broadcast footage and take photographs of both the event and the venue;

4.2.7 Insurance

Usually, the venue owner will already have existing general/public liability insurance in place at the venue. The event organiser may wish to obtain a warranty that such insurance is in place and the extent of such insurance. The event organiser may wish to be noted as an additional party on such insurance policy. This usually involves a cost, which should be covered by the event organiser.

Alternatively, there may be an obligation on the part of the event organiser to take out general/public liability insurance.

A further aspect which will need to be resolved is insurance to the venue itself. Again, this will usually be covered by an existing policy taken out by the venue owner. The existence and terms of such a policy should be confirmed. This will cover damage to the venue itself.

Some venue owners may not wish to claim under an insurance policy for damage to the venue. They may have to pay an excess under that policy or the policy may only cover certain types of damage. In such a case, the venue owner may require that the event organiser repairs the damage. If so, the event organiser should stipulate that the repair work will be carried out by contractors appointed by it rather than the venue owner.

The event organiser will usually be responsible for insuring against loss or damage to the property and effects of the event organiser, its employees, and its sub-contractors. The event organiser can exclude liability for loss or damage to the personal effects of the attendees at the event by including such an exclusion clause in the ticket terms and conditions, which govern the conditions of

---

[4]   See paragraphs 4.2.1 and 1.5.1 above.

access to the venue. Such an exclusion of liability should also be expressed on signboards at the venue. The venue owner will want to expressly state that it has no responsibility for any loss or damage to equipment, materials or property of any kind brought into the property by the event organiser, its employees, its sub-contractors or its agents, or by the attendees at the event.

The venue owner may also request that cancellation insurance be taken out by the event organiser in respect of the event, although it should be noted that this is often expensive to obtain.

It is common for the venue owner to ask for an indemnity from the event organiser for any costs, liabilities or expenses as a result of claims from third parties against the venue owner arising out of the event, particularly where the event organiser has been negligent. For instance, if a temporary structure which has not been erected properly falls and injures a third party, and that third party sues the venue owner, the venue owner would want to obtain an indemnity from the event organiser for any losses it suffers as a result of the negligence of the event organiser.

Finally, the parties should consider whether liquor liability insurance is necessary.

A more detailed explanation of the types of insurance available is provided in Chapter 6.

4.2.8   Exclusivity

The success of an event can be affected by the presence of a competing event held at the venue at around the same time. This is particularly the case for trade shows. For this reason, event organisers often try and negotiate an 'exclusivity' arrangement with the venue owner. A typical arrangement would preclude the venue owner from hosting a similar event within 30 days before or after the event. As long as there are other available venues or the chosen venue, if deemed to be essential, is not monopolised for an entire year, such an arrangement will generally be permitted.

4.2.9   Regulatory Issues

There are a number of general regulatory issues to consider in relation to venues. These will vary from country to country (and sometimes from region to region and state to state) but will generally include the following:

- Planning requirements (particularly during any periods of construction and redevelopment)
- Health and safety regulations
- Liquor licensing regulations

- Entertainment licensing regulations
- Fire certification

An understanding of relevant health and safety legislation, in particular, is absolutely essential for event organisers. For this reason, a whole chapter has been dedicated to this (see Chapter 6).

It is recommended that event organisers take specific legal advice in respect of all the above aspects, to ensure that they are compliant.

a) United Kingdom

There are a number of pieces of legislation in the United Kingdom which are relevant for venue owners or those in control of a venue.

I) Occupiers Liability Act 1957

It is important to note that any person in occupation, control or possession of premises owes a duty of care to all visitors under this Act. The occupier should take such care as is reasonable to ensure that the visitors to the premises will be safe in using the premises for the purpose for which they were invited or permitted to attend there. The obligations of the occupier will vary according to the circumstances and according to the nature and age of the visitors, but the standard of care is broadly the same as that in an ordinary case of negligence. Event organisers may try to limit their liability by way of providing appropriate warnings of potential dangers which may arise at the venue, for example by erecting sign boards[5].

II) Disability Discrimination Act 1995

The provisions of this Act require service providers (including venue owners) to take reasonable steps to alter any policy, practice or procedure which makes it impossible or difficult for disabled persons to use a service (such as attending at a venue). It would also require venue owners to take reasonable steps to put in place mechanisms to facilitate use of a venue by disabled persons.

III) Safety of Sports Grounds Act 1975

Following tragic incidents at sports grounds, regulations were introduced relating specifically to the licensing and control of large sports stadia (those with a capacity of over 10 000 visitors or otherwise designated by the Secretary of State). This

---

[5] It should be noted that under the Unfair Contract Terms Act 1977 it is not possible to exclude liability for death or personal injury where the venue is occupied by an occupier for the purposes of his business. Where the granting of access to the venue forms part of the business of the occupier, then that will be considered to be a business purpose. It is also a principle of English law that a venue owner or occupier cannot exclude liability for death or personal injury arising from its own negligence. For these reasons, it is advisable to obtain public liability insurance.

obliges the venue owner to obtain a current safety certificate issued by a local authority. The certificate deals with matters such as the number of spectators allowed into the stadium and the number, size and location of entrances. The local authority also has the power to issue restrictions on the use of the venue when it considers that certain risks are present.

iv) Football Spectators Act 1989

An association football club must also comply with the requirements of this Act. This sets out a programme for the licensing of football grounds and a related national football membership scheme at specified matches in England and Wales. Licences are issued by the Football Licensing Authority to venue owners and operators.

v) Alcohol Control and Licensing

General provisions relating to alcohol licensing are set out in the Licensing Act 2003 (this is discussed further in paragraph 8.3.1(a)). In addition to this, however, regulations have been introduced under the Sporting Events (Control of Alcohol etc) Act 1985 (subsequently amended in 1992), in terms of which certain time periods for the sale of alcohol before and after a game are imposed.

vi) Health and Safety at Work Act 1974

This Act imposes an obligation upon an employer to ensure that the work environment is safe and without risk to the health of employees. This means that venues owners and event organisers with employees who work at the venue may also be bound by these regulations if the venue is regarded as the workplace under this Act. This is dealt with further in paragraph 6.4.2(c) below.

vii) Entertainment Licensing

Under the Licensing Act 2003, those venues providing entertainment to the public require a 'Premises Licence' after 24 November 2005 in order to provide such entertainment. This licence is also required for those venues providing late night refreshment (providing hot food or drink to members of the public between 11 pm and 5 am). This Act only applies to England and Wales. In certain circumstances an event organiser can obtain a Temporary Event Notice (TEN), which is a form of temporary licence. This is dealt with further in paragraph 8.3.1(a) below.

b) United States

i) Americans with Disabilities Act (ADA)

This Act is a federal civil rights law designed to prevent discrimination against those individuals who have a physical or mental disability or impairment. Events companies falling within this Act must ensure that individuals with such disabilities have equal opportunities to apply for jobs and to work in jobs for which they are qualified; that they have equal access to benefits; that they are not harassed by virtue of their disability; and that they an equal opportunity to be promoted once hired[6].

The ADA is also of significance to event organisers and venue owners because it provides protection for disabled persons in the area of public accommodations. Public accommodations are private entities that affect commerce and include hotels, theatres, concert halls, stadiums, convention centres, auditoriums, museums, parks, restaurants and even golf courses. In addition, entities which are not in and of themselves public accommodations, such as a trade association, may become a public accommodation when it leases space at a convention centre, hotel or stadium.

The ADA generally requires entities responsible for public accommodations to make reasonable modifications in policies, practices or procedures to accommodate persons with disabilities, unless making such modifications would substantially or fundamentally alter the nature of the goods, services and facilities offered. Such modifications will include the removal of architectural barriers to entering and using facilities e.g. installing ramps, making curb cuts at sidewalks and entrances, widening doorways, installing bars in bathrooms and adding Braille to elevator control buttons.

Convention and conference organisers should also note that the ADA requires that 'auxiliary aids and services' be provided when necessary to ensure effective communication with individuals with hearing, vision or speech impediments. These aids include interpreters, headsets, television captioning, telecommunication devices for deaf persons and Braille materials, for instance. However, such aids are not required where provision would impose an undue burden on the organisers e.g. a significant administrative difficulty or expense.

The ADA places legal responsibility for compliance on the shoulders of both venue owners and event organisers.

ii) Occupational Safety and Health Act (OSHA)
This Act relates to workplace conditions and therefore includes venues at which employees will be working. The Act provides for a number of health and safety requirements of which event organisers and event owners should be aware, particularly if the venue qualifies as a workplace under this Act[7].

---

[6] Under this Act employers are required to make reasonable accommodations or adjustments so as to enable employees to maintain equal employment opportunities. Employers are not obliged to make an accommodation if it would present an undue hardship. The question of undue hardship will depend on the circumstances of each situation.

[7] See paragraph 6.4.2(c) below.

c) South Africa

i) *National Building Regulations and the Building Standards Act 103 of 1977*

These pieces of legislation set standards for technical performance for all buildings constructed in South Africa to ensure the health and safety of occupants[8].

ii) *Disability Legislation*

The arrival of democracy in South Africa saw the implementation of a number of acts of parliament and policies designed to improve accessibility to venues for the disabled. Apart from the anti-discrimination principles enshrined in the South African Constitution and Bill of Rights 1996, the government introduced the White Paper on an Integrated National Disability Strategy 1997 and the Promotion of Equality and Prevention of Unfair Discrimination Act 2000. In addition, the governing is currently reviewing Part S of the National Building Regulations (which provides access to venues for wheelchair users) and the related SABS Codes of Practice to remove the current loopholes which have prevented the enforcement of these regulations in the past. Section 9 of the Promotion of Equality and Prevention of Unfair Discrimination Act 2000 partly addresses this problem by making it an offence to contravene the SABS Codes of Practice relating to accessibility[9].

iii) *Occupation Health and Safety Act 85 of 1993*

As is the case in the United States and the United Kingdom, this primary piece of legislation on health and safety deals imposes an obligation upon an employer to ensure that the work environment is safe and without risk to the health of employees. This means that venues owners and event organisers with employees who work at the venue may be obliged under law to ensure that the venue is safe if the venue is regarded as a workplace under that Act.

iv) *The Safety at Sports and Recreational Events Bill*

As the title suggests, this piece of legislation is currently only a bill and has not yet been passed by Parliament in South Africa. However, this bill when it is passed is likely to have far-reaching consequences and, as such, it is worth mentioning here.

The purpose of the legislation is to determine, maintain, protect and ensure the safety and security of spectators and participants (and their property) at sports and recreational events at a stadium or a venue or its precincts in South Africa.

---

[8] See also SANS 10400 on the application of the National Building Regulations.

[9] See SABS 0400: 1990 and SANS 10400 regarding the application of the National Building Regulations and SABS 0246: 1993 which establishes the minimum design requirements for access to and circulation in buildings and related facilities to permit general use by disabled persons.

The legislation imposes a number of obligations on event organisers as well as venue owners. As these cover safety and security issues, they are dealt with in Chapter 6 in more detail[10].

4.2.10 Codes of Practice and Guidelines

There are a number of comprehensive codes of practice or guidelines which have been issued by governments or quasi-governmental bodies in different countries relating to event management and venue safety. These do not generally have the force of law. However, it is important to be aware of these codes or guidelines as it is not uncommon for a clause to be included in the contract to the effect that the venue owner or event organiser shall comply with the requirements of such codes of practice.

For example, in the UK the Health and Safety Executive issued *The Event Safety Guide: a Guide to Health, Safety and Welfare at Music and Similar Events* (also known as 'The Purple Book') in 1999[11]. The Home Office in the UK has also issued other guides such as *The Guide to Fire Precautions In Existing Places of Entertainment and Like Premises*[12] and *The Guide to Safety at Sports Grounds*[13] (also known as 'The Green Guide').

In South Africa, the obvious example is the SABS code of guidelines, which do not have legislative effect.

As these codes and guidelines relate to health and safety primarily, they are dealt with more detail in Chapter 6[14].

4.3 Specific Considerations for Convention Centres

Event organisers should be aware that many convention centres are owned and operated by cities or other governmental entities. Traditionally, these entities are less willing to make changes to standard-form contracts which have been developed especially for their convention centres. Many of these contracts contain one-sided provisions. However, that does not mean that an event organiser cannot make reasonable requests or negotiate changes to the contract.

4.3.1 Parties

Event organisers should take care to establish whether they will be negotiating and contracting with the convention centre directly or with a city's convention and

---

[10] See paragraph 6.4.2(c)(i) below.

[11] First published as *The Guide to Health, Safety and Welfare at Pop Concerts and Similar Events* 1993, ISBN 0113410727. 1999 issue by the Health and Safety Executive under ISBN 0717624536.

[12] March 1990, ISBN 0113409079.

[13] The Stationery Office, 1997, ISBN 01130000952.

[14] See paragraph 6.4.2(e) below.

visitor's bureau. Often a convention and visitor's bureau may have the right and ability to reserve space in a convention centre well in advance of the event, although the actual convention centre contract is only entered into with the convention centre a few months before the event. In such a case, the event organiser may have to sign the contract on the terms stipulated by the convention centre because by that late stage all other alternative venues are no longer available.

Also ensure that the person signing the contract on behalf of the convention centre has authority to sign on behalf of the centre.

4.3.2   Binding Contract

Event organisers should ascertain up-front when and if a contract has been entered into for the hiring of space. Often a reservation will have been made for the hiring of a convention centre on a tentative basis (this is sometimes referred to as a 'tentative first option'). Usually this will not constitute a binding contract but will be an offer which must be specifically accepted by the event organiser. In these circumstances there will be no obligation on the centre to hold the "option" or offer open.

However, sometimes parties make a reservation on a 'definite basis' and then find that they have mistakenly entered into a binding contract. As a general rule, an event organiser should not accept the space on a 'definite basis' unless it intends to sign the final contract of hire.

4.3.3   Duration

Although this might seem obvious, it is vital to ensure that the centre is booked on the correct days, particularly when the booking is made well in advance. This is one of the major problems giving rise to disputes between an event organiser and convention centre. It is also one of the most difficult and costly problems to correct. Note that Easter, Passover, Rosh Hashanah and Yom Kippur do not fall on the same date or even in the same month every year.

4.3.4   Move-in/Move-out Costs

Often a convention centre will provide a certain number of complimentary move-in and move-out periods to allow for the setting up of the venue. Do not assume this is automatic – this should be expressed in the contract. If more than the complimentary allotment of move-in/move-out time is required, a special rate for the extra days may be negotiated.

4.3.5   Rates

The rates charged for the hire of space in a convention centre can vary substantially. For instance, there may be different rates charged for different types of events held in the convention centre. In addition, the centre may charge on a daily basis or on net square footage actually used. The parties may also agree a revenue sharing arrangement on ticket sales for the event which will affect the rates charged[15]. The rates and the basis for charging these rates should be agreed and stipulated in the contract. It should also be noted that if the event organiser is not using sections of the rented space to generate revenue, it may be able to negotiate reduced rental payments. Similarly, check if a reduction can be negotiated for any space cancelled or not used.

Take special note of any late or accelerated payment provisions in the contract in the event that an instalment is missed. It is also not advisable to agree to pay for unspecified charges to be determined at a later date or by the convention centre. If such charges are foreseeable but are unable to be determined at the time of signature of the contract, provisions should be included dealing with precisely how and when such charges will be determined. In general, a vague agreement to agree the charges at a later date will be unenforceable, however a clause stating that such charges will be determined by the convention centre will be enforceable.

4.3.6   Additional Charges

The rates for hire may exclude a number of additional charges. Event organisers should be warned that these charges may quickly accumulate. The parties should clarify in the contract whether the rates will include the following in particular:

* The provision of chairs, tables, podiums, drapes, microphones etc;
* Set-up of any meeting rooms or halls;
* Set-up and provision of a PA system, sounding boards or screens for presentations;
* On-hand technical support for the above;
* Dial-up facilities and use of the internet;
* Re-setting of meeting rooms during the event;
* Locking and unlocking of meeting rooms between periods of use;
* Provision of beverages for meetings e.g. bottled water, tea, coffee etc;
* Provision of air-condition and heating units.

4.3.7   Remodelling/Expansion/Refurbishment

Changes in the physical aspects of the convention centre may have a negative impact on the event. Even minor construction can affect access, parking, traffic or the building's appearance. It is not uncommon for convention centres to omit mention of these changes to an event organiser. Provisions should be included

---

[15] See paragraph 4.2.3 above.

in the contract requiring notification of such circumstances and permitting cost concessions or even cancellation if the event is to be compromised in any way.

4.3.8   Other Events

An event organiser may want to specify that it will not share the centre with a competitive event, or ask for a specific period of time in which a competitive event will not be scheduled. The event organiser should certainly specify that the centre must ensure that the sounds and activities arising from other events in the centre do not negatively impact on the event (the same may be required for the event organiser, however).

4.3.9   Approval for Promotion and Advertising of the Event

The convention centre may try and specify that approval is required over all promotional and advertising materials in relation to the event, particularly if the event is a public one. The event organiser will want to try and avoid this restriction. In addition, provisions should be included governing the use of logos belonging to the event organiser and the convention centre, if required for the promotion of the event.

4.3.10   Exclusive Service Providers

The convention centre may have exclusive arrangements with certain designated service providers e.g. decorating, cleaning, security etc. This can sometimes gives rise to disputes. For example, the Jacob Javits Center in New York was involved in a dispute over lobby advertising with a trade show operator who wanted to contract with a company to provide specialist TV monitors. The Center claimed to have an exclusive contract with another supplier.

If such an arrangement does exist, the event organiser needs to be aware of the exact nature of the services to be provided and the costs thereof. The event organiser should, where possible, negotiate out of this provision so that it will have the right to appoint its own service providers for the event. If this is not possible, the event organiser should try and negotiate a special financial or service benefit for agreeing to use the convention centre's service providers.

4.3.11   Waste Disposal and Cleaning

The obligation to remove waste and litter from the venue usually rests with the event organiser. However, it is not uncommon for convention centres to assess additional charges for trash removal, particularly if waste, litter or any other items are left behind at the venue. Furthermore, it should be made clear in the contract who is responsible for the placement and emptying of bins during the event if the event is to run over a period of several days.

The parties should confirm who will be responsible for cleaning the venue during the event (including the toilets which, during a busy convention, need constant attention).

Does the venue owner expect the venue to be cleaned after the convention and, if so, who will bear the costs of this?

4.3.12 Access for Convention Centre Officials

The convention centre may require that their officials will have access to the venue and the event. This is not usually problematic, although event organisers should insist that notice is given of their attendance. They should also insist that such officials do not bring guests or prospective clients (certainly not competitors) through the centre during the event without their permission.

4.3.13 Convention Centre Terms and Conditions

The contract to hire the convention centre or part thereof may refer to additional standard terms and conditions of the convention centre. Event organisers should be aware that these additional terms and conditions will be incorporated into the contract by reference and will therefore form part of the contract. Accordingly, it is vital that event organisers obtain a copy of these terms and conditions and read them carefully.

If a contract is signed well in advance of the event, the standard terms and conditions may have changed at the time of the event. However, the terms and conditions at the time of signing will be the applicable terms and conditions unless otherwise agreed by the parties.

4.4 Specific Considerations for Hotel Contracts

Hotel contracts are usually highly negotiable. Apart from room rates, meeting space and dates, additional items such as complementary rooms, up-grades, cut-off dates, attrition/cancellation provisions, staff rates, limo service, VIP amenities, parking, complementary food and beverages and complementary health treatments are all usually negotiable.

However, as a general rule, if the event organiser is going to negotiate with a hotel sales representative, the event organiser must:

- Understand the competitive marketplace in which the hotel operates i.e. its strengths, weaknesses and occupancy patterns;
- Understand how a hotel evaluates business; and
- Promote the event in the best possible manner, using detailed information to support the business case.

In most cases, the party in the negotiation who is better prepared will reap the rewards. This will usually be the hotel, since the hotel is likely to know more about the event organiser and the event than the event organiser knows about the hotel industry and the specific hotel in question.

4.4.1   Parties

It is important for an event organiser to ensure that the hotel is correctly named in the contract. In almost all cases the hotel will simply operate under a trade name, such as the "Boston Marriott". However, the actual entity with whom the event organiser will be contracting will be the property or management company which owns the hotel (usually a chain of hotels). The event organiser may never have even heard of the company who owns the hotel. It should check the identity of the party with whom it is entering into the contract to avoid any misunderstandings.

4.4.2   Binding Contract

As is the case with convention centres, the event organiser should take great care in clarifying when a binding contract will come into existence with a hotel for the hiring of space or rooms. The contract provided by the hotel will usually amount to an offer, which must then be specifically accepted by the event organiser in order for a contract to exist.

4.4.3   Rates

Usually an event organiser will be hiring rooms and meeting/conference facilities from the hotel for the event. In addition, because the event is taking place in the hotel and guests are also staying in the hotel, the hotel will also usually be providing food and beverages to the guests during the event. Rates should be negotiated bearing in mind the overall financial benefit to the hotel.

Sometimes bookings are made years in advance and it may be tempting to leave the room rates to future negotiation. However, this is inadvisable. Rates can always be set as a percentage of then-current "rack" rates or be linked to a consumer price index.

Often a hotel will provide meeting rooms at no cost if a certain number of rooms are booked in the hotel or if a large number of guests will be eating and drinking in the hotel itself.

4.4.4   Attrition Clauses

Attrition clauses (often also referred to as performance or slippage clauses) provide for the payment of damages to the hotel when an event organiser fails to fully use the room block specified in the contract. Most hotels regard the requested room block as a contractual commitment by the event organiser to fill the number of rooms specified, particularly if the bookings are made by the event organiser as opposed to the individual guests.

A reasonable attrition provision should provide the event organiser with the ability to reduce the room block by a specific percentage (e.g. 10 to 20%) up to a specific time before the event (e.g. 6 to 12 months) without incurring damages. If the stated threshold is crossed, damages should only accrue if the event organiser fails to use a specified percentage (e.g. 85 to 90%) of its adjusted (not the original) room block. Occupancy should be measured on a cumulative room-night basis, not on a night-by-night basis.

Damages for failure to meet a room block commitment should never be payable if the hotel is able to resell the rooms. The contract should stipulate that the hotel shall use its best endeavours to resell the rooms and, if possible, resell the rooms in the event organiser's block first.

Damages should be expressed as "liquidated damages" or a "genuine pre-estimate of loss" and not as a penalty, since the law generally does not recognise penalty clauses.

As an alternative, hotels sometimes charge a meeting room rental fee if there is a failure to meet a room block commitment, based on a sliding scale. If so, damages should not be payable in addition to this as described above.

Some event organisers have attempted to insert a clause which is the direct opposite of an attrition clause. This clause states that if the group exceeds the room block by a specified percentage (often the same as the attrition percentage) the hotel would provide a specified amount to the event organiser's master account, in recognition of the additional revenue generated for the hotel. Although there is some justification for such a clause in that it is merely reciprocal to the attrition clause, hotels are usually reluctant to agree to such a provision.

4.4.5   Cancellation

The event organiser should reserve the right to cancel a meeting or room reservations without penalty or damages if:

* There is an adverse change in the hotel's quality rating;
* The hotel ownership or management is changed;
* Notice of cancellation is given by a certain time (giving the hotel ample opportunity to re-sell the space);
* The hotel does not perform satisfactorily at an earlier event (e.g. in the case of a multi-year contract for an annual event);
* If the size of the event outgrows available hotel space; or
* An event of 'force majeure' arises, such as a strike, severe weather or transportation difficulties.

If cancellation triggers a monetary payment to the hotel, the payment should be based on actual losses suffered. For instance, if the hotel is able to re-sell the space or the rooms, so that no loss is actually suffered, no payment should be made to the hotel.

As in the case of attrition, damages should be expressed as "liquidated damages" and not as penalties.

Damages triggered by cancellation are sometimes stated on a sliding scale basis, with greater amounts being paid the closer to the event the cancellation occurs.

In general, the contract should be drafted so that damages are payable in the event either party cancels without a valid reason.

4.4.6   Re-allocation

Hotels may try and reserve the right to re-allocate rooms or meeting rooms. Event organisers should try and resist this unless they approve of such re-allocations.

4.5   Specific Considerations for Exhibitions

In the case of an exhibition, the event organiser will enter into a venue hire or licensing agreement with a convention centre or hotel. Relevant considerations for this contract are dealt with above. However, the event organiser will also enter into contracts with individual exhibitors who hire space (usually a booth or stand) at the exhibition.

Exhibitor contracts are usually signed in the year leading up to the exhibition. However, some event organisers, particularly those with new or growing events, may provide long term contracts to exhibitors, offering them reduced rates for long term commitment. Courts have generally held that such favourable or lower rates are a commercially reasonable practice and therefore will not usually be subject to legal challenge by a later exhibitor who pays more for similar space[16].

The exhibitor contract itself will usually consist of a cover sheet recording the basic terms and a set of regulations attached.

Apart from general provisions dealing with booth rates and payment, times and dates for the event, times for the installation and dismantling of the booth, booth passes and booth construction, the following should also be considered:

---

[16] Similarly, if an event organiser provides favourable rates to members of an association or repeat customers, or provides a 'protected window' for signing up, this will not generally be held to be an anti-competitive practice, unless the event organiser is exercising monopolistic control over an essential venue.

4.5.1 Official Contractors

The event organiser will usually want to appoint official contractors to provide exposition servicing and decorating. This will assist exhibitors with the construction and dressing of the booth (including the provision of utilities and furniture, if necessary). Exhibitors will be required to use the services of the official contractors, unless notice is provided by the exhibitor within a certain period of time.

4.5.2 Care of the Venue

The exhibitor should undertake not to deface the walls or floor or any other part of the venue. The exhibitor should be held liable for any damage caused to the venue by the exhibitor or its officers, employees or agents.

4.5.3 Circulation and Solicitation

The event organiser may want to prevent the exhibitor from distributing marketing or other materials beyond the confines of the booth.

4.5.4 Direct Selling

Usually the event organiser will require that if the exhibitor engages in on site sales transactions at the event, the exhibitor will be responsible for complying with all tax legislation relating to such transactions. The event organiser may also wish to obtain an indemnity from the exhibitor for any penalties or liabilities imposed on the event organiser in this regard.

4.5.5 Food and Beverages

It is common for the event organiser to place restrictions on the service and sampling of food and beverages at the booth.

4.5.6 Liability and Insurance

The event organiser will not wish to be liable for any damage caused to the booth or the property of the exhibitor, except perhaps when damage has arisen through its own negligence. Usually, it will insist on the exhibitor taking out its own insurance for damage to property or personal injury. Often the event organiser will make available exhibitors' liability insurance to the exhibitors[17]. It will also seek to obtain an indemnity from the exhibitor for all losses arising from claims against it as a result of the conduct of the exhibitor.

4.5.7 Health and Safety

The exhibitor should be asked to undertake to comply with all relevant health and safety regulations, including those pertaining to fire safety, electrical wiring

---

[17] This may or may not include insurance of own exhibits.

and the environment. Most event organisers will insist that all exhibit booths or stalls are made of flame-proof materials.

4.5.8 Music Licensing

Music licensing for exhibitions or trade shows is often a controversial issue. Many trade show organisers obtain a music licence directly from the music licensing authorities. Usually only one licence is required to cover the entire trade show. The trade show organiser will either absorb the cost as a cost of running the trade show or charge slightly higher fees to exhibitors who use the music to offset the cost. If the event features hospitality suites at which music is played, the trade show organiser's licence can be written to include such suites.

Some trade show operators refuse to obtain a licence, arguing that this is the responsibility of the individual exhibitor who plays the music at the booth. However, there are some cases which suggest that the trade show organiser can still be held vicariously liable for failing to obtain a licence if the organiser has the right or ability to supervise the performance of the music and has a direct financial interest in the performance i.e. benefits financially from the performance[18]. Accordingly, if a trade show organiser is going to play music at the trade show or allow exhibitors to play music, the most prudent course of action would be for the trade show organiser to obtain the music licence.

4.5.9 Activities

The event organiser may wish to restrict various activities at the booth, such as loud music, social functions or receptions, smoking etc.

4.6 Conclusion

The venue is a key part of an event. It houses the event. It can play a major role in the success of an event. It can also be the downfall of an event and give rise to costly legal claims. Event organiser and venue owners in particular need to consider all the legal issues arising from the venue and how these may affect the delivery and success of the event.

---

[18] See *Shapiro, Bernstein & Co v H.L. Green Co.*, 316 F.2d 304 (2nd Cir. 1963) and *Artists Music Inc v Reed Publishing (USA) Inc.*, 63 USLW 2015, 1994 WL 191643 (S.D.N.Y. 1994), two United States cases.

CHAPTER FIVE

Ticketing

This chapter covers those events for which tickets are required for admission.

5.1 Purpose of Ticket Terms and Conditions

It should be noted that the sale of a ticket to an event is in fact a legal contract. The purchaser will be paying consideration in return for which he or she is granted access to the event. In addition, access may be granted to the purchaser on certain specified terms and conditions, which are usually reflected on the ticket itself.

For small, simple events (such as a pantomime in the local town hall) it may not be necessary to impose any terms and conditions on entry to the event. In such a case, a ticket may be printed without any accompanying terms and conditions and simply exchanged for payment.

However, for larger, more complex events, it is often necessary and desirable for an event organiser to impose terms and conditions of entry. Through the imposition of these terms and conditions, an event organiser is able to expand upon the legal nature of its relationship with an attendee and thereby exercise more control over the behaviour of the attendee at the event.

As explained in Chapter 1[1], in many countries, including England, South Africa and other countries in the Commonwealth, there are no proprietary rights in an event itself. Accordingly, one of the key ways for an event organiser to ensure that it has control over the event, and is able to offer, exploit and protect its commercial rights with confidence, is to ensure that it has control over access to the event.

In the ticket terms and conditions, for instance, the event organiser can specify that the purchaser is not entitled to film or record footage of the event whilst attending at the event. This protects the event organiser's ability to offer valuable broadcasting rights to a third party.

---

[1] See paragraphs 1.4.3 and 1.5 above.

The law of contract gives the event organiser the right not only to impose terms and conditions of entry, but also to exclude those who do not accept or will not abide by those terms and conditions. In addition, a person who enters onto land without permission may be guilty of trespassing under civil law of tort or delict or, in some cases, under criminal law[2].

5.2   Notice of Ticket Conditions

The enforceability of ticket conditions is generally a complex matter. This is because purchasers of tickets are often unaware of ticketing conditions, or may successfully argue after the fact that they were unaware of ticketing conditions at the time of purchasing the ticket (which is when the contract between the seller and the purchaser of the ticket comes into force).

In the United Kingdom, ticket conditions are only enforceable if they were brought to the attention of the purchaser, and thereby incorporated into the contract of sale, prior to the sale taking place[3]. In South Africa, the situation is very similar. The general position is that the seller must take such steps as are necessary to draw to the attention of a reasonable customer the ticket terms. What steps are considered necessary will depend on the facts of each case.

There are a number of steps which can be taken to bring the ticket conditions to the attention of the purchaser.

Notices may be placed at and outside the venue, in the form of ground regulations, stating clearly that entry is subject to express terms and conditions and then listing those terms and conditions. It should also be stated that entry to the venue constitutes acceptance of those terms and conditions. However, it should be noted that attendees could argue that these conditions were not brought to their attention at the time they purchased the ticket and therefore they are not bound by these conditions.

Accordingly, efforts should be made to bring the ticket conditions to the attention of the attendee at the time he or she is purchasing the ticket. This can be a relatively simple matter if there is a single, central, ticket distribution office. However, these days it is common for tickets to be sold via a number of distribution channels. For instance, tickets may be sold by a ticket office at the venue, in person and by mail; over the internet, via the issuer or event organiser's website; by a commercial ticket agency such as Ticketmaster (by phone or via

---

[2]   In this case reasonable force may be used to evict a trespasser, but only after the trespasser has been asked to leave and refuses to do so. Only that amount of force that is reasonably necessary to remove the trespasser from the premises is permitted. Excessive force may subject the event organiser (and/or the security company acting on their behalf) to a claim for damages if injuries arise during the course of eviction.

[3]   *McCutcheon v David MacBrayne Ltd* [1964] 1 All ER 430, [1964] 1 WLR 125; *Thornton v Shoe Lane Parking* [1971] 2 QB 163, [1971] 1 All ER 686, CA.

their website); to member clubs (or, via those clubs, to their members); to stadium debenture-holders; or as part of hospitality packages by official operators.

Written confirmation should ideally be obtained from the purchaser to the effect that the purchaser has had the ticket conditions brought to his or her attention prior to the purchase and acknowledges and accepts them as conditions of sale. For instance, the application form for tickets for the All England Championships at Wimbledon reproduces the ticket conditions in full on the back of the form and the purchaser is required to complete and sign a slip confirming that he accepts them.

If tickets are purchased on the internet, event organisers or their ticket agents should ensure that, before purchasers can proceed to purchase a ticket, they are given clear notice that ticket conditions apply. The ticket conditions should be listed in full. Ideally, purchasers should then have to tick a box indicating that they have read the conditions and accept them.

If tickets are sold telephonically, ticket sellers should be encouraged to offer to read out the ticket conditions to purchasers. Nowadays telephonic ticket sales are usually automated. In such a case, the recorded message should indicate that ticket terms apply and then either list such conditions or give purchasers the option to listen to them. As in the case of on-line sales, purchasers should subsequently be required to acknowledge that they have heard the conditions and accept them.

5.3 Key Legal Issues

There are a number of key legal issues which should be covered in the ticket terms and conditions. Sample ticket terms and conditions have been included in Appendix 3.

5.3.1 Acceptance

The event organiser should expressly state that purchase of the ticket constitutes acceptance of the terms and conditions. The event organiser may also wish to state that the terms and conditions are also subject to certain external regulations, such as the rules and regulations of a governing body.

5.3.2 Access

As mentioned in paragraphs 1.5 and 5.1 above, the event organiser will want to control access to the venue for a number of reasons.

Firstly, the event organiser may wish to reserve the right to refuse access to the venue to any person or eject any person from the venue. This may be expressed as a blanket refusal at its discretion or restricted to situations where such person has failed to comply with the terms and conditions. This allows the event organiser to refuse access for security reasons for instance and is of particular use if the event organiser has established security checks at the venue.

Secondly, the event organiser may wish to grant access on certain conditions only e.g. that the ticket holder is over a certain age or that the ticket holder carries no recording or broadcasting equipment.

Thirdly, the event organiser may wish to specify that access shall only be permitted to certain specified areas of the venue. This of importance for music concerts and sporting events in particular. Those sports which have a big fan base may wish to reserve certain areas of a stadium to a certain segment of fans e.g. 'home' fans or 'away' fans.

Fourthly, the event organiser may wish to preclude certain behaviour at the event, for example, recording the event, or transmitting audio or audio-visual content from the event. Modern technology now allows a 'fan' to bring in a range of handheld recording devices into the venue through which content can be transmitted to those outside the venue. As discussed previously, a clause preventing any such recording is a particularly important mechanism to protect the value of any broadcasting rights which may be granted to a broadcaster by the event organiser.

5.3.3 Ownership

The event organiser will want to specify that, notwithstanding the purchase of the ticket, the ticket remains the property of the event organiser at all times. This may sound nonsensical. However, remember that what the purchaser is purchasing is not the actual right in the ticket itself, but a *right of access* to the event (albeit subject to certain terms and conditions).

In 2004 UEFA, the European football (soccer) governing body, filed a number of injunctions against English companies preventing them from unlawfully selling match tickets for the Euro 2004 tournament. The various defendant companies were unauthorised re-sellers of match tickets who had obtained the tickets from agents of authorised UEFA ticket sellers and who then sold the tickets as part of a travel package to the host nation Portugal. UEFA successfully argued that legal title in the ticket was retained by UEFA and that the right of access to the venue had not been transferred contractually to the defendants. The injunctions obtained by UEFA included orders that the unauthorised re-sellers be stopped from selling further tickets, that they be restrained from buying more tickets, that they provide details of those from whom they bought or obtained tickets in order to be able to cancel those tickets, and that they provide details of those to whom they sold tickets to enable UEFA to seek to recover the ticket from the ultimate recipient to prevent onward sale or use.

This case has important implications for those in the United Kingdom and other countries in the Commonwealth. Fans travelling to sports matches may find that tickets bought over the internet as part of a holiday package or from an unauthorised ticket agency do not provide legitimate entrance to the match.

5.3.4 Transferability of Tickets

The event organiser will usually want to restrict the ability of the purchaser to transfer the ticket to a third party. Of particular concern to the event organiser will be its ability to restrict the commercial sale of the ticket by the purchaser. This is usually included to prevent operators from buying up large numbers of tickets and then on-selling them to third parties at a profit i.e. the trading of tickets by unofficial operators.

In general, ticket agencies and event organisers will want to ensure that official status is granted to a single ticket agency or a limited number of ticket agencies and that appropriate controls are put in place to prevent the unauthorised re-selling of tickets for a profit.

In some countries, event organisers are assisted in this regard by specific legislation that has been passed in respect of ticket 'touting' or 'scalping', as it is sometimes known[4].

The event organiser will also want to specify that the ticket may not be used as part of a hospitality package or a competition, unless the event organiser has consented to such use.

5.3.5 Cancellation or Postponement

The event organiser may wish to include terms dealing with the cancellation or postponement of the event. In particular, the event organiser may wish to specify whether or not a refund is permitted and under what circumstances it is permitted.

5.3.6 Physical Activity

If the event requires a degree of physical activity on the part of the purchaser of the ticket, the event organiser may wish to obtain an acknowledgement of the risks inherent in attendance at, or participation in, the event. The event organiser may also wish to exclude liability for any losses suffered as a result of an injury sustained by the purchaser of the ticket by virtue of his or her participation in, or

---

[4] In the United Kingdom, for example, under s166 of the Criminal Justice and Public Order Act 1994 it is a criminal offence for an unauthorised person to sell, or offer or expose for sale, a ticket for a designated football match in any public place. The Home Secretary has the power to extend the application of s166 to other sporting events. In South Africa, the draft Safety at Sports and Recreational Events Bill prohibits any form of ticket touting.

attendance at, the event. Such an exclusion clause may not be valid under the laws of particular countries in certain circumstances, and local advice should be taken in this respect[5].

5.3.7 Right to Film Attendees

If the event organiser wishes to film the event or photograph the attendees at the event, it may wish to reserve such a right in the ticket terms and conditions. It may also wish to reserve the right to broadcast or publish such content.

5.3.8 Regulations

In some countries there may be legislation, regulations or by-laws governing the sale and distribution of tickets. This is rare. However, there appears to be a movement in many countries towards greater controls in this area. For instance, in South Africa the draft Safety at Sports and Recreational Events Bill sets out a number of requirements for the design, content, sale and distribution of tickets for certain types of events[6].

5.4 Appointment of a Ticket Agency

The event organiser may wish to appoint a ticket agency to manage ticket sales for the event. This is not a straightforward matter, and will require a detailed contract in its own right.

5.4.1 Key Legal Issues

In addition to the standard terms outlined in Chapter 2, the following terms should be considered:

a) Exclusivity

The ticket agent will wish to be appointed as the exclusive ticket agent for a specific territory. The extent of the territory will need to be defined, but if the agency is a large one, the extent of the territory may well be worldwide.

b) Financial Provisions

The parties will need to set out the financial arrangement between them as regards the services to be provided by the ticket agency. Although this is essentially a commercial issue, which will vary from contract to contract, usually remuneration will be in the form of commission on ticket sales.

---

[5] For example, in the United Kingdom, one cannot exclude liability for personal injury or death arising from negligence under the Unfair Contract Terms Act 1977.

[6] See section 27 of the draft Bill. This applies to all events held at stadiums or venues with a capacity of over 2000 at any one time.

The parties should indicate in the contract whether commission is based on gross ticket revenues or whether certain costs, such as the costs of producing the tickets, will be deducted before the commission is calculated. In addition, consideration could include a transaction fee per customer sale/ticket sale, which could vary according to the price of the tickets or the number of tickets sold.

The party with control over the accounts in respect of ticket sales will usually be required to account fully in respect of such sales. This could be via access to those accounts (upon reasonable request) or via regular provision of statements of account. The other contracting party may also wish to reserve the right to appoint an auditor to conduct an audit in respect of such accounts.

As mentioned above, the parties should clearly record who is responsible for the costs relating to the design, production and distribution of tickets. It is common for the event organiser to control branding on the tickets and to set the ticket prices, although it may wish to consult with the ticket agency in this regard.

The parties should also record their arrangement in respect of cancellations and postponements. The parties may wish to set aside a certain percentage of the revenues from ticket sales for possible refunds, which are usually permitted in the event of cancellation or postponement of an event.

c) Service Levels

The level of ticket sales may well depend on the degree of service provided by the ticket agency. For this reason, the event organiser will want to include in the contract certain terms and conditions relating to the performance of the ticket agency. Obligations may include:

- Ensuring that a call centre is established to manage calls;
- Ensuring that the staff manning the call centre are adequately trained and have a reasonable knowledge of the ticketing procedures;
- Ensuring that a sufficient number of telesales staff are on duty at any one time to handle requests for tickets;
- Ensuring answering response times within a certain specified period;
- Ensuring that abandoned calls not to exceed a certain percentage over a given period; or
- Ensuring that tickets are despatched within a certain time period from booking.

The event organiser should stipulate that if the service levels are not met for any reason, a meeting shall be called between the respective parties to address the service levels. If the required level of service is still not forthcoming, the event organiser should include a right to terminate the contract on written notice.

d) Logistics

Although this may be viewed as a commercial issue, there could be legal implications if the respective obligations of the parties in this regard are not recorded clearly in the contract.

For instance, the parties should specify who will be responsible for designing, producing and distributing the tickets. Will logos be placed on the tickets? Who will be responsible for keeping track of ticket sales and relaying this information? Will priority booking periods be implemented and which groups will receive priority? Will any parties receive free or discounted tickets and on what terms will these be distributed? Who will be responsible for ticket stock and how will this be managed? Who will be responsible for the provision, training and management of on-site ticket staff? Will any complementary tickets be issued and, if so, on what basis?

The event organiser will usually wish to impose certain marketing obligations on the ticket agency. At the very least, the event organiser will want the ticket agent to market the event to its database and on its website. Terms to this effect should be included in the contract.

e) Data

Of particular importance to the event organiser will be the details of all ticket purchasers. The event organiser will want to capture these details so that it has information on its customers. It may also want to undertake marketing activities in respect of these customers. For this reason, access to, and ownership of, such details and data will essential for the event organiser. The event organiser will want to ensure, at the very least, that it has the right to view and use such data. If necessary the data can be licensed to the ticket agent for its use.

The party collecting that data may have additional obligations imposed upon it under legislation. For instance, in the UK, the collector of such data will be required to comply with the Data Protection Act. Accordingly, the event organiser may ask for a warranty from the ticket agent that the agent has complied with relevant data protection laws and/or an indemnity for any losses it may suffer as a result of non-compliance on the part of the ticket agent with such laws.

f) Event Information

The provision of correct and accurate information regarding the event is usually crucial to the sale of tickets for the event. Certain pieces of information will also be recorded on the face of the ticket. For this reason, ticket agency contracts sometimes contain provisions relating to event and/or ticket information.

For instance, the ticket agent may wish to record when such information shall be provided to it by the event organiser and the extent of such information. What happens if the event information on the ticket is wrong? The ticket agent will usually wish to specify that the event organiser is responsible for the accuracy of such information and that it shall indemnify the ticket agent for any losses its sustains as a result of the content of, or omissions from, such information or any material changes thereto.

5.5   Conclusion

It is evident from the above that a ticket can be a very important instrument in relation to an event. Far from merely providing revenue, it serves as a mechanism for controlling the conduct of the ticket holder when attending the event. As a result it serves to protect both the integrity of the event and the value of the commercial rights arising from the event.

However, event organisers need to take active steps to ensure that ticket terms and conditions are brought to the attention of the purchaser at the time of purchase of the ticket, otherwise the ticket terms and conditions may be very difficult to enforce.

CHAPTER SIX

Risk Management, Health & Safety and Insurance

In this chapter we look at the legal implications of risk management and health and safety, two topics which have become increasingly important in the field of event management in recent years. We will also discuss briefly the different types of insurance that should be considered for an event.

6.1   What is Risk Management?

Risk management is the process of considering and then controlling risk. Whether the proposed event is a small or large-scale affair, it will not take place in a vacuum. There will usually be a need for risk assessment and management at some level.

Briefly, comprehensive risk management of an event involves the event organiser:

- Assessing the nature of the event and identifying damaging incidents that might occur during, or as a result of, the event;
- Evaluating the likelihood of such incidents occurring;
- Considering the severity of the consequences were such incidents to occur;
- Establishing and implementing a strategy to minimise or eliminate the risk of such incidents occurring relative to the financial and other resources available to the event organiser; and
- Consider insuring against those risks that can't be avoided, assumed or transferred.

6.2   Why is Risk Management Important?

Risk management for an event is important for a number of reasons:

- An event organiser will want to ensure that the event runs smoothly and is a success;

- The existence of a risk management programme will usually result in reduced premiums payable for insurance. As some form of insurance will be required for most events, this is likely to be important to an event organiser. In addition, an event organiser will usually obtain better terms for legal expenses cover if it can show that it has a risk management programme in place that reduces the prospects of claims against it;
- It will be essential from a public relations point of view. Incidents can create negative publicity that may have a significant effect on the success of an event. It also sends a message to the public that the event is being staged professionally and that the event organiser cares about the well-being of all those persons involved in the event;
- Effective risk management will have legal implications – for example, a sound risk management programme will assist the event organiser in complying with its legal obligations in staging the event. It will also significantly reduce the likelihood of claims against the event organiser as a result of an incident. Also, if a claim is made as a result of an incident, an event organiser that can show that it took all reasonable steps to manage risk would be more likely to successfully defend a claim or minimise the amount of damages awarded against it.

In this chapter, we will be focussing on the fourth reason in particular, namely the legal implications of risk management.

6.3   Legal Consequences of an Incident

The full consequences of an incident at or during an event may not be foreseeable by the event organiser in the early stages of planning. However, these consequences can often be far-reaching.

Let us take the real-life example of the spectator who, wearing a kilt and carrying a placard, mysteriously appeared on the Silverstone racetrack during lap 11 of the Formula 1 British Grand Prix in 2003[1].

If an accident had occurred resulting in injury to a driver, the driver may well have had a claim against the venue owner or event organiser. Apart from a claim for the injuries suffered, there may well have been consequential losses arising from the driver having to forego various commercial opportunities outside of his racing contract, or from an inability to fulfil other third party contracts as a result of the injury. The event organiser may have had its licence to hold the event revoked by the relevant local authority for failing to secure a safe venue. In addition, the sport's governing body, the FIA, may have imposed its own

---

[1] A similar incident occurred at the German Grand Prix in Hochenheim in 2000, when a spectator wandered around the course and crossed the track in front of oncoming cars.

sanction where a breach of safety was found to have occurred. Finally, the event organiser may have found itself in breach of its agreement with a sponsor to ensure that a safe event was run.

There have been a number of highly publicised incidents that have occurred at events that have had significant legal implications.

For instance, in England, there have been the tragic football (soccer) stadium collapses at Ibrox and Hillsborough in 1969 and 1989 respectively, resulting in extensive loss of life. In October 1994 part of a stand collapsed at a Pink Floyd concert at Earl's Court in London, injuring several people. In South Africa, a stampede at Ellis Park Stadium caused by overcrowding at a football match in 2001 resulted in the death of 43 people. In the same country, a power shortage halted a crucial World Cup rugby match played under floodlights in Port Elizabeth in 1995. In the United States, bizarre incidents at events are well-documented. One example is a brawl which broke out between Indiana Pacers players and Detroit Piston fans at an NBA basketball game in November 2004.

Whilst the above events were all fairly large events, event organisers of small events will still need some form of risk analysis and management. Medieval dinner organisers have to plan for the theft of important props, school fête organisers will need to assess the risks inherent in holding an evening fireworks display and corporate events companies will need to consider the likelihood of injury to participants in an outdoor team-building event.

Each event will have its own unique blend of risks to be considered. These risks will almost certainly have legal implications. Civil claims in particular are usually a consequence of poor risk management. We live in an increasingly litigious world where one claim can mark the end of an otherwise successful events business.

6.4 Assessment of Risk

6.4.1 Risks Arising from the Event Itself

A thorough assessment of the possible risks arising out of the actual event should be undertaken, following which a report should be drafted. The risk management report, whether conducted by the event organiser or by a professional organisation on its behalf, should identify the possible risks, assess the likelihood of each risk becoming a reality and grade the severity of the consequences of each risk.

Even for a simple event such as a wedding, there are a number of risks to be considered, many of which have legal implications. A list of the type of considerations for such an event is included in Appendix 4 by way of example.

6.4.2 Risks Arising from Legal Duties and Obligations

Apart from the risks arising from the event itself, there will usually be risks arising from various legal duties and obligations on the part of the event organiser. These could arise contractually (by virtue of contracts entered into by the event organiser), in tort or delict (by virtue of a duty of care owed by the event organiser) or under statute (by virtue of legislation or regulations).

a) Contractual Duties and Obligations

Entering into a contract will create certain duties and obligations between the parties entering into that contract. These duties and obligations will be set out expressly in the contract itself. However, there may also be additional implied duties and obligations under the laws in each specific country. A risk management assessment should include a review of *all* the contracts relating to the event, in terms of which the potential risks arising from those contracts should be identified and assessed.

Ensuring that contracts are skilfully drafted and negotiated by suitably qualified lawyers will go a long way towards minimising the risks arising from those contracts. A shrewd lawyer will seek to exclude liability altogether for certain risks on behalf of a party or, alternatively, apportion liability between the contracting parties where possible. Warranties can be obtained from the other contracting party in respect of key elements of performance under a contract[2]. A party could request indemnities for losses arising as a result of various acts, omissions or breaches of contract on the part of the other contracting party[3].

'Force Majeure' or 'Act of God' clauses are another means through which liability can be excluded for risks arising from incidents that are beyond the control of the contracting parties. The topic of 'force majeure' is considered in more detail in paragraph 2.3.9 above.

b) Duties and Obligations Arising in Tort (Delict)

A court of law may establish liability on the part of a party even though there is no contract between them, under tort law (known as 'delict' in some countries). Negligence is a tort under the law of many countries.

In order to be liable for negligence, the claimant will usually have to prove certain things. First, there must be what is known as a 'duty of care' owed by one party to another by virtue of their respective circumstances. In considering whether or not a duty of care exists, the conduct of the offending party will be

---

[2] For an explanation of the nature of a warranty, see paragraph 2.3.6 above.
[3] For an explanation of the nature of an indemnity, see paragraph 2.3.10 above.

measured against accepted standards within that activity and in general. In many countries, including the United Kingdom, the United States and South Africa, the conduct of the offending party will be measured against that of the fictional 'reasonable man' and will be based on the facts and circumstances of the case in question. It has also been argued that if an event organiser holds itself out as being a *professional* event organiser or planner (by virtue of a special certificate or association membership, for example) then it may be held to the standard of care expected by other *professional* event organisers or planners in the same circumstances i.e. it may be held to a higher standard of care[4].

In the events industry, an event organiser's duty of care encompasses the duty to investigate all aspects of the event and act accordingly, the duty to warn attendees and participants of known hazards as may be necessary, the duty to plan for the safety and well-being of attendees and participants, and the duty not to subject attendees and participants to unreasonable risks of harm.

If a court has found that a duty of care does exist, it will need to decide to whom it is owed, whether or not that duty of care has been breached, whether the breach arose as a direct result of the negligent act or omission of the offending party, and whether the innocent party has suffered loss or damage as a result of the offending party's negligence. Courts have traditionally been reluctant to allow recovery for 'emotional distress' suffered as a result of negligence, although they will permit recovery for actual financial loss suffered.

Let us take the man running on the racing track at Silverstone as an example by way of illustration.

If a driver had an accident as a result of the man running on the racing track, there could a claim for negligence against the event organiser, particularly if it can be established that the event organiser failed to take reasonable steps to prevent such an incident from happening. If, for instance, the event organiser had failed to erect adequate fencing on that part of the track when it really ought to have done so, and as a result of that omission the man had gained access to the track, thereby causing an accident, the event organiser could well be found to have breached the duty of care to the drivers[5].

In one real-life example in Canada, an advertising agency was held to be liable as a result of the negligent planning of an event for some of its top executives. DDB Needham Advertising Agency had to pay $1.1 million in damages to the survivors of an individual who was killed on a company-sponsored rafting trip. The group

---

[4] See *The Law of Meetings, Conventions and Trade Shows: Selected Articles on Meetings and Liability* by John S. Foster, pg 1, published by John S. Foster in 1999.

[5] There may also be a claim for negligence against the venue owner as well if it can be established that the venue owner also failed to take reasonable steps to prevent the incident from happening.

of executives travelled to British Columbia to raft the rapids on the Chilko River. During one part of the trip, the raft hit a boulder and all eleven participants fell out of the raft. Five of the men never surfaced and drowned. The claimant or plaintiff successfully maintained that the advertising agency had breached its duty of care in that it had (1) failed to inquire about the physical fitness or rafting experience of each participant; (2) failed to investigate the weather and river conditions at the time of the rafting trip; (3) failed to hire a licensed river guide; (4) actively misrepresented the safety of the proposed rafting trip; (5) failed to provide adequate transportation to those not wanting to raft; (6) failed to provide adequate safety equipment such as helmets, wetsuits and life jackets with crotch straps; (7) overcrowded the raft; and (8) failed to provide radios, safety boats or spotters in case of an incident.

In a similar occurrence in South Africa, an events company was sued as a result of a tubing incident in which 13 people died on the Storms River in March 2000.

Part of the risk management assessment will involve consideration of the necessary steps to be undertaken by an event organiser in order to ensure that it reduces the likelihood of a claim in tort law. An event organiser will only be required to take such steps as are *reasonable* in the circumstances.

For instance, in the Silverstone example, it would probably have been sufficient if the event organiser had erected a high wire fence in order to prevent spectators from gaining access to the track. If the spectator had cut the fence using special heavy-duty clippers in order to gain access to the track, a court would probably find that the event organiser had taken reasonable steps to prevent such an incident from occurring i.e. it had done what could be considered reasonable in the circumstances. In such a case, a court would probably find that there was no negligence on the part of the event organiser. In considering what steps would be considered reasonable in any given situation, it is obviously advisable to err on the side of cautiousness.

If an event organiser or venue owner is aware that a certain part of a facility or venue is a potential hazard to those using the facility or venue, it will almost certainly be held to have breached its duty of care if it did not take any steps to remove that hazard and an attendee was later injured because of the hazard. Even if the event organiser or venue owner was not aware of the hazard, but ought to have been aware of the hazard, it may be held to have breached its duty of care to the injured attendee. In short, attendees and participants have a legal right to expect the event organiser to take steps to alleviate or avoid health and safety problems to which the attendee or participant may be exposed.

Another real life example, which indicates the nature of such legal duties owed by hotels and event organisers in particular, is the well-known 'Tailhook' case in the United States. The Tailhook Association held an annual event at the Las Vegas Hilton for active and retired naval aviators. Lt Paula Coughlin was an attendee at a particular annual conference. She won a $6.7 million dollar claim against the hotel for the hotel's failure to provide adequate security in preventing a longstanding Tailhook tradition known as the 'gauntlet', during which she was accosted in an inappropriate manner in a hotel hallway by a group of drunken attendees[6]. The lack of control and supervision exercised by the hotel in the circumstances, and its failure to adequately manage what was a potential (and actual) hazard, resulted in a successful claim against the hotel.

Event organisers should ensure that first aid facilities are available at the event and that any first aid will be carried out by appropriately trained personnel. It should also ensure that written procedures exist on how to handle emergency situations such as fires, attendee illness or injury. In a well-known case in the United Kingdom, the British Boxing Board of Control, which acts as the governing body for boxing within that country, was held liable for its negligent failure to ensure adequate medical facilities were available at ringside[7].

Event organisers can often take relatively simple steps in order to both minimise risk and avoid costly claims. For instance, erecting signs indicating any risks involved in attending at or participating in an event is helpful. Erecting a sign with a disclaimer (excluding liability) at a venue is also an option available to an event organiser[8]. However, if such a step is taken, the event organiser should do its utmost to bring both the risks and the contents of the disclaimer to the attention of the attendees. This can best be achieved by including properly drafted and clear wording on registration forms, invoices, tickets and safety-deposit forms[9]. Disclaimers which are vague, general or unclear will not generally be upheld by a court of law. If the wording of the disclaimer is approved by the insurance company, this can often help to reduce insurance premiums.

---

[6] See *Coughlin v Tailhook Association & the Las Vegas Hilton Corporation*, US 9th Circuit Court of Appeals, No 95 – 15909 DC No CV-93-00044. As is evident from the citation, Lt Coughlin also filed suit against the Tailhook Association, but the latter settled out of court for an undisclosed sum a few days before the trial started. Although the settlement was in no way an admission of liability or guilt, it was undoubtedly prompted by the judge's finding that there was evidence to suggest that the Association could be held liable for failing to plan properly.

[7] See *Watson v BBBC* (1999) 143 Sol Jo LB 235, (1999) Times, 12 October, Court of Appeal [2001] QB 1134, CA, 19 December 2000.

[8] In the United States, these are sometimes called 'exculpatory clauses' because they attempt to exclude a party from liability.

[9] It should be noted that whilst these clauses are useful and effective on the whole, in some countries, these exclusion clauses or disclaimers may not be upheld by the courts in every instance. In the United States and in South Africa, for example, in some cases these clauses have been upheld and in other cases they have not – in general, the courts do not look favourably on clauses attempting to exclude liability for negligence, particularly where insufficient notice is given to the disclaimer, the language is vague and unclear, there is

Another means of reducing the risk of claims is hiring suppliers who are experts at managing certain parts of the event. In this way responsibility and liability can be shifted to the supplier. For example, in the river rafting case discussed above, the advertising agency could have hired a supplier who was an expert in planning and carrying out rafting trips. It would have been the rafting company's job, as the expert, to have specialist knowledge of the river and weather conditions and to provide necessary equipment.

Finally, it is important for an event organiser to remember that it will also be liable for the acts of its employees (and perhaps volunteers whom it has engaged), provided that such employees were acting in the course and scope of their employment at the time when the act was committed.

c) Statutory Duties and Obligations

Those involved in the events industry are often oblivious to the fact that they may be bound by legislation. It is important to note that breaches of statutory provisions usually give rise to fines or penalties, and in some cases even criminal prosecution. Statutory breaches can also serve as an important basis for civil claims. Unfortunately, as the saying goes, ignorance of the law is no excuse! For this reason it is essential to consult with a suitably qualified local attorney who can advise on the relevant obligations arising under statute.

i) Health and Safety Legislation

Many countries have specific legislation dealing with health and safety that will be relevant to the events industry in that country. Governmental or advisory bodies or associations will usually have been established, from whom general advice can be sought on the relevant health and safety legislation in that country. Some examples are set out below:

United Kingdom[10]

In the United Kingdom, an organisation which acts as an employer (such as an events company) will be subject to various statutory duties imposed by the Health and Safety at Work Act 1974 ("HSWA 1974"). For instance, section 2 of the HSWA 1974 imposes a duty on employers to ensure, as far as is reasonably practicable, the health, safety and welfare of its employees. This requires that

---

a clear inequality of bargaining power between the parties or the disclaimer is contrary to public policy. It should also be noted that in the United Kingdom, it is not possible to exclude liability for death or personal injury arising as a result of negligence under the Unfair Contract Terms Act 1977. Accordingly, when drafting disclaimers, it is advisable to consult with a local and suitably qualified lawyer.

[10] For further information on the legislation mentioned below, see the Health and Safety Executive's *Event Safety Guide: A Guide to Health, Safety and Welfare at Music and Similar Events*, the website ww.hse.gov. uk and *Essentials of Health & Safety at Work (3rd edition)*, HSE Books, 1994, ISBN 071760716X.

employers provide a safe place of work[11], adequate supervision, guidance and training. Section 3 of the same Act imposes a duty on an employer to ensure that no person (regardless of whether or not they are employed by the employer) is exposed to health and safety risks by the employer's business activities.

There is also a duty in relation to all public buildings to meet minimum fire safety standards.

If an organisation has five or more employees, it is obliged to implement a health and safety policy under the HSWA 1974. Often an events organiser will call upon the assistance of volunteers in running an event. The health and safety requirements do not apply in full where the organisation has no employees and is run by volunteers. It is considered best practice, however, to comply with the health and safety requirements under the Act even in such circumstances.

The Workplace (Health, Safety & Welfare) Regulations 1992 cover a wide range of basic health, safety and welfare issues, such as ventilation, heating, lighting, workstations, seating and welfare facilities.

The Management of Health and Safety at Work Regulations 1992 require all employers and self-employed persons to assess the risks to workers and others who may be affected by their work. The purpose of this risk assessment is to identify hazards that could cause harm, assess the risks that may arise from such hazards and decide on adequate measures to eliminate, or manage, the risks. These regulations also deal with evacuation procedures, which will be of relevance to all events organisations, particularly venue owners. They also govern the erection and dismantling of temporary stages, grandstands and other temporary platform requirements.

Events organisations should also take care to comply with the provisions of the Fire Precautions Act 1971 and the Fire Precautions (Workplace) Regulations 1997. The latter also applies to any tent or moveable structure, such as a marquee. Owners of sports stadiums, or event organisers who plan an event at a sports stadium, will also need to comply with the provisions of the Fire Safety and Safety of Places of Sport Act 1987.

All safety signs, notices and graphic symbols must conform to the Health and Safety (Safety Signs and Signals) Regulations 1996.

In addition, events organisations need to be wary of legislation dealing with pollution. Nearly every event will produce waste of some kind. Section 34 of the Environmental Protection Act 1990 introduced a duty of care for waste management which applies to anyone who produces, carries, treats or disposes

---

[11] This will include a venue at which an employee may be working temporarily.

of controlled waste. Controlled waste is defined as any commercial, industrial or household waste.

Legislation concerning the management of waste itself includes the following:

- the Environmental Protection Act 1990
- the Environment Act 1995
- the Controlled Waste Regulations 1992
- the Waste Management Licensing Regulations 1994
- the Special Waste Regulations 1996

For events that are likely to produce large amounts of noise, the Noise at Work Regulations 1989 and HSWA 1974 should be consulted. Both of these pieces of legislation require the protection of workers and the audience from noise.

Other regulations have been produced to govern:

- the lifting and carrying of loads[12]
- the use of lifting and rigging equipment[13]
- the use and maintenance of lift trucks[14]
- the use of personal protective equipment[15]
- the installation and use of electrical equipment[16]
- the provision of toilets and washing facilities in the workplace[17]
- the supply, acquisition and use of fireworks[18]
- first-aid for employees and event workers[19]
- the assessment and control of hazardous substances[20]
- the use of visual display units[21]
- the display of health and safety information in the workplace[22]

United States[23]

In the United States, the Occupational Health and Safety Act (OSHA) [1970] governs workplace conditions for health and safety. OSHA also established the National Institute for Occupational Safety and Health, which falls under the Department of Health and Human Services. OSHA covers a wide range of activities. Owing to the fact that the employees of events companies are often

---

[12] See the Manual Handling Operations Regulations 1992.
[13] See the Lifting Operations and Lifting Equipment Regulations 1998.
[14] See the Provision and Use of Work Equipment Regulations 1998.
[15] See the Personal Protective Equipment at Work Regulations 1992.
[16] See the Electricity at Work Regulations 1989.
[17] See the Workplace (Health, Safety and Welfare) Regulations 1992.
[18] See the Fireworks (Safety) Regulations 1997.
[19] See the Health and Safety (First Aid) Regulations 1981.
[20] See the Control of Substances Hazardous to Health Regulations 2002.
[21] See the Health & Safety (Display Screen Equipment) Regulations 1992.
[22] See the Health & Safety Information for Employees Regulations 1989.
[23] For more information on this section refer to the website www.osha.gov.

involved in activities with some element of danger (such as moving heavy objects, working with high-voltage equipment, or working in unusually high places), an events company should have good knowledge of the Act to ensure compliance.

Events companies should take particular note of the Occupational Health and Safety Standards. These are set out in PART 1910 of the OSHA Regulations and cover a range of issues relevant to the events industry including:

- Working surfaces (including scaffolding)
- Evacuation
- Platforms and manlifts
- Noise exposure
- Personal protection equipment
- Environmental controls (including sanitation)
- Medical and first-aid
- Fire protection
- Lifting, handling and storage of materials
- Electrical risks

OSHA encourages each state to develop and operate its own health and safety standards. States must establish job health and safety standards that are at least as effective as comparable federal standards. States also have the option to promulgate standards covering hazards not addressed by federal standards. About half of the states in the United States have developed their own OSHA-approved State Plans. Event companies should contact the Occupational Safety and Health State Plan Association to find out whether or not they are bound by the standards set out in a State Plan or by the federal Standards.

If notified of a potentially dangerous condition or circumstance in the workplace (which will generally include an event site at which employees may be working), representatives of OSHA may come in and conduct an audit or inspection. As a result of such an audit or inspection, it may impose a fine on the organisation or require that the dangerous condition or circumstance be removed.

In addition to the above, event organisers and venue owners will be monitored by inspectors from the state health and sanitation departments. Local inspectors will check for compliance with state health and sanitation codes and municipal ordinances dealing with issues such as restroom facilities and a safe water supply.

Regulations relating to food hygiene are dealt with in paragraph 8.3.2 below.

Event organisers and venue owners should take care to comply with the fire safety regulations set out in the Federal Fire Prevention and Control Act of 1974 (which established the United States Fire Administration and its National Fire

Academy) and those promulgated at state level. Failure to comply with fire safety laws constitutes negligence per se.

In relation to fire safety, it is worth noting that as a means of encouraging compliance with the Hotel and Motel Fire Safety Act of 1990, the use of federal funds to organise or stage a meeting, convention, conference or training seminar in a place of public accommodation is prohibited unless the facility in which the event is being held is equipped with a hard-wired (i.e. not battery powered) smoke detector in each room and an automatic sprinkler system, both meeting National Fire Protection Association standards.

The Environmental Protection Agency (EPA) is an independent agency of the federal government. Established in 1970, its mission is to 'permit co-ordinated and effective government action on behalf of the environment'. Many EPA directives are implemented by state and local governments. Directives relating to the control and removal of waste will be relevant to event organisers and catering and hospitality companies.

South Africa[24]
In South Africa, employers in the events industry will be bound by the Occupational Health and Safety Act 85 of 1993 ("OHS") which requires the employer to bring about and maintain, as far as reasonably practicable, a work environment that is safe and without risk to the health of its employees. As is the case under the British Act (HSWA 1974), the OHS Act also provides for the protection of persons other than employees from hazards arising out of or in connection with the activities of persons at work.

The OHS Act provides for the appointment of health and safety representatives and health and safety committees in the workplace. Every employer who has more than 20 employees under employment at any workplace is required to designate in writing health and safety representatives for that workplace.

The Minister of Labour incorporates various regulations, on specific topics, into the OHS Act from time to time. It is important to note that, in terms of the OHS Act, any regulations made in terms of the Machinery and Occupational Safety Act 6 of 1983 ("MOS") will still be in force and in effect. The OHS Act and the regulations made in terms of the MOS Act interface and cover different aspects of safety.

Other health and safety regulations to which events organisations should refer

---

[24] For more information, see the book *The Hospitality Industry Handbook Series: Legal Requirements for South African Students and Practitioners* by Gordon-Davis and Cumberlege (Juta & Co Ltd 2004) and the website www.nosa.co.za or contact the National Occupational Safety Association.

include SABS 0400 (dealing with fire safety), the MOS Act General Safety Regulation R1031 (dealing with first aid requirements), and the Health Act 63 of 1977 (dealing with food hygiene).

It should also be noted that a very significant piece of legislation is intended to be introduced in South Africa relating to safety and security at stadiums and venues. The legislation, currently in the form of a bill, is called the Safety at Sports and Recreational Events Bill 2005 and is likely to have a significant impact on event organisers and venue owners alike if introduced in its intended format. It is arguably the most extensive piece of legislation produced worldwide dealing exclusively with event safety and security at stadiums and venues.

The purpose of the legislation is to determine, maintain, protect and ensure the safety and security of spectators and participants (and their property) at sports and recreational events at a stadium or venue or its precincts in South Africa. Those stadiums and venues which qualify are those which have an audience or attendee capacity of at least 2000 people at any one time.

The legislation creates a new body known as the National Event Inspectorate, which falls under the auspices of Sports and Recreation SA, and imposes a host of obligations on a number of different role-players in the events industry, including controlling bodies, event organisers, venue owners and any other person or body with a material interest in an event (even a sponsor!).

All controlling bodies have to submit annually a written list of proposed and envisaged events to be hosted at a stadium or venue at least 6 months before the start of each calendar year. Along with that list, the controlling body must include a categorisation of risk for each event, based on a number of factors. In addition, controlling bodies and stadium or venue owners will need to apply to the National Event Inspectorate for a range of safety certificates under the legislation, including certificates for planned stadiums or venues. Inspectors will conduct annual audits of qualifying stadiums and venues.

Apart from the above, the legislation imposes extensive requirements in relation to medical care and facilities, spectator access control, ambush marketing, security service providers (including private security service providers), emergency services, so-called venue operation centres, event ticketing, public liability insurance, accreditation, corporate hospitality, vendors and tobacco usage, amongst others. Owing to the high public interest element, the penalties for non-compliance with the act are high. Non-compliance with the legislation will be a criminal offence and may give rise to a fine or to imprisonment (for a term not exceeding 10 years) or both.

A copy of the above bill can be obtained from the Department of Sport and Recreation SA. For general advice and assistance with health and safety issues, event organisations in South Africa should contact the National Occupational Safety Association, an association that assists organisations to identify and control safety issues in the workplace.

ii) Other Legislation

Apart from health and safety legislation, there may well be other legislation that is relevant to the events industry in the country in which you live. It is common for countries to have statutes relating to provisions for employees in general, the disabled, discrimination, occupiers liability and the environment, for example, all of which will have some bearing on the events industry. Some examples are listed below.

United Kingdom

The Employment Rights Act 1996 is the primary piece of legislation in the United Kingdom dealing with employees, whether in the events industry or otherwise. The Employment Rights (Dispute Resolution) Act 1998 deals with the procedures and methods of dispute resolution. Employment and other policies should be reviewed to ensure compliance with the Sex Discrimination Act 1975, the Disability Discrimination Act 1995 and the Race Relations Act 1976. Venue owners and event organisers should note in particular that, under section 21 of the Disability Discrimination Act, service providers are under a duty to ensure that there is suitable access to venues for disabled people[25].

The Occupiers' Liability Act 1957 requires that an 'occupier' must take such care as is reasonable to ensure that a visitor will be reasonably safe in using the premises or venue for the purposes for which he or she is invited or permitted to be there. An occupier is deemed to be anyone in control of a venue. In the case of the spectator on the race track, failure to provide adequate fencing could give rise to liability under this Act.

It should be noted that the Employers' Liability (Compulsory Insurance) Act 1969 requires employers to take out insurance against accidents and ill health to their employees.

United States

In the United States, engaging employees means having to comply with a host of laws at both federal and state level. These laws deal with a variety of issues, such as non-discrimination due to gender, colour, religion, race and age (Title VII of the Civil Rights Act of 1964, the Equal Pay Act of 1963, the Age Discrimination

---

[25] See 4.2.9(a) above.

in Employment Act of 1967, Title 1 and V of the Americans with Disabilities Act of 1990, and the Civil Rights Act of 1991); family leave (Family and Medical Leave Act); and how employees are remunerated (Fair Labor Standards Act). Companies in the events industry should consult with an attorney and accountant in drafting a company policy manual recording the issues arising under these laws, and ensure that each employee has a copy of the policy manual.

The Americans with Disabilities Act is a federal civil rights law designed to prevent discrimination against those persons with a mental or physical impairment. This Act only applies to those companies with 15 or more employees. Such companies must make sure that persons with disabilities have equal opportunities to apply for jobs and to work in jobs for which they are qualified, equal opportunities to be promoted once employed and equal access to benefits[26].

Employers need to be sure that they do not contravene the Fair Labor Standards Act, in particular. This Act lays down minimum wage and overtime pay and regulates the employment of minors. Under this Act, employees are entitled to time and a half for any hours worked over 40 in any given week unless they are specifically exempted by statute[27]. Thus if a non-exempt employee works a few extra hours in the days building up to an event to complete all the work for that event, the employee must be paid overtime.

Overtime pay cannot be avoided by a promise to provide compensatory time off in another work week, even if the employee agrees to the procedure. The only way so-called 'comp time' is legal is if it's given in the same week in which the extra hours are worked, or in another week of the same pay period, and if the extra time off is sufficient to off-set the amount of overtime worked (i.e. at time-and-a half).

The Immigration Reform and Control Act (IRCA) may also be relevant. This Act prohibits employers from knowingly hiring illegal persons for work in the United States, either because the individual is in the country illegally, or because his or her immigration and residency status does not permit employment. Under the Act employers are required to verify that all employees hired after 6 November 1986 are legally authorised to work in the United States. It is worth noting that IRCA applies to organisations of any size and to both full and part-time employees.

---

[26] See 4.2.9(b) above.

[27] The most generally recognised exceptions are the so-called 'white collar' exceptions for professional, executive and administrative employees. According to the Department of Labor regulations, an administrative employee is one whose primary duty is the performance of non-manual (i.e. office) work directly related to management policies, and who, in the course of that work, generally exercises discretion and independent judgement. An administrative assistant is not exempt from overtime just because he or she exercises discretion over such things as office supplies and stationery or the processing of meeting or convention registrations, for example.

Each state regulates employment and employer/employee relationships within its borders. Generally, issues such as worker-related unemployment benefits and workers' compensation will be dealt with by the state entity charged with these responsibilities, usually a branch of the Employment Security Agency.

South Africa

Event organisations with employees in South Africa will need to have a good understanding of the Labour Relations Act 66 of 1995 ("LRA"), around which labour law revolves in that country. Almost every employer and employee is covered by the LRA[28]. The LRA aims to promote economic development, social justice and peace and democracy in the workplace. It also promotes the right to fair labour practices and provides for conciliation and negotiation as a way of settling labour disputes.

In addition to the LRA, event organisations should have reference to the Basic Conditions of Employment Act 75 of 1997, the Unemployment Insurance Act 63 of 2001, the Compensation for Occupational Injuries and Diseases Act 130 of 1993, the Skills Development Act 97 of 1998, the Employment Equity Act 55 of 1998 and the Promotion of Equality and Prevention of Unfair Discrimination Act 4 of 2000[29].

Given South Africa's legacy of discrimination on the basis of race, gender and disability, the Employment Equity Act 55 of 1998 and the Promotion of Equality and Prevention of Unfair Discrimination Act 4 of 2000 are of particular significance. These two Acts were developed on the back of the fundamental rights relating to equality set out in the country's first constitution[30].

Events organisations should also have reference to the Regional Services Council Act 109 of 1995 (relating to the payment of levies for basic services), the Liquor Act 2003 (dealing with the manufacture, distribution and sale of liquor[31]) and the Tobacco Products Control Act 83 of 1993 (dealing with the manufacture, sale, supply, consumption and use of tobacco products) as these Acts will all be likely to have some bearing on an event.

d) Licences and Permits

Events companies are usually obliged to obtain licences or permits in order to carry out certain activities. For example, licences and permits may be required in

---

[28] People who are considered to be independent contractors are not employees and are not therefore bound by the LRA (or by other labour legislation). The LRA does also not apply to members of the National Defence Force, the National Intelligence Agency and the South African Secret Service.

[29] For further details on these statutes, see Section 3 of *Legal Requirements for South African students and practitioners* by Gordon-Davis and Cumberlege (Juta & Co Ltd, 2004).

[30] Chapter 2 of the Constitution of the Republic of South Africa 108 of 1996, which contains the Bill of Rights.

[31] See paragraph 8.3.1 below.

relation to fire safety, alcohol, noise, music, food, pyrotechnics, gaming activities and vehicle access. The larger the event, the more likely that licences and permits will be required. Usually, the requirements for obtaining a licence are more stringent than for obtaining a permit and require due diligence (evidence of some element of worthiness) prior to issuance. Failure to secure a necessary licence is likely to have serious consequences. More than one event has had to be cancelled because of failure to obtain a necessary licence. If a licence is obtained, it is likely to be granted subject to terms and conditions with which the events organisation must comply. Working closely with the various regulatory bodies in respect of the procedures, time frames and conditions of licences and permits will help to ensure compliance is achieved successfully and the event proceeds without undue interruption.

Vendors are usually well-acquainted with licensing requirements in their particular area. However, for large events, a local authority or local attorney should be consulted to give guidance. Event companies should take care to specify in their contracts which party is responsible for obtaining the necessary licences or permits. Often a party is required to provide a warranty that it has obtained all the necessary licences and permits. Parties should also clarify who is responsible for the costs of such licences or permits. Although the costs are usually minimal, unless this is clarified, it can lead to misunderstandings and conflict between the various stakeholders.

Alcohol licensing is usually a primary concern for events companies, given that events companies operate in the entertainment industry. In some countries, such as the United Kingdom, additional regulations have been imposed in relation to the service of alcohol at sports events[32].

These days music is also an essential feature of most events. Music licences will need to be obtained to use certain songs legally. This is discussed in more detail in Chapter 10 which deals with entertainment-related contracts.

e) Guidelines

Although codes of practice or guidelines relating to the events industry are usually advisory (not legally binding) in nature, a party may include a duty to comply with certain codes or guidelines in its contract with another party in order to ensure that services are delivered to a certain standard.

For instance, the codes of ethics developed by the International Special Events Society (ISES) or Meeting Professionals International (MPI) are sometimes incorporated by reference into event contracts.

---

[32] See the Sporting Events (Control of Alcohol etc) Act 1985 and the Sporting Events (Control of Alcohol etc) Amendment Act 1992.

In the United Kingdom, the Health and Safety Executive have produced a number of very useful and comprehensive health and safety guides which can likewise be incorporated by reference into a contract e.g. the *Event Safety Guide: a Guide to Health, Safety and Welfare at Music and Similar Events*, the *Guide to Fire Precautions in Existing Places of Entertainment and Like Premises* and the *Guide to Safety at Sports Grounds*[33].

In the United States, the National Institute for Occupational Safety and Health (NIOSH) has produced a number of publications and guidelines for health and safety in the workplace. NIOSH is the federal agency responsible for conducting research and making recommendations for the prevention of work-related injury and illness. NIOSH is part of the Centers for Disease Control and Prevention (CDC) in the Department of Health and Human Services. It provides research, information, education and training in the field of occupational safety and health[34]. NIOSH also operates programmes in every state through the respective Departments of Health[35]. In addition, the Food and Drug Administration, through the Food Code, has produced a number of guidelines in relation to food safety[36].

In South Africa, the South African Bureau of Standards (SABS) has developed a variety of codes of practice. Some of these, such as those dealing with fire safety, have already been incorporated into law and are therefore mandatory[37]. Others, such as those dealing with food hygiene, are merely considered to be best practice and are required only if an organisation wishes to acquire SABS certification. At present, a technical committee is working on an SABS code for health and safety at live events. The ISO 9000 series of guidelines is also recognised as a symbol of management (including safety) excellence.

6.5　Insurance

Proper risk assessment and management will go a long way towards minimising an organisation's potential exposure. However, it is impossible to eliminate all risk. Event organisations, particularly event organisers and suppliers, would be wise to consider taking out insurance to cater for residual risks. Suitably qualified insurance brokers should be consulted with a view to obtaining relevant and necessary insurance policies. Leading insurers such as Marsh and E & E specialise in advising on insurance policies in relation to events held all over the world.

---

[33] See Chapter 4, n 11, n 12 and n 13.
[34] See www.cdc.gov/niosh.
[35] See www.cdc.gov/niosh/statosh.html.
[36] See paragraph 8.3.2(b).
[37] See paragraph 6.4.2(c)(i) above.

6.5.1 Nature of Insurance Contracts

Insurance policies are contracts in their own right, with legal implications. The contract will be between the insurance company (the insurer) and the person or company (the insured) in terms of which the insurer agrees, in return for payment of a premium, to pay the insured a sum of money (or its equivalent) on the happening of an uncertain event in which the insured has some interest. The contract effectively exposes the insurer to identified risks of loss from events or circumstances occurring or discovered within a designated period.

The insured will usually complete a proposal form and submit it to the insurer for consideration. Once the insurer agrees to insure, a document setting out the terms of the contract of insurance is issued by the insurer. This is referred to as an insurance policy. The proposal will usually form part of the insurance policy.

As with any contract, there will need to be agreement between the insured and the insurer on the material terms of the contract, the most important of which are described below.

6.5.2 Key Terms

a) Undertaking by the Insured to Pay a Premium

The insured undertakes to pay a premium to the insurer. This is usually a sum of money, payment of which is a condition for the insurance policy to take effect.

b) Undertaking by the Insurer to Pay a Sum of Money

The insurer may undertake to pay the insured a fixed amount of money if the event insured against takes place[38]. Alternatively, the insurer may undertake to pay the insured a determinable amount of money, to be calculated after the occurrence of the event insured against by determining the extent of the damage[39]. In the latter case, it is common for an insurer to include an excess clause in the contract, in terms of which the insured must bear a specific proportion of the loss him or herself.

c) The Risk

The uncertain event insured against is referred to as the risk. It is important for both parties to be clear on the precise nature of the risks insured against. A description of the risk usually includes:

- The object insured e.g. a motor car;
- The hazard insured against e.g. theft; and
- Circumstances affecting the risk e.g. limitations of liability

---

[38] This is often referred to as 'non-indemnity insurance'.
[39] This is often referred to as 'indemnity insurance'.

As regards the last-mentioned point, events companies should take special note of any exclusion or limitation clauses upon which the insurer will seek to rely in order to exclude or limit liability in certain circumstances.

d) Insurable Interest

It is a basic requirement of an insurance contract that the insured must have an insurable interest in the subject matter of the insurance. This is because it is the person or entity with the insurable interest that will suffer the loss when the risk that is insured against actually occurs.

6.5.3 Types of Policies

The specific insurance requirements will vary, and hence the contracts with vary. The policies need to be tailored to suit the nature of the event and the particular risks relating to that event.

The types of policies that should be considered and discussed with your insurance advisors are set out below:

a) Liability Insurance

Liability insurance usually covers claims from the public in the event of personal injury, death or damage to property. Event organisers and venue owners may be the recipient of such claims and accordingly such cover should be considered by these parties. Although venue owners will usually have some type of liability insurance in place to cover claims from the public at an event, it is not unusual for event organisers to also take out such insurance in relation to an event as well. The extent to which a party may be required to take out such insurance will also depend on what has been negotiated between the parties contractually in relation to the event[40].

Litigation can be an expensive business, even if it only includes the filing of a defence for a frivolous claim. Liability insurance policies will also usually cover the legal expenses involved in defending any claims brought against an events company, but this should be checked. Where legal expenses are covered, the insurance company will want to take control of the legal proceedings and appoint its own lawyer to defend the claim.

For large events, consideration should also be given as to whether or not to cover volunteer staff for claims against them arising from their involvement in the event. Volunteers play a vital role in many large events and it is considered best practice to protect them to ensure their continued support.

---

[40] See paragraph 4.2.7 above.

In the United States, liability insurance is usually referred to as 'general liability insurance' and, apart from claims for personal injury and damage to property, may cover a broad range of liability including:

- Claims for slander and libel;
- Claims for false arrest;
- Liquor liability;
- Contractual liability (to cover indemnities given in a contract, for example);
- Fire damage;
- Medical payment coverage;
- Burglary and robbery coverage;
- Accidental death and dismemberment;
- Independent contractors coverage;
- Door receipts coverage;
- Valuable papers coverage; and
- Office contents coverage.

In the United Kingdom, South Africa and other countries within the Commonwealth, liability insurance is usually referred to as 'public liability insurance' and is much narrower in scope than 'general liability insurance'. The former generally only covers claims from the public for personal injury, death or damage to property.

It should be noted that in some countries it may be mandatory for an event organiser to have some form of public liability insurance in place[41].

Event organisers are advised to take the trouble to ascertain the contents and extent of their liability insurance and also consider whether or not the level of cover is appropriate, given the large amounts of potential claims in this day and age.

b) Employer's Liability/Workers' Compensation Insurance

In some countries it is a legal requirement that an employer takes out insurance cover against liability for personal injury or disease arising in the course and scope of employment[42]. This would usually cover accidents to staff employed to work at a venue e.g. slipping on a wet floor, a stage collapsing, falling lights etc. It is considered best practice to extend such cover to include volunteer staff, as in the case of liability insurance.

---

[41] For example, in South Africa the draft Safety at Sports and Recreational Events Bill makes it mandatory for event organisers and venue owners to have public liability in place for certain events. See section 42 of the Bill, which at the time of writing is yet to be passed by Parliament.

[42] In the United Kingdom, this is governed by Section 1 of the Employers' Liability (Compulsory Insurance) Act 1969. In the United States, all states require public and private sector employers to provide some form of mandatory workers' compensation insurance. In South Africa, the Compensation for Occupational Injuries and Diseases Act 130 of 1993 (COID) provides compensation for disablement caused by injuries and diseases sustained in the workplace, through the Compensation Fund.

Additional employment-practice liability insurance, which covers companies
claims from their employees that their legal rights have been violated, is ob~~~~~~
in some countries[43]. This is intended to cover employers against claims for sexual
harassment, discrimination, failure to hire or promote, wrongful termination, breach
of employment contract and infliction of emotional distress, for example.

c) Contingency/Cancellation Insurance

These days it is possible to insure against almost any contingency, from adverse
weather conditions to acts of terrorism. The size and financial implications of
the event will largely determine the need for such insurance. In some cases,
the cancellation or postponement of an event as a result of an incident can have
massive financial implications. Where entities borrow against future income to
be generated by an event (as a result of ticket sales, for instance), the need for
such insurance increases. This is common in the United States in particular,
where the securitisation of future income has become relatively common.

Since the September 11 terrorist attacks, both the need and the cost of cancellation
insurance have increased greatly. For the Olympic Games in Athens in 2004, the
International Olympic Committee took out cancellation insurance for the first
time, reportedly seeking £170 million worth of cover![44] A policy can cover as
much or as little finance as is required in the circumstances. However, the loss
must be reasonably ascertainable. Insurance can be taken out to cover loss of
expenses incurred in organising an event, to cover business interruption[45] and
even to cover the non-appearance of a star performer at an event.

d) Professional Indemnity Insurance

In cases where an organisation has professionals involved in its activities, it should
consider taking out insurance to protect the organisation and the individual for
claims that a person has breached their professional duty or been negligent[46].

---

[43] In the United States, for example, this can usually be obtained, although it is not offered as part of a typical
liability policy, but as stand-alone insurance.

[44] This was announced at an IOC press conference, as reported in the *Daily Times* on 28 April 2004 and
several other news publications. This insurance covered total or partial cancellation in the event of a
disaster (such as terrorism, flooding, an earthquake or a landslide). According to the IOC, similar policies
will be taken out for the 2006 Turin Winter Games, the 2008 Beijing Games and the 2010 Vancouver
Winter Games.

[45] This is common in the United States. Business interruption insurance covers the loss of income resulting
from having to shut a business down temporarily because of fire, flood, hurricanes or other disasters that
disrupt the operation of the business. If the events company is located in California, New Orleans or Florida,
earthquake, flood and hurricane insurance should also be considered.

[46] Professional liability could also extend to those who hold themselves out as having a greater than average
level of skill or expertise in a certain area or sell their services based on their professional status. This is
usually evidenced by some kind of degree or qualification. In the United States, for example, travel agents
have been held responsible for professional liability and it has been argued that this could also apply to
independent meeting planners and specialist event organisers.

For instance, where an event organiser employs medical staff or professional coaches, such insurance may be appropriate. Professionals may already have insurance in place. However, existing policies may not cover that person if their involvement in the event is outside of their usual activities.

e) Product Liability Insurance

This type of insurance may be relevant for suppliers, particularly where the success of an event depends on the provision and reliability of equipment or specialised products. For instance, a supplier of timekeeping devices for an athletics event may wish to obtain such insurance. Likewise, the supplier of equipment for rides at a funfair may wish to consider such insurance.

f) Key Person Insurance

This type of insurance cover helps to deal with injury to, or the loss of, a key person. If there are key people in the events organisation without whom the business or event would seriously suffer, this insurance cover should be considered. Key person insurance can be taken out to cover incidents such as death, injury, illness or loss of revenue. In some countries, this is known as 'personal accident and life insurance'.

For practical reasons a key person should be made aware of the policy terms and be asked to comply with those terms. The organisation should also be noted as payee on the insurance policy in the event that the policy is paid out.

g) Director and Officers' Liability

It is common for the constitutional documents of a company to include an indemnity in favour of directors or officers for losses they incur in acting in their official capacity for the organisation. This indemnity constitutes an additional risk in respect of which insurance can be obtained.

h) Property

Insurance can be obtained on fixed property or real estate (which is recommended if you are a venue owner) and also on moveable property, such as equipment and motor vehicles. The latter is likely to be important if an events company owns or operates a number of vehicles, such as trucks, or expensive equipment, such as lighting[47]. Events companies working extensively with electrical equipment should insure for damage caused by fire. Insurance can also usually be obtained to cover damage to, or loss of, company records including data and accounting records.

---

[47] In most states in the United States, if a company owns vehicles, it usually must carry commercial liability insurance on the vehicles. If vehicles are leased long term, the leasing company may handle the insurance and charge it back to the events company.

i) Exhibitor Liability Insurance

For trade shows or exhibitions, event organisers may wish to consider exhibitors liability policies, which provide protection to the organisation for damaged caused by exhibitors.

6.5.4 Purchasing Insurance

Purchasing insurance can be an expensive exercise. However, the following steps can be taken to reduce the cost of obtaining insurance:

- Don't leave it until the last minute. Certain types of insurance can be difficult to obtain in some markets. Also, the earlier you start shopping for it, the better. If you shop for insurance when the event is around the corner you will have less time to shop around and may be forced to take out a package on terms which don't necessarily suit you;
- Reduce your insurance premiums by adopting sound risk management techniques and policies. If you are able to record these techniques and policies and share them with your insurer, this will also help to prove that you do not represent an excessive risk;
- Select insurance companies that are familiar with your business or the events industry. This will reduce the amount of time and trouble it takes in obtaining relevant and appropriate insurance for the event; and
- Compare prices and policies. Both of these are likely to differ slightly from insurer to insurer.

6.6 Conclusion

Risk assessment and management is an area that is often overlooked by those in the events industry. However, the increasingly complex nature of the events industry now requires successful events organisations to be knowledgeable about, and competent in, this area of expertise.

Risk assessment and management is not just about maximising the chances of success of the event. Incidents can have dire legal consequences. Accordingly, risk assessment and management is also about knowing your legal obligations arising from the event. As the old saying goes, ignorance of the law is no excuse. Event organisers need to know exactly where their legal responsibilities start and end.

CHAPTER SEVEN

Supplier/Vendor Contracts

Event organisers will usually require the supply of goods of services from a supplier (sometimes called a vendor) for the successful running of the event. For example, the organiser of a conference may require flower arrangements to be supplied. The organiser of a sports event may require the supply of sports equipment. The organiser of a music event may wish to contract for the provision of security services. The type of goods or services to be supplied can vary greatly, depending on the nature of the event. Examples of the types of suppliers include[1]:

- Airlines
- Audio-visual, staging and lighting companies
- Décor companies
- Florists
- Invitation and Print Material companies
- Caterers
- Hospitality companies
- Special effects companies
- Transportation companies
- Tourist Boards
- Performers and entertainment management companies
- Security and crew/staffing companies
- Public relations companies
- Professional advisors e.g. lawyers, accountants
- First-aid providers

Ideally a supplier contract should be entered into between the event organiser and the supplier, the nature of which is discussed below[2].

---

[1] Venue providers, ticket companies and performers could also be deemed to be suppliers. These contracts are sufficiently unique and important so as to merit separate attention. They are dealt with in Chapters 4, 5 and 10 respectively.

[2] For advice on general commercial aspects of supplier contracts, see *The Business of Event Planning* by Judy Allen (John Wiley & Sons) 2002.

7.1　The Nature of the Supplier Contract

The basis of the supplier contract is simply this: the supplier contracts to provide goods or services to the event organiser in return for which the supplier receives remuneration and/or certain rights in relation to the event.

Usually, the contractual process is initiated when the event organiser sends out what is often referred to as an 'RFP' (request for proposal)[3]. A proposal is then prepared by the supplier. The proposal (sometimes submitted with the supplier's standard terms and conditions or 'rider') is either accepted by the event organiser, revised or rejected. In the first two cases, it very often becomes the contract. The event organiser signs the proposal, indicating acceptance, and that is that.

However, neither party is usually as fully protected as it could and should be and, moreover, it leaves the door open for disputes (and potential litigation) relating to those subjects not dealt with in the proposal.

It pays to have proper contracts drafted by a lawyer that knows and understands your business. In addition, if a comprehensive contract is drafted, it can be used as a useful template going forward, so as to avoid repeat costs on other similar projects.

Finally, some supplier contracts may be fairly complex in nature, particularly where the supplier procures an official designation and acquires branding or advertising rights at the event. The exact scope of the different rights and obligations of the parties should be carefully recorded in the contract.

In this chapter, we will focus on the more detailed supplier contracts, as these can always be edited to suit the needs of a simpler arrangement. A sample supplier/vendor contract is set out in Appendix 5.

7.2　Key Legal Issues

Apart from the general terms and conditions which are described in Chapter 2, the following terms and conditions should be considered:

7.2.1　Term

In contracts of this nature, the duration of the contract usually only extends from the time of contracting to the end of the event, or in some cases only for the duration of the actual event itself. Parties should take care to define the exact term so that this aspect of the contract is clear.

---

[3]　For assistance in drafting an RFP, refer to *Meeting and Event Planning for Dummies* by Susan Friedmann (Wiley Publishing Inc) 2003, Chapter 12.

7.2.2 Timing

Owing to the nature of the events industry, the timing of the supply of the goods or services is usually crucial. As a result, the time for delivery of the goods or services should be defined with precision. Sometimes contracts are sent out and concluded before these details are known. If so, the contract should be amended once the details are known or a letter should be signed by both parties recording the additional details and stating that it is part of the contract.

The event organiser may wish to impose penalties for late delivery of the goods or services. Under the law of some countries, imposing penalties in a contract is not permitted, so it is worth checking this point with a local lawyer in the area in which you are contracting[4].

7.2.3 Remuneration

Usually, the supplier will be paid a fee for the provision of the goods or services. Where this is the case, the event organiser will want to try and ensure that most of the fee (or perhaps even all of it) is paid after the goods or services have been provided. Conversely, the supplier will want to ensure that a good portion of the fee is paid in the form of a deposit before the goods or services are provided. Usually the fee, however it is paid, will be paid on the provision of an appropriate invoice provided by the supplier or within a certain period of provision thereof.

In some cases, the supplier may agree to provide goods or services for free (as so-called 'benefits in kind'). Where this occurs, the supplier will usually want to negotiate commensurate value in the form of a grant of rights in relation to the event. The content of such rights is dealt with in more detail at paragraph 7.2.5 below.

Where 'benefits in kind' are being provided as part of the consideration, it is important when entering the contract to have clarity on the value of the goods or services being provided. How are the goods or services to be valued? Are they to be valued at wholesale or retail selling price? Who decides the prices?

Ideally, a price list should be used to obtain agreement on the value of the goods being provided. However, this may not be appropriate for all contracts. It is often sensible to include a clause that provides a procedure for settling disputes in respect of the value of the 'benefits in kind' (perhaps reference to an independent third party evaluator, for instance).

Finally, it is important to establish which party will be responsible for any expenses incurred on the part of the supplier. For example, if a transport company

---

[4] Cancellation charges based on actual losses incurred or "liquidated damages" (based on a genuine pre-estimate of loss) will usually be permitted however see paragraph 2.3.10 above.

is contracted to provide transport, will the costs of petrol be covered by the transport company (as is usually the case) or the event organiser? Which party will be responsible for the costs of obtaining any necessary licences and permits? If this is not agreed, the event organiser may receive an untimely invoice in the post asking them to cover these expenses.

7.2.4 Goods or Services

In contracts of this nature, it is imperative to define the extent or nature of the goods or services to be provided. This may sound obvious, but all too often, for example, the services are not adequately described or defined, so that conflict or confusion arises as to whether or not the services have been provided in full.

Where services are to be provided, the event organiser will want to break the provision of services down into specific deliverables, to be provided by the supplier at a particular time or place. The event organiser will also want an undertaking on the part of the supplier that the services will be provided with the necessary level of skill and expertise as may be expected in similar contracts of this nature. Ideally, the event organiser will have ensured that the supplier has the requisite level of skill and expertise to carry out the services properly by conducting some level of due diligence in respect of the supplier.

It may be that the supplier will be contracting with third parties to hire additional personnel for the delivery of the services. For instance, a security company may contract with independent contractors for a specific event, or a catering company may bring in the support of kitchen staff and waiters. It is important for the event organiser to stipulate that the supplier will be responsible for the acts and omissions of its contractors (including volunteers) when providing the goods or services.

Where goods are being provided by the supplier, it is likely that the quality of the goods will be material to the success of the event. For instance, if someone is supplying equipment for a particular event, the event organiser will want to know that the equipment is of sufficient quality to ensure that the event is successful. The event organiser may wish to include a warranty in the contract that the goods are fit for the purpose for which they are to be used. The event organiser may also insist that the supplier takes out product liability insurance in respect of the goods, if such insurance is not already in place. Finally, the event organiser may wish to include an indemnity in the contract in terms of which the supplier indemnifies the event organiser for any loss it may suffer as a result of any claims arising from third parties for defective goods provided by the supplier.

For example, if a supplier provides defective gym equipment for a gymnastics competition and a participant injures him or herself as a result of that equipment, that participant may issue a lawsuit against the event organiser. In such a case, the event organiser may wish to have the benefit of an indemnity from the supplier for any losses it may suffer as a result of that lawsuit (rather than issuing a lawsuit against the supplier, in turn).

Where goods are to be provided, it is worthwhile to specify in the contract which party will be responsible for the costs of delivering or transporting the goods, particularly if the costs are likely to be substantial. Usually, these costs will be borne by the supplier.

7.2.5 Rights

The event organiser may choose to grant certain rights to the supplier in exchange for the provision of the goods or services. This may be as an alternative to payment of cash or to supplement a payment of cash.

Examples of the types of rights that might be granted to a supplier are set out in Chapter 3 at paragraph 3.5.2. The most common are:

- Designation – the right to be referred to as 'the Official Supplier of X to ABC Event', or simply 'Official Supplier to ABC Event' (in the case of the latter, this may be non-exclusive);
- Use of the event trade marks;
- Advertising and branding rights – these are usually rights which are secondary to those granted to a sponsor;
- Hospitality rights – for example, tickets.

Where the supplier is given the right to use the event trade marks or a designated title, the parties should clarify the manner in which these are permitted to be used. For example, will the supplier be entitled to use the event trade marks and/ or designation on its website and on its letterhead? Will it extend to television advertising? Will the event organiser have the right of approval over all usage of the event trade marks and/or designation?

It is worth noting that in some countries the right to use the 'Official Supplier' designation may be constrained by competition rules. For instance, in the Danish Tennis Federation case[5], where a tennis ball supplier was entitled to use the designation 'DTF Official Balls' on its packaging, the European Commission

---

[5] Case Nos IV/F-1/33.055 and 35.759, [1996] 4 CMLR 885. In this case, the Danish Tennis Federation ('DTF') granted Slazenger and Tretorn the exclusive right to supply tennis balls for use in all official tournaments in Denmark for a three-year period. The suppliers obtained the right to use the DTF logo and the designation 'DTF official balls' on their packaging, in a manner that effectively allowed them to prevent parallel imports. They were also permitted to say the balls were 'approved by' or 'selected by' the DTF. Various other manufacturers complained that this restricted their ability to compete and the European Commission agreed. The DTF subsequently revised its arrangements.

found that the sports body could not grant their 'official' stamp of approval to give a chosen manufacturer an edge over its competitors that is not justified on the basis of technical quality. The case also suggests that sports bodies would be well advised to ensure that the appointment process for suppliers of equipment is fair and open and does not unreasonably shut out certain companies from the market.

7.2.6   Cancellation Charges

Often the supplier will incur costs and expenses prior to delivering the services. For example, a décor company may have manufactured or sourced certain items for the event, or a florist may have sourced, and paid for, certain flowers for the event. The supplier may wish to impose cancellation charges, or seek reimbursement of those costs and expenses, if the event is cancelled or postponed for any reason.[6]

It may be that specific time periods for cancellation need to be negotiated. For instance, if the event organiser cancels the event three months before it is due to take place, no cancellation fees may be charged, but if it is cancelled three days before the event then cancellation charges may be payable. Cancellation charges could also be staggered, if necessary.

This would also apply to requests to change the nature and scope of the goods or services to be supplied.

Where cancellation or postponement occurs as a result of a circumstance outside the control of the contracting parties, it may be that neither party will be held liable for their obligations under the contract. This will usually depend on whether a so-called 'force majeure' or 'Act of God' clause is included in the contract.[7]

7.2.7   Substitutions

In some supply contracts, the event organiser may wish to include a clause dealing with substitutions. Specifically, it may state that substitutions in relation to the goods or services to be provided are not permitted without prior consent. For instance, a florist will not be permitted to change the type of flowers for the floral arrangements without consulting with the event organiser and obtaining their permission. In any event, if substitutions are permitted, the event organiser

---

[6]   See paragraph 2.3.10. If these cancellation charges are deemed to be penalties, they may be illegal in some countries.

[7]   See paragraph 2.3.9 dealing with 'force majeure' clauses. If there is no force majeure clause, both parties may still be relieved from their duties under the contract if the contract has been frustrated so that the contract is impossible to perform. See paragraph 2.3.9 in relation to frustration of contracts.

will want to specify that suitable substitutions are located and that it will not be liable for any increased cost in this regard.

7.2.8 Insurance

In supplier contracts, insurance is always likely to be an important issue[8].

Firstly, the event organiser or organiser will be relying on the supplier to provide goods and services of sufficient quality. Where goods are being provided, as mentioned above, the event organiser should insist that the supplier has adequate product liability insurance in place.

Secondly, where services are being provided, professional indemnity insurance should also perhaps be considered.

Thirdly, for both the provision of goods and services, the supplier should have general/public liability insurance in place to cover claims by the public arising from the delivery of the goods or services.

Finally, provision should be made in the contract for the storage and insurance of the goods, particularly if the event is to endure for a period longer than one day. The supplier may wish to impose an obligation in the contract on the event organiser to store the goods safely and ensure that it has necessary insurance in place to cover damage to, or theft of, the goods, particularly if the goods are valuable. Guests at events have been known to help themselves to anything not nailed down, especially props, candlesticks, pot-plants and vases!

The event organiser may wish to be noted on the insurance policy as an interested party. Note that this may involve paying a fee, so the parties should agree who will be responsible for payment of this fee.

7.2.9 Indemnity

The event organiser will not want to be on the end of a lawsuit as a result of the acts or omissions of the supplier. The event organiser may, for example, receive a claim from a member of the public who is injured because of a falling light which was not secured properly by the lighting supplier. The event organiser should seek to obtain an indemnity to cover it for any losses arising from claims from third parties as a result of the provision of the goods or services from the supplier.

7.2.10 Regulations, Licences and Permits

The provision of goods or services may be covered by specific legislation or regulations, or be subject to a licence or permit. This will usually be the case

---

[8] For a more detailed explanation of insurance in relation to events, see paragraph 6.5 above.

if catering services, special effects or electrical equipment are being provided[9]. The parties need to record which party will be responsible for applying for and obtaining any necessary licences or permits and who will bear the costs thereof.

7.2.11 External Documents

The supplier may refer in the contract to the provisions of certain external documents, such as policy documents or guidelines. The terms of these documents could be incorporated into the contract by reference. If the event organiser accepts this clause, it will need to ensure that it has had sight of such documents and agrees to the terms contained therein.

7.2.12 Restrictive Covenants

Event organisers or planners who may be acting on behalf of a client are often concerned that suppliers will make contact with, and eventually do business directly with, their client. If this is the case, they may wish to include a clause in the contract restricting the ability of the supplier to contract directly with the client for a certain period after the event. This may also include a restriction on the handing out of business cards or the holding of business-related discussions at the event, particularly if this involves disclosing confidential information about the contract between the event organiser and the supplier.

7.3   Catering Contracts

Catering contracts are essentially supply contracts, in that the catering company is providing goods (in the form of food) and services in exchange for consideration.

Owing to the importance of these contracts in the events industry, an entire chapter is devoted to these contracts at Chapter 8.

7.4   Conclusion

Almost every event will require the contracting for services of some kind or other. By far the most important part of this contractual relationship is defining the exact nature and scope of the services to be provided by the supplier. This will help to eliminate disputes about whether or not the services have actually been provided. Taking the time to spell this out in the contract will go some distance towards ensuring that both the event organiser and the supplier are happy with the arrangement.

---

[9] Regulations, licences and permits are usually implemented for health and safety reasons. For further details on health and safety legislation and related regulations, licences and permits, refer to Chapter 6 on risk management, health & safety and insurance.

CHAPTER EIGHT

Catering Contracts

The catering industry has grown substantially in the last decade and is now a major industry in its own right. Catering contracts are an essential part of almost every major event these days. Accordingly, this subject warrants a separate chapter on its own.

8.1 The Nature of the Catering Contract

Catering contracts are essentially supplier or vendor agreements in their own right[1]. One party (the caterer, for example) is providing goods and services to another (the event organiser) in return for consideration and/or rights in the event. A sample catering contract is set out in Appendix 6.

8.2 Key Legal Issues

Apart from the standard terms and conditions contained in Chapter 2 which should be included in the contract as a matter of course, the general terms and conditions described in Chapter 7 (relating to supplier or vendor contracts) should be reviewed. The following specific terms and conditions should also be considered:

8.2.1 Term

In most cases, the term of the contract will run from the time of signature up to the end of the event. This will be the case if there are obligations on the parties that must be fulfilled before the event starts e.g. payment. Alternatively, the contract can run from the time of the start of the event to the end of the event, even though this may be a very short time.

8.2.2 Timing

Further to paragraph 7.2.2 above, this is one type of supplier contract where the timing for the delivery of the goods and services may be crucial. If the caterer is simply supplying a stand selling hotdogs at a music concert, this aspect may

---

[1] See Chapter 7 and paragraph 7.1 in particular.

not be so important. However, if a caterer is providing a four-course lunch in a corporate box at a football match, the exact timing of the delivery of the catering services will certainly be of importance. The parties should take the time to specify with precision when the food and beverages will be served.

If an event organiser is contracting with a restaurant for a private event or group seating in a reserved section, it is important to spell out in the contract the exact times the space will be available for the group and specify a cut-off time after which the public will not be seated in the reserved area prior to the group's arrival. This will prevent the restaurant from having lingering customers in the reserved section whilst the guests are left standing waiting for the customers to leave.

8.2.3 Services

On the face of it, this seems simple. The caterer is obliged to provide food and beverages at a particular venue at a particular time. However, there is more to this than meets the eye.

Firstly, the type of food and beverages to be served will almost certainly be a matter of great importance. Usually, the event organiser will have been presented with (and perhaps tasted) a list of potential items or menus, and there will have been some discussion around the appropriate items or menu to be served. It seems obvious to say that the list of items or menu will need to be agreed carefully. However, on more than one occasion disputes have arisen with caterers over the items or menu to be served because of a lack of communication between the event organiser and the caterer.

The caterer will need to be sure that the selected dishes will be available, and the parties should discuss the right to substitute dishes if there is any likelihood that any of these dishes may not be available for the event. The parties will need to consider any special dietary requirements. The event organiser may also wish to insist on the exclusive use of quality branded products, although this will obviously have an affect on the pricing.

Ideally, the list of selected items or menus should be attached to the contract as a schedule. If there is a likelihood that the list will change from the time of signature of the contract to the event, provision should be made in the contract to allow for an amendment and substitution of the schedule by agreement between the parties.

A price list should also be attached to the contract. This may include a list of sale prices (prices at which the items will be sold to the public) or payment prices (prices at which the food and beverages will be sold to the event organiser).

The caterer will need to know the number of people to whom it is expected to provide the services. Again, this may sound obvious, but lack of attention to detail in this area could give rise to costly errors and also affect the success of the event. If it is likely that the numbers will change substantially, provision should be made in the contract for notification and an adjustment to pricing, if necessary. Caterers will usually make provision for a slight change in numbers, but this something that should be clarified up-front with the caterer. It is a matter of commercial negotiation whether or not to agree a minimum amount of food and beverages to be provided. A caterer will usually try to quote their prices based on a certain minimum number of meals and beverages, and will want to charge the same fee even if fewer numbers are actually sold.

Part of the delivery of the services will be the provision of personnel to assist in preparing and serving the food and beverages. Depending on the nature of the event, the event organiser may wish to merely include a general clause in the contract to the effect that the caterer will provide sufficient and adequately trained personnel to provide the services. Alternatively, the event organiser may wish to agree and specify exactly:

- how many personnel will be available to provide the services;
- how they will be dressed;
- their required degree of experience in the catering business;
- that a chef of suitable experience will be provided; and
- that a warranty will be included in the contract to the effect that the services will be provided with all necessary skill, care and judgement.

The parties also need to specify what facilities or equipment (such as plates, glasses, candlesticks, tables, chairs, silverware etc) will be required for the delivery of the services and who will be responsible for ensuring the facilities or equipment will be available. Again, this will depend on the type of event. A caterer providing a hotdog stand at a music event will usually provide the stand and all the necessary cooking-related equipment. A caterer providing food in a corporate box at a football match may want to have access to and use the facilities and equipment at the sports ground.

If equipment being provided is extensive and valuable, the party providing such equipment may wish to record in an inventory (to be attached as a schedule) the items being provided. The parties will need to record who will be responsible for the cleaning, maintenance and insurance of both the facility and the equipment.

Caterers conducting the food preparation off-site will need to agree additional logistical arrangements with the event organiser. What happens if hot food becomes cool or even cold during transit? Is this likely to affect food delivery time?

One item that will almost always be required for the successful delivery of catering services will be electricity. Caterers providing a food and beverage stand at an event cannot simply assume that they will have access to an electrical power source nearby. This is an item that is often overlooked, and the caterer will need to ensure that the event organiser is obliged to provide such a facility on the site.

Caterers should do the same check in respect of water and an accessible water supply.

Another element of the services that is often overlooked is that of waste. Catering services often generate a large amount of waste. The event organiser should record in the contract, for the avoidance of doubt, that the caterer will be responsible for the removal of waste from the venue (unless agreed otherwise).

Other logistical aspects of the services that should be clarified and recorded in the contract may be the following:

- responsibility for the delivery and setting of tables and chairs;
- approval of any equipment (such as plates, glasses, candlesticks, silverware) to be provided by the caterer;
- the production and delivery of menus;
- facilities for the suitable storage of food and beverages;
- security personnel to safeguard food and beverages of high quality;
- access to the venue for the caterer and its staff.

Finally, it is interesting to note that, in the United States at least, there would appear to be a trend towards caterers extending their skills (and their revenue streams) to provide event management services in addition to catering services[2]. In such a case, a combination of an event management contract and a catering contract may be required to allow for the diverse issues that will arise[3].

8.2.4 Remuneration

The amount that the caterer will be paid for providing the goods and services will need to be recorded in the contract.

Usually, a set fee will be charged by the caterer, taking into consideration factors such as the nature and amount of food and beverages to be supplied, the number of guests to be served, the number of personnel required, the use of facilities and equipment and the extent of the services that will be required. A fixed price list can be used as a basis from which to calculate and agree the total remuneration.

---

[2] See *Special Events* by Dr Joe Goldblatt, John Wiley & Sons (2002), pg 167.
[3] See Chapter 14 on Event Management Contracts.

If a caterer is contracted to provide a stand at an event, the above pricing structure will not usually be applied. In this case, a price list will usually be agreed, and the event organiser will negotiate a percentage of revenues generated at the event. There is no fixed formula in calculating such a percentage. It will depend on factors such as the type of event, the number of other stands at the venue, the exact site on which the stand is to be located, the number of expected attendees at the event and the size of the stand required.

If such an arrangement is agreed, the parties should specify in the contract whether such percentages are based on gross or net revenues. In the case of net revenues, the types of costs and expenses will need to be agreed. In addition, the event organiser will usually wish to insist on some accounting mechanisms, including access to the sales figures or books of account.

The parties should specify who will be responsible for the costs of utilities, such as water, gas and electricity. The costs are likely to accumulate quickly, particularly if the event is run over a period of several days.

8.2.5 Obligations

Express obligations on the part of the caterer may include the following:

- appointing a representative to manage the relationship between the event organiser and the caterer, who shall be responsible for all management, compliance and operational issues arising in respect of the catering services;
- notifying the event organiser of any complaints received in respect of the catering services and promptly addressing such complaints;
- obtaining at its own cost all necessary licences (including liquor licences), registrations, permits, health and safety certificates, consents and other authorisations necessary for the provision of the catering services;
- providing the catering services in accordance with all relevant laws, regulations, health and safety provisions, governmental decrees and court orders (including perhaps the event organiser's prescribed hygiene standards and emergency procedures);
- notifying the event organiser immediately in the event of any change to legislation regulating the sale of alcohol at the event (if applicable) and discussing with the event organiser the impact on the provision of the catering services;
- responsibility for contracting and paying any staff required for the delivery of the catering services, including the payment of all taxes in relation to staff (if applicable);
- putting in place adequate controls for the handling of all monies received for the provision of the catering services (if applicable), including opening and

maintaining separate books of account in respect of all revenue generated during the event;

- Providing reports and other necessary information on the delivery of the catering services (if applicable);
- Notifying the event organiser immediately of any accident or breach in health and safety regulations; and
- Removing all waste from the facility or venue arising from the provision of the catering services, in accordance with health and safety regulations.

Express obligations on the part of the event organiser may include the following:

- payment of the agreed fees on the dates specified in the contract;
- making available certain facilities or equipment at the venue, as agreed;
- notifying the caterer of any complaints made by third parties relating to the catering services;
- maintaining all facilities and equipment in good condition, including effecting all repairs, if necessary (assuming that such facilities and equipment are owned by the event organiser); and
- providing suitable access to the venue for the caterer and its staff.

8.2.6   Rights

If something were to go wrong and the full extent of the catering services could not be provided at the last minute, the event organiser may wish to reserve the right to appoint another caterer to provide residual or replacement services at the last minute without being in breach of the catering contract.

The event organiser may also wish to reserve the right to monitor the delivery of the services, including carrying out random checks of the foods, beverages and facilities. The parties should work to agree an approach that is not intrusive or disruptive to the delivery of the services.

The caterer may wish to secure the right, in turn, to use the designation 'Official Caterer to XYZ Event' or 'Official Supplier to XYZ Event'. This may or may not include the right to use the brand or logo of the event organiser[4]. If the event organiser wishes to grant the caterer the right to use its brand or logo, it should detail the terms and conditions under which such brand or logo may be used.

8.2.7   Insurance

This is dealt with in more detail at paragraph 7.2.8 above. With regards to catering contracts in particular, the following types of insurance should be considered.

---

[4]   For further details on the right to a designation in a supplier contract, see paragraph 7.2.5 above.

Firstly, the caterer should have liability insurance in place to cover claims from third parties as a result of the services. Claims could arise from an executive who slips and falls on a floor which is not kept dry. Claims for negligence could also arise in the event of food poisoning.

In 1990 approximately 300 people attending a convention in a downtown Chicago hotel were sent to local hospitals with food poisoning as a result of salmonella, prompting a Chicago Tribune headline "Convention Illness Linked to Salmonella". It was unclear whether the food poisoning resulted from food prepared by the hotel or as a result of canapés served at the reception prepared by a local caterer. The Chicago Health Department were called in to investigate.

Threats of claims against the caterer and the hotel were made after the 1995 Rugby World Cup final in Johannesburg, South Africa. The New Zealand rugby team claimed that a large part of their team were subjected to food poisoning at the team hotel two days prior to the final.

It is not unusual for food service providers to be held liable for personal injury from serving unwholesome or unhealthy food. In most cases, the afflicted consumer will have to prove that the food service provider failed to use reasonable care in the preparation or service of the food[5].

Secondly, the parties may also wish to ensure that either of them has insurance in place to cover damage to, or theft of, the equipment whilst it is at the venue, particularly if the equipment is valuable (e.g. silver candlesticks, silverware, microwaves etc).

In addition to the above, and in the United States in particular, liquor liability insurance should be considered by caterers or event organisers serving alcohol. Under the so-called 'dram shop' laws, a caterer or event organiser may be held liable for injuries incurred by a guest or by an innocent party as a result of the alcohol consumption by a guest. These laws may vary from state to state, but if there is a risk of such claims, both caterers and event organisers should consider this type of insurance.

Finally, an event organiser may wish to stipulate that a caterer has insurance to cover a claim by the event organiser under an indemnity granted by the caterer. This is dealt with in the paragraph below.

---

[5] In the United States, the afflicted consumer can also sue for a breach of warranty under the Uniform Commercial Code (UCC), which has been adopted in almost every state. Under the UCC, it is not necessary to prove that the food service provider was negligent, only that the food service provider, as the seller of the food, breach the implied warranty that the food is wholesome and fit for human consumption (the same form of liability may attach to the food suppliers who supplied the food to the hotel or caterer). It should also be noted that in some states, neither proof of negligence nor breach of warranty is required and the afflicted consumer need only prove that the food he or she ate made them ill (this is so-called 'strict liability').

8.2.8   Indemnity

It is precisely because of the risks of the claims referred to above that the event organiser will seek to obtain an indemnity for any losses incurred by it from claims arising from the provision of the services by the caterer. If the event organiser does incur such losses it can then claim for reimbursement of those losses under the indemnity.

8.2.9   Cancellation Charges

Cancellation charges will usually be of relevance in catering contracts, as the caterer is likely to incur costs in the event of cancellation or postponement of the event, particularly if such cancellation or postponement is last minute.

This is dealt with at paragraph 7.2.6 in more detail.

Cancellation charges in the catering industry should be staggered, as the caterer will not usually suffer any losses if the event is cancelled one month before it is due to take place, whilst the caterer may well suffer losses if the event is cancelled one day before it is due to take place. The caterer may also seek to implement cancellation charges in the event of material changes to the number of attendees for whom it will be catering.

8.3   Regulations, Licences and Permits

This will most definitely be an issue in catering contracts. This is because the food and beverage industry is highly regulated in most countries in the world today.

Health and safety issues are dealt with in more detail in Chapter 6 on risk, health & safety and insurance[6]. This section will deal with alcohol service and licensing and food hygiene in particular.

8.3.1   Alcohol Service and Licensing

Many events will have alcohol of some kind being served at the venue. Attendees at events usually expect to be able to buy a beer or a glass of wine. It is all part of the entertainment (although it also substantially increases the risk of unfavourable incidents at events and, as such, it should be considered an integral part of the risk assessment and management programme carried out an event[7]).

Some countries or states have very strict liquor laws. Legislators in Utah were criticised for their stringent liquor laws imposed at the 2002 Winter Olympic

---

[6]   See paragraphs 6.4.2(c) and 6.4.2 (d) in particular.

[7]   For a detailed analysis of potential risks arising from alcohol at an event, refer to Chapter 3 of *Event Risk Management and Safety* by Peter Tarlow (2002), John Wiley & Sons Inc.

Games. Some Muslim countries prohibit the consumption of liquor altogether, at least for their local populations. On the other hand, people from Scandinavia, large parts of Western Europe and Israel are used to their governments taking a more relaxed attitude towards the sale and consumption of alcohol.

a) Liquor Licences

Notwithstanding this diversity in approach amongst the countries of the world, a licence will almost always be required to serve and sell alcohol at the event. In many cases, the venue may already be a licensed facility and this will not be an issue.

However, both the event organiser and the caterer will need to be clear on the liquor licensing requirements and who is responsible for obtaining and holding the licence.

In almost all cases a licence to sell liquor at the venue will be granted by a local or state authority. In the United States, each state has its own alcohol and beverage commission (known as an 'ABC') that will set liquor licensing conditions in that state. The ABC's job is to establish policy regarding who may receive a liquor licence and under what conditions, what taxes are to be paid, and what the state's policy is concerning the use of alcoholic substances.

In England and Wales, there has recently been a transition from an old licensing regime to a new one. The Licensing Act 2003 established a new single, integrated regime for licensing premises which are used for the supply of alcohol, to provide regulated entertainment or to provide late night refreshment. The new regime became effective on 24 November 2005. Permission to conduct some or all of these activities is now contained in a single licence – the 'Premises Licence'. This brings together the six old licensing regimes (alcohol, public entertainment, cinemas, theatres, late night refreshment houses and night cafes) thereby cutting down on red tape. The new Act transfers alcohol licensing from licensing justices to licensing authorities which are democratically accountable[8]. The sale of alcohol must be authorised by a 'Designated Premises Supervisor' who is in day to day control of the premises. He or she must hold a 'Personal Licence'. To allow people to apply for the necessary Premises and Personal Licences a six months transition period was implemented between 7 February 2005 and 6 August 2005. During this period holders could apply to convert licences under the old regime to a new licence. If such an application was not made, licences under the old regime would

---

[8] The main licensing authorities as defined in the Act are: 1) the council of a district in England 2) the council of a county in England in which there are no district councils 3) the council of a county or county borough in Wales or 4) the council of a London borough.

expire on 24 November 2005[9]. On that date all premises that supply alcohol, provide entertainment or provide late night refreshment must have a 'Premises Licence' or they will no longer be able to operate.

Event organizers can apply for a Temporary Event Notice (TEN) to authorise the supply of alcohol, the provision of regulated entertainment and the provision of late night refreshment on a temporary basis. A TEN can cover a period of up to 96 hours and there may be 12 TENs per year in respect of any particular premises. A TEN can only authorise an event where the number of persons attending (including audience, competitors, staff etc) is less than 500.

It should also be noted that in the United Kingdom, additional regulations have been imposed in relation to the service of alcohol at sports events in particular[10].

In South Africa, liquor legislation has recently undergone significant changes. In August 2004 the Liquor Act 27 of 1989 was replaced by the new Liquor Act 59 of 2003 and nine provincial liquor acts. The new Liquor Act deals primarily with the manufacture, distribution and wholesaling of liquor whilst each of the provincial liquor acts deal with liquor retailing. Under the South African Constitution, retail liquor licensing is deemed to be within the ambit of provincial government and not national government. The nine Provincial Liquor Boards consider application for liquor licences, grant such licences and also impose conditions on such licences.

In South Africa, event organisers and venue owners also need to be aware of the provisions of the draft Safety at Sports and Recreational Events Bill, which imposes a range of obligations in relation to the sale or service of alcohol at events held at stadiums or venues with a capacity of over 2000 people at any one time.

Generally speaking, the requirements and conditions of liquor licences will vary from region to region, state to state and country to country. Both the event organiser and the caterer should be aware of the requirements and conditions of the licence, as a breach of the licensing terms may have disastrous consequences both for the event and for the organisation in breach. In many countries, including

---

[9] For more information, see *Alcohol and Entertainment Licensing Law* by Colin Manchester, Susanna Poppleston and Jeremy Allen, Cavendish Publishing (2005), ISBN 1859416721.

[10] See the Sporting Events (Control of Alcohol etc) Act 1985 and the Sporting Events (Control of Alcohol etc) Amendment Act 1992. Under s 3 of the 1985 Act, where licensed premises are located within the area of a designated sports ground (as defined under s 9 of the Act), intoxicating liquor may not be sold or supplied in the premises or consumed in or taken off the premises from two hours prior to the start of such an event until one hour after the event. Under s 5 A of the Act, an exception to this rule may be made by an order of the local licensing justices. Such an order may specify the exact hours when intoxicating liquor can be supplied subject to any conditions they wish to impose.

the United States, the United Kingdom and South Africa, contravention of the licensing regulations can lead to criminal prosecution.

b) Liquor Liability

Remember also that in most countries it is an offence to serve or sell liquor to those under age. If there is a risk of this happening at an event, the event organiser and the caterer need to take steps to eliminate or limit this risk, or they themselves run the risk of prosecution.

Those in the United States will need to be aware of the so-called 'dram shop' laws. These laws impose liability for the acts of others on those who serve alcohol negligently, recklessly or negligently. For instance, a person who pours the alcohol may be legally responsible if a person being served overindulges and causes injury to himself or other parties. Each state has different interpretations of the dram shop laws. These laws will usually only apply to commercial sellers of alcohol. More than 40 states have some form of 'dram shop' liability.

In addition, in some states in the United States liability may also extend to 'social hosts' (i.e. unlicensed servers such as associations or companies which organise meetings or employee parties) who provide liquor to a person who is obviously intoxicated or underage and that person causes injury to another. A social host may be found negligent if the host had control over the liquor supply, was in a position to observe the condition of the guest, and knew or ought to have known that the guest constituted a reasonably foreseeable danger or risk of injury to a third party but did not take reasonable precautions to prevent such injury.

An event organiser can try to avoid such liability by taking the following steps:

- Ensuring that bartenders are professionally trained and giving them instructions (preferably written) not to serve persons who are either underage or noticeably intoxicated;
- Requiring the venue or catering company to have its own insurance policy;
- Inserting a clause in the venue or catering contract that shifts liability to the venue owner or caterer as the servers or sellers of alcohol;
- Establishing a monitoring system to ensure that intoxicated persons and those underage are not served alcohol e.g. checking IDs;
- Appointing staff members or volunteers to be designated drivers for obviously intoxicated persons, or arranging for cabs to collect these persons;
- Avoiding self-service bars, kegs of beer and happy hours if possible;
- Setting reasonable limits on the amount of alcohol that can be served if possible e.g. provide guests with drink tokens;
- Ensuring that a good selection of non-alcoholic drinks are available and placing free water in certain locations;

- Serving food whilst guests are drinking if possible (preferably not salty food which can encourage more drinking);
- Setting bar opening and closing times and not announcing a last call.

Alternatively, event organisers in the United States could ensure that their general liability insurance cover includes liquor liability.

Interestingly, in Brazil, a totally different system applies to that of the United States and the legal system places the responsibility firmly on the drinker rather than the server[11].

In South Africa, it is an offence for the holder of an on-consumption licence to allow drunkenness or licentious conduct on the licensed premises[12]. The licence holder may not sell or supply liquor to someone who is drunk, as to do so is also an offence.

In the United Kingdom, under the Licensing Act 2003 it is an offence to, amongst other things, allow disorderly conduct on a licensed premises, permit the sale of alcohol to an under 18 or allow a child under 16 to be on a licensed premises unaccompanied by an adult where the main purpose of the premises is the supply of alcohol for consumption on the premises.

c) Conclusion

Owing to the varied views that different governments or states take towards alcohol in general, it is advisable to consult a local and suitably qualified lawyer in your area to confirm the relevant legislative and regulatory requirements relating to the service and sale of alcohol at the event. It is far too important an issue to be overlooked.

As far as the catering contract is concerned, the parties should take care to specify who is responsible both for obtaining the liquor licence and ensuring that the terms thereof are not breached.

8.3.2   Food Service and Hygiene Legislation

Food hygiene law basically governs the handling, transportation, storage and sale of food to the general public. These laws are in place to protect the consumer against any potential risk of contracting food poisoning or a food-borne illness. These laws also protect the food industry from legal claims by giving them a framework of rules within which to operate.

It is very important that events organisers are aware of food hygiene laws to ensure that they, and any caterers whom they contract, are compliant with these laws.

---

[11] *Special Events* by Dr Joe Goldblatt (2002) John Wiley & Sons, pg 315.
[12] This type of licence allows the liquor to be consumed where it is bought but not taken off the premises.

For caterers, it is simply essential that they have a good understanding of food hygiene law as this is a material aspect of their business and can result not only in legal action and prosecution, but in the closing down of their business.

a) United Kingdom

In the United Kingdom there is a plethora of legislation governing food and food hygiene in particular. The BSE crisis has meant that issues of food safety and consumer health have become paramount. In this section merely a summary of the legislation is provided and the reader is encouraged to read further for a comprehensive study on the topic of food law in the United Kingdom[13].

The Food Safety Act of 1990 is the main piece of legislation which regulates the food industry in the United Kingdom today. This Act is principally an enabling piece of legislation but it also provides for offences and defences in law and defines food and the enforceable authorities and their responsibilities.

The Act creates a number of offences and a number of additional offences are created in individual regulations made under the Act. The two most important food safety offences laid down in the Act relate to rendering food injurious to health and selling food not complying with the food safety requirements.

Section 7 of the Act makes it an offence for a person to add a substance to a food or treat the food in such a way that it is rendered injurious to health when that person intends that the food will be sold for human consumption. Food will be considered injurious to health if the probable effect on any consumer who eats the particular food, or the cumulative effect of eating similarly constituted food in ordinary quantities, would be to cause any permanent or temporary impairment.

Under Section 8 of the Act, it is an offence to sell or offer for sale food which fails to comply with 'food safety requirements'. Food will fail to comply with 'food safety requirements' if it is rendered injurious to health under Section 7, if it is unfit for human consumption, or if it is so contaminated that it would not be reasonable to expect it to be used for human consumption in that state.

There are many regulations dealing with the specific requirements of food and food hygiene. Two of the most important are the Food Safety (General Food Hygiene) Regulations 1995 and the Food Labelling Regulations 1996.

The basis of the implementation of the Hazard Analysis Critical Control Point (HACCP) system is provided for in Regulation 4(3) of the former, which requires a proprietor of a food business to 'identify any step in the activity of the food business which is critical to ensuring food safety and ensuring that adequate

---

[13] See *Food Standards and Product Liability* by O'Rourke, Palladium Law Publications Limited (2000) and *Food Standards Regulation: the New Law* by Iain Macdonald and Amanda Hulme, Jordans (2000).

safety procedures are identified, implemented, maintained and reviewed'. A number of requirements for premises are set out in Schedule 1 of these same Regulations, including those dealing with wash basins, ventilation, running water and drainage. There are specific requirements for moveable and/or temporary premises (such as market stalls, marquees and mobile sales vehicles) or premises used occasionally for catering purposes.

Enforcement of food legislation in the United Kingdom is the responsibility of local authorities. Each local authority employs different officers to ensure that the different food laws are properly enforced. There are two main types of officers – environmental health officers and trading standards officers. The former will usually enforce those aspects of UK food law dealing with food hygiene and controls on food unfit for human consumption as outlined in the Food Safety Act 1990. The trading standards officers will, on the other hand, be involved in the enforcement of those matters relating to trade, labelling and composition of foodstuffs.

To help achieve a uniform interpretation and application of the law, the body LACOTS (Local Authorities Co-ordinating Body on Food and Trading Standards) assists to ensure that trading standards officers and environmental health officers apply the law in a uniform way. LACOTS has established a system whereby most companies only have to deal with one local authority and any complaints are discussed with that authority. Notwithstanding this elaborate system of governance, many gaps and loopholes emerged in the system and enforcement has been irregular for many years.

The Food Standards Act of 1999 attempted to address this problem in part.

The Food Standards Act of 1999 gave rise to the new Food Standards Agency in the United Kingdom. Established in 2000, this Agency now regulates food safety standards throughout the food chain. It has powers to commission research and to publicise findings, regulate and monitor local authority enforcement and even take action in the event of failing authorities.

In all cases where a company is providing or serving food on a commercial basis at an event, the above laws will apply.

b) United States

In the United States, as a company involved in the service of food for value, you have a legal obligation to only sell food that is wholesome, and to deliver that food in a manner which is safe.

That responsibility arises from the Uniform Commercial Code (UCC) as well as other state and local laws. Under the UCC, when a merchant (such as a catering company) enters into a contract to sell food or drink, there is an implied warranty that the food or drink is merchantable (the warranty applies even if the parties do not mention it). The food or drink must be fit for consumption. In other words, it must not make you ill or give rise to injury (poor tasting food will not give rise to liability). A catering company is required to operate their service facility in a manner that protects guests from the possibility of foodborne illnesses (i.e. bacteria) or any other injury that may arise from the consumption of unwholesome food or drink[14].

A catering company could also be held liable under strict products liability, which has been adopted by most states in the United States. In order to bring a claim under this law is that it is not necessary to show that there was a contract governing the relationship, which is a requirement for a breach of the warranty of merchantability. Under strict products liability, a plaintiff need only prove that the defendant sold a product in a defective condition (e.g. the food was unhealthy or unwholesome), the plaintiff was injured and the injury was caused by the defect.

Apart from the above, a food server, whether it be the event organiser or a contracted caterer, can be held liable on normal principles of negligence if the food server or its employees was careless or reckless in the preparation or service of the food and that caused injury to a guest or attendee at an event.

Each local health department will have regulations relating to food handling and will conduct routine inspections of catering and food production facilities. They may also provide training and certification classes for those who handle food.

The advertising of food and drink is also regulated through the federal and state 'truth in menu' laws in the United States. These laws, which could more aptly be described as 'accuracy in menus' laws, are designed to protect consumers from fraudulent food and drink claims. The various 'truth in menu' laws currently in effect are voluminous, and are overseen by many different agencies and administrative entities[15]. Menus must accurately reflect the food to be served[16] and the price to be charged[17]. Accuracy is also required when describing many

---

[14] The courts usually apply one of two tests to determine whether or not a foodservice company is liable to a guest for any damages suffered from eating unwholesome food. One test seeks to determine whether the questionable article or substance found in the food is foreign to the dish or a natural component of it. The other test, which the courts are increasingly favouring, is a test which seeks to determine whether the item could reasonably be expected to be found in the food by a guest. Liability will depend on the facts of each case.

[15] The federal government, through either the Food and Drug Administration or the Department of Agriculture, has produced guidelines for accurately describing menu items. The National Restaurant Association has also produced education material designed to assist foodserving companies when writing and preparing menus.

[16] For example, 'fresh' food must indeed be fresh and 'Maine lobster' must be caught in Maine.

[17] If the menu price is to include a mandatory service charge or cover charge, these must be brought to the attention of the guest. This will not usually be an issue for events, as the event organiser will usually pay a set price to the catering company and there will be no additional service or cover charge.

food attributes including the preparation style, ingredients, origin, portion sizes, and health benefits. In addition, if a menu carries a nutrient or health claim, the regulations under the Nutrition Labelling and Education Act will apply and certain additional nutritional information must be provided upon request.

The Food and Drug Administration (FDA) is a federal agency that oversees the food industry. Its aims include promoting public health by ensuring foods are safe, wholesome, sanitary and properly labelled. The FDA issued a Food Code, which is a set of model ordinances that provides guidance on food safety. An important part of this Code is the Hazard Analysis Critical Control Point system (HACCP), which is a quality assurance scheme designed to identify and minimise spoilage and contamination problems during the manufacturing and service of food. Compliance with this system certainly helps prevent and reduce liability for defective food.

In addition, the National Restaurant Association, through its ServSafe programme, is a very useful guide to ensuring food safety[18]. ServSafe is a national education programme designed to assist foodservice operations in ensuring food safety.

c) South Africa

The Health Act 63 of 1977 is currently the main Act that regulates food handling in South Africa. However it is believed that the new National Health Act will repeal the Health Act and that food regulations currently provided for under the Health Act will be incorporated into the Foodstuffs, Cosmetics and Disinfectants Act 54 of 1977. These food regulations are regulations R918 of July 1999 governing 'General Hygiene Requirements for Food Premises and the Transport of Food'. These regulations are enforced by municipal health inspectors or environmental health officers, who process applications for health certificates, inspect premises and issue certificates.

The R918 Regulations deal with the application for, and issuance of, a 'Certificate of Acceptability for Food Premises', standards and requirements for food premises (e.g. ventilation, wash-up facilities, waste disposal systems, storage space etc), standards and requirements for facilities on food premises (e.g. work surfaces, food preparation equipment, chilling and freezing facilities etc), standards and requirements for food containers, standards and requirements for the display, storage and temperature of food, standards and requirements for protective clothing, duties of the person in charge of the food premises, duties of a food handler, standards and requirements for the handling of meat and standards

---

[18] See the National Restaurant Association website www.restaurant.org and www.nraef.org which is the official site of the NRA Education Foundation.

and requirements for the transport of food. Any person who contravenes the regulations, or allows a contravention to take place, will be guilt of an offence.

In addition to the above, each municipal authority is allowed to create specific by-laws for governing health and hygiene in its area. These are usually created to address a specific problem in a specific area.

The Department of Health has also made provision for the implementation of the Hazard Analysis Critical Control Point (HACCP) system for food hygiene management (any sector in the industry may apply to the Minister of Health for application of the HACCP to their industry), although these regulations are not yet applicable to the catering or hospitality industry in South Africa.

The South African Bureau of Standards (SABS) has compiled codes of practice relating to food handling and chilled and frozen food storage[19]. These are merely guidelines for good practice but compliance with these guidelines is required in order to obtain SABS certification.

Finally, the Department of Health's Directorate of Food Control has a number of valuable documents on their website, such as 'Guidelines for the Management and Health Surveillance of Food Handlers'[20].

8.4 Conclusion

Catering is an important part of many events. As is evident from the above, catering is not simply about a company turning up on the day of the event and randomly serving guests with a tray of snacks. There are some complex issues involved, many of which have legal implications. In most cases, a licence to serve food and beverages will be required. A host of different issues will need to be agreed between the event organiser and the catering company. The regulations relating to food hygiene and alcohol licensing will usually be extensive. For this reason, parties should pay great attention to the terms of the catering contract and, if necessary, take specialist legal advice in this regard.

---

[19] Code of Practice for Food Hygiene Management, SABS No 049-1989 and Code of Practice for The Handling of Chilled and Frozen Foods, SABS No 0156-1979.

[20] See www.doh.gov.za/department/dir_food-contr-f.html.

CHAPTER NINE

Hospitality Contracts

9.1   What is Hospitality?

The term 'hospitality' generally refers to a package of benefits secured by an official provider in relation to an event and then on-sold to a third party (often a company looking to entertain its guests). The package generally includes tickets to the event, entertainment, food and beverages. These are the main elements. However, a hospitality package may also include transport (to and from the venue), accommodation, booking facilities and management and administration services.

Hospitality is particularly popular for sporting events, which are deemed to offer a relaxed and informal environment to discuss business.

An official provider of hospitality will contract with the event organiser to secure the tickets and sites for entertainment. Unofficial providers will usually acquire tickets and sites for entertainment from unauthorised sources. In each case these providers, whether official or unofficial, will package the tickets and sites with hospitality in the form of entertainment, food and beverages and charge a premium for this. Hospitality has become an important source of revenue for venue owners and event organisers. Accordingly, it has become common for venues (such as sports stadia) to be re-designed or rebuilt to maximise the opportunity for selling hospitality packages. One example is the £100m development of Chelsea Football Club's Stamford Bridge stadium in London. The West Stand, renovated at a cost of £30m, now contains six large hospitality areas, including an upper tier of corporate suites to accommodate up to 600 people.[1] In the United States, the new 80,000-seater Giants stadium in New Jersey, to be built by 2009 at an estimated cost of $750 million, will feature a large entertainment-retail complex, the Giants Hall of Fame, a variety of themed restaurants and 200 luxury suites[2].

---

[1] See www.sportsvenue-technology.com
[2] Associated Press release 22/04/05.

9.2   The Nature of the Hospitality Contract

Unofficial hospitality activity, including the sale of 'hospitality packages' the value and content of which are questionable, has undoubtedly increased in recent years. The best security for purchasers is provided by buying hospitality packages from official providers as they are more likely to provide the package advertised and ensure the benefits are of a reasonable standard. From an event organiser's point of view, making an 'official provider' appointment provides an additional revenue stream, reduces the prevalence of unofficial activity and secures the provision and quality of hospitality packages.

Hospitality contracts in this context therefore refer to the contract between the event organiser and the official provider, in terms of which the event organiser guarantees both the provision of the benefits that make up the hospitality packages and the 'official' status of the provider in return for agreed consideration paid by the provider.

Although hospitality usually does involve catering and therefore the previous chapter is of undoubtedly of relevance, the nature of the catering contract is that of a supplier contract, whilst the hospitality contract of the type referred to above is more akin to a licensing agreement. The official provider is securing certain key benefits from the event organiser and also the rights to sell hospitality packages, use the event name and logo and use the designation 'official hospitality provider'.

A sample hospitality contract is set out in Appendix 7.

9.3   Key Legal Issues

The general terms and conditions outlined in Chapter 2 should be considered as per normal.

In addition, the following key terms should be considered:

9.3.1   Appointment

An appointments clause will usually record the appointment of the provider as an official provider of hospitality in relation to the event.

This clause should specify whether or not the appointment is exclusive. The official provider will usually try and negotiate to have an exclusive appointment. From the official provider's point of view, an exclusive, official appointment will:

- Enable it to distinguish itself from unofficial providers and provide the best quality benefits in the best locations for the event;
- Enable it to use the event name and logo exclusively (in relation to the sale of

hospitality), which will bring credibility to the packages and instil confidence in the eyes of the consumer; and

- Minimise the risk of any potential contraventions under criminal law[3].

The event organiser may try and resist an exclusive appointment. If the event is a very large event, it may wish to appoint a handful of official providers. However, from the event organiser's standpoint, an exclusive, official appointment will:

- Protect the value and integrity of the event marks, as it can control the use of the marks under the terms of the contract with the official provider;
- Generally maximise the value of the hospitality rights;
- Facilitate the policing of both the official and unofficial hospitality market in relation to the event; and
- Save time and money, in that only one hospitality contract will need to be negotiated.

If the appointment is exclusive, the official provider will want it recorded that neither the event organiser nor anyone else authorised by it can sell hospitality for the event. For large events in particular, the official provider may seek to obtain a warranty from the event organiser that there are no other contractual arrangements with third parties which conflict with or prejudice the rights of the official provider in relation to the event. For instance, it is common for the event organiser to provide some hospitality rights to sponsors and other commercial partners. In addition, the venue owner may have arrangements with debenture or box holders in terms of which guests are provided with hospitality. These issues should be dealt with at the outset and if conflicting rights do exist, they will need to be expressly excluded from the rights granted to the official provider. Also, if such conflicting rights do exist, the official provider will usually want to ensure that it secures the premium locations at the venue for providing the hospitality if possible.

The official provider will also usually require some assistance on the part of the event organiser to protect its position in so far as unauthorised hospitality providers are concerned. Whilst the event organiser cannot provide a guarantee that unofficial operators will not procure tickets and sell hospitality at the event, it may agree to assist the official provider by taking some of the following steps:

- Referring any parties interested in procuring hospitality to the official provider only;
- Publicising the fact that exclusive hospitality rights have been granted to the official provider (via press releases, published materials and on the event website, for example).

---

[3] See paragraph 9.4 below.

- Taking legal action against unauthorised providers or informing the official provider of the existence of unauthorised providers so that the official provider can take legal action. If the official provider insists on the former, the event organiser may wish to secure an indemnity in respect of legal costs;
- Establishing a telephone hotline whereby members of the public can confirm the validity of hospitality packages (particularly tickets) and obtain related information;
- Including clauses in contracts (including on the tickets themselves) with those to whom the event organiser sells or supplies tickets, preventing them either from using the tickets for hospitality purposes or from transferring them without the event organiser's consent;
- Ensuring that all tickets bear a security code or number and a means of identifying the original recipient of the ticket[4];

Finally, it is important to note that exclusive hospitality arrangements can be regarded as anti-competitive. The relevant competition or anti-trust regulations will vary from country to country or region to region, but the key question is usually whether the arrangements in question have a material adverse effect on competition in the relevant market[5]. If so, the event organiser may be forced to restructure their arrangements and could also face a fine[6].

Although hospitality contracts for most events are unlikely to give rise to competition concerns, where the event is a large event, exclusive rights are given to an official provider for a long period and ticket distribution channels are severely limited or restricted, the probability of such concerns arising is greater. Proper legal advice should be taken in relation to this aspect of the event and, where necessary, discussions should be held with the relevant competition authorities to gain some comfort in relation to the proposed arrangements.

---

[4] See Chapter 5 on Ticketing Contracts and paragraph 5.3 in particular.

[5] In the European Union, for instance, Article 81(1) of the EC Treaty prohibits agreements which may affect trade between Member States and which have as their object or effect the prevention, restriction or distortion of competition.

[6] Although not dealing with hospitality contracts specifically, the 1992 European Commission decision relating to the distribution of package tours for the 1990 World Cup is relevant. The event organisers of the 1990 World Cup granted a package tour operator exclusive rights worldwide to acquire ground entrance tickets for the purpose of selling package tours that included those tickets. The European Commission held that the exclusive rights granted infringed Article 81(1) of the EC Treaty because the effect was to restrict competition between tour providers in the common market. In 1999 the Commission held that the ticketing arrangements for the 1998 World Cup in France were anti-competitive. The event organiser was held to have acted in breach of the EC Treaty by abusing its dominant position in distributing over 570,000 tickets only to those with an address in France and 181,000 tickets for the final stage games at a draw in Paris six months before the event. The event organiser was only fined €1000.

9.3.2   Territory

The parties should agree and define the geographical area for which the hospitality rights are granted. The rights may be granted worldwide or only in respect of one specific area.

Major events with international appeal usually have at least one official travel and tour provider providing packages of tickets along with travel and/or accommodation for those attending the event from other countries. The official provider may wish to sell competing packages itself or appoint agents to do so. The event organiser may seek to limit the official provider's right to sell packages outside the country where the event is being held unless an agreement is made with the official tour provider. There may be potential for conflict here. As a result, these issues should be discussed fully at the time of entering into the contract.

One issue with regard to territoriality that has arisen in recent years is the advertising of hospitality packages for sale over the internet. As websites can be accessed globally, the official provider may risk being in breach of any territorial restrictions imposed on it if a purchaser located in another country (beyond the defined territory) were to buy a package. It has become possible recently to arrange for website functionality to restrict or limit such a risk[7] and if this is an issue for the event organiser it should secure some form of contractual undertaking on the part of the official provider to take certain steps to eliminate this concern.

9.3.3   Rights

As mentioned above, in considering what rights can and will be granted to the official provider, the event organiser will need to consider what rights it has granted to other third parties. In order to protect its position, the official provider will usually wish to obtain warranties in respect of the rights provided to it.

The most important rights are the following:

- The right to buy tickets from the event organiser of the desired quality and quantity. Location of the tickets will usually be an important issue as it will affect the value of the hospitality packages and the reputation of the official provider[8];

---

[7]   The website may require address details for the sale of packages and not permit entry of addresses outside the permitted jurisdictions (for example, by only including certain countries or regions in the 'country' part of the address).

[8]   It is important to clarify, either on a map attached as a schedule to the contract, or in the contract itself, the exact location of the seats provided. Where it is not possible to provide specific allocations at the time of contracting, wording can be included referring to 'highest face value tickets' or certain nominated stands or sections at the venue.

- The right to such tickets at a certain price[9];
- The right to sell hospitality packages (as defined in the contract) to third parties;
- The right to 'official status'. The official provider will usually seek to obtain the right to refer to itself as 'Official Hospitality Provider' in respect of the event[10]. This is important in giving comfort to the public as to its ability to deliver the benefits under the hospitality package. As in the case of supplier contracts, the manner in which the official provider is entitled to use the designation should be discussed and agreed (e.g. on its letterheads, on its website, on all promotional material issued in respect of the event etc);
- The right to use the event logo. The official provider will want to use the event logo (usually in conjunction with the designation) in its sales and promotional material. This will also provide some credibility to the official provider. This will require a licensing of the event logo by the event organiser. Again, details regarding the form and manner in which the logo may be used will need to be agreed. This is usually dealt with in a separate section of the contract dealing with intellectual property rights;
- The right to use photographs of those participating in the event. The official provider will usually wish to use these photographs in its sales and promotional materials. If the photographs are of sportsmen and women or artists and entertainers, the event organiser may not have authority to grant this right. This will depend on the rights obtained by the event organiser in respect of the event. Either the official provider must secure permission from the performers themselves, or seek a warranty from the event organiser that the event organiser has secured all necessary consents, licences and authority to give the official provider access to, and the right to use, photographs of the participants; and
- The right to have access to certain sites at the venue. The official provider will want to secure the right to use certain facilities for the purposes of catering and entertainment e.g. rooms, electricity, water[11].

The event organiser may wish to reserve for itself some of the following rights:

- The right to prior approval of all sales and promotional materials using the event logo;
- The right to veto any sales and promotional materials that it considers of sub-standard quality;
- The right to conduct inspections of the hospitality services being provided.

---

[9] The price or face value of the tickets will be important in pricing hospitality packages and calculating potential profit margins for the official provider.

[10] As in the case of supplier contracts, this may have competition/anti-trust implications. See 7.2.5 above.

[11] See paragraph 8.2.5 above in relation to catering. The obligations should be imposed on the event organiser under this contract.

9.3.4   Consideration/Remuneration

Payment for the rights granted above is usually in one of four forms:

- A fixed amount paid by the official provider to the event organiser. This may be paid in the form of a licence fee paid up front for use of the event name and logo or a minimum guaranteed amount of the hospitality sales revenues. If it is the latter, this is generally paid in instalments, after the execution of the contract but prior to the event itself. The event organiser may seek to obtain a guarantee from the official provider in respect of the payment instalments. The minimum guarantee will relate to a fair valuation of the rights granted to the official provider. This valuation will be based on various assumptions, such as the price of tickets, the number of participants and the number of events. The official provider may wish to include in the contract the right to vary the minimum guaranteed amount if any of the assumptions prove to be false. This can be dealt with by warranties or via agreed terms for a reduction of the amount;
- A percentage of revenues arising from hospitality sales, or a percentage of profits derived from such sales;
- The cost of tickets. Where tickets prices have not been determined at the time of contracting a mechanism for calculating the price can be agreed. Where the tickets are priced in more than once currency, clauses dealing with currency conversion will also be required; or
- A combination of the above.

The event organiser will usually want to secure a fixed fee, paid upfront, for the rights, so that it does not have to rely solely on hospitality sales. Where the event organiser is to receive a share of the revenues or profits arising from hospitality sales, however, it may wish to impose certain obligations in the official provider in respect of accounting (the opening of separate books of account, providing statements of account, the right to request an audit etc).

As mentioned above, the event organiser may require that the official provider furnish some form of security for the payments. Such security may be provided in the form of a bank guarantee or letter of credit arranged by the official provider. A bank will usually insist on its own standard guarantee or letter of credit terms and require a counter-indemnity from the official provider. A guarantee may also be provided by a parent company of the official provider, if such a company exists. The parent company could also be asked to guarantee the performance obligations of the official provider, if appropriate.

Sometimes the event organiser may insist that a pre-agreed amount of the official provider's revenue is held on trust for the event organiser in a trust account to meet the cost of providing the packages to the purchasers should the official provider fail to deliver. In this way funds can be released on reaching certain performance-related milestones, such as the provision of packages for the early rounds of a tournament.

9.3.5 Warranties

Lack of time often prevents a comprehensive due diligence exercise from being undertaken by the official provider, leaving it reliant on warranties being provided in the contract[12].

The official provider may wish to include the following warranties and undertakings in the contract:

- That the event organiser has the necessary authority to grant the rights to the official provider, including the right to access designated sites for the purposes of providing the hospitality;
- If the arrangement is exclusive, that it has not entered into any conflicting arrangements in respect of the rights granted to the official provider;
- That the event organiser has the right to grant the licences under the contract so that the use of the logo will not infringe third party intellectual property rights;
- That the quality of participants in the event is of a certain agreed standard (if applicable);
- If the arrangement is exclusive, that all enquiries regarding hospitality will be referred to the official provider;
- That the event organiser has insurance in place to cover for cancellation or postponement of the event and that the official provider has an insurable interest under that policy; and
- That the event will take place at a certain time, at specified venues and be of a certain format.

The conduct of the official provider may reflect on the reputation of the event organiser. As a result, the event organiser may want to include the following warranties and undertakings on the part of the official provider:

- That the quality of the benefits or services that the official provider provides will be of a certain standard;
- That it will report any complaints about itself or about the event to the event organiser; and
- That it will inform the event organiser if it is aware of any third party infringement of the event organiser's intellectual property rights.

---

[12] See paragraph 2.3.6 for an explanation about the nature of a warranty.

9.3.6 Obligations

Additional obligations, not necessarily in the form of warranties, may also be included. Some of these are set out at paragraph 8.2.5 in the chapter dealing with catering contracts.

9.3.7 Restrictions on Official Providers

The event organiser may wish to impose certain restrictions on the official provider's activities. These may include:

- A prohibition on the sale or supply of tickets to unofficial operators, including ticket agencies or ticket touts;
- A prohibition on the official provider from sourcing additional tickets from third parties;
- Restrictions on the manner in which the event logo can be used;
- Restrictions on the use of income received by the official provider from hospitality sales prior to the delivery of the packages;
- Restrictions on sub-contracting to caterers or other hospitality providers without the consent of the event organiser; and
- Restrictions on the ability of the official provider or its clients from branding the hospitality sites.

9.3.8 Cancellation

The event organiser may wish to reserve the right to cancel the event without penalty up to a certain number of days before the event. As in the case of catering contracts, cancellation charges should be staggered depending on the time of cancellation[13].

9.4 Criminal Liability

In some countries or states legislation may have been enacted which could give rise to criminal liability on the part of those providing hospitality packages or elements thereof. Examples include the following:

- It may be an offence for an unauthorised person to re-sell a ticket to an event[14];

---

[13] See paragraphs 8.2.9 and 7.2.6 above.

[14] In the United Kingdom, for example, it is an offence under s166 of the Criminal Justice and Public Order Act 1994 to sell a ticket for a 'designated' football match in any public place or place to which the public has access. This includes most cup or league matches in England or Wales. If a hospitality package provider supplies a ticket to such a match without being authorised to do by the event organiser, it will have committed an offence under this Act. At present, this only applies to designated football matches, but the Home Secretary has the power to extend this section of the Act to other sporting events as well.

- It may be an offence for an unauthorised person to re-sell a ticket without giving certain information, prior to the supply, about the ticket[15];
- There may be specific safety and security measures imposed in relation to the provision of hospitality[16];
- There may be travel and tourism-related regulations placing restrictions on the supply and sale of hospitality packages that include travel and accommodation[17]; and
- It may be an offence under trading regulations to make any statement in the course of trade or business which is knowingly false or reckless in relation to the provision of services, accommodation or facilities[18].

Specialised advice should be sought from a local attorney or solicitor in order to ensure that parties are not contravening the law in this area.

9.5 General

A number of the key terms outlined in 8.2 in relation to catering may also be relevant for hospitality and these should be reviewed and applied if appropriate.

For instance, the event organiser may insist that the official provider has necessary liability insurance in place to cover claims from third parties making use of the hospitality.

It may also require an indemnity for any losses it incurs as a result of claims from third parties arising from the provision of the hospitality. For example, if an employee of an official provider pours boiling water over a guest, the event organiser will want to be indemnified for any losses arising from a claim by the guest against it[19].

---

[15] For example, in the United Kingdom, it is an offence under Regulation 4 of the Price Indications (Resale of Tickets) Regulations 1994 for an unauthorised person to re-sell tickets without providing information (prior to the supply of the ticket) of the original price or 'face value' of the ticket, the rights conferred to the ticket holder, the seat location and other factors which would adversely affect the ticket purchaser's enjoyment of the ticket. This applies to the re-sale of tickets for any exhibition, performance, game, sport or similar event.

[16] For example, in South Africa the draft Safety at Sports and Recreational Events Bill sets out specific safety and security measures for corporate hospitality, including the securing of hospitality areas, accreditation and the provision of a safety and security plan.

[17] It is common in many countries for regulations to have been enacted to regulate the travel and tourism industry. In the United Kingdom, the Package Travel, Package Holidays and Package Tours Regulations 1992 may apply to hospitality packages that include travel and/or accommodation in addition to tickets. This may include the obligation on the provider to register with a formally recognised association and to provide some form of bond or guarantee to refund consumers in the event of insolvency. Where the package includes a flight, the provider must have an Air Travel organisers' licence (ATOL) issued by the Civil Aviation Authority.

[18] For example, such a provision exists under s 14 of the Trade Descriptions Act 1968 in the United Kingdom.

[19] In some cases the official provider may provide the catering services directly. Alternatively, it may contract out such services to a caterer and will seek a reciprocal indemnity from the caterer in respect of any such claims.

The parties may also wish to include a reference in the contract to specific codes of practice developed by interest groups and governing bodies. These codes of practice will usually refer to certain standards in the industry which may be imposed on the parties by incorporating the code into the contract by reference[20].

Finally, owing to the fact that the provision of tickets will usually form part of the hospitality package, readers should also refer to the issues raised in paragraph 5.3 relating to ticketing.

9.6   Conclusion

The hospitality industry is a fast-growing industry. Hospitality itself has become a big part of many events. It has also become a fairly significant additional revenue stream for event organisers. The main concern of the event organiser will be to ensure that no unofficial hospitality packages are sold. This will reduce the value of the commercial rights arising from the event. It may also undermine the integrity and standing of the event. The hospitality provider will, on the other hand, be concerned with obtaining exclusivity with respect to the sale of the hospitality packages and/or ensuring that it has sufficient access to, and control over, the venue so as to deliver on the hospitality itself.

---

[20] Codes of practice may be imposed by virtue of membership of an association e.g. the Corporate Hospitality and Event Association (CHA) in the United Kingdom.

CHAPTER TEN

Entertainment Contracts

With the exception perhaps of business conferences, events usually provide some form of entertainment. Depending on the size and nature of the event and the importance of the entertainment to the success of the event as a whole, the event organiser may wish to enter into a contract with participants, performers or entertainers. In this way the event organiser can ensure that the entertainment that it is offering is going to be provided and also that it will be provided in accordance with the agreed terms of the contract.

10.1   The Nature of the Entertainment Contract

The nature and form of the entertainment contract may vary substantially.

In some cases, artists and entertainers may be asked to perform at the event. This may require the event organiser (or sometimes a promoter) entering into a performance contract with the artist or entertainer or their management agency to procure their services.

Very often an event organiser may wish to use music at the event. In almost all cases it will need to ensure that it has the necessary permission and licence to use such music. This may require entering into a licensing contract with a music rights organisation. These organisations, usually non-profit in nature, grant the relevant licences to event organisations and collect fees on behalf of composers of the music for onward distribution to them[1].

In other cases, such as large sporting events, the event organiser may wish to enter into participation contracts with certain teams or governing bodies who will be providing the entertainment. These will set out the terms and conditions governing the participation of the teams or athletes in the event. This is dealt with more fully in the following chapter.

---

[1]   Usually a deduction is made for the administration involved in collecting the fees before distribution.

10.2 Performance Contracts

Whether an event organiser is staging a large event and merely wishes to procure the services of an artist or entertainer for a very short part of the event, or whether it is a promoter of a music event and wishes to secure the services of the artist or entertainer for the whole event, it is prudent to enter into a comprehensive performer's contract setting out the terms and conditions relating to the performance.

The performance contract can be likened to a supplier contract, similar in nature to that discussed in Chapter 7. The entertainer, usually an independent contractor, will be providing services to the event organiser in return for payment. As a result, the general terms and conditions contained at paragraph 7.2 should be considered.

A sample performer's contract is set out in Appendix 8.

The following key terms should be considered:

10.2.1 Key Legal Issues

a) Services

It is important to specify the exact scope of the services to be provided at the event. This can be done in the main body of the contract or in a rider or schedule to the contract.

Details in relation to the following should be agreed and recorded:

- The exact length of the performance by the entertainer;
- The exact time the performance is to be delivered;
- The manner of performance (the extent to which this is agreed will vary depending on the type of performance);
- If a group of entertainers are involved (such as a band), the exact identity of the performers;
- The location of the performance;
- The number of encores (if appropriate);
- The priority of billing and order of performance, where there are a number of entertainers performing at the event;
- Additional appearances to be made e.g. for autographs, interviews, press conferences etc.

b) Remuneration

The remuneration paid to the entertainer may be in the form of a fixed fee. The event organiser will want to try and negotiate to pay this amount after the performance has been provided. The entertainer will usually try and negotiate for at least part of the payment to be paid upfront (either before or on signing of the contract, by way of a non-refundable deposit) and the balance on completion of the performance.

Alternatively, or by way of addition to the fixed fee, the entertainer may be paid a percentage of the revenue generated by ticket and/or merchandising sales. If this is the case, the parties should clarify whether the percentage will be based on gross or net receipts. If net receipts, the parties should take great care to specify what will be deducted from the gross receipts e.g. the fixed fee mentioned above, certain costs etc.

Depending on the negotiating power of the entertainer, he or she may wish to secure an upfront payment as a minimum guarantee against revenue generated by ticket and/or merchandising sales.

If the fee is related to ticket sales, the records relating to such sales should be made available to the performer. The performer will want assurances that the event organiser or promoter will use its best endeavours to promote the event. The performer should also note whether the event organiser or the promoter is charging a ticket price in excess of that previously stated to the performer, as this will have an effect on ticket sales.

The parties should also record whether or not the fee will include the cost of the performer's travel, accommodation, lighting, equipment hire, personnel and other expenses. It is worth noting that the value of these items may have to be added onto the fee for the calculation of local withholding tax, if relevant.

c) Cancellation Charges

Entertainers are notoriously fickle and temperamental in nature. It is not unusual for an entertainer to cancel a performance at the last minute. For this reason only part of the fee should be paid upfront. The event organiser or promoter will want to specify that this part-payment is a deposit and will be refunded to it in the event that the entertainer cancels the performance, except where such cancellation occurs as a result of a so-called 'force majeure' event and is beyond the control of the entertainer[2]. The entertainer will similarly want to retain the deposit in the event that the event organiser or promoter cancels the performance after a particular period of time.

The event organiser or promoter may wish to obtain cancellation insurance if the performance is material to the event[3].

The event organiser or promoter may well have incurred costs prior to cancellation e.g. venue hire charges, costs of hiring security etc. It may therefore also wish

---

[2] See paragraph 2.3.9 above.
[3] See Chapter 6 and in particular paragraph 6.5 relating to insurance.

to include an indemnity in the contract in terms of which it is indemnified by the entertainer for any costs incurred by it as a result of cancellation by the entertainer.

d) Practical Contractual Matters

There are a number of practical issues which may be relevant. These matters should be recorded in the contract to avoid dispute at a later stage. These issues are often included in a rider or schedule attached to the contract. Although some of these may appear to be relatively minor issues, resolution on these issues at an early stage will go some distance towards ensuring that the performance is successful.

- Travel arrangements – this may be particularly important if the performance is part of a tour;
- Stage – the responsibility for stage construction and design should be clarified;
- Equipment – the provision and installation of necessary equipment (including lighting, sound mixers, monitors etc) may be a vital part of the performance;
- Expertise – depending on the extent and complexity of the performance, specialist personnel may be required, such as a production manager, a lighting director, a sound mixer, an audio technician and a cameraman. The parties will need to establish who will bear the responsibility for contracting with, and paying for, these personnel;
- Support act – if there is a to be a support act of any kind, the entertainer will usually want to ensure that the support act's material is sufficiently compatible, that the support act is not seriously competitive with the entertainer (but is supplementary to the entertainer's act) and that the duration of the support act's performance is relatively short;
- Free tickets – the entertainer will usually be provided with a specified number of free tickets for the best seats;
- Backstage passes – a specified number of backstage passes may be required for the entertainer and his or her management. If separate onstage passes are produced for the performance these will also need to be dispersed to the appropriate people;
- Security – there is usually an express obligation on the part of the event organiser or promoter to provide adequate security for the entertainer. This might range from the provision of a secure locker for personal possessions to security personnel and personal bodyguards;
- Auditorium and stage requirements – these will vary according to the extent and complexity of the performance;
- Dressing room facilities – over the years the nature of dressing room facilities has changed. Today, these facilities may range from a simple changing room to the provision of sofas, a full bar facility, a television and a masseuse!

- Access to the venue for rehearsals, sound checks etc – this will normally be required to ensure that the performance is successful but will depend largely on the extent and complexity of the performance;
- Personnel – a number of personnel may be required, such as electricians, sound specialists, personal assistants etc;
- Work permits and visas – this will most definitely be an issue if the entertainer is coming from outside the country to perform at the event. This obligation often rests with the event organiser or promoter, but it is essentially a matter of negotiation between the parties. The contract should be conditional upon visas and permits being obtained in good time. It is doubtful whether failure to obtain a visa or work permit will fall within the definition of 'force majeure'[4].

e) Unauthorised Recordings of the Performance

A major problem facing entertainers is the making of unauthorised recordings of live performances, from which CDs, DVDs and tapes are made and sold. Apart from the non-payment of royalties, the quality of the recording is usually poor.

The entertainer will usually seek an undertaking from the event organiser or promoter to ensure that no person (with the exception of perhaps the entertainer) shall be permitted to make any audio or audio-visual recording of the performance[5]. This may include express obligations on the part of the event organiser or promoter to appoint additional security for the purposes of searching attendees at the event.

Event organisers or promoters will be aware that preventing unauthorised recordings has become much more difficult with the technological development of hand-held devices. Video-recorders now fit into the palm of the hand and can be easily concealed. Mobile phones can now produce short audio and audio-visual recordings for transmission and the day will soon come when they will be able to produce lengthy recordings of a high quality.

For these reasons, the event organiser or promoter may want to restrict their obligation to use their 'best endeavours' to prevent such activity from taking place.

If the performance is recorded by the event organiser, promoter or entertainer for commercial or other purposes, the issue of intellectual property rights in the

---

[4] There will inevitably be some debate over whether or not the failure to obtain a visa was beyond the reasonable control of the entertainer. See paragraph 2.3.9 above for more information on 'force majeure' events and their effect on the contract.

[5] If the entertainer is a musician, this may cause the musician to be in breach of his or her exclusive recording contract with a record company.

recording will need to be dealt with in the contract. Under copyright law, usually these rights will vest in the person who makes the recording or the broadcaster (if the event is being broadcast). However, the owner of the copyright may be asked to contractually waive or assign such rights in favour of another party[6]. If the entertainer wishes to make a live recording of the performance, or film the performance, the entertainer may also have to obtain the consent of the venue owner.

Ownership of the performance, as opposed to a recording of the performance, is dealt with in paragraphs 1.5.3(a) above and 10.4 below.

f) Merchandising

If the entertainer is popular, additional merchandising revenues may be generated through the sale of merchandise (such as t-shirts, key-rings, caps and posters) at the venue.

Where the entertainer has already granted the exclusive merchandising rights to a professional merchandising company, the event organiser or promoter must be prohibited in the contract from conducting unauthorised merchandising operations, whether directly or indirectly.

If the entertainer is free to grant merchandising rights to the event organiser or promoter, and the event organiser or promoter wishes to exercise those rights, the contract should include terms dealing with the following[7]:

- The items of merchandise that may be sold. These will need to be approved by the entertainer in advance, particularly the use of trade marks and logos[8];
- The royalty to be paid to the entertainer. This may be in the form of a percentage of revenues generated through sales of the merchandise. The parties should take care to define whether the royalty is payable on gross or net revenues;
- A definition of the area in which the sales can take place. This will not be an issue if the sales will take place only at the venue, but if there are a number of performances in different venues this should be clarified;
- The dates and times when the merchandise can be sold. Again, this is more likely to be an issue if there are a number of performances;
- Control, storage and distribution of stock;

---

[6] In the United Kingdom, the performer may also have what is known as a 'performance right' under s183 of the CDPA. Performance rights are the right not to have one's performance of a work exploited (in particular, recorded for commercial exploitation) without one's consent. Note that sports events will not qualify as a 'performance' under this section of the CDPA, but a musical or dramatic performance will qualify.

[7] This will essentially involve the granting of a licence to the event organiser or promoter and, as such, the reader should refer to Chapter 12 on Merchandising Contracts.

[8] See paragraphs 12.3 and 12.4 below.

- The rights granted to the event organiser or promoter should be non-exclusive if the entertainer has a contract with a record company, because the record company may also be promoting the entertainer by distributing small quantities of merchandise.

g) Local Regulations, Licences and Permits

Where an entertainer is performing at an event, certain additional licences and permits may be required, such as entertainment licences and licences to use smoke machines or pyrotechnics. Local regulations may also stipulate noise restrictions, crowd control, traffic control and closing times at the venue. This is dealt with further in Chapter 6.

The responsibility for securing any licences and permits for the performance will usually rest with the event organiser or promoter and the entertainer may wish to obtain a warranty or undertaking that the necessary consents have been obtained.

h) Insurance

This is also dealt with in Chapter 6.

The question of insurance should be considered in some detail where an entertainer is performing at an event, as the level of risk will undoubtedly increase. For example, the risk of claims for personal injury will rise. The value of equipment used in the performance will also be considerable and thought should be given to appropriate cover for loss of, or damage to, such equipment. Cancellation insurance should also be considered, as entertainers are prone to cancelling the performance at the last minute.

i) Termination

Specific clauses relating to termination may be also be included in the contract. The parties may wish to reserve the right to terminate the contract immediately in the event of certain circumstances or if certain conditions are not fulfilled. Examples may include the following:

- If the security provided is so inadequate that there is a real danger of personal injury to the entertainer or to members of the audience;
- If the venue or its facilities are so inadequate that there is a genuine fear of personal injury or substantial damage to or loss of essential equipment;
- If the venue is entirely unsuitable for the staging of the performance. In one real life example, it turned out that the venue had an automatic control mechanism which would cut the power in the event that the sound reached a particular level, resulting in continuous power cuts during the sound check;
- If the entertainer or the event organiser or promoter is unable to procure a necessary work permit or visa for the entertainer to enter the relevant country;

- If the entertainer is ill or incapacitated[9]. The parties should specify that if this causes cancellation of the performance the entertainer will need to verify such illness or incapacity with a doctor's certificate. The event organiser or promoter may wish to stipulate that the entertainer be examined by an independent medical practitioner. If the event organiser or promoter has insured the event against cancellation on a 'force majeure' basis, for either expenses wasted or loss of profit to a particular level, his or her insurance company may also demand to inspect the entertainer for a medical opinion if it has any doubt that cancellation was justifiable. It is less likely to enforce this if the event organiser or promoter has obtained an independent medical opinion already.

If the disability is self-inflicted or is prolonged unnecessarily by the unreasonable refusal of the entertainer to seek or accept proper medical treatment, or to comply with doctor's orders, it would be inequitable for the entertainer to cancel the performance without compensating the event organiser or promoter. A further clause may be included to this effect.

j)   Governing Law and Jurisdiction for Disputes

Special mention is made of this issue here, as it may be more complex than meets the eye. If one considers that the event organiser or promoter may reside in one country or state, the entertainer in another, and the event or performance is going to take place in a third, then one begins to appreciate the complexities that may arise when it comes to interpretation of the contract and jurisdiction for disputes arising under the contract.

The event organiser or promoter will usually want to insist that the law to be applied to the interpretation of the contract and the courts of competent jurisdiction should be that of his or her country or state of residence, or that of the country or state in which the event is to take place. A high-profile entertainer, however, may insist that this be the law and courts of his or her country or state.

k)   Taxation

The liability for local income tax or withholding tax on revenues arising from a performance in a foreign country should be dealt with in the contract, if relevant. In most cases the liability to pay the tax falls on the entertainer as the recipient of the income, but there may also be a liability on the promoter to withhold that tax from the money due to the entertainer. Local regulations will differ in each country. Depending on the financial arrangements with the entertainer, the

---

[9]   A singer may lose his or her voice, for instance.

event organiser or promoter will usually either withhold the appropriate tax and pay it to the relevant Revenue Authorities or will bear the liability for the local tax itself, and will not deduct it from the fee paid to the entertainer. This would mean that the value of the fee to the entertainer would be increased by that amount. The exact obligations should be recorded in the contract, after taking appropriate tax advice.

l) Promotion and Marketing

The parties should specify who will be responsible for the promotion and marketing of the performance. Usually the event organiser or promoter will be responsible for this. The entertainer may wish to record specific obligations in this regard e.g. publicise the performance in certain magazines, on radio etc.

m) Image Rights/Rights of Publicity

The entertainer will usually want to protect the use of his or her image rights or rights of publicity in relation to promotion and marketing of the event or performance. These may include use of the entertainer's name, image, likeness, logos, signatures, biographical information, computer-generated representation and the like[10].

The event organiser or promoter will usually want to use the name and image of the entertainer to promote and market the event or performance, at the very least. If so, the entertainer (or his or her management team) may wish to reserve the right to approve any materials using his or her name and image prior to such materials being released into the public domain. If the entertainer insists on this, a 'deemed approval' clause should also be included in the contract, in terms of which such materials shall be deemed to be approved if no response is received within a certain time period. This allows the event organiser or promoter to move ahead swiftly with any necessary promotion and marketing without unnecessary delays.

---

[10] The degree to which these rights are recognised and may be protected will vary from country to country. Many states in the United States recognise an independent right of publicity which protects a person's name, voice, image or signature from being used or associated with any products or services without their consent. This is based on the concept that everyone has the right to control the commercial use of their identity or persona. In addition, at a federal level, s43 of the Lanham Trade Mark Act prohibits the false use of a name in association or connection with the goods, services or commercial activities of another. Canada recognises a similar right. However, in the United Kingdom and South Africa, an individual must rely on piecemeal protection through one of a number of disparate legal doctrines that do not recognise separate, legally enforceable image rights per se (e.g. defamation, passing off, copyright or malicious falsehood). For further details on this subject, refer to the author's (co-written) chapter on image rights in *Sport: Law and Practice* by Adam Lewis and Jonathan Taylor, Butterworths (2003).

n) Indemnity

Once the entertainer is actually performing, the event organiser or promoter has very little control over the content of such performance, notwithstanding what might have been agreed beforehand with the entertainer. The event organiser or promoter should look to obtain an indemnity from the entertainer for all losses it may suffer as a result of any libellous, obscene or defamatory material included in the performance.

An example of this is Janet Jackson's alleged 'wardrobe malfunction' during the Superbowl half-time show in 2004. MTV was the producer of the half-time show. If MTV's contract was cancelled as a result of Ms Jackson's activity and assuming this was not part of the agreed script[11], such an indemnity may have been useful to recover the losses MTV would suffer as a result of losing that contract.

o) Confidentiality

Finally, both parties will want to ensure that the terms of the contract are kept strictly confidential. A term should be included to this effect in the contract. In the past the media have sought to publicise the demands of high-profile entertainers and the entertainer will want to try and prevent this in so far as this is possible. Of course, once this information is the public domain there is very little that the entertainer can do about it, but he or she would at the very least have a claim for damages based on a breach of the contract[12].

p) Noise Regulations

Noise regulation is a factor which should be taken into account when considering entertainment contracts, particularly where a band is being contracted to perform live at an outdoor venue. Event organisers need to be aware of noise levels and any local regulations which may be relevant in this regard[13]. Where an event organiser or promoter contracts with a band and there is a risk that the band may contravene the noise regulations, the event organiser or promoter may wish to obtain a warranty that the band will perform in accordance with such regulations. It may also wish to obtain an indemnity from the band for any fines or other losses that it may incur as a result of such contravention.

---

[11] According to both Janet Jackson and Justin Timberlake, neither the broadcaster CBS nor MTV were aware of the incident and it was not included in rehearsals.

[12] This would depend on whether the law of the relevant country recognises such claims. It will also depend on whether it can be proven that the entertainer has suffered loss or damage as a result of the disclosure of the confidential information.

[13] This is discussed in Chapter 6 dealing with health and safety.

10.3   Music Licensing

It is common for an event organiser to use recorded music during the event. In most developed countries in the world this is not permitted without the payment of a licensing fee to a music licensing organisation that is responsible for collecting those fees in the relevant territory on behalf of composers and performers[14]. Depending on the power and authority of such organisations, licensing fees may be payable by the event organiser even for small events, such as meetings, conventions, trade shows, seminars and conferences. This is the case even where the music is only played in the background[15]. However, usually these fees are not payable for events that are small gatherings of people who are known to you. As a result, events such as weddings, birthday parties and other informal social gatherings will generally be exempt from the payment of licensing fees.

The costs of licensing fees are usually minimal. The assessment of fees may be based on the number of daily attendees at the event or the number of times a particular song is played or a similar formula. Separate formulas may also be applied for recorded and live music and if both forms of music are used, the costs may be higher.

How is the use of unlicensed music monitored? Usually, the music licensing organisation will have 'spotters' who will visit events randomly and investigate organisations that are using their licensed works unlawfully. The penalties for non-compliance can be substantial. It is far cheaper to obtain a licence than defend a lawsuit.

Event organisers should contact the relevant music licensing firm in that country or region for details on the terms and conditions relating to the use of music at an event. Some examples of music licensing operations in the United States, United Kingdom and South Africa are set out below.

10.3.1   United States

In the United States, the two major licensing firms collecting fees from those wishing to use their licensed music are the American Society of Composers, Authors and Publishers (ASCAP) and Broadcast Music Inc (BMI)[16]. The majority of popular is music is licensed through ASCAP, but very often an event organiser will have to sign licensing contracts with both these organisations to cover the full range of songs it wishes to use during an event. These two agencies, together

---

[14] Copyright law will usually require that one must obtain permission from the copyright holder before playing a piece of live or recorded music.

[15] It is usually the event organiser (and not the hotel, convention centre or stadium) who is responsible for obtaining the licence, although often the venue owner will have already obtained such a licence.

[16] See www.ascap.com and www.bmi.com respectively for more information on these organisations.

with the smaller agency SESAC[17], cover approximately 95% of the songs ever written, including foreign songs.

ASCAP and BMI have separate standard licensing contracts that require careful consideration by the event organiser. These contracts were negotiated in 1990 by a music licensing task force representing ASAE (American Society of Association Executives), MPI (Meeting Planners International), PCMA (Professional Convention Management Association) and RCMA (Religious Conference Management Association). These contracts govern both recorded and live music.

Both ASCAP and BMI assess fees based on the daily attendance at each event, depending on whether recorded or live music is used. Some associations, such as the International Association for Exposition Management (IAEM), have signed separate contracts with ASCAP and BMI governing the payment of licensing fees by members of the association.

What music is covered? Basically any musical work within the portfolios of ASCAP and BMI, which includes 'Happy Birthday'! Note that the licensing requirements do not apply to music over 75 years old that has not been revised and copyrighted. For music licensed after 1978 the copyright protection expires 50 years after the death of the last surviving composer or author[18].

There are several narrow exceptions whereby the user of music would not be required to obtain a licence to use the music. Under one exception, an organisation would be exempt if the following four conditions are all met: 1) the music is not received beyond the place from which it is performed; 2) the performance is made without any direct or indirect commercial advantage to the organisation; 3) the performers, promoters or organisers do not receive a fee or any other compensation for the performance; and 4) there is no direct or indirect admission charge[19].

Accordingly, if an organisation wished to play a CD or tape in the same room that the player's speakers are located as background music for a presentation to which there is no admission charge, they will not require a licence.

Other exceptions include:

- Music played during a religious ceremony or part of a worship service e.g. a wedding;

---

[17] See www.sesac.com.

[18] For further information, see *Copyrights and Trademarks for Media Professionals* (Broadcast and Cable Series) by Arnold P. Lutzker (Focal Press).

[19] An admission fee can be charged if the proceeds are applied exclusively for religious or charitable purposes or are used exclusively by an educational institution for educational purposes.

- Music played as part of face to face teaching at a non-profit educational institution;
- Music played by a governmental body or non-profit agricultural or horticultural organisation, in the course of an annual agricultural or horticultural fair or exhibition conducted by such body or organisation; or
- Music performed at a gathering of a family circle and its social acquaintances e.g. a birthday party.

10.3.2 United Kingdom

In the United Kingdom, the Copyright, Designs and Patents Act 1988 provides a copyright in the public use of sound recordings (records, cassette tapes, CD's etc). As a result the companies or organisations who make sound recordings have legal protection against unauthorised public performance or broadcasting of their sound recordings.

Phonographic Performance Limited (PPL) is a non-profit making company which administers public performance and broadcasting rights centrally[20]. It also issues licences to all those who wish to use the sound recordings in the public arena[21]. This means anything outside the family or domestic circle. Playing the music in a club is deemed to be a public performance, but a wedding reception would generally be regarded as a private performance, even if it is held in a public hall. The income generated from the collection of licensing fees (less administration costs) goes back to its members and to performers and artists who have assigned the public performance and broadcasting rights to PPL.

Event organisers who wish to use sound recordings at the event are usually responsible for securing a PPL licence. This does not necessarily mean that the event organiser is solely liable. In some cases there may be a number of parties causing sound recordings to be heard in public and they may each be liable in their own right.

PPL's licence gives permission to use any or all of the recordings at any time included in the repertoires of the organisation's members for the purposes stipulated on the licence. Without the central 'blanket' licence of PPL, it would be necessary to obtain individual licences from all the individual recording companies concerned.

PPL has a variety of standard tariffs covering the different kinds of public performance. As in the case of ASCAP and BMI in the United States, these tariffs are often negotiated with national representative bodies or associations. PPL's licence usually lasts for one year. PPL may also consider issuing licences

---

[20] See www.ppluk.com.
[21] This would include background music used for conferences, exhibitions and receptions.

for shorter periods or for 'one-off' events where a renewal would not be required.

If a PPL member's recordings are used without authorisation, PPL may secure an injunction in the High Court preventing any further use of the recording.

Event organisers may also require a licence from the Performing Rights Society (PRS). This is a separate organisation solely concerned with composers' and music publishers' rights. Whenever copyright musical works are performed in public (whether live or recorded) a PRS licence will be required.

10.3.3 South Africa

In South Africa, the event organiser will need to obtain a licence from the South African Music Rights Organisation (SAMRO) in Johannesburg. This organisation is a section 21 company (non-profit) that controls the performing rights in music in South Africa.

Regulation is comprehensive and tariffs are required to be paid for licensed music used in church halls, school halls, reception and waiting areas, fitness centres, hairdressing salons, use of incidental music before and after religious services and use of background music in shops and offices.

10.4 Ownership of the Performance

Can a performance itself be owned and, if so, who owns it?

This is a complex question and will largely depend on the intellectual property laws of the country in which the performance is given. It will also depend on the nature of the performance. In general, however, because a performance is an *expression* of an idea, as opposed to just the idea itself, it may be protectable under law as a 'dramatic work'[22]. This would usually include any performance by an entertainer at the event, such as a singer, dancer, actor or mime artist[23]. However, it will not include a performance at a sports event, except perhaps in exceptional circumstances, as explained below.

It is important to note that ownership of any copyright for a dramatic work will vest in the performer and not the event organiser, as the performer will be regarded as the 'author' of the work.

---

[22] This is the case under s3 of the CDPA 1988 in the United Kingdom and s102(a) of the Copyright Act of 1976 in the United States, but not under the Copyright Act 98 of 1978 in South Africa. In South Africa, performances are protected under the Performer's Rights Act of 1967.

[23] This would also include an address, speech or sermon at a conference, for example. See *Sport Business: Law, Practice and Precedents* by Verow, R., Lawrence, C., and McCormick, P., Jordan (2005), pf 4.2.8.8.

A particular play or move at a sports event is not considered to be protectable in most countries. This has long been a question of debate in the United States in particular. The current position is that a 'slam dunk', 'quarterback sneak' or 'googly' does not belong to anyone in particular and will not be protectable[24]. This is because the sporting spectacle as a whole is by its nature not scripted but improvised, and the outcome thereof is inherently uncertain[25]. On the other hand, where performances are entirely scripted or choreographed there may be room for arguing that these are protectable as dramatic works under copyright law[26]. Examples include figure skating, gymnastics and synchronised swimming. Even in such a case, however, the athlete would still have to show that the work is original and not copied from another work. That does not mean that the athlete cannot use common knowledge or existing material. But he or she must have put sufficient independent skill or labour into the work such that it can be regarded as original. The extent to which a variation on an existing or well-known move will give rise to originality will no doubt depend on the facts of each case.

Sometimes an event organiser will want to make audio or video tapes of certain speakers or performers at an event, either for the purpose of selling copies to attendees (and perhaps those who could not attend) or for archival purposes. Recordings of a performance will generally always be protectable under copyright law. However, the event organiser should obtain permission from the speaker or performer in order to record the presentation or performance and to sell the recordings made of the presentation or performance[27].

Finally, if the event organiser wishes to use the image rights or rights of publicity of the performer (including his or her name, image or likeness) in promoting the performance, the event organiser should also obtain the consent of the performer[28].

10.5 Conclusion

Contracts to perform at an event are often concluded verbally. Alternatively, they may be concluded on a half a page of text. If all goes well, this will be sufficient. However, this is not recommended, particularly where you are dealing with a star

---

[24] See *Can Sport Move in Mysterious Ways?* by Warren Phelops, Copyright World (63), September 1996.

[25] This was the reasoning given by the Federal Court of Appeal in Canada in a case brought by the governing bodies of, amongst others, American football and ice hockey (*FWS Joint Sports Claimants v The Copyright Board and Others* (1991)), where the Court held that there was no copyright in the playing of a sports game.

[26] This is particularly the case in the United States, where choreographic works are protected under s102(a) of the Copyright Act of 1976.

[27] See Chapter 10, n 6 above.

[28] See paragraphs 10.2.1(e) and 10.2.1(m) above and Chapter 10, n 10.

performer or a high profile event. It is necessary to have a sound contract to fall back on if something were to go wrong. Janet Jackson's 'wardrobe malfunction' at the Superbowl in 2004 is a case in point. The parties need to have a very clear idea of their respective rights and obligations. A performer is certainly more likely to honour a properly drafted and professionally presented contract rather than a simple verbal agreement.

CHAPTER ELEVEN

Participation Contracts

For most events, a participation contract will not be necessary. This chapter will only be relevant to situations where a number of different individuals, teams or groups may be participating in the event. In such a case, the event organiser may wish to enter into a contract with each individual, team or group governing the terms of their participation in the event.

11.1 The Nature of the Participation Contract

Contracts with individuals governing the terms of participation in an event are usually fairly short and simple. An example may be the terms and conditions signed by an athlete in order to participate in an athletics event. These terms and conditions are usually set out in, or attached to, the entry form for the event.

However, where an event organiser is contracting with a number of teams or representative bodies in relation to participation in a large event, the contract will be more complex. An example of this may be a participation contract entered into by the organisers of an international sports event with each participating team or nation. Such a contract will set out all the terms and conditions of participation and will be signed by an authorised representative of each team or representative body.

In order to ensure that each individual team or group member is also bound by the terms of such a contract, each individual should be asked to sign a brief statement of acceptance indicating that he or she has read the terms and conditions of the participation contract and agrees to be bound by it.

The operational rules of the event do not usually form part of the main body of the participation contract, but are attached as an appendix to the contract. The operational rules usually deal with the way in which the event will be run. They do not generally deal with the rights and obligations of the parties and should therefore be separated from the main body of the contract.

Whether a team, representative body or individual, the participating entity is essentially an 'entrant' in the event, and will be referred to as such in the remainder of this chapter.

A sample participation contract is set out in Appendix 9.

11.2   Key Legal Issues

11.2.1 Sanction

If the entity staging the event does not own the rights in the event itself, or wishes the event to count as part of an official national or international programme of events, it may have to obtain 'sanction' or permission from a governing body to run the event. In such a case, the parties may wish to record that the event organiser has been granted the rights to stage the event. This may be recorded in the recitals section of the contract or the main body of the contract itself.

11.2.2 Participation

The parties should record that the entrant will participate in the event in accordance with the terms and conditions contained in the participation contract (including any appendices containing event or tournament rules)

An obligation should also be imposed upon an entrant which is a participating team or representative body to procure that each and every member of the team shall abide in every respect with the terms and conditions contained in the participation contract. This should include an obligation to procure that every member of the team signs the statement of acceptance accepting the terms and conditions of the participation contract. In this way the event organiser has a contractual relationship with each participating team and individual.

The event organiser may require that the entrants participate in accordance with additional rules and regulations aside from the event or tournament rules attached to the participation contract. For example, some large sporting events may be subject to certain rules and regulations imposed by a national or international governing body. In addition, participation may also be subject to the established or official laws of the game as published. If so, there should be an additional obligation on the part of the entrant to participate in the event in accordance with such rules and regulations.

11.2.3 Title of the Event

The event organiser may wish to record the formal name of the event and require that every entrant refers to the event by that name. This may be particularly important if the event is a high-profile event and the event organiser wishes to maintain a consistent message for the purposes of promoting and marketing the event. If the event has a title sponsor, this is an additional way of ensuring that the sponsor obtains maximum value for its sponsorship.

11.2.4 Obligations

The primary obligations on the part of the event organiser will usually include the following:

- To organise and stage the event in a professional manner and in accordance with the standards expected for an event of that nature;
- To provide all the necessary administration in order to run the event successfully. This may include providing and running an administrative office (for the purposes of dealing with queries, requests etc.), hosting briefing sessions and arranging transport for the participants and officials to and from hotels to the venue;
- To distribute relevant information, documents and other materials to the entrants (such as event rules and manuals, programmes etc);
- To provide a safe and suitable venue for the event[1];
- To provide first-aid and emergency treatment facilities, if appropriate.

The primary obligations on the part of the entrant will usually include the following:

- To participate in the event in accordance with the terms and conditions of the participation contract, the event or tournament rules, the rules and regulations of the governing body and the laws of the game, to the extent that this has not been dealt with under the clause dealing with participation;
- Not to do or permit anything to be done which may bring the event or the relevant game (if appropriate) into disrepute.

11.2.5 Liability and Indemnity

Particularly in the case of sports events, where there is usually some element of risk, the event organiser will want to exclude liability for any claims arising from death, personal injury or damage to property in so far as this is possible[2]. It will also be helpful if a clause is included in terms of which the participant acknowledges the risks in participating in the event and accepts those risks.

The event organiser may also wish to seek the comfort of an indemnity for any losses it may suffer as a result of the breach of the participation contract or the negligence or recklessness of the entrant.

In a rally event, for example, a bystander was injured as a result of a car leaving the road and sued the event organisers as well as the driver of the car. In such a case, had the event organisers suffered financial loss as a result of the negligence of the driver of the car, they would have been able to recover such loss under the indemnity.

---

[1] The event organiser will have procured the use of a safe and suitable venue under the venue hire contract between the event organiser and the venue owner.

[2] See Chapter 6, n 9 with regard to exclusion clauses.

11.2.6 Insurance

In circumstances where the entrants are participating in a sporting event which carries some element of physical activity giving rise to risk of injury, special consideration should be given to insurance provisions. The different types of insurance that should be considered are discussed in more detail at paragraph 6.5 above.

Whilst the event organiser will usually be responsible for taking out insurance such as liability insurance, cancellation insurance and insurance for damage to property, it may impose an obligation on the part of the entrant (particularly if the entrant is a representative body) to take out death, accident and/or permanent health insurance on behalf of itself and/or the members of a team.

11.2.7 Power to Make Rules and Other Provisions

During the staging of large events involving a number of teams or entrants, it is inevitable that issues will arise that have not been foreseen and therefore are not the subject of specific provisions in the contract or otherwise. Alternatively, such unforeseen circumstances may fall within the scope of a particular clause, but the application of that clause to the unforeseen circumstance would have an unintended effect.

Swift resolution of such issues will be very important to the smooth running of the event. The event organiser will usually be under time pressure (particularly if the event is in the form of a competition) and will need to ensure that there are no disruptions to the event.

Accordingly, it is very important that the event organiser expressly reserves the right to make any additional rules or give any directions as to the conduct of the event and the entrants. Such additional rules and decisions should be deemed to be included in the participation contract upon publication[3].

The power to deal with unforeseen circumstances and issues that arise during the event may be expressly delegated to an event or tournament director, or to

---

[3] The legal question may arise as to whether any supplementation or alteration of the Participation Contract (or event or tournament rules) would amount to a unilateral variation of the contractual terms and would not be binding unless specifically agreed to by the participant/entrant and supported by the payment of consideration. Where the event organiser has an express power in the contract to deal with unforeseen circumstances or issues which require resolution during the event, and simply exercises that power, it is unlikely that a court would challenge this power and find that the exercise of such was unfair. However, where the event organiser in dealing with the unforeseen circumstance actually amends or varies the existing participation contract (or event or tournament rules), then such an amendment or variation could be open to challenge on the basis that it amounts to a unilateral amendment or variation and is therefore not enforceable. Whether or not such a challenge will be successful will depend on the law of each country or state.

an event technical committee established to handle the day to day running of the event.

The event organiser may wish to stipulate that its decision, or the decision of the event director or event committee (as appropriate), shall be final and binding upon all parties. However, owing to the breadth of the power given to supplement or amend the participation contract (or the event or tournament rules), it is recommended that an appeal mechanism be put in place to enable the entrant to appeal against the new term or rule imposed. The grounds for appeal should be limited (e.g. the term or rule is illegal, irrational, disproportionate or procedurally unfair, for instance) and provision should be made for a quick and efficient hearing of the appeal so as not to disrupt the event. As regards the appeal process, the reader should refer to the section below dealing with the resolution of disputes that take place during the event.

11.2.8 Resolution of Disputes

Perhaps the most important terms in the participation contract are those dealing with disputes. If the event is of a competitive nature, it is highly likely that disputes will arise during the event. The event organiser will want to ensure that these disputes are not only dealt with fairly, but quickly and efficiently.

Disputes may be quite different in nature. They may range from complaints about the way the event is being run, to disputes concerning incidents taking place during participation in the event, to disputes between competing entrants.

The contract should specify that all complaints should be referred to the event or tournament director. He or she will deal with the day to day management and administration of the event as he or she deems fit.

In the event of an alleged breach, the starting point is the participation contract. If the entrant breaches a material term in the participation contract (including the event or tournament rules), then the event organiser will usually have the right to terminate the contract and exclude the entrant from participating further in the event.

If the infringement is of a relatively minor nature, the event or tournament director may wish to impose a fine or some kind of penalty (perhaps a docking of points, if the event is a competition). Usually an indication of infringements and suitable penalties are set out in the event or tournament rules, the rules of the governing body or the official laws of the game. An example was the 2 shot penalty imposed under a PGA ruling on golfer Ian Woosnam in the 2001 British Open golf tournament at Royal Lytham & St Annes for carrying too many clubs in his bag.

The event organiser should try to ensure that the event or tournament rules attached to the participation contract deal, in particular, with doping and disciplinary infringements. The extent to which these infringements may take place will depend on the type of event. For large-scale sporting events, both will be important. For doping offences in particular, event organisers may wish for the matter to be dealt with under the World Anti-Doping Agency (WADA) code. More and more sports are adopting this code as a standard[4].

If any financial sanctions are imposed on the entrant, such as a fine, such should be fair and proportionate to the infringement committed. Some countries have special laws relating to the imposition of financial penalties and these should be considered[5].

On occasion an infringement may occur which is not dealt with in the rules. In such a case, the event or tournament director should have the express power in the contract to impose a suitable sanction. In this way, most issues, complaints or infringements can be dealt with expeditiously.

If the entrant believes that the complaint or infringement has not been dealt with appropriately by the event or tournament director, the entrant should have the right to declare a dispute in writing and refer the matter to the event technical committee. Sometimes referred to as a 'disputes committee', this committee should ideally consist of three or five members and be as independent and impartial as possible. Decisions of the committee should be made by majority. Formal notice of the matter referred and all relevant documentation and material relating thereto should be delivered to the event technical committee within a specified period of time after the declaration of the dispute.

The event technical committee should have full discretion as to its procedures and as to what evidence it may require in hearing the dispute, provided that the proceedings are conducted with reasonable notice, in a fair manner and with a reasonable opportunity for relevant parties to present their case[6]. Again, this is to ensure that the dispute is resolved fairly but quickly.

---

[4] See www.wada-ama.org.

[5] In the United Kingdom, for instance, such a financial sanction must be a genuine pre-estimate of loss and commensurate to the seriousness and extent of the relevant breach or infringement.

[6] What will be regarded as fair will depend on the circumstances. In some instances, written submissions may be sufficient. In other cases, the parties should have the option of a full oral hearing at which to present evidence and arguments. The event technical committee should also give direction as to whether representation should be allowed (in particular, legal representation) and whether parties are entitled to call or cross-examine witnesses. There is usually no obligation on the event technical committee to give reasons for its decision. However, it is considered prudent to do so, particularly if there is an appeal process.

The event technical committee should have the power to determine the following issues:

- Declarations of a dispute arising from decisions of the event or tournament director dealing with unforeseen circumstances;
- Declarations of a dispute arising from decisions of the event or tournament director dealing with complaints;
- Declarations of a dispute arising from decisions of the event or tournament director dealing with infringements of the rules (including the event or tournament rules, the rules of a governing body or the official laws of the game);
- Acting as an appeal committee on decisions taken pursuant to any doping or disciplinary hearings under the event or tournament rules[7].

The procedures relating to the declaration of a dispute, the hearing and adjudication of the matter by the event technical committee and the form, manner and publication of the decision should all be dealt with in the contract. Examples of these provisions are set out in clauses 12 and 13 of the sample contract provided in Appendix 9. These can be adapted to suit the event in question.

The event technical committee should have broad powers in respect of sanctions to be imposed on the entrants. These should include the power to:

- Expel an entrant and/or its team from participating further in the event; and/or
- Expel any team member from participating further in the event; and/or
- Suspend or otherwise discipline an entrant and or a team and/or a member thereof; and/or
- Impose restrictions on entry into official designated areas of the venue(s); and/or
- Impose any fines which may be appropriate and deduct or set-off any sums due in respect of such fines from any monies due to the entrant as a result of participation in the event;
- Increase any fines imposed under the event or tournament rules or rules of the governing body, where aggravating circumstances exist that warrant such an increase; and/or
- Cancel and/or vary the result of any match and/or the points awarded in relation thereto (if relevant); and/or
- Issue a warning, caution or reprimand as to future conduct of the entrant or members of its team; and/or

---

[7] Consideration should be given to whether the event technical committee would have the expertise to hear a doping-related appeal.

- Make any legal costs orders in relation to the matter as it deems appropriate; and/or
- Adjudicate on whether there has been a breach of the event or tournament rules; and/or
- Adjudicate on whether an event constitutes a 'force majeure' event[8]; and/or
- Take any other step which in the exercise of its powers the event technical committee considers would be appropriate in order to deal justly and efficiently with the matter in question.

The last point above attempts to act as a 'catch-all' clause which gives the event technical committee as broader powers as possible in respect of sanctions.

Consideration should also be given as to whether the decisions of the event technical committee should be final or whether an appeal against these decisions should be permitted. There are advantages and disadvantages to both.

The advantage of having an appeal procedure is that it greatly reduces the risk of a successful challenge to the ultimate decision on procedural grounds. The lack of an appeal mechanism is not per se a breach of the duty to act fairly (in a procedural sense) but it would certainly make a challenge on procedural grounds much easier.

However, setting up an appeal mechanism may be costly, both from a financial and administrative point of view (e.g. increased administrative burden, fees of adjudicator, cost of setting up the structure etc). Also, allowing for an appeal procedure very often prevents a final decision being taken expeditiously, which could be disruptive for the event.

If an appeal procedure is instituted, consideration should be given to the structure and nature of the body to which the appeal is made. Perhaps the most important factor is to provide for the independence of this body. Also, assessing the speed with which this body would be able to deal with the appeal should be an important factor. The Court of Arbitration for Sport (CAS), based in Lausanne, Switzerland, have reacted to this concern by establishing the Ad Hoc Division of CAS, which provides for quick, efficient arbitration in accordance with standard rules designed specifically for sporting tournaments[9]. Whatever the nature of the body, the event organiser will need to spell out in the clause dealing with appeals the exact rules relating to the appeal procedure. Provisions should be included relating to the following:

- The grounds of appeal;

---

[8] See paragraph 2.3.9 above.

[9] See for example the Arbitration Rules for the XVII Commonwealth Games in Manchester which is available on the CAS website at www.tes-cas.org. The Ad Hoc Division consists of arbitrators that are selected from a designated list, a President and a Court Office on-site.

- The filing and time period for the filing of a notice of appeal;
- Security for costs in the event of failure of the appeal;
- The constitution of the appeal panel;
- The procedures for the hearing of the appeal (e.g. written/oral arguments, representation etc);
- The time-scales for the appeal;
- The form and manner of the decision (the decision of the appeal panel should be in writing, giving reasons for the decision); and
- The power to increase on appeal any sanction imposed by the event technical committee.

It is worth noting that, notwithstanding the existence of an appeal procedure from decisions taken by the event technical committee, there is a likelihood that disputes could still be referred to the courts. It is very difficult to immunise decisions made by or on behalf of an event organiser entirely from review by the courts. The courts will generally not accept or recognise any attempt to oust their supervisory jurisdiction over such bodies. Therefore, provisions should be considered for inclusion in the contract to manage this risk.

Courts will generally recognise and enforce jurisdiction clauses and/or arbitration clauses attempting to confer exclusive jurisdiction on one court or arbitration body. The event organiser should consider including a clause to the effect that a referral to such a court or body should only take place after the event, so as to minimise any disruption to the event[10].

11.2.9 Commercial Contracts

For large events in particular, the event organiser will have entered into a number of commercial contracts (such as sponsorship and supplier contracts) with third parties who wish to be associated with the event. The event organiser will want to protect its relationships with these sponsors and suppliers. It will not want the entrant, be it a team or individual, to promote other third parties whilst participating in the event, particularly if such third parties are competitors of its sponsors or suppliers[11]. This will undermine both its relationship with its sponsors and suppliers and the value of the rights granted under the commercial contract.

A good example of this is the well-publicised dispute that arose in relation to the ICC Champions Trophy, a cricket tournament held in September 2002.

---

[10] It must be noted, however, that there may be circumstances where a court may feel justified in intervening during an event (e.g. a tournament) and ordering urgent relief e.g. participation in the final of the tournament. If the circumstances were compelling enough, it is doubtful whether a court would refuse to intervene because the parties have agreed that any challenges could only be made after the event.

[11] This may include equipment or accessories used in the event by the entrant.

The international governing body for cricket, the ICC, had sold the central commercial rights (including sponsorship rights) to this tournament and other ICC events (including the 2003 and 2007 Cricket World Cups) to Global Cricket Corporation for $550m. As part of the contract, the ICC promised that teams and players participating in these events would not be permitted to conclude sponsorship endorsement deals that conflicted with the exclusive sponsorship rights granted by Global Cricket Corporation to event sponsors. Disputes in relation to the Indian team's sponsorship by Sahara (in conflict with event sponsor South African Airways) and to the stipulation that players not conduct any endorsement activity for sixty days either side of the event, resulted in threats of boycotts and litigation which were only avoided at the 11th hour[12].

Accordingly, the event organiser may wish to obtain a warranty from the entrant to the effect that it or he or she has not entered or will not enter into any contract with a third party to promote that party or its products during the event. The event organiser may seek additional assurance that the clothing or kit to be worn during the event (and perhaps also whilst travelling to and from the event) will not carry the name of any third party. In this way, the event organiser can ensure that either the kit is clean of any references to third parties or it can contain a reference to the official sponsor(s) of the event.

An exception is sometimes made for kit manufacturers. The event organiser may allow the entrants (usually teams) to wear kit displaying the logo of a kit manufacturer with whom that entrant has its own contract. If so, the event organiser will usually want to specify the size and placement of such logo.

If the event organiser wants to ensure that the entrant wears kit containing a reference to the official sponsor(s) or the event logo, an obligation should be included in the contract to this effect. To ensure control over this process, the event organiser may wish to supply the entrant with kit for use in participating in the event or, alternatively, supply the entrant with the necessary logos to be attached to the kit.

The event organiser may also wish to include clauses to the effect that:

- the entrant will not, and will procure that members of the team will not, exercise any rights in relation to the event which compete with the commercial rights;

---

[12] More recently, a similar case arose in the West Indies in March 2005. The West Indian Cricket Board dropped a number of their leading players who had private endorsement deals with Cable & Wireless, because these deals were in conflict with a central deal between the Board and competitor Digitel in relation to a series in which the West Indies team were due to play. Contracts between the Board and their players prevented the endorsement of private sponsors in direct conflict with a commercial partner of the Board.

- the entrant shall not allow its name, or the name of the members of the team to be used in association with the event for the purposes of advertising or endorsement;
- the entrant will not, and will procure that the members of the team will not, make any recording of the event or parts thereof. If the entrant wishes to make a recording for internal training purposes only, this is usually permitted, provided that the entrant agrees not to make more than one copy and assigns all rights in such a recording to the event organiser.

11.2.10 Interviews and Press Conferences

The event organiser may wish to include an obligation on the part of the participants to participate in interviews and press conferences before, during or after the event. This may be particularly important if the event is being broadcast and the event is likely to feature high-profile participants.

11.3 The Event or Tournament Rules

A handbook should be compiled containing the event or tournament rules, as well as details on logistic matters. These rules should be attached to the contract and referred to therein as part of the legally binding contractual documentation.

11.3.1 Rules

The nature and extent of the rules will depend on the type of event being staged. The rules are usually designed to govern the conduct of the parties whilst participating in the event. Whilst they may be legally binding on the participants (as part of the contractual documentation), they will not usually have the force of law. For events which include a competition or tournament, fairly detailed rules may be required. These may include:

- Rules governing the structure of the competition or tournament;
- Rules relating to the selection and nomination of teams (if relevant);
- Rules relating to the draw;
- Rules relating to scoring;
- Rules relating to non-attendance or non-participation;
- Rules relating to awards, prizes and medals;
- Rules relating to designated officials and their conduct;
- Rules relating to eligibility;
- Rules relating to medical fitness, medical information and insurance;
- Rules relating to drug testing[13];
- Rules relating to disciplinary proceedings;
- Rules relating to dress code and kit;

---

[13] These may be imposed by a national or international governing body or by another external body, such as the World Anti-Doping Agency.

- Sanctions for non-compliance with the rules;
- Rules relating to dealing with the media; and
- Rules relating to kit and the use of logos and trade marks on such kit.

11.3.2 Logistics

The handbook should also deal with logistical issues (if relevant), such as:

- A schedule of activities or matches;
- Travel;
- Accommodation;
- Baggage, laundry and kit storage;
- The role of any liaison officers and managerial staff;
- Access to and use of the tournament office;
- Access to the event or tournament director and/or members of the event technical committee;
- Requests for information;
- Provision of kit and/or equipment;
- Tickets and programmes;
- Accreditation;
- Facilities for meetings;
- Venue guides, if necessary; and
- Briefing sessions, award ceremonies and other relevant functions.

11.4 Statement of Acceptance/Adherence

As mentioned above, if the event organiser is contracting with an entrant who is a representative body or team, it will want to ensure that it also has a direct contractual relationship with each individual member of the team or body itself. It can achieve this by attaching to the contract a short Statement of Acceptance (sometimes known as a 'Statement of Adherence') to be signed by each member of the team or body.

The Statement of Acceptance should, in its simplest form, contain a statement that each individual entrant agrees to be bound by the terms and conditions contained in the participation contract, including the event or tournament rules and any other schedules attached to the participation contract.

If participation in the event carries some element of risk, there should also be a clause under which the participant acknowledges the risks and the event organiser is excluded from liability arising from injury, death or damage to property, insofar as this is possible under the laws of the relevant country or state[14].

---

[14] See Chapter 6, n 9 above.

If the event or performance is being filmed, the entrant should be asked to consent to being filmed and to the use of his or her image rights or rights of publicity (including name, image, likeness, signature and biographical information) in relation to the event in perpetuity for the purposes of advertising and promoting the event[15]. In addition, he or she should be asked to assign in perpetuity to the event organiser any rights in the recorded material and consent to the exploitation of such material in any media[16].

As to rights in the actual performance by the participants, the reader is referred to paragraph 10.4 above. Copyright or performance rights will usually vest in the participant, unless such rights are assigned to the event organiser in the Statement of Acceptance.

Finally, consideration should be given to paragraph 11.2.9 above in relation to commercial contracts. The participant should be asked to acknowledge the commercial rights defined in the contract and undertake not to commit any act that interferes with or prejudices such rights, including wearing any kit containing logos or trade marks not authorised by the event organiser.

A version of a Statement of Acceptance is set out in Appendix 9.

11.5 Personal Information

It may be prudent to attach a personal information sheet to the contract to be completed by the participant. This is particularly useful if the event is being broadcast or publicised and personal information is being sought on the participants. This information can also be used in an event programme. It would normally include statistics and other relevant historical data rather than unnecessarily intrusive information.

11.6 Conclusion

As mentioned at the outset of this chapter, for most events it will probably not be necessary to enter into a participation contract. However, for those events in which a number of teams or individuals are participating or competing, such a contract will be crucial. Indeed, it is the only way to regulate the conduct of such participants during the event. Even if the participation contract is limited to a simple waiver and indemnity, the event organiser should ensure that each participant who participates in the event signs the document as a condition to participation in the event. In this way a direct contractual relationship will be established with the participant.

---

[15] See Chapter 10, n 10 above. This could also include the right to use the participant's image rights or rights of publicity in relation to any commercial projects arising from the event e.g. a computer game.

[16] See Chapter 10, n 6.

CHAPTER TWELVE

Merchandising Contracts

Merchandising contracts, as they relate to the events industry, involve the sale of merchandise by reference to the event itself. A manufacturer will produce a range of products carrying the logo or trade marks of the event in the hope of selling such products to those attending the event. We have all seen people wearing shirts or caps containing the logos and trade marks of an event. People wish to be associated with events carrying a high profile or significant status. They also wish to collect memorabilia from the event.

Merchandising at events can be big business. Major events such as the Olympics sell merchandise as diverse as branded underwear, postcards, and key rings. Usually the event organiser will not wish to manufacturer and sell the products itself. It will want to appoint a merchandiser to produce and sell 'official' products carrying the event logo and trade marks.

In recent times the sale of 'unofficial' merchandise by those who are not authorised to use the event logo or trade marks has become commonplace. Successful merchandising centres on the control by the rights owner (in this chapter we will assume this is the event organiser) of protectable intellectual property rights that it can grant to the merchandiser, together with a programme to prevent counterfeiters from selling 'unofficial' goods. The event organiser will wish to enter into a merchandising contract setting out the terms and conditions under which the intellectual property rights can be used.

12.1 The Nature of the Merchandising Contract

The merchandising contract is essentially a licensing contract. The intellectual property rights owned by the event organiser will be licensed to the merchandiser (the licensee) under certain terms and conditions. In exchange, the event organiser will usually be paid a royalty on the sales of the licensed products.

A sample merchandising contract is set out in Appendix 10.

12.2 Establishing Ownership of the Intellectual Property Rights

In order to license the rights the event organiser must be the rights holder i.e. the owner of the intellectual property rights[1]. This can be a complex issue in itself. The subject is discussed in more detail in paragraph 1.5.3 above.

Many countries will have a system of trade mark registration, in terms of which the event organiser can register an event name, logo, a team or an individual name or nickname[2]. Trade mark registration will generally provide the strongest protection from infringement, providing civil remedies to rights holders and criminal offences for infringers. Trade marks are usually registered in certain categories. The event organiser will need to ensure that the categories in which the marks are registered will cover the required product range. Even if an event or individual name or logo are not registered as trade marks, some protection may still be offered under the common law of the relevant country[3].

As regards the licensing of trade marks, additional requirements may be imposed under legislation in the relevant country. For instance, in the United Kingdom, the Trade Mark Act 1999 stipulates that a trade mark licence must be in writing. Unless the licence states otherwise, there is also an obligation on trade mark owners to take action for infringement if the licensee requires them to do so[4].

The event organiser may also be able to claim some protection over the event logo under copyright law. Copyright law usually protects an original artistic work such as a logo or emblem. There is generally no registration requirement for copyright to subsist in a work. The position will however vary from country to country. In the United States, for example, copyright should be registered for full protection. Literary works will also be protectable in most cases under copyright law. An event programme would therefore be protected. The names of events or individuals will not generally qualify for protection as literary works, although a signature, slogan or quote may well qualify.

Photographs included as part of the merchandising property will also generally be protected as an artistic work under copyright law. Photographs will be owned by

---

[1] The event organiser could also be a licensee, having obtained the rights from the licensor e.g. a governing body.

[2] The general requirement is that the name or logo must be distinctive in itself and not descriptive or generic in nature.

[3] Event organisers may also have a 'passing off' action under tort law, if there is confusion in the minds of the public as to the authenticity of the goods purchased as a result of misrepresentations by the infringer, and this has also caused damage to the event organiser. If such a cause of action exists, the event organiser may be able to obtain an injunction or interdict preventing the further sale of the unauthorised goods until a trial resolves the issues in full.

[4] See ss28 to 31 of the Trade Mark Act 1994.

the photographer as he or she will be the originator or creator of the work. The copyright in the photographs can either be licensed to the event organiser and then on-licensed to the merchandiser for commercial exploitation or alternatively licensed directly by the photographer to the merchandiser.

In some countries, such as the United Kingdom and South Africa, there may also be design right protection for merchandising property. A registered design protects, usually by way of registration on a territorial basis, the appearance of an article, as opposed to any engineering aspect thereof. Protection incorporates the features of the design, including the lines, contour, shape, colours and texture of a product or its ornamentation. In order to be registrable, a design must be new and have individual character. A design right may also exist in a product even if it is not registered, as it usually arises automatically when the design is created. Ownership of the design and design rights used in a merchandising programme should be discussed and clarified in the contract if necessary.

A successful merchandising programme relies on the ability to protect the intellectual property rights in relation to the event. It is therefore essential for an event organiser running such a programme to take specialist advice from a local attorney or solicitor in order to ensure that these rights (particularly rights in the event or individual's name and logo) are fully protected.

12.3   Key Legal Issues

12.3.1 Parties

The parties will usually be the event organiser (assuming it is the rights holder or authorised licensee of the rights holder) and the party wishing to exploit the rights (commonly known as the licensee or sub-licensee). If the event organiser has appointed an agent to exploit the merchandising rights on its behalf, the agent may be a party to the contract and may even grant the rights.

12.3.2 Grant of Rights

The contract will need to specify the nature of the intellectual property rights to be licensed to the merchandiser. As discussed above, these rights may be a combination of trade marks (registered or unregistered), copyright (words and pictures) and perhaps designs (registered or unregistered). The rights are usually defined in the contract and set out in full in a schedule to the contract.

The rights will normally be granted for a particular category of products that are to be manufactured by the merchandiser. The range of products will need to be discussed by the parties and defined carefully in the contract. The event organiser may wish to license the rights in a certain product category (e.g. clothing) to one merchandiser and the rights in other product category (e.g. pendants) to another merchandiser. The definition of the product categories will therefore also need to be discussed and documented.

The merchandising contract permits the merchandiser to combine the intellectual property rights with the defined products to produce what is usually known as the 'licensed products'. These are the approved products which can be manufactured by the merchandiser and are the subject matter of the contract.

12.3.3 Exclusivity

The event organiser will need to consider whether the grant of rights to the merchandiser is exclusive or non-exclusive. The granting of rights on an exclusive basis can prevent anyone else from exercising the merchandising rights, in the agreed territory[5]. The granting of rights may be limited in other ways, e.g. duration or on condition that certain sales targets are reached.

The right to manufacture the licensed products may not necessarily be limited to a particular territory. This will enable the manufacturer to have the licensed products manufactured in territories outside those in which they are permitted to sell the licensed products. The merchandiser may wish to have the licensed products manufactured abroad, for example.

The right to use the intellectual property rights will usually be non-exclusive as the event organiser will wish to grant these rights to other parties and to use them itself. It may wish to grant these rights to other merchandisers (for other territories), to sponsors, suppliers, broadcasters or other commercial partners.

The event organiser will commonly grant an exclusive licence to use the intellectual property rights on certain products for sale in a defined territory for the duration of the contract. The territory will be a specified geographical area. Constraining merchandising sales to a particular territory allows the event organiser to enter into identical arrangements with other merchandisers in other territories.

If the marketing and sale of the licensed products are exclusive to a particular territory and this includes the right to market and sell such products on-line, certain controls may need to be put in place to ensure that such products are not available for purchase by third parties outside the territory. This is discussed further in paragraph 9.3.2 in relation to the sale of hospitality packages over the internet.

Where the granting of rights is exclusive, the parties will need to take advice

---

[5] An exclusive appointment usually also prevents the event organiser from exercising the rights itself, although this should be clarified if this is likely to be an issue. This is the position in the UK and South Africa.

on any national or regional laws relating to competition and free movement of goods.

12.3.4 Term

The period during which the licensed products may be manufactured and sold should be defined in the contract. Sometimes these periods may be different. For instance, the merchandiser may wish to have the right to manufacture the licensed products for a certain period, but to have the right to sell the licensed products for a slightly longer period.

The term of the agreement will usually cover the period of the event and perhaps a short period thereafter. If the events are part of a series (such as a music tour, for instance), the merchandiser may wish for the licence to cover the entire period of the series.

The length of the term may occasionally be linked to financial targets. For instance, if the merchandiser has not reached a particular target by a particular date, the licence may come to an end. If the event organiser is concerned about the level of commitment and experience of the merchandiser in a particular territory, it may wish to grant a licence for a short period but reserve for itself a unilateral option to extend the term.

The merchandiser may request a right of first negotiation or a matching rights clause to extend the term. These rights are examined in further detail in paragraph 2.3.4 above.

In general, the event organiser will be interested in developing its brand and maximising profits through merchandising sales. It will not wish to be tied into long term merchandising contracts and should retain some flexibility in the contract to allow for this.

The main objective of the merchandiser, on the other hand, will be to retain those rights which are profitable and to recoup any advance or fees it has paid the event organiser as soon as possible.

12.3.5 Payment

The payment provisions for a merchandising contract can be complex. The event organiser will normally receive a royalty on sales of the licensed products. However, the manner and structure of the payments may vary substantially.

The royalty will usually be calculated as a percentage of the sales price on total sales of the licensed products. The parties should take care to establish whether the percentage will be based on the merchandiser's published retail price or on the wholesale price. Percentage rates for retail sales vary between 10 and

20% of the retail price, although this is really a matter of negotiation between the parties. If the calculation is on wholesale price, the event organiser should expect to receive an increased percentage. Care should also be taken to define whether any costs or taxes will be deducted from the wholesale or retail price before the royalty percentage is calculated.

The event organiser may negotiate an upfront payment in advance of royalties or guaranteed minimum payments. These payments are usually non-returnable but recoupable against sales of the licensed products. Alternatively, there may be a sliding scale royalty percentage which decreases as sales increase. These payment mechanisms serve as additional incentives for the merchandiser to actively market and promote the licensed products.

A licence fee may also be paid on signature of the contract by the merchandiser. This fee is not usually recoupable. It is regarded as a one-off payment to obtain the licence. However, the merchandiser can insist that part of the fee is repaid in the event that certain conditions are not met e.g. the event is not held, certain participants don't appear in the event, attendances do not reach a minimum figure, no television coverage is secured etc.

The merchandiser may wish for the term of the contract to be directly related to the recoupment provisions. If at the end of the contract the advance has not been fully recouped by the merchandiser, the term of the contract may be extended until such time as the advance has been recouped. In such a case the event organiser should insist on a clause in the contract giving it the right to buy the merchandiser out of the contract.

12.3.6 Obligations on the Merchandiser

a) Manufacturing, Promoting, Distributing and Selling

Usually the merchandiser will be required to manufacture, promote, distribute and sell the licensed products. The merchandiser may be entitled to outsource some of these activities. The event organiser will want to specify certain dates by which these activities will be undertaken and completed. This is really a matter of negotiation between the parties and will depend on the size, nature and timing of the event. The payment terms will be structured so that there is an incentive on the part of the merchandiser to maximise sales. However, the event organiser should at the very least require that the merchandiser uses its best endeavours to manufacture, promote, distribute and sell the licensed products.

In addition to the obligation to manufacture the licensed products, the event organiser should ensure that the merchandiser manufactures the goods to the highest standard and in accordance with all relevant legislation and regulations. This should cover product safety legislation as well as any local or national labelling regulations. Specialist advice should be taken and reference should be made to specific pieces of legislation if this is an area of concern for the event organiser.

As regards promotion and advertising, the costs of such activities should be borne by the merchandiser. The event organiser may wish to specify a minimum level of spend for these activities. It may even go as far as stipulating certain advertising and promotional activities to be undertaken by the merchandiser. On the other hand, it will want to restrict the merchandiser to advertising and promotional activities inside the exclusive territory.

As regards distribution and sale of the licensed products, the event organiser may wish to agree a suitable programme in this regard with the merchandiser. The licensed products will almost always be sold at the event itself and on the event website, if any. However, they may also be sold to certain wholesalers and retailers for on-sale. The event organiser may seek an undertaking that the licensed products will not be sold to vendors, hawkers, peddlers and the like.

The event organiser may also wish to specify that the licensed products will not be sold at reduced or discount prices, or given away by the merchandiser as so-called "premiums", without the prior written consent of the event organiser. In addition, the event organiser should ask for an assurance that the merchandiser will not offer products on sale or return and that there will be no financial reserves held against such products.

b) Approval over the Licensed Products

The event organiser will want to check both the quality of the licensed products and the use of the intellectual property rights. The merchandiser should therefore be required to submit (at its own expense) samples of the licensed products to the event organiser for approval in writing. The event organiser will seek to withhold such approval in its absolute discretion and have the right to alter the goods if it is not satisfied with them. On the other hand, the merchandiser may require that the approval may not be unreasonably withheld.

Time periods for the approval process should be stipulated in the contract. The merchandiser will want to ensure that approval is deemed to be given if it receives no reply as to the suitability of the goods within the specified time period.

Each new design or variation of the licensed products should be submitted for approval. In addition, the approvals process should also apply to all advertising and promotional materials produced by the manufacturer if such materials make use of the works or logos of the event organiser.

In addition to the above, the merchandiser may be required to:

- Ensure that the licensed products comply in all respects with the samples it has submitted for approval;
- Manufacture the licensed products in accordance with a strict set of guidelines produced by the event organiser (including guidelines as to how the intellectual property rights can be reproduced and used);
- Attach a label to all licensed products with specified trade mark and copyright notices and wording to the effect that the licensed products represent 'official merchandise' and are manufactured under license of the event organiser; and
- Permit inspection of the licensed products at any stage of manufacture, promotion, distribution or sale.

c) Intellectual Property Rights

The trade marks and logos belonging to the event organiser should be attached as a schedule to the contract. This is to ensure that they are used in correct form by the merchandiser.

There should also be a general obligation on the part of the merchandiser to do its utmost to protect the intellectual property rights. However, notwithstanding all efforts on the part of the merchandiser, infringements may still occur.

The parties will need to agree a course of action in the event that the intellectual property rights are infringed in any way by a third party. It is in the interests of both the event organiser and the merchandiser that these rights are protected.

An exclusive merchandiser may be required to sue infringers under the terms of the contract, although in that case the merchandiser may seek repayment of any costs incurred in the action and any sums recovered from any damages received from an infringer. Alternatively, the event organiser may require that all actions against infringing parties be taken by it. In either case, there should be an obligation on the merchandiser to inform the event organiser of any third party infringements and to assist in any litigation proceedings, if necessary[6]. Unless otherwise agreed between the parties in the contract, it will be the owner of the trade marks that will conduct any litigation to protect the marks.

In addition to the above, the merchandiser may be required to:

- Give an undertaking that it will not challenge any of the registered trade marks if the contract terminates;

---

[6] Trade mark owners in the UK should also note that unless the trade mark licence states otherwise, they are bound to take action for infringement if the licensee requires them to do so.

- Give an undertaking that it cannot manufacture any products other than the licensed products using the intellectual property rights;
- Give an undertaking that it will not do anything which might impair the intellectual property rights or the reputation of the event organiser in any way;
- Acknowledge that the intellectual property rights are owned by the event organiser and will remain so owned both during and after the contract; and
- Acknowledge that any enhancements or improvements made to the intellectual property rights are assigned to the event organiser free of charge.

12.3.7 Obligations on the Event Organiser

The primary obligations on the event organiser will be to deliver and protect the intellectual property rights which will be required by the merchandiser in order to successfully sell the merchandise.

Firstly, the merchandiser will usually want a warranty that the event organiser owns the intellectual property rights, in particular the marks to be used on the merchandise itself[7]. The event organiser may be asked to provide details of any registrations undertaken in respect of the marks in a schedule attached to the contract. The schedule should also contain examples of the marks and guidelines as to their use.

Secondly, the event organiser should be expected to maintain these rights and their registrations, at its cost.

The merchandiser will also require the event organiser to take legal action to protect its marks in the event of infringement by a third party. This is because infringement of these rights may affect the value and sales of the products. The event organiser may wish to resist an absolute obligation to take legal action in the event of infringement. If the event organiser does take legal action against infringers, it will want to ensure that it controls the litigation process in this regard.

12.3.8 Termination

Apart from the usual termination provisions discussed in Chapter 2, additional provisions may be considered dealing with the following:

- The right to terminate the contract if the merchandiser fails to manufacture and produce the licensed products for sale by a particular date;

---

[7] If the event organiser has itself been licensed to use the intellectual property rights by the rights holder or licensor, the merchandiser will wish to obtain a warranty that the event organiser has indeed obtained such a licence from the rights holder and that it is entitled to sub-license those rights to the merchandiser.

- The right to terminate if particular sales targets are not reached (or the right to terminate only the exclusive arrangement in such a case);
- The right to terminate if the merchandiser ceases or abandons merchandising activities, such as sales or advertising; or
- The right to terminate in the event that adequate accounting processes are not put in place or suitable reporting is not forthcoming.

12.3.9 Effect of Termination

Clauses should be included in the contract dealing with events after termination of the contract.

The contract will normally come to an end in two instances: it will either come to an end with the effluxion of time (i.e. at the end of the agreed term of the contract) or as a result of termination because of breach of the contract by one of the parties.

In the case of termination of the contract at the end of the agreed term, provision is usually made for a run-off period, during which the merchandiser is granted a non-exclusive licence to sell off its existing stock of the licensed products. The duration of this period is a matter of negotiation between the parties but it will usually last for one additional accounting period at least. During this run-off period, the merchandiser should be required to continue to adhere to the accounting process and to pay any royalties due to the event organiser.

If provision is made for a run-off period, the event organiser should require that, during the last two or three accounting periods of the contract, the merchandiser should not be entitled to manufacture more than the average amount of licensed products for the previous accounting periods. This is to prevent the merchandiser from manufacturing and stockpiling products towards the end of the contract for sale in the run-off period after the contract. The event organiser should also stipulate that no licensed products should be sold at a discounted rate or given away by the merchandiser without its consent during the run-off period.

Once the run-off period has ended, the event organiser will want an undertaking on the part of the merchandiser that it will cease to manufacture, promote and sell the licensed products and destroy any remaining licensed products in its possession or control (or sell them to the event organiser). The event organiser may wish to appoint another merchandiser in the territory, and will not want to be restricted by virtue of the terms of the previous contract in any way.

If the contract is terminated by the event organiser as a result of a breach of the contract by the merchandiser, the merchandiser will usually not have the benefit of the run-off period. It should be required to immediately cease from all merchandising activities and to undertake a final accounting process following which all amounts owing to the event organiser should be paid to it. Provision should also be made for the immediate return of all materials provided to the merchandiser by the event organiser before or during the contract.

12.3.10 Insurance

The event organiser will want to stipulate that the merchandiser has adequate product liability insurance in place. It may even require that the merchandiser has sufficient product liability insurance to cover a specified minimum amount in respect of any one claim and that its interest is noted on the insurance policy.

12.3.11 Indemnity

Owing to the prominence of the event organiser's marks on the licensed products, there may be a risk of claims against the event organiser from third parties who buy and use the products. This will largely depend on the nature of the products.

If there is such a risk of claims, in addition to product liability insurance, the event organiser should seek to obtain an indemnity for any losses it may suffer from claims made against it by third parties arising from the manufacture or sale of the licensed products by the merchandiser.

12.3.12 Accounting

In this type of contract, as is the case in all licensing contracts, accounting provisions will be of some importance, particularly for the event organiser. The event organiser will be receiving a royalty payment on the sales of the licensed products. However, the proceeds from the sales of the licensed products will be collected and administered by the merchandiser. Hence the event organiser will need some assurance in the contract that, at the very least, the merchandiser will maintain full and adequate books of account reflecting the sales of the licensed products.

The event organiser should consider including provisions enabling it or its auditors to have access to such books of account for the purposes of conducting an audit and, if necessary, to enable them to make copies of the books of account or extracts thereof. The costs of such an audit are usually borne by the event organiser, unless the audit reveals a material discrepancy in respect of the amount due, in which case such costs should be borne by the merchandiser. A material discrepancy is usually agreed by the parties as being a figure of three to ten percent of the actual amount due to the event organiser.

In addition, the parties should include provisions in the contract dealing with:

- The definition of the accounting periods during the term of the contract;
- The provision of statements of account for each accounting period and/or any interim statements of account to be provided by the merchandiser;
- The level of detail to be provided in the statements of account; and
- The continuation of accounting provisions during any run-off period.

12.4 Character Merchandising

The above section dealt with the sale of licensed products where the products contained intellectual property rights relating to an event. In such a case the intellectual property rights will usually be owned by the event organiser.

However, a performer may also wish to license rights to his or her name, nickname and logo for the purposes of producing and selling merchandise at an event. An example of this is a singer who performs a concert. This is often referred to as character merchandising as it involves the sale of products referring to a real character.

There is very little difference between such a merchandising contract and the type of contract referred to above. The only real significant difference is in the nature of the marks being licensed to the merchandiser. The merchandiser will be seeking a licence to use the image rights or personality rights of the performer, including the name, nickname, image, biographical details and signature[8]. For example, the merchandiser will usually want to produce T-shirts, caps or key rings using the name, nickname or image of the performer. The merchandiser may also wish to use photographs of the performer for the purposes of producing an event programme[9].

The contract will be between the performer and the merchandiser in this case. However, the issues raised in paragraph 12.3 above will still apply and should be considered by the parties.

12.5 Conclusion

Merchandising contracts will usually only be necessary for large, high-profile events where there is a market for products bearing the name and logo of the event. In the merchandising contract, the event organiser will be most concerned with the protection of the goodwill attached to these intellectual property rights and with ensuring that the goods or products manufactured and sold are of sufficient quality. As the event organiser will be relying on the merchandiser to collect the revenue and pay to it a royalty in most cases, it should also ensure that it has access to the books of account reflecting the sales of the licensed products. From the merchandiser's point of view, the products will be largely worthless without the proper and protected use of the name and logo of the event. It will therefore seek to ensure that it has adequately secured the use of such rights.

---

[8] See Chapter 10, n 10.

[9] These photographs may not belong to the performer. They may belong to a photographer or agency, for instance, and the rights to use such photographs may have to be licensed separately from such photographer or agency.

CHAPTER THIRTEEN

Broadcasting Contracts

The business of broadcasting is an extensive topic which can be dealt with in a book of its own. This chapter will focus almost entirely on television broadcasting of events which, at the time of writing, is still the most popular means of broadcasting an event.

The event broadcasting contract is regarded as being the most valuable to an event organiser. Not only will it be a major source of revenue for the event organiser, but it will enable the event to be brought to thousands, if not millions of people in their own homes. Broadcasting contracts of high-profile events will likewise be of great value to broadcasters, who are likely to compete for the rights to broadcast the event.

In recent years the rights fees paid by broadcasters to broadcast an event have increased dramatically. This has largely been as a result of the increasing influence of satellite and cable channels and the arrival of pay-per-view and digital television. Although the amount and variety of coverage of good quality events has increased, so have the number of broadcasters looking for good quality content.

The broadcasting market keeps growing and developing. Broadcasting is no longer reserved to the major broadcasters such as the BBC or NBC. Sports clubs, mobile telephone companies and entrepreneurs are increasingly discovering ways to exploit broadcasting rights. Successful sports clubs such as Manchester United and the New York Yankees have established their own dedicated subscription television channels through joint venture agreements[1].

With the development of 3G mobile telephony, it will not be long before events will be broadcast in full via mobile phones[2]. Broadcasting of major events over

---

[1] MUTV is a joint venture with Sky and YES (Yankee Entertainment and Sports Network) is 60% owned by Yankees owner George Steinbrenner and 40% owned by investment bank Goldman Sachs.

[2] At the time of writing, one mobile telephone company is already advertising the first full-length pop concert to be relayed live to its customers.

the internet is already occurring. Viewers could watch certain events taking place at the Olympics in Athens in 2004 via the internet, for example.

The exploitation of current and back catalogue event footage through re-broadcasts and sales of videos and DVDs is another important source of revenue for event organisers.

Although this chapter will focus on the exploitation of broadcasting rights for television, broadcasting should not be thought of as being limited to this medium. Audio broadcasting via radio remains a lucrative market, particularly for sports events. Moreover, the development of the internet and mobile telephony as additional broadcasting mediums is likely to have a significant impact on the business of broadcasting in years to come.

13.1   Legal Basis of Broadcasting Rights

As discussed earlier[3], the law of many countries does not recognise that there is a separate and distinct proprietary right in an event. The lack of formal legal protection in this area will be of concern to the broadcaster, who is being granted rights to broadcast the event in the knowledge that the event organiser does not legally 'own' rights in the event itself. Notwithstanding this, the granting of broadcasting rights for an event is deemed to be a valuable 'property' and such rights are traded or sold by way of sophisticated commercial contracts.

For the broadcaster, the delivery and protection of broadcasting rights rests on the ability of the event organiser to control access to the event and the venue in which the event is to take place.

By controlling access to the venue, the event organiser can impose conditions of entry on the attendees. In particular, the broadcaster will want assurances from the event organiser that no third party is entitled to record footage at the venue for commercial purposes. This will go some distance towards ensuring exclusivity for the broadcaster, particularly if the event organiser is also required to take active steps towards preventing the recording of any footage of the event.

Where the event organiser is not the owner of the venue, the broadcaster will also need assurance that the venue owner has granted rights of access to the event organiser to allow for broadcasting from the venue and, in addition, has not separately granted anyone else the right to access the venue and set up their own equipment for broadcasting. The event organiser will need to secure such assurance itself in its contract with the venue owner for the hire of the venue.

Where the event is held in a public place, there may be obvious problems of

---

[3] See paragraph 1.4 above.

control over access to the venue. However, the event organiser can still seek the co-operation of any local and public authorities to help prevent unauthorised broadcasting. For instance, the event organiser may be able to block off key areas in which the event takes place in order to prevent unauthorised broadcasters from setting up their equipment. The event organiser can try and control the air space of the event and buildings that overlook it to prevent unauthorised broadcasters from setting up any equipment. It may also work with the authorities to reserve key areas for the authorised broadcaster by setting up platforms or scaffolding.

Where there are performers taking part in the event, the event organiser will be expected by the broadcaster to have secured the rights to take footage of these performers in the event. The degree to which the performer will be able to protect and exploit his or her image rights/personality rights and performance rights will vary from country and country. The event organiser will need to secure such rights under the participant contract with the performer. The performer will usually grant such rights in return for a fee, the right to earn prize money, a share of broadcasting or ticket revenue or simply for the right to participate in the event itself.

It should be noted that broadcasting itself is, in most countries, a regulated industry. It may be regulated by legislation and by binding codes of practice. Specialist advice should be sought to ensure that the parties to the broadcasting contract comply with any relevant regulations.

Finally, intellectual property rights will usually arise in the film or sound recording as well as the broadcast of the footage. This is dealt with in the following paragraph in more detail.

13.2 Intellectual Property Rights and Broadcasting

One should be careful not to confuse broadcasting rights (i.e. the right to broadcast an event) with rights in the broadcast itself (i.e. the rights in the recording or transmission). These are two different things.

It is only at the stage where the event is actually recorded or broadcast that any rights of the latter nature arise. At this point, copyright will usually arise in the film or sound recording of the event as well as in the broadcast and/or cable transmission of it[4]. This will of course depend on the copyright law in the country where the recording and transmission take place. Although at the time of entering into the broadcasting contract these rights will not have arisen yet,

---

[4] This will generally be regarded as a creative work capable of protection in its own right.

the contract should deal with the ownership and exploitation of the copyright that arises, as this will be a material issue for the parties.

The initial owner of the copyright will usually be the broadcaster and/or the production house that has actually created the recording. This is because they are the parties that will be deemed to have created the 'work' which gives rise to the copyright.

The event organiser may require that the copyright in the recording and/or broadcast is assigned or licensed to it. In this way, the event organiser can copy and distribute any recording for DVD and video release or grant broadcasting rights to other broadcasters in different territories, for example. If it wishes to do this, terms will need to be included in the contract to this effect. Again, how these rights are dealt with will be a matter of negotiation between the parties and depend on the relative bargaining power of the parties and, to a large extent, on the copyright laws of the country in question.

It is important to remember that where commentary or music is added to the broadcast then there may be additional copyright issues which arise. In the case of commentary, copyright will vest in the commentator him or herself or the broadcaster (by virtue of a contract with the commentator). In the case of music, the broadcaster may have to obtain permission to use the music from a music rights holding body in that country[5].

13.3   The Nature of the Broadcasting Contract

In the broadcasting contract, the event organiser will grant the broadcaster the rights to broadcast the event in a certain defined territory. In return, the broadcaster will usually pay a rights fee, which will vary substantially according to the level of popularity and perceived value of the event.

A sample broadcasting contract is set out in Appendix 11.

13.4   Key Legal Issues

Apart from the general clauses referred to in Chapter 2, the following key issues should be considered:

13.4.1 The Parties

The parties to this contract will usually be the event organiser and the broadcaster itself. As mentioned, the broadcaster will want some assurance from the event organiser that it is in a position to deliver the rights to the broadcaster. It will normally seek this assurance in the form of warranties, which are discussed further below. Likewise, the event organiser will seek a warranty

---

[5] See paragraph 10.3 above.

from the broadcaster that it has authority to enter into the contract. In complex broadcasting arrangements where the rights fees are substantial, the broadcaster may need to demonstrate that it has approval from its board to enter into the contract and that it has sufficient funds to pay the rights fee.

13.4.2 The Event

The parties will need to ensure that they define the subject matter of the broadcast. It may be that the entire event will be broadcast from start to finish. But will this include pre-event and post-event interviews or award ceremonies, for example? Coverage may also be limited to certain parts of the event. If the event is a competition of some kind, it may be that only the final rounds of the competition will be broadcast.

The parties should also discuss and agree the timing as well as, in some cases, the location of the events. This may have both technical and commercial implications. For instance, the broadcaster may wish to ensure that there is sufficient time between intervals or parts of the event to include broadcast sponsorship credits and advertising sales space.

13.4.3 Facilities and Access

The practical mechanics of creating a broadcast will require some consideration by the parties.

The primary audio and/or visual aspects of the broadcast are commonly known as the 'event feed'. The venue itself will usually be the inception point for the creation of the feed. The event organiser will need to consider who will be responsible for the actual production of the feed itself.

There are usually two alternatives in this regard. On the one hand, the event organiser may appoint a production house to create the event feed. The event feed will then be fed on to the various appointed broadcasters under licence for broadcasting in the respective territories. On the other hand, the event organiser may appoint a host broadcaster who will also be responsible for creating the event feed. The host broadcaster will either use its own equipment or else appoint a producer to create the event feed itself.

Where the broadcaster will be producing the event feed itself, it will require full and unrestricted access to the venue and all relevant sites in and around the venue. The broadcaster will need to introduce its own outside broadcast units and equipment to the venue. It will require adequate parking for all its broadcast vans and related equipment. It will need to ensure it has a sufficient power supply and access to the venue before, during and after the event for relevant staff. It will also need to ensure that adequate facilities will be put in place to enable the event to be recorded e.g. gantries, camera platforms, scaffolding etc. Additional facilities may need to be made available for the broadcaster's commentary team, if any. The broadcaster may also wish to secure access for its cameramen to certain areas of the venue e.g. backstage areas, the player tunnel or entrance and changing rooms.

The event organiser may wish to insist that the broadcaster provides feed of the event (including commentary) to various boxes, dining rooms or hospitality tents at the venue. For particular kinds of events, the event organiser may also request that giant screens be erected at the venue for the purposes of relaying live coverage of the event to the attendees.

Even where the event organiser is providing a full feed to the broadcaster for it to use, the broadcaster will usually have some requirements for facilities and access to the venue. For example, at the very least it will seek to ensure rights of access for its commentary team so that it can elaborate on the event feed and create its own style of content.

13.4.4 The Broadcaster's Rights

Provisions should be included in the broadcasting contract that deal specifically with both the medium or delivery system of the broadcast and the specific type of coverage to be provided.

13.4.5 Broadcast Medium

Traditionally broadcasting would be exclusively via terrestrial free-to-air television. However, with the development of new technologies, we have seen the arrival of cable, satellite, pay-per-view, internet and now mobile telephony as mediums for broadcasting. The result is that the parties should define carefully which broadcast mediums will be covered by the contract in question.

Owing to the pace at which new broadcasting mediums are developing in general, the parties should consider how they will deal with any new or developing delivery methods. The event organiser will want to exclude these from the contract so it can further exploit such opportunities as they arise, whilst the broadcaster will want to include these in the definition of 'broadcasting'.

13.4.6 Types of Coverage

The nature of the rights granted to the broadcaster will also be defined by the type of coverage that the broadcaster will choose to adopt. These may include the following:

- Live coverage;
- 'As live' coverage (full coverage of the event but a delayed broadcast, often referred to as a 'replay right');

- magazine packages;
- highlight packages; or
- news footage.

The specific rights will attach to a specific medium of delivery.

The rights may be split into different packages e.g. live coverage of the event via satellite and cable and highlights on standard terrestrial or free-to-air television. The rights may be further sub-divided with reference to exclusivity, duration and territory of the rights being granted.

13.4.7 Exclusivity

Most broadcasting contracts will provide the broadcaster with complete exclusivity within a particular territory for all types of coverage and all broadcast mediums. Exclusive rights tend to be more valuable for event organisers, broadcasters and other commercial partners, such as broadcast sponsors.

Exclusivity may relate to a number of different aspects of the rights.

Exclusivity may attach to the types of coverage as well as the different broadcast mediums. The event organiser may grant one broadcaster exclusive rights in relation to live and delayed broadcast for all broadcast mediums and another broadcaster exclusive rights in relation to highlights and magazine packages for all broadcast mediums, for instance. Alternatively, the event organiser may grant exclusivity to a broadcaster only in respect of certain broadcast mediums.

Although this is essentially a commercial issue to be negotiated between the parties, the parties should take care to define the extent of any exclusivity granted in the contract.

Special news-access agreements, codes of practice or regulations may exist in certain countries to allow for a small amount of footage for the event for the purposes of news reporting[6]. The event organiser may also wish to reserve the right for itself to record footage of the event for news reporting, documentaries or promotional purposes. Whether or not these considerations apply, the parties should set out in the contract what rights other broadcasters have to broadcast the event.

The event organiser may be asked by the broadcaster to give warranties that it will not grant rights to any other third parties which would impact on the ability of the broadcaster to exploit its rights under the contract.

---

[6] In the United Kingdom, the New Sports Access Code provides for access to footage of important events for news purposes amongst UK-based broadcasters. The case of *BBC v BSC* [1991] 3 WLR 174 also established that the fair dealing provisions of the Copyright Design and Patents Act 1988 applies to the use of recorded material from live transmissions for news purposes.

It should also be noted that in some countries or regions the granting of exclusive rights packages may be regarded as anti-competitive. This will depend largely on the nature of the exclusivity provided to the broadcaster and the duration of the grant of the rights. This is a complex subject in its own right and it is advisable to seek specialist advice in this area for the purposes of ensuring compliance with any national or regional directives.

13.4.8 Territory

As in the case with merchandising contracts, the definition of the territory in which the broadcasting rights may be exploited will be of importance.

The event organiser should make it clear in the contract that the broadcasting rights do not extend beyond the territory. Where transmission is via satellite, it may be possible for reception to be obtained by a viewer outside the territory unintentionally. This is sometimes referred to as 'overspill'. Usually the event organiser will acknowledge that such overspill will not amount to a breach of the territorial restrictions included in the contract.

Where a host broadcaster is appointed who will also produce the feed, the event organiser will need to ensure that necessary copyrights are granted to itself so that it can in turn grant rights to broadcasters in other territories.

13.4.9 Term

The contract may cover a particular event, such as the Mandela '4664' concert, or a series of events, such as Formula 1. This will be a matter for negotiation between the parties. It may also be designed to cover an agreed number of transmissions within a certain period of time.

The event organiser will usually want to specify that the broadcasting rights (and any intellectual property rights in the footage itself) will revert to it after the term of the contract.

As mentioned above[7], the duration of the contract will be one of the factors examined by any competition or anti-trust authority in considering whether any grant of rights is anti-competitive.

13.4.10 Secondary Rights

The broadcaster may wish to secure additional rights that go beyond the mere broadcasting of the event. For instance, it may wish to acquire the right to compile DVDs or videos using the footage of the event and then distribute and sell these items within the territory. Or it may wish to grant the right to a mobile

---

[7] See paragraph 13.4.7 above.

phone company to allow certain highlights of the event to be downloaded by its customers. In such a case the event organiser should seek to obtain a royalty on the revenues generated from the exploitation of these rights.

Alternatively, the event organiser may wish to reserve these rights for itself expressly in the contract.

If the rights are defined in general terms, without consideration of these issues, the event organiser may find that the broadcaster has acquired these rights in addition to the rights to broadcast the event.

13.4.11 Rights Fees

The 'rights fee', as it is sometimes known, represents the sum of money paid by the broadcaster to acquire the rights to broadcast the event. The amount will depend on many factors, such as the popularity of the event, the unique nature of the event, its appeal across a diverse audience, the timing of the event and the competition between broadcasters to broadcast the event. The amount will also depend on whether or not the production costs will be covered by the broadcaster. Accordingly, the amount can therefore range from tens of millions of dollars or pounds to nominal consideration.

If the event is sure to find a television audience but is not considered 'hot property', the broadcaster may enter into a barter agreement with the event organiser, in terms of which the former agrees to broadcast the event at no cost to the broadcaster, with perhaps an equal split on advertising revenue.

Another option, usually the least appealing and most expensive for an event organiser, is to purchase airtime directly from the broadcasting station. In this case, the event organiser will be responsible for producing the entire event programme and for selling all the advertising spots.

The contract should clearly set out the terms of payment, including whether or not any tax is payable on the rights fees.

The event organiser will, unsurprisingly, want the rights fee paid upfront in a lump sum. On the other hand, the broadcaster will usually try and negotiate to pay the amount in instalments.

13.4.12 Obligations

a) Broadcaster's Obligations

The event organiser should ensure that the obligations of the broadcaster are described in the contract sufficiently clearly.

The exact nature of the obligations will depend on the complexity of the arrangement with the broadcaster.

If the broadcaster is responsible for producing the feed, this should be spelt out in the contract, particularly if the broadcaster is sourcing out this obligation to a third party producer.

If the broadcaster has undertaken to commit to broadcasting the event at a particular time or for a certain number of hours, this should also be specified in the contract.

As previously mentioned, it is highly likely that there will be statutory and regulatory provisions governing the broadcasting of the event. Although these will no doubt vary from country to country, there should be a general requirement on the broadcaster to comply with these statutory and regulatory obligations. In addition, there should be an obligation on the broadcaster to obtain any consents, licences or clearances that may be necessary to broadcast the event in the manner anticipated.

Owing to the fact that the broadcaster will have de facto control over the broadcast, the event organiser should insist that the broadcaster undertakes not to commit any act which might be prejudicial or defamatory to the name and image of the event organiser or the event in question.

The event organiser may require that the broadcaster provide it with statistics relating to the size, location and profile of the audience in question. It may also require that the broadcaster provide copies of all broadcast coverage for its own purposes.

b) Event Organiser's Obligations

The broadcaster will be looking to include in the contract an obligation on the part of the event organiser to grant the broadcasting rights to the broadcaster, at the very least.

The broadcaster will be unable to comply with its own obligations under the contract unless it is provided with the rights of access to the venue and facilities described in paragraph 13.4.3 above. As a result, the broadcaster is likely to require that these are listed as express obligations in the contract.

In addition to the rights of access already mentioned, the broadcaster may also require access to:

* Team sheets, statistics or biographical information on the participants;
* Key participants, managers and coaches before, during and after the event for the purposes of conducting interviews;
* Backstage, red carpet or dressing room areas for the purposes of conducting these and other interviews.

There may also be obligations on the part of the event organiser to deliver additional rights to the broadcaster which are similar to those usually granted to a sponsor, such as the right to advertising at the venue and in the event programme, the right to receive a certain number of free tickets and the right to use of hospitality facilities at the venue.

13.4.13 Commercial Partners

The event organiser will not only want to protect its commercial partners (i.e. those parties with whom it has entered into commercial contracts) but it will also want to ensure that it can deliver on any rights which it has granted to those commercial partners.

For instance, a title sponsor may require that the event organiser and any broadcaster that is appointed by the event organiser refer to the event using the full and correct title at all times, including in any trailers, credits, commentary, interviews and award ceremonies.

Sponsors of the event may try and seek some assurance from the event organiser as to the extent of coverage given to them. For instance, a sponsor may seek to ensure in the sponsorship contract that the broadcast contains a certain amount or duration of footage of their logos, advertising boards and signage. Event organisers should resist giving these types of assurances, as this may be outside the control of the event organiser. Moreover, many countries have regulations and codes of practice which apply restrictions on the degree to which such references are emphasised in the broadcast[8]. As a result, both the event organiser and the broadcaster will need to ensure that they comply with any restrictions that apply by virtue of relevant regulations or codes of practice.

Notwithstanding the above, the event organiser should still seek an undertaking from the broadcaster that the camera locations will not unnecessarily exclude, obscure or restrict coverage of any advertising boards, signage and logos placed at the venue.

Where the event organiser has granted sponsorship rights which include advertising at the venue for the specific purpose of securing broadcast coverage, it will need to ensure that it can deliver on those rights. For instance, if a sponsor has been given a right for its name to appear on a backboard during interviews, but the broadcaster is unaware of this right and conducts the interview in a slightly different location (without the backboard), the event organiser may be in breach of its contract with the sponsor.

The broadcaster cannot be expected to be aware of all the rights granted to its

---

[8] In the UK, for instance, the Broadcasting Acts 1990 and 1996 will apply, as well as the ITC codes of practice.

commercial partners by the event organiser. It will therefore be incumbent upon the event organiser to make the broadcaster aware of any rights which have been granted to these parties which may be affected by the broadcasting of the event.

13.5   Broadcast Sponsorship

What is broadcast sponsorship?

Broadcast sponsorship usually refers to a situation where the cost of production or transmission is met by an advertiser with a view to promoting its own or another's name, trade mark, image, activities or other commercial interests[9].

The right to appoint a broadcast sponsor will be a matter of negotiation between the event organiser and the broadcaster and will ultimately depend on the bargaining power of the parties.

Event organisers may argue that they own the broadcasting rights and therefore also the right to appoint broadcasting sponsors. On this basis, event organisers sometimes contend that the sponsorship fees paid by a broadcast sponsor should rightfully be paid to them. However, broadcasters tend to argue to the contrary. They believe that once they acquire the rights to broadcast the event, it is their time to sell and therefore they should have the right to appoint broadcast sponsors and enjoy the benefits of any sponsorship fees in order the set-off the costs of production and the costs of acquiring the broadcasting rights. They also argue that ultimately the obligation to comply with broadcasting regulations and codes of practice rests with them and they run the risk of losing their licence or paying heavy fines if they do not comply with such regulations or codes of practice.

Accordingly, the broadcaster will usually insist that it retains the right to appoint broadcast sponsors. The event organiser will try to obtain a right of approval over those broadcast sponsors appointed by the broadcaster or the right to exclude certain categories of sponsors in order to ensure that no broadcast sponsor is appointed which is a competitor of one of the event organiser's own sponsors. The event organiser may also try to secure a right of first refusal in favour of its own sponsors, so that a broadcaster is bound to offer the broadcast sponsorship rights to the existing event sponsors before offering these rights to other third parties.

The event organiser may wish to acquire broadcast sponsorship rights from the broadcaster either by way of payment or a reduction of the rights fee. This can be quite expensive as the broadcaster may ask for a rights fee equivalent to the amount it would have secured from broadcast sponsors. The advantage for the

---

[9]   This is the definition given by the UK's Independent Television Commission (ITC) in its code on programme sponsorship. The ITC was established under the Broadcasting Act 1990.

event organiser in acquiring broadcast sponsorship rights is that it can then offer an integrated package of sponsorship rights (including both event sponsorship and broadcast sponsorship) to its own sponsors.

The broadcast sponsorship contract itself will usually be between the broadcaster and the sponsor and be much like a regular sponsorship contract[10]. The contract should identify the parties, the rights being granted, the degree of exclusivity, the duration, the territory and the fee involved.

Under the contract, the sponsor will pay a fee to the broadcaster and in turn the broadcaster will grant the sponsor the right to sponsor the agreed transmission using what is generally referred to as the 'sponsor's credits'. This is the agreed visual and/or audio-visual recorded sequence usually incorporating the trade mark and logo of the sponsor together with associated words which are also agreed between the parties.

As mentioned, in many countries, the sponsorship of broadcasting is regulated. For instance, there may be regulations or codes of practice governing the type, nature and extent of the credits which a sponsor can receive. These regulations and codes are generally designed to protect the editorial independence of the broadcaster and the integrity of the broadcast itself[11]. The parties will therefore need to ensure that they comply with the regulatory regime in place. This will usually be recorded as an express term of the contract.

If the sponsor is creating or commissioning visual, audio-visual and/or oral credits then the issue of ownership of the intellectual property rights in such credits may arise. Usually the sponsor will want to retain or acquire the copyrights and related intellectual property rights in such credits. If so, it will need to grant a licence to the broadcaster to use and broadcast the credits. In order to avoid possible disputes at a later point, provisions relating to these issues should be inserted in the contract.

13.6   Licensing of Broadcast Footage

This section briefly deals with additional terms which may be relevant when licensing footage of an event. Footage can be licensed for a number of purposes. It can be licensed to other broadcasters for broadcast in different countries, to third parties for the purposes of manufacturing and selling DVDs and videos, to mobile phone companies for the purposes of producing clips for distribution

---

[10] See Chapter 3 on Sponsorship Contracts and the sample contracts provided in Appendix 1A and 1B.

[11] For example, in the United Kingdom, the ITC code on sponsorship requires that programme integrity must not be distorted for commercial purposes. In this respect the sponsor is not permitted any influence on either the content or the scheduling of a programme in such a way as to affect the editorial independence of the broadcaster (see Rule 9 of the code). Rule 10 of the same code also prohibits the undue prominence of goods or services in a programme.

to customers, to the event organiser for promotional purposes or to the event organiser's commercial partners, for example.

The licensing of the footage will usually be subject to a separate licensing contract between the relevant parties mentioned above.

13.6.1 Key Legal Issues

a) Parties

It is important to establish at the outset that the party purporting to license the footage has the right to do so in the first place. The party granting the licence will usually either be the event organiser or the broadcaster. Owing to the fact that the footage will be protected by copyright in most cases, the licensor of the footage must be in a position to show that it has the right and title to license the footage. Since copyright in the footage will usually vest in the broadcaster or producer in the first instance, the event organiser will be expected to show that copyright in the footage has been assigned or licensed to it if the event organiser is the party on-licensing the footage.

b) Rights

The terms of the contract must indicate what rights are being granted in the footage.

Assuming that the event organiser is licensing the rights in the footage to a broadcaster, then the broadcaster will require the right to broadcast the footage concerned. It may also require the right to:

- Copy, alter or edit the footage;
- Appoint broadcast sponsors and insert advertising[12];
- Sub-license news clips or excerpts from the footage to third parties; or
- Produce trailers and still photographs for promotional use.

The licensee will also want assurance that the event organiser has obtained all the necessary consents and clearances from third parties in respect of the footage. For instance, the footage may contain commentary, music, graphics, logos and trade marks, the rights in which are owned by third parties. Likewise, if the footage contains performances which are protected by copyright legislation, the event organiser will need to have acquired consent in order to on-licence that footage[13].

---

[12] See paragraph 13.5.

[13] In the UK, certain performances are protected by copyright law under Part II of the CDPA 1988. Sports performances are not protected in this manner.

c) Territory and Exclusivity

As in the broadcasting contract itself, the territory for the use of the licensed footage should be clearly defined in the licensing contract. If the licence is exclusive to a particular territory, that should also be stated clearly.

d) Duration

The duration of the licence will depend on the needs of the licensee and will be a matter of negotiation between the parties. It may be restricted to a specific time period or a certain number of transmissions within that time period.

e) Fees

If the rights are being licensed to a broadcaster, a licence fee will usually be payable by the broadcaster to the event organiser. This may be payable in a lump sum or in instalments. If the footage has not yet been created by the time of the execution of the licensing contract, the broadcaster will not wish to make any payment until such time as the footage has been created or delivered to it in acceptable form.

If the footage is being exploited by a third party for the purposes of DVD, video or mobile phone distribution, the financial terms will vary. These terms will usually include the payment of an advance, royalty payments on sales and/or royalties on revenues generated from downloads[14].

If the event organiser is going to be receiving a royalty, it should impose suitable accounting obligations on the licensee[15].

f) Obligations

The primary obligation on the part of the event organiser is to make available the footage to the licensee for it to use. The parties will usually agree a date for delivery of the footage. Time may well be of the essence in such a contract, so that if delivery is late, the licensee may reserve for itself a right to terminate the contract.

In addition, the licensee will expect the footage to be in a suitable form and of an appropriate standard, both technically and commercially. If the licensee is a broadcaster in particular, the exact requirements of the broadcaster in this regard should be discussed and documented. Where the footage is not suitable or appropriate, the event organiser should be given the opportunity to alter or amend the footage and re-submit it to the licensee without being in breach of the contract. If the licensee still believes that the footage is not suitable or

---

[14] See Chapter 12 on Merchandising Contracts for payment variations.
[15] See paragraph 12.3.12 above in relation to accounting provisions.

appropriate, it will usually seek a right to terminate the contract and obtain a refund for any rights fees paid to the event organiser. Alternatively, the licensee may wish to take over the production of the footage. In such a case it will seek to deduct the costs of putting the footage into the appropriate form from any further fees payable to the event organiser under the contract or recover those costs directly from the event organiser.

13.7 Conclusion

A broadcasting deal remains the cherry on the cake for an event organiser. Not only is it a major source of revenue (depending on the nature and standing on the event) but it has the potential to bring an event into the homes of people in far flung corners of the earth. For the event organiser, two of the key issues will be the right to exploit the footage commercially and ownership of the footage itself. The broadcaster will want to ensure that, at the very least, it is able to obtain access to the venue and if necessary to the participants so that it can secure good quality footage of the event. For the value of the broadcast will depend to a large extent on the ability to obtain such good quality footage.

CHAPTER FOURTEEN

Event Management Contracts

The rights holder (i.e. the entity owning or controlling the rights to the event, if any) may not necessarily wish to actually organise and stage the event itself. It may wish to appoint an event manager to do this. Event managers will vary in size and nature. Some event managers consist of a small enterprise with one or two personnel who specialise in organising and staging functions such as weddings and parties. Other event management companies specialise in organising and staging corporate team-building events. Then there are those companies who specialise in the management of large-scale events, such as concerts, sports events and international conferences. As each event will be different in nature, the array of services to be provided by the event manager may vary substantially.

Two precedent event management contracts have been included in Appendix 12 to cover the situations described above. One is a simple set of terms and conditions that could be used by an event management company for a small function. The other is a comprehensive contract to govern the management of a large-scale event. The legal issues described below will be of relevance to both potentially.

14.1 The Nature of the Event Management Contract

The contract between the rights holder and the event manager is essentially a contract for the supply of services. The event manager will usually provide a range of event management services in return for payment of a fee. As such, the terms and conditions set out in Chapter 7 will be relevant to this contract.

14.2 Key Legal Issues

14.2.1 Appointment

The contract should record that the event organiser appoints the event management company to be the event manager for the event. The event should, for the sake of certainty, be defined in the definitions section of the contract.

The appointment is usually exclusive, but the parties should nonetheless record that this is the case, if indeed that is the intention.

14.2.2 Term

The parties should define the term of the contract. The contract may cover a single event or a series of events.

14.2.3 Services

The parties should record in some detail the exact services to be provided by the event manager. Usually the services are described in a schedule to the contract. They may include the following:

- Arranging all aspects of venue preparation and management, including venue hire, branding and signage, decorations, communications, security, stewards, turnstile operators, event staff and all necessary equipment;
- Determining the style, content and format of the event[1];
- Arranging all matters in relation to event personnel, officials and participants, including travel and accommodation;
- Ensuring the attendance of first-aid and medical officers and equipment, where necessary;
- Managing all aspects of hospitality and catering in relation to the event, including civic hospitality, VIP hospitality and catering, participant and staff catering and media catering;
- Organising any prize giving or award ceremony, including prize money, medals, gifts and 'goodie bags';
- Liaison with all necessary local authorities, including the police and traffic authorities;
- Liaison with all venue announcers, production managers, camera crew and commentators;
- Ensuring the provision of an accurate results service;
- Arranging for the production of all necessary printed materials for the event, including accreditation, event stationery, ticket printing and distribution, programme production, invitations and certificates;
- Arranging all necessary production and broadcasting facilities, such as sound, lighting, electricity, scoreboard facilities, platforms and scaffolding, where necessary;
- Managing arrangements with the press and media, including press conference facilities, photographers and interview facilities; and
- Managing all aspects of event entertainment, including liaison with performers

---

[1] The rights holder may wish to retain these rights and have the event manager act in accordance with its directions in this regard.

and managers, arranging props, providing backstage and changing facilities, stages and lighting.

Apart from these typical event management services, it is not uncommon for an event manager to also undertake, or be asked to undertake, the following additional services in relation to the event:

- Arranging insurance in relation to the event, particularly general/public liability insurance;
- Conducting promotion and marketing of the event, including liaison with the press and media, PR and the production of promotional materials;
- Arranging all necessary accounting and legal advice in relation to the event, where necessary;
- Liaising with the commercial partners of the event organiser and, in particular, managing the delivery of the commercial rights to the commercial partners;
- Assisting the event organiser in combating any ambush marketing activities, including dealing with any unauthorised advertising and merchandising activities;
- Ensuring that adequate facilities are provided for doping control and disciplinary enquiries;
- Ensuring that the venue is cleaned and all litter is removed after the event;
- Liaising with all relevant governing bodies regarding the event and obtaining any necessary sanctions, where relevant; and
- Preparing and managing an event budget.

The nature of event management is such that the scope of the services may change from time to time. The parties should provide that the schedule of services may be amended by agreement between the parties in writing. However, if the scope of the services is amended substantially during the contract or additional services are added to the schedule, the event manager will be expected to request an increase in the fee. For this reason, it is again advisable to specify the exact nature of the services to be provided, so that there can be little doubt as to what is included in the services.

14.2.4 Payment

As consideration for the event management services to be provided by the event manager, the rights holder will be expected to pay a fee. The event manager will try to ensure that this is paid up-front in one lump sum usually. On the other hand, the rights holder will want to pay the amount in instalments, particularly if it is waiting for funds to come in from other commercial partners, such as sponsors. It will also want to withhold the final payment until after the event has taken place. This is a matter of negotiation between the parties.

The fee is sometimes calculated as a percentage of the event budget. Percentages tend to range anywhere from 10 to 25% of the event budget. If payment is based on a percentage of the event budget, the parties should agree the event budget when they enter into negotiations.

Some event management companies will charge a fee based on the number of hours that it takes to manage the event. In such a case, the rights holder should negotiate a cap on the amount, because it can be the case that hours mount up unbeknown to the rights holder and the rights holder is left with a large bill at the end of the event which was not anticipated. The event manager should also be asked to account for the time spent and to keep a daily dairy in such a case, to avoid dispute at a later point.

14.2.5 Accounting

One aspect that parties should deal with in detail is accounting.

It is inadvisable to manage an event without an event budget. The event budget will be the budget from which funds will be paid to organise and stage the event. Whilst, the rights holder will be the party who ultimately benefits from the revenue generated from the exploitation of the commercial rights in relation to the event, it will also usually be the party who is funding the organisation and staging of the event. Therefore, it will want to draft or approve the event budget.

At the same time, it is very difficult for the event manager to manage the event properly without some control over the event budget. The event manager will be expected to arrange flowers and pay the florist, appoint and pay a caterer, pay a deposit for the venue hire etc.

The event budget should be agreed between the rights holder and the event manager and should be based on set quotations obtained from vendors and other relevant third parties, where possible. A separate account should be established for the management of the event budget. The event manager will want to ensure that it is able to make payments from the event budget to various third parties quickly and easily. The rights holder should permit the event manager to make these payments provided that provision has been made for these amounts in the event budget. The event manager should not be permitted to incur any expenditure in excess of the itemised amounts provided for in the event budget without the prior written consent of the rights holder.

Notwithstanding the operation of an agreed event budget, it is likely that there will be small expenses and costs which are not itemised in the budget. It is not necessarily practical for the event manager to have to obtain consent for incurring such expenditure. The rights holder may consider including a provision that expenses below a certain amount can be paid out of a 'sundry expenses' provision in the event budget without its consent.

The rights holder should insist on being provided, at regular intervals, information regarding the progress of the event organisation, expenditure incurred to date, estimates of any likely variations to the event budget and copies of all relevant contracts, invoices and receipts.

If the event manager has complete control over the account for the event budget, it should be required to maintain full and proper books of account in this regard and to allow the event organiser to inspect and, if necessary, audit the books of account. The event organiser should also be entitled to request copies of all accounting records and related documentation on reasonable notice.

14.2.6 Event Manager's Obligations

The primary obligation on the part of the event manager is to provide the defined event management services in a professional manner and with the necessary skill and expertise as is required for an event of the nature in question.

The rights holder should also seek to obtain a warranty from the event manager that it will organise and stage the event in accordance with all relevant legislation, regulations, rules or codes of practice imposed by any local, national or international authority. This should include, for the avoidance of doubt, any health and safety regulations. If the rights holder is to be responsible for obtaining any specific licences, consents or sanctions, this should be clearly stated in the contract.

The rights holder will want to ensure that it has regular meetings with the event manager. The rights holder should seek to make it an express term of the contract that the event manager will make itself available at all reasonable times and on reasonable notice for the purposes of meeting with the rights holder and providing all necessary consultation and advice in relation to the event.

In addition to the above, terms may be included in the contract requiring the event manager to:

- Comply with the reasonable instructions of the rights holder in relation to the organisation and staging of the event;
- Provide an undertaking that it will not make any statements and take part in any activities which are or may be prejudicial or detrimental to the name, image and reputation of the rights holder or the event;
- Provide an undertaking that it will not issue any press releases or press statements in relation to the rights holder or the event without the prior written approval of the rights holder;

- Ensure that sufficient personnel of suitable levels of experience are available at all times to carry out the services to be provided by the event manager;
- Agree that it will not itself sign any contracts in relation to the event and shall refer all contracts to the rights holder for consideration and execution[2]; and
- Agree that it will not hold itself out as having authority to bind the rights holder in any way[3].

14.2.7 Rights Holder's Obligations

The primary obligations on the part of the rights holder will be to pay the event management fees to the event manager on the dates agreed in the contract, provide and agree an event budget for the purposes of organising and staging the event, and keep the event manager fully informed of all relevant matters relating to the event.

In addition to the above, terms may be included in the contract requiring the rights holder to:

- Obtain all licences, consents and sanctions necessary to organise and stage the event or, if this is agreed as an obligation on the part of the event manager, assist the event manager in procuring any such authorisations where necessary;
- Provide a written statement confirming the event manager's appointment under the contract; and
- Provide an undertaking that it will not engage any other party to manage the event or provide the services (as defined).

14.2.8 Intellectual Property Rights

For large events, where the rights holder has developed intellectual property rights in relation to the event and wishes to protect those rights, the rights holder will wish to license the use of the intellectual property rights to the event manager. The most important of these rights will be the use of trade marks. The licensing of the trade marks will usually be on a royalty-free non-exclusive basis. The trade marks in question should be attached as a schedule to the contract.

In this way, the event manager will be able to use the marks in carrying out its various activities. This will be particularly important if the event manager is producing any materials for the promotion and marketing of the event.

The event manager may be asked to expressly acknowledge that such rights belong to the rights holder and that it will not do anything to interfere with the rights holder's ownership of these rights.

---

[2] See 14.2.10 below.
[3] See 14.2.10 below.

It is quite likely that the event manager will also be required to notify the rights holder if it becomes aware of any infringements by third parties of these rights and assist the rights holder in preventing such infringements.

14.2.9 Insurance

As is the case with all events, insurance is likely to be a material issue for the parties. It is a basic commercial principle that insurance follows risk. Whilst it may be expected that the rights holder should be the party required to take out insurance in relation to the event, the event manager does bear the risk of claims against it from third parties simply by virtue of the degree of control it exercises over the production of the event. As such, the event manager should look to take out its own insurance in relation to the event, or require that it is noted as an interested party on any insurance policies taken out by the rights holder. The parties should consider this issue and record their agreement in this respect in the contract, including which party shall be responsible for the costs of any notations on existing policies.

14.2.10 Approvals

Whilst the event manager will have de facto control over the day to day planning and operational aspects of the event, in general the rights holder will want to have right of approval over certain important issues.

The parties will need to consider whether or not the event manager should have the capacity to enter into contracts in its own name, or on behalf of the rights holder, in relation to the event. Where the event manager is organising a function or party, the rights holder may wish for the event manager to negotiate and execute contracts with third parties (such as caterers, decorators, suppliers etc), provided that expenditure incurred under these contracts falls within the agreed event budget.

However, where the event is a large event involving a number of complex contracts, the rights holder may wish to specify that all contracts will be entered into by it, notwithstanding the fact that the event manager may have negotiated the terms of such contract on its behalf.

In most cases, the rights holder will at the very least want to be aware of all contracts entered into by the event manager with third parties and perhaps have the opportunity of authorising those contracts. For large events, where there may be a number of contracts, the parties may agree a suitable level of materiality e.g. all contracts over a certain value will require authorisation.

In general, the event manager will want to avoid entering into long, complex agreements with third parties because when it becomes a party to those contracts it will inevitably be assuming risks under those contracts in its own capacity. It will want the rights holder to enter into the contracts with the third parties directly, or alternatively it will want to make it clear that it is entering into such contracts only as agent on behalf of the rights holder.

Whatever the parties agree in this regard, this is an important legal and practical issue and the terms should be recorded in the contract for the avoidance of doubt.

In addition to the above, where the event manager produces any promotional material in relation to the event (and particularly when it uses any trade marks belonging to the rights holder), it should be required to submit such materials to the rights holder for approval. These materials could include posters, brochures, invitations and the like.

14.2.11 Indemnity and Liability

The event manager will usually assume control over the staging of the event. In the event that the rights holder incurs costs or losses as result of a claim by a third party in relation to the negligent acts or omissions of the event manager, the rights holder will want to obtain an indemnity from the event manager in respect of those costs or losses.

In addition, if the event manager has control over security at the venue, the rights holder may wish to seek an indemnity for any costs or losses it incurs as a result of a claim by a third party for loss or damage to property as a result of the acts or omissions of the event manager.

If the rights holder has to terminate the contract because of a breach of the contract by the event manager, it may have to cancel or postpone the event. There is a very real possibility that it will incur losses in such circumstances. The event manager will seek to exclude all liability for indirect or 'consequential' losses (as they are sometimes known) arising out of the contract. However, the rights holder may consider that this is unacceptable by virtue of the fact that any such consequential losses may be substantial. As a result this issue may be fiercely negotiated[4].

14.2.12 Termination

Apart from the standard termination clauses already discussed[5], the parties should consider consequences of termination, as these can be far-reaching.

---

[4] Underlying this issue is the general legal principle established in many countries that one can only claim for losses actually caused by the unlawful actions of another. A sufficiently close causal relationship will generally need to be established between the unlawful actions of the event manager and the loss actually incurred. In addition, the rights holder will generally have an obligation to take steps to reduce or mitigate its losses e.g. appointing another event manager as soon as possible.

[5] See paragraph 2.3.8 above.

If the contract is terminated prior to or during the event, the rights holder will need to be assured that the event can still be staged, if at all possible. In the first instance, it should require that the event manager return all documents relating to the organisation and staging of the event to it upon termination. The event manager may insist that any documents prepared by it in this respect belong to it and, under the law of copyright, it may be correct in this regard. The rights holder may get around this by requiring in the contract that any such documents drawn up by the event manager will belong to the rights holder and the event manager will assign any copyright and any other relevant intellectual property rights in such documents to the rights holder on demand.

Secondly, the rights holder will be concerned about the performance of certain contracts between the event manager and third parties in relation to the event. If the rights holder has entered into the contracts directly with the third parties, this should not be a problem. However, if the event manager has entered into the contracts with the third parties, the rights holder will not be in a position to enforce those contracts directly. In addition, it will not have an established relationship with those third parties.

In order to deal with this, the rights holder should insist that a term be included in the contract that in the event of termination of the contract, any contracts with third parties should be assigned or transferred to the rights holder by the event manager[6]. In order to ensure that this clause is effective, the rights holder will need to stipulate that in all contracts with third parties, the event manager should have the right to assign or transfer the contract to the rights holder.

Finally, if the contract terminates, the rights holder will want to ensure that the licence to use its intellectual property rights also terminates immediately.

14.2.13 Appointment of Sub-contractors

In the case of large events, the event manager may wish to appoint a sub-contractor to carry out certain of the services. The rights holder may resist this, on the basis that the contract is personal to the event manager and the reason that the rights holder appointed the event manager is because it wanted the event manager to carry out the services. The parties may agree a compromise, in terms of which the rights holder may have the right to approve the appointment of any sub-contractors. In general, if the appointment of the sub-contractor is going to assist with the successful organisation and staging of the event, the rights holder will not object to this.

---

[6] In strict legal terms, this will usually require a contract of novation, in which it is stipulated that the rights holder will step into the shoes of the event manager with respect to the contract.

14.3   Event Manager Terms and Conditions

A comprehensive contract of the type provided in the Appendix 12A may not necessarily be appropriate for a company that is providing event management services for a small function, such as a wedding, party or exhibition.

Event management companies who specialise in these sorts of events often simply require a basic terms and conditions of business which they can simply attach to a quotation and give to a customer who wishes to engage their services[7].

Although this can be an effective and easy way of doing business, there is often uncertainty around when, or indeed if, a contract has been entered into between the customer and the event manager.

In practice, the customer will usually approach the event manager and discuss his or her requirements for the event, after which he or she will ask for a written quotation. The provision of the quotation will generally be regarded in law as an invitation to do business (or an 'invitation to negotiate', as it is known in the United States) and not an offer to contract. The terms and conditions should clarify this. If the quotation is accepted by the customer, he or she should be asked to sign the terms and conditions of business and return same to the event manager. The signing of the terms and conditions of business and the provision of this document to the event manager should be regarded as a formal offer. The event manager should then also sign the terms and conditions. This should be regarded as an acceptance of the offer and a legal and binding contract will now be in place.

What often occurs in practice is that the event manager will be asked to provide a written quotation, following initial discussions between the parties. The event manager will provide the quotation together with the proposed terms and conditions of business. The customer will then verbally request that the event manager go ahead and provide the services for the event. The customer will not sign the terms and conditions and the event manager will either choose not to insist that they are signed or will simply forget to insist that they are signed. The event manager will then proceed with the organisation and staging of the event. When disputes later arise, questions will generally be asked as to:

- whether or not there is indeed a contract in place between the parties; and
- whether or not the terms and conditions of business will still be valid and binding as between the parties.

The answer to the first question is usually relatively simple. There will be a partly verbal, partly written contract in place between the parties. This is because

---

[7]   The customer will be the 'rights holder' in this case, although he or she will not usually be referred to as such.

there will have been a verbal offer from the customer when the quotation was accepted. There will also have been an express and/or implied acceptance of that offer by virtue of the fact that the event manager has agreed to provide, and has provided, some or all of the services. There will also have been an agreement on the price (by virtue of the written quotation) and agreement on the services to be provided (either because a breakdown of the services will have been provided in the quotation itself or this will have been agreed during the discussions which took place initially).

The second question is not quite as straightforward. Will the written terms and conditions be regarded as valid and binding as between the parties?

The key legal question in this case is usually this: can it be said that both the parties intended for the terms and conditions to apply[8]?

If the quotation indicates clearly that the services will be provided (or the quotation is provided) subject to the attached terms and conditions, and these terms and conditions have been provided to the customer, the event manager may be able to successfully argue that, even though the terms and conditions were not signed, it was indeed intended by both the parties that the terms and conditions of business would govern their relationship.

If the quotation does not clearly indicate that the services will be provided (or the quotation is provided) subject to the terms and conditions, or if no reference has been made to the terms and conditions at all, and the customer then argues that he was unaware of the existence of the terms and conditions, the event manager will generally have a much tougher mountain to climb in proving that the terms and conditions should govern their relationship.

Accordingly, it is advisable for event managers to avoid the above situation and insist on the customer signing and returning the terms and conditions. The effect of this is also that the customer is more likely to read through the terms and conditions and comply with them.

A second issue which often arises in these simpler contracts is the issue of payments to third parties. For small functions, a comprehensive event budget may not have been agreed with the customer. There may not be a fund from which suppliers (such as caterers, florists etc) can be paid. In such a case, often the event manager will contract with a third party supplier and will request that payment be made by the customer. The customer may not pay the supplier timeously or, worse still, refuse to pay the supplier for some reason. The event

---

[8] This test will vary from country to country.

manager may then be in breach of its contract with the supplier. In addition, the event organiser could face claims from the supplier for outstanding payments, even if the customer is ultimately to blame for failing to pay and if the event manager is contracting as agent for, and on behalf of, the customer[9].

There are a number of ways to avoid this.

Firstly, the event manager could insist that the customer contracts directly with the third party suppliers. The event manager will source the supplier and negotiate with it, but it will insist that the customer actually contracts with the supplier itself.

Secondly, the event manager could insist on payment of a lump sum to cover payments to third party suppliers. The event manager will have agreed in preliminary planning discussions what kind of suppliers will be necessary to organise and stage the event and will in most cases be aware of the approximate costs of engaging those suppliers from past experience.

Thirdly, the event manager could insist on receiving payment from a customer in respect of a specific contract with a supplier before actually entering into a contract with that supplier.

Another issue which regularly arises in the organisation and staging of smaller functions, such as wedding and parties, is that of damage to property. Event managers often report that a hall has been damaged, props have been stolen and furniture and equipment has been ruined. One event manager even reported that pot plants had been stolen from the venue!

If any of the equipment or props belongs to the event manager, it should seek to include an indemnity from the customer in the contract to cover for damage to, or loss of, such property. This indemnity should cover damage or loss to such property howsoever caused (i.e. it should not be limited to damage or loss of property caused by the customer). Damage to the venue itself will usually be covered by a deposit for the hire of the venue, which will be non-returnable in the event of damage. If the deposit has been paid by the customer to the venue owner directly, this will not usually be a problem. If the deposit has been paid by the event manager to the venue owner, the event manager will want to ensure that it is refunded any shortfall by the customer in the event that part of the deposit is held by the venue owner. Either way, the event manager should ensure that it is a term of the contract that the customer will be responsible for any damage to the venue by attendees at the function.

---

[9] In such a case, the event manager may in turn have a claim against the customer for breach of contract.

14.4   Conclusion

The role of an event manager can range from organising a small party or function to the staging of a series of large international competitions. For these reasons, two separate forms of sample contracts have been provided for this chapter.

In either case, the issues are likely to be the same. Issues such as the control and management of the event budget, the ability of the event manager to enter into binding agreements in relation to the event, and the exact nature of the event management services to be provided are likely to give rise to a dispute if not clarified with precision in the contract.

CHAPTER FIFTEEN

Souvenir Programme Production Contracts

For medium to large-scale events, it is often necessary or desirable to produce an official guide or souvenir programme for the event. This is particularly the case where you will have a large number of attendees at the event.

There are a number of reasons for this.

Firstly, it is a good way for an event organiser to create additional revenue from the event. Although the cost of the official programme will usually be fairly insignificant in the greater scheme of things, if a large number of people are attending the event (perhaps over a few days) the revenue generated from the sales of the official programme can accumulate quickly.

Secondly, it presents an additional marketing opportunity, not only for the event organiser but also for its commercial partners. The event organiser can sell additional branding and advertising opportunities to an event sponsor or official supplier, for instance. Alternatively, the event organiser can include these additional branding and advertising rights in the overall package to the commercial partner to make the package more attractive to them.

Thirdly, a well-produced glossy programme can help to create a good impression of the event for attendees, participants and media at the event.

Finally, the event organiser can use the official programme as a means of distributing information on the event itself, on the participants in the event and on the commercial partners.

15.1 The Nature of the Souvenir Production Contract

In the souvenir programme production contract the event organiser will contract with a third party (usually a graphic designer or publishing company - hereinafter for ease of reference simply referred to as 'the production house'), in terms of which the latter will agree to provide certain services to the event organiser in exchange for a fee.

This type of contract is really a combination of a merchandising licence agreement and a supplier agreement. On the one hand, the event organiser will be licensing certain rights to the production house (including the right to use the event marks) and the production house will be producing a product that is similar to event merchandise. On the other hand, the production house will also usually be supplying services to the event organiser, such as the marketing and selling of the official programme.

Apart from the contents of this chapter, the reader should therefore also have regard to the contents of Chapters 7 and 12 dealing with supplier and merchandising contracts respectively.

A sample Souvenir Programme Production Contract is set out in Appendix 13.

15.2 Key Legal Issues

The key issues identified below should be dealt with in the contract.

15.2.1 Appointment and Grant of Rights

The production house will usually be expressly appointed as the company that will be providing the services, namely the production, marketing and selling of the official programme. This is essentially a grant of rights, in that the company will be granted the right (usually the exclusive right) to produce, market and sell the official programme. It will also acquire the right to use the event marks in relation to the programme, including the name and logos of the event.

The production house may seek to obtain additional rights in relation to the event, including the following:

- The right to use the name, image and biographical details of those participating in the event (the event organiser will need to have acquired these rights in a participation contract with the participants);
- The right to a certain number of free tickets for the event;
- The right to hospitality at the event;
- The right to sell advertising in the official programme (see paragraph 15.2.3 below); or
- The right to advertise its own business in the official programme.

In some cases, the production house may also request the right to sub-license various activities to a third party e.g. marketing, distribution, typesetting etc. If this is the case, the event organiser may wish to insist on approving the identity of such third parties and/or insisting that such third parties expressly agree to abide by the terms and conditions of the contract between the event organiser and the production house.

15.2.2 The Services

As in the case where any third party is providing services for the event, the services will need to be clearly defined in the contract. These can be detailed in the body of the contract or in a schedule or rider at the back of the contract.

The parties should define the exact nature of the official programme that will be produced for the event. For example, the parties should agree on the look and feel of the programme, the size of the programme, the length of the programme, the content of the programme and the sale price of the programme.

One of the most important aspects to be agreed is the date for the production and delivery of the official programme. Clearly in this contract time will be of the essence, because if the programme is not produced and delivered in time for the event, the whole purpose of the programme will be defeated.

Usually the event organiser will want the production house to sell advertising space in the official programme. If this is the case, the production house will seek to secure a commission, or a share of the revenues, in relation to such sales. The event organiser should expressly provide in the contract that the production house will use its own personnel to conduct the marketing and sale of advertising space.

In many cases the event organiser will also want the production house to use its own personnel to market and sell the programme at the venue and other locations in and around the venue. Some production companies are able to provide this service. If they are not able to, either the event organiser or the production house will have to hire temporary personnel to conduct these activities.

Either the event organiser or the production house will need to ensure that it has any necessary consents to sell the official programme at various locations outside the venue. This usually involves obtaining a temporary licence from the local authorities at the cost of a small fee.

15.2.3 Consideration/Payment

There are a number of different payment mechanisms in a souvenir production contract, depending on the type and extent of the services to be provided by the production house.

The most common form of payment is royalty system, whereby the production house will pay a portion of the revenue generated by the official programme to the event organiser.

Remember that there are potentially two revenue streams arising from the official programme. The royalty can be based on a percentage of the revenue generated from the sale of the actual programme itself or from the sale of advertising space in the programme, or both.

The percentage paid will depend on the bargaining power between the parties and the expected revenue arising from the above activities. It is essentially a matter of negotiation between the respective parties.

In the event that a royalty is paid to the event organiser, the parties will need to define whether or not the royalty is payable on gross or net revenues. If it is to be paid on net revenues, the parties should agree up-front on the nature of costs that can be deducted from the gross revenue in order to arrive at the net revenue figure. This will eliminate any disputes arising at a later point in this regard.

If the production house is simply producing the official programme and is either not selling advertising space or there is to be no advertising in the official programme at all, payment may be in the form of a set fee to be paid by the event organiser based on the services provided. An additional commission may be added to the set fee based on sales of the programme if such sales are undertaken by the personnel of the company.

15.2.4 Advertising

Even if the event organiser does not wish to sell advertising space to third parties in the official programme, it will usually want to reserve advertising space in the programme for itself and for commercial partners, such as sponsors and official suppliers. It can either sell these additional branding and advertising opportunities directly to the commercial partners or, as is usually the case, combine them as additional rights in the rights packages sold to the commercial partners.

If the production house is going to sell advertising space in the official programme, the event organiser should stipulate that the production house will not sell such space to any competitor of one of the event commercial partners.

The event organiser may also want to take the opportunity to advertise its own or related businesses in the official programme.

15.2.5 Right of Approval

It is common for the event organiser to seek right of approval over the final version of the official programme (including editorial copy, layout and advertising) before going to print. The production house will be on a tight deadline and in most cases will therefore insist on obtaining feedback within a certain period of time, failing which the final version will be deemed to be approved.

15.2.6 Accounting

As mentioned in paragraph 15.2.2 above, the event organiser and production house may decide to base the latter's remuneration on the revenue generated from the sale of the official programme and/or the sale of advertising therein.

In such a case the production house will be the party managing the sales. It will contract with advertisers. It will also collect the revenue from the sale of the programmes by the sellers of the programme. It will then pay a percentage of those sales to the event organiser. Accordingly, the event organiser should insist on a provision in the contract stipulating that the production house must keep and maintain separate books of account in respect of the sales. The event organiser should also insist on having access to those books of account and the right to request an audit of those books of account if necessary.

15.2.7 Termination

Owing to the fact that the date for the production and delivery of the official programme will be crucial to the event organiser, the event organiser should expressly reserve the right to terminate the contract immediately if the official programme is not produced and delivered by that date. This makes 'time of the essence', so to speak[1].

The event organiser should also make it clear that in such circumstances it will be able to appoint any other third party to produce the programme. As a matter of law, once the contract is terminated the event organiser will have this right, but it is always best to spell this out in the contract.

15.2.8 Intellectual Property Rights

The production house will usually be the party who is the ultimate author and creator of the official programme. Accordingly, under copyright law it will be the owner of the content in the official programme[2], unless the event organiser has written and provided parts of the content for the company (e.g. an editorial piece) in which case the ownership of that part of the content will vest in the event organiser.

If the event organiser wishes to own the copyright in the content of the official programme, it will need to include a term in the contract recording that the copyright will be assigned to the event organiser.

In many cases, the event organiser may not wish to actually acquire copyright in the content of the official programme. It may only wish to use the content from time to time. If so, it will be sufficient for the production house to grant a licence to the event organiser to use such content as and when it wishes. Such a licence is usually granted on a royalty-free basis in perpetuity.

---

[1] See paragraph 2.3.8(e)(iv) above.
[2] This is the position in the United States, United Kingdom, South Africa and most European countries.

15.2.9 Indemnity

The production house will be in control of the content of the official programme, notwithstanding any right of approval that the event organiser has over the final copy. As such, the event organiser will usually seek to obtain an indemnity for any losses it may suffer as a result of claims against it arising from the content of the official programme. This will cover the event organiser in the event of any material which is defamatory, libellous or slanderous.

15.3 Conclusion

An official programme can play a surprisingly important role in an event. Not only does it generate revenue, but it can also give an impressive air to the event. In addition, it can be a useful tool in communicating information on the event itself and promoting the commercial partners, such as sponsors and suppliers. As such, it is sensible to have a sound contract in place governing the production of the official programme. The existence of such a contract will go some distance towards ensuring that the expectations of the respective parties to the contract are met.

Appendices

Precedents

Notes:

1. These sample contracts propose potential terms for consideration when formulating a contract between relevant parties for an event. Local advice should always be taken in finalising the contract and each contract should be tailored to account for unique circumstances which may be present in a particular case.

2. Square brackets have been inserted to emphasise certain terms which may or may not be appropriate given the circumstances of a particular case or to simply indicate that further information should be provided.

APPENDIX 1A

SHORT FORM SPONSORSHIP CONTRACT

Parties: [insert party]	[insert party] whose registered office address is at [insert address] ("EventCo"); and	
[insert party]	[insert party]("the Sponsor")	
Effective Date:	[insert date]	**Term:** From the Effective Date until [insert date]
Event/Event Title:	[insert details]	
Designation:	[e.g. Official Sponsor of XYZ Event]	
Sponsorship Rights:	See Schedule 1	**Date of Event:** [insert date]
Brand Sector:	[e.g. Alcoholic Beverages/Telecommunications/Financial Services]	
Sponsor's Marks:	Means the trade marks and logos belonging to the Sponsor attached at Schedule 2, the right and title to which belongs to the Sponsor.	
Charges:	Sponsorship Fee: [(excluding relevant taxes)]	Payment Terms:
EventCo Marks	Means the trade marks and logos belonging to EventCo (including any composite mark produced by EventCo using the Sponsor Marks and the EventCo Marks) and attached at Schedule 3.	
Contact Details:	EventCo	The Sponsor
Contract Managers:	[insert details]	[insert details]
Tel:	[insert details]	[insert details]
Fax:	[insert details]	[insert details]
Email:	[insert details]	[insert details]

The parties each agree to the terms of this Agreement (which expression includes the attached Terms and Conditions and the attached Schedules).

Signed by:	Signed by:
For and on behalf of	For and on behalf of
[insert party]	**[insert party]**

TERMS AND CONDITIONS

1. **KEY OBLIGATIONS OF EVENTCO**

EventCo represents, warrants and undertakes:

(a) to deliver or procure the delivery of the Sponsorship Rights to the Sponsor;

(b) that it owns or controls all rights in and to the Event;

(c) to organise and administer the Event in a professional manner;

(d) to use the Sponsor Marks in the manner and form illustrated in Schedule 2;

(e) not to enter into any Sponsorship Agreement with any Brand Sector competitor of the Sponsor in relation to the Event;

(f) to keep the Sponsor informed with respect to material developments or changes to the Event which may affect the Sponsorship Rights;

(g) that no further party will be authorised to use the EventCo Marks in conflict with the Sponsorship Rights granted to the Sponsor;

[(h) not to engage more than [insert number] further Sponsors of the Event;]

[(i) to use all reasonable endeavours to procure broadcast coverage in [insert countries] of the Event although EventCo shall not be liable to the Sponsor in anyway should the Event not be broadcast.]

2. **KEY OBLIGATIONS OF THE SPONSOR**

(a) The Sponsor represents, warrants and undertakes:

(i) to pay the Sponsorship Fee on the dates specified in this Agreement;

(ii) to be responsible for the costs relating to the manufacture, delivery and storage of materials associated with the provision of the Sponsorship Rights;

(iii) not to use or exploit any rights of a commercial nature connected with the Event (the "Commercial Rights") other than as set out in this Agreement;

(iv) not to establish an internet website relating to the Event;

(v) not to engage in any joint promotional activity without the prior written approval of EventCo;

(vi) that it shall not do anything or permit anything to be done which might adversely affect the rights of EventCo or any of the Commercial Rights.

(b) The Sponsor grants to EventCo a non-exclusive, royalty free licence for the duration of the Term to use the Sponsor Marks for promotional and/or commercial use in connection with the Sponsor's involvement with the Event.

(c) The Sponsor agrees and consents to EventCo's use and reproduction of the Sponsor Marks and any audio or visual or electronic recordings of the same.

(d) The Sponsor shall only use the EventCo Marks (including any composite mark) in accordance with Schedule 1 and shall not produce any merchandise, premiums or other give-away items without the consent of EventCo.

3. TERMINATION

3.1 Either party shall have the right at any time to terminate this Agreement immediately by giving written notice to the other in the event that:

(a) the other party has committed a material breach of any obligation under this Agreement which breach is incapable of remedy or cannot be remedied in time for the Event;

(b) the other party has committed a material breach of any of its obligations under this Agreement and has not remedied such breach (if the same is capable of remedy) within fourteen days of being required by written notice so to do;

(c) the other party goes into liquidation whether compulsory or voluntary or is declared insolvent or if an administrator or receiver is appointed over the whole or any part of that other party's assets or if that other party enters into any arrangement for the benefit of or compounds with its creditors generally or ceases to carry on business or threatens to do any of these things; or

(d) either party undergoes a change of control or ownership.

3.2 EventCo shall have the right to terminate this Agreement by providing [3 month's] notice in writing to the Company in the event that it no longer wishes to stage the Event. [Upon termination of this Agreement pursuant to this clause EventCo shall immediately repay to the Sponsor such proportion of the Sponsorship Fee that has been paid, and no further instalments (if any) shall be payable by the Sponsor.]

4.   LIABILITY

(a)   Under no circumstances shall either party be liable for any actual or alleged indirect loss or consequential loss howsoever arising suffered by the other, including, but not limited to, loss of profits, anticipated profits, savings, business or opportunity or loss of publicity or loss of reputation or opportunity to enhance reputation or any other sort of economic loss.

(b)   The Sponsor undertakes and agrees that it will indemnify and hold EventCo harmless from and against all costs and expenses (including without limitation reasonable legal costs), actions, proceedings, claims, demands and damage arising from a breach of the Sponsor's representations, warranties or undertakings contained herein or arising from the acts or omissions of the Sponsor or its respective officers, employees or agents.

(c)   A party will not be liable for any failure or delay in performing its obligations under this Agreement to the extent that such failure or delay is the result of any cause or circumstance beyond the reasonable control of that party and that failure or delay could not have been prevented or overcome by that party acting reasonably and prudently.

5.   GENERAL

(a)   This Agreement shall be binding on the parties.

(b)   The parties acknowledge that they intend to negotiate and enter into a further long form sponsorship agreement, whereupon this Agreement shall terminate. If the parties fail to enter into such long form agreement, this Agreement shall remain in force and shall govern the terms of relationship between the parties.

(c)   This Agreement is subject to [insert governing law] and the parties submit to the non-exclusive jurisdiction of the [insert courts with jurisdiction].

SCHEDULE 1

SPONSORSHIP RIGHTS

[1. **Naming, Advertising and Promotional Rights**

1.1 EventCo shall use the Event Title with regard to all references made by it to the Event [and shall also communicate to its broadcast and media partners that the Event Title is the official name of the Event and should be used in all visual, written and verbal references].

1.2 Subject to EventCo's prior approval, the Sponsor shall have the exclusive right within the Brand Sector to use the following Designation on the Sponsor's promotional and marketing materials ("the Sponsor Materials") to be used solely in connection with the Sponsor's products and/or services:
[insert appropriate Designation e.g. Official/Title Sponsor of XYZ Event]

1.3 The Sponsor shall have the right to use the EventCo Marks on the Sponsor Materials solely in connection with the Sponsor's products and services provided that the prior approval of EventCo is obtained in respect of such use.

2. **Signage, Advertising and Other Branding Rights**

2.1 The Sponsor shall have the right, subject to the Sponsor meeting the cost of production of copy to be included in such advertising space, to display the following advertising in the Official Guide:

[front cover/back cover/inside/sponsors' credit page etc]

2.2 The Sponsor shall have the right to have any composite mark appear on all official printed material produced by EventCo for public distribution in relation to the Event.

2.3 The Sponsor shall have the right, subject to the prior approval of EventCo and subject to the Sponsor meeting the cost of production thereof, to the following signage boards at the Event:
[insert details]

3. **Tickets and Hospitality**

3.1 The Sponsor shall have the right to receive [insert number] tickets free of charge for the Event for use by Sponsor personnel and their guests (which shall be in the best available areas designated by EventCo), subject to compliance by such Sponsor personnel and their guests with the conditions of entry applicable to such ticket.

3.2 The Sponsor shall have the further right to purchase up to [insert number] additional tickets (which shall be in the best available areas designated by EventCo) for the Event together with hospitality packages, both tickets and hospitality to be subject to availability and to sufficient notice being received by EventCo.

3.3 Subject to availability and to the standard terms and conditions of use and to the Sponsor meeting the costs consequent on the provision of such hospitality, the Sponsor shall have the right to use the best available hospitality facilities as designated by EventCo or any reasonable alternative proposed by EventCo (which shall be for the exclusive use of the Sponsor) at or near the event venue.

3.4 Each individual enjoying a hospitality package at the Event shall receive a free copy of the Official Guide.

3.5 EventCo shall procure up to [insert number] invitations for Sponsor personnel and guests to attend any suitable Event-related activities, at no further charge to the Sponsor.

4.   Internet, Database and Mobile Service Branding Rights

4.1 EventCo shall provide or facilitate the provision of:

(a) a reciprocal hyper-text link between the Official Website home page and the Sponsor Website;

(b) the Event Title to appear on the Official Website in a prominent position on each page and no less than:

(i) one button of no less than 120 x 60 pixels (6K file) on each page;

(ii) one banner ad of no less than 468 x 60 pixels (12K file) on each page;

(iii) up to two advertisements in the week preceding the Event;

4.2 EventCo and the Sponsor shall further work together in good faith to provide co-branded features for the Sponsor Website and the Official Website.

4.3 Subject to the provisions of all relevant data protection regulations, EventCo agrees to mail, at the Sponsor's cost, advertising and promotional materials for the Sponsor's products and services in a form approved by EventCo to those persons whose names and addresses are held on EventCo's database(s) PROVIDED THAT such persons have not objected to receiving information relating to the Event commercial partners and PROVIDED THAT such mailings shall be limited to one such mailing in [insert period of time].

5.   Further Rights

5.1   The Sponsor shall have the right to stage a press conference announcing the Sponsor's sponsorship of the Event, the time and location to be agreed between the parties and all costs in relation to such event to be borne by the Sponsor.

5.2   Subject to available space, all applicable regulations, and any contractual restrictions relating to the same, the Sponsor shall have the right to conduct advertising promotions at the Event subject in every case to the approval of EventCo.

5.3   The Sponsor shall have the right to present an award at the Event and the right to branding on the awards podium.

5.4   The Sponsor shall have such additional rights as EventCo may make available to the Sponsor on such terms as may be agreed between the parties from time to time.]

SCHEDULE 2

SPONSOR'S MARKS

[insert details]

SCHEDULE 3

EVENTCO MARKS

[insert details]

APPENDIX 1B

LONG FORM SPONSORSHIP CONTRACT

This Agreement is made the   day of

BETWEEN:

(1)   [insert party] of [insert address] ("EventCo"); and

(2)   [insert party] of [insert address] (the "Sponsor")

WHEREAS:

(A)   EventCo owns or controls all rights in and to the Event; and

(B)   The Sponsor wishes to acquire certain sponsorship rights in relation to the Event and EventCo wishes to grant such rights upon the terms and conditions of this Agreement.

OPERATIVE PROVISIONS:

1.   DEFINITIONS

1.1   In this Agreement the words and expressions set out below shall, save where the context otherwise requires, have the following meanings:

Brand Sector   means [insert brand sector e.g. alcoholic beverages/ telecommunications/financial services];

Commercial Rights   means any and all rights of a commercial nature connected with the Event including, without limitation, broadcasting rights, so-called new media rights, interactive games rights, sponsorship rights, merchandising and licensing rights, ticketing rights, promotional rights and catering and hospitality rights;

Composite Mark   means a joint logo featuring a composite of the EventCo Mark and the Sponsor Mark owned and applied in accordance with the provisions of Schedule 4;

Designated Account   means the bank account of EventCo, details of which are as follows:
[insert bank details]

Designation	means any designation set out at paragraph 1.2 of Schedule 1 and such other designations as EventCo may approve in writing;
Effective Date	means [the date of signature of this Agreement];
Event	means [insert details] taking place on [insert details];
Event Title	means [insert event title];
EventCo Marks	means the event titles, words and logos which are owned or controlled by EventCo and which are set out in Schedule 3;
Event of Force Majeure	means any circumstance not foreseeable at the date of this Agreement and not within the reasonable control of the party in question, including but not limited to any strike, lock-out or other industrial action (not due to the acts of any party to this Agreement); any destruction (temporary or permanent), breakdown, malfunction or damage of or to any premises, plant, equipment (including computer systems) or materials; any civil commotion or disorder, riot, invasion, war or terrorist activity or threat of war or terrorist activity; any action taken by a governmental or public authority of any kind (including not granting a consent, exemption, approval or clearance); and any fire, explosion, storm, flood, earthquake, subsidence, epidemic or other natural physical disaster;
Official Guide	means the guide produced and/or published by or on behalf of EventCo relating to the Event;
Official Website	means that internet website situated at [insert website] or such other website as EventCo may notify to the Sponsor;
Premium	means any item featuring the Composite Mark or which is otherwise connected with the Event, offered by the Sponsor free of charge or for minimal consideration to the public in connection with the promotion of the Sponsor's Brand Sector products or services;

Sponsor Marks	means those Sponsor trade marks and logos as set out at Schedule 2;
Sponsor Materials	means any and all items and/or samples of Sponsor product and/or services and/or promotional, marketing or advertising materials and/or Premiums produced by or on behalf of the Sponsor which bear the EventCo Marks, Composite Mark and/or any Designation or which otherwise associate the Sponsor with EventCo and/or the Event;
Sponsor Website	means the website situated at [insert website] wholly owned and controlled by the Sponsor;
Sponsorship Fee	means the sum of [insert amount] [(plus VAT)/other applicable taxes], payable by the Sponsor to EventCo in accordance with Clause 4.1;
Sponsorship Rights	means those rights in relation to the Event set out in Schedule 1;
Term	means the term of this Agreement described in Clause 2;
Territory	means [insert territory];
Venue	means [insert venue] where the Event is to be held.

1.2   Unless the context otherwise requires words denoting the singular shall include the plural and vice versa and words denoting any one gender shall include all genders and words denoting persons shall include bodies corporate, unincorporated associations and partnerships.

1.3   References in this Agreement to Schedules are to Schedules to this Agreement.

2.   TERM

2.1   This Agreement shall take effect on and from the Effective Date and shall continue subject to Clause 7 until [insert relevant date]("the Term").

[2.2   The Sponsor shall have the option to extend this Agreement on the same terms and conditions by a further period of [insert period] by notifying EventCo in writing by no later than midnight on [insert date].]

[2.3 Upon the Sponsor's request, EventCo shall negotiate exclusively with the Sponsor from [insert date] to [insert date] ("the Exclusive Negotiating Period") with the intention of renewing this Agreement.

2.4 If despite the parties' best endeavours within the Exclusive Negotiating Period the parties are unable to settle on mutually satisfactory terms for a new agreement between them, then EventCo shall be free to negotiate with any third party an agreement covering any or all of the rights and benefits described herein. If EventCo receives a bona fide offer from any third party for such rights and benefits, it shall notify the Sponsor in writing of the material financial terms of the bona fide third party offer in the form of a true copy which shall be on the offeror's letterhead or other identifiable stationery or imprint which the Sponsor can readily verify as having originated from such third party offeror. If within twenty (20) business days from its receipt of notice of the bona fide third party offer the Sponsor agrees to match or better the material financial terms of such third party offer, the parties shall forthwith document such agreement in a new agreement upon such terms. If the Sponsor fails or declines to match or better such third party offer within such twenty (20) day period, EventCo shall not be restricted in any way from accepting that bona fide third party offer but only on the terms so notified to the Sponsor.]

3. GRANT OF RIGHTS

3.1 In consideration of and subject to the payment to EventCo by the Sponsor of the Sponsorship Fee, EventCo grants to the Sponsor the Sponsorship Rights for use throughout the Territory during the Term.

3.2 All rights not expressly granted to the Sponsor under this Agreement are hereby reserved to EventCo. The Sponsor acknowledges and agrees that:

(a) EventCo owns or controls all rights in and to the EventCo Marks;

(b) EventCo owns or controls all the Commercial Rights in and to the Event; and

(c) The Sponsor shall not be entitled to exploit or enter into any commercial or other agreement to exploit any of the Commercial Rights other than as set out in this Agreement.

[3.3 In the event that for whatever reason EventCo is unable to deliver any of the Sponsorship Rights precisely as set out at Schedule 1, EventCo shall be entitled to substitute alternative rights in the nature of the

Sponsorship Rights to an equivalent value without penalty, subject to the approval of the Sponsor of the alternative rights offered, such approval not to be unreasonably withheld or delayed.]

[3.4   In the event that, following 30 days of negotiations in respect of the provision of alternative rights under Clause 3.3 the parties are unable to agree a suitable alternative, the parties shall negotiate in good faith a proportionate reduction in the Sponsorship Fee to reflect the reduced value of the Sponsorship Rights calculated in relation to the period of time during which non-delivery continued.

3.5   If within 30 days of the commencement of such further negotiations to agree any reduction the parties are unable to agree the reduction in the Sponsorship Fee, the matter shall be referred to an expert ("the Expert") agreed upon between the parties who shall be a person independent of all parties. If the parties are unable to agree upon an Expert then the Expert shall be appointed by [insert party]. The parties shall procure that there is made available to the Expert such information as he or she reasonably requires to determine the relevant reduction.

3.6   The Expert shall be deemed to be acting as an expert and not an arbitrator and his or her decision shall be final and binding on the parties, save in the case of manifest error. The costs and expenses of the Expert will be divided equally between the parties.

3.7   If the Sponsor elects to seek a reduction of the Sponsorship Fee pursuant to Clause 3.4 then and in such event any reduction will be the sole remedy of the Sponsor to the exclusion of all other rights and remedies available to the Sponsor under this Agreement or in law in respect of the relevant non-delivery.]

4.   CONSIDERATION

4.1   In consideration of the grant of the Sponsorship Rights, the Sponsor agrees to pay into the Designated Account the Sponsorship Fee in the sums and on the dates set out below:
[insert details]

[4.2   The Sponsor acknowledges and agrees that its obligation to pay to EventCo the Sponsorship Fee described in Clause 4.1 in its entirety arises upon signature of this Agreement, notwithstanding the instalment dates set out in Clause 4.1.]

4.3 Interest shall be payable by the Sponsor to EventCo on any late payments at the rate of [%] per annum above the base rate of [insert name of bank] in force from time to time.

4.4 Payment of the Sponsorship Fee shall be made in full without any set off, deduction or other withholding whatsoever.

5. OBLIGATIONS OF EVENTCO

5.1 In consideration of the payment of the Sponsorship Fee, EventCo represents, warrants and undertakes to the Sponsor as follows:

(a) subject to Clause 3.3, to deliver or procure the delivery of the Sponsorship Rights to the Sponsor;

(b) it has full right and title and authority to enter into this Agreement and to accept and perform the obligations imposed on it under this Agreement;

(c) to organise and stage the Event in a professional manner;

(d) to ensure that none of its directors or employees makes any defamatory or derogatory statements or takes part in any activities which are or might be derogatory to or are or might otherwise be detrimental to the reputation, image or goodwill of the Sponsor;

(e) to use the Sponsor Marks in the manner and form illustrated in Schedule 2;

(f) that EventCo will not enter into any sponsorship agreement with any Brand Sector competitor of the Sponsor in relation to the Event. For the avoidance of doubt, nothing in this Agreement shall prevent EventCo from offering rights similar in nature to the Sponsorship Rights to third parties other than Brand Sector competitors of the Sponsor;

(g) that it shall keep the Sponsor informed as promptly as reasonably practicable with respect to material developments or changes to the Event which might affect the Sponsor's enjoyment of the Sponsorship Rights;

(h) that it owns or controls the EventCo Marks and no third party will be authorised by EventCo to use the EventCo Marks in conflict with the Sponsorship Rights granted to the Sponsor during the Term;

(i) that it shall use its best endeavours to prevent any third party from conducting any ambush marketing campaigns in relation to the Event that may impact adversely on the rights granted to the Sponsor under this Agreement;

[(j) that it shall not, without the prior written approval of the Sponsor (such approval not to be unreasonably withheld or delayed), engage more than [insert number] further sponsors of the Event PROVIDED ALWAYS that nothing in this Agreement shall prevent EventCo from engaging licensees, media partners or other commercial partners.]

[(k) it shall use all reasonable endeavours to procure broadcast coverage in [insert name(s) of country/countries] of the Event though EventCo shall not be liable to the Sponsor in any way should the Event not be broadcast.]

6.   OBLIGATIONS OF THE SPONSOR

6.1   The Sponsor hereby represents, warrants and undertakes that:

(a) it shall pay the Sponsorship Fee to EventCo in the amounts and on the dates specified in Clause 4;

(b) it shall be responsible for the reasonable costs arising from the manufacture, delivery and storage of materials associated with the provision of the Sponsorship Rights;

(c) it has, and will continue to have throughout the Term, full right and title and authority to enter into this Agreement and to accept and perform the obligations imposed on it under this Agreement;

(d) it shall exercise the Sponsorship Rights strictly in accordance with the terms of this Agreement. For the avoidance of doubt, the Sponsor shall not be entitled to use or exploit any of the Commercial Rights (other than the Sponsorship Rights) in any way;

(e) it shall not establish an internet website relating to the Event nor use the Sponsorship Rights in connection with any internet website save as expressly provided for in this Agreement;

(f) it shall not without the prior written approval of EventCo engage in any joint promotional activity or otherwise exploit any of the Sponsorship Rights with or in connection with any third party nor exercise the Sponsorship Rights in such a manner that a confusion may arise in the minds of the public as to the identity of the person to whom EventCo has granted the Sponsorship Rights;

(g) it shall not do anything or permit anything to be done which might adversely affect the rights of EventCo in or to any of the Commercial Rights or the value of the Commercial Rights and shall provide all reasonable assistance to EventCo in relation to the exploitation by EventCo of the Commercial Rights;

(h) it shall promptly observe and comply with all reasonable instructions, directions or regulations issued by or on behalf of EventCo in relation to the Event;

(i) it shall ensure that neither it nor any of its directors, employees, or other members of staff makes any defamatory or derogatory statements or take part in any activities or use the Sponsorship Rights in any manner which is or might be derogatory to or is or might otherwise be detrimental to the reputation, image or goodwill of EventCo or the Event;

(j) it owns the Sponsor Marks and such marks do not infringe the intellectual property rights of any third party.

6.2 The Sponsor hereby grants to EventCo a non-exclusive, royalty-free licence for the Term of this Agreement to use the Sponsor Marks for promotional and/or commercial use (including, without limitation, in relation to the Composite Mark) or otherwise PROVIDED THAT such use is restricted to use in connection with the Sponsor's involvement with the Event and that the Sponsor Marks shall not be used in a manner which implies endorsement by the Sponsor of any product or service.

6.3 The Sponsor shall only use the Composite Mark on and in connection with Sponsor Materials and shall not be entitled to produce any merchandise, Premiums or other give-away items without the prior approval of EventCo.

6.4 All Sponsor Materials and other branding produced by or on behalf of the Sponsor under this Agreement are subject to the following approvals process:

(a) the Sponsor shall submit to EventCo for its prior written approval, representative samples or artwork accurately illustrating all Sponsor Materials prior to the production, publication or use of the relevant Sponsor Materials;

(b) the Sponsor shall not manufacture, distribute, issue, publish, circulate or otherwise make use of any Sponsor Materials without the prior written approval of EventCo;

(c) following any approval of Sponsor Materials as specified in sub-clause 6.4(a) above, the Sponsor shall ensure that the Sponsor Materials do not deviate from the sample artwork approved by EventCo in any material respect and shall submit further representative samples of such Sponsor Materials for approval whenever reasonably requested to do so by EventCo;

(d) if at any time any Sponsor Materials fail to conform to any approved representative artwork, sample or other submission, the Sponsor shall, forthwith upon notice from EventCo, withdraw or procure the withdrawal of any and all such Sponsor Materials from circulation; and

(e) if EventCo has failed to respond to any request for approval within [ten working days] of receipt of any such request, the Sponsor Materials shall be deemed to have been approved by EventCo.

7. TERMINATION

7.1 Either party shall have the right at any time to terminate this Agreement immediately by giving written notice to the other in the event that:

(a) the other party has committed a material breach of any obligation under this Agreement which breach is incapable of remedy or cannot be remedied in time for the Event;

(b) the other party has committed a material breach of any of its obligations under this Agreement and has not remedied such breach (if the same is capable of remedy) within fourteen days of being required by written notice so to do;

(c) the other party goes into liquidation whether compulsory or voluntary or is declared insolvent or if an administrator or receiver is appointed over the whole or any part of that other party's assets or if that other party enters into any arrangement for the benefit of or compounds with its creditors generally or ceases to carry on business or threatens to do any of these things; or

(d) either party undergoes a change of control or ownership.

7.2 EventCo shall have the right to terminate this Agreement by providing [3 month's] notice in writing to the Company in the event that it no longer wishes to stage the Event.

8. CONSEQUENCES OF TERMINATION

8.1 The expiry or termination of this Agreement shall be without prejudice to any rights which have already accrued to either of the parties under this Agreement.

8.2 [Upon termination of this Agreement pursuant to Clause 7.2 or 9 EventCo shall immediately repay to the Sponsor such proportion of the Sponsorship Fee that has been paid, and no further instalments (if any) shall be payable by the Sponsor.]

8.3 Upon expiry or termination of this Agreement:

(a) the Sponsor's right to exercise the Sponsorship Rights shall forthwith terminate and all Sponsorship Rights shall forthwith revert to EventCo;

(b) the Sponsor shall not use or exploit its previous connection with EventCo or the Event, whether directly or indirectly;

(c) EventCo shall be entitled to grant all or any of the Sponsorship Rights to any third party; and

(d) each of EventCo and the Sponsor will promptly return to the other all of the property of the other within its possession.

9. FORCE MAJEURE

9.1 Neither party to this Agreement shall be deemed to be in breach of this Agreement or otherwise liable to the other as a result of any delay or failure in the performance of its obligations under this Agreement if and to the extent that such delay or failure is caused by an Event of Force Majeure and the time for performance of the relevant obligation(s) shall be extended accordingly.

9.2 A party whose performance of its obligations under this Agreement is delayed or prevented by an Event of Force Majeure:

(a) shall immediately notify the other party of the nature, extent, effect and likely duration of the circumstances constituting the Event of Force Majeure;

(b) shall use all reasonable endeavours to minimise the effect of the Event of Force Majeure on the performance of its obligations under this Agreement; and

(c) shall (subject to Clause 9.3 below) immediately after the Event of Force Majeure has ended notify the other party and resume full performance of its obligations under this Agreement.

9.3 If any Event of Force Majeure delays or prevents the performance of the obligations of either party for a continuous period of [three months], the party not so affected shall then be entitled to give notice to the affected party to terminate this Agreement with immediate effect without penalty. Such a termination notice shall be irrevocable except with the consent of both parties and upon termination the provisions of Clause 8 shall apply.

10. LIABILITY

10.1 Under no circumstances shall either party be liable for any actual or alleged indirect loss or consequential loss howsoever arising suffered by the other, including, but not limited to, loss of profits, anticipated profits, savings, business or opportunity or loss of publicity or loss of reputation or opportunity to enhance reputation or any other sort of economic loss.

10.2 The Sponsor undertakes and agrees that it will indemnify and hold EventCo harmless from and against all costs and expenses (including without limitation reasonable legal costs), actions, proceedings, claims, demands and damage arising from a breach of the Sponsor's representations, warranties or undertakings contained herein or arising from the acts or omissions of the Sponsor or its respective officers, employees or agents.

10.3 [EventCo shall maintain at its own expense comprehensive [general/ public/] liability insurance in such amount as may be adequate to protect the EventCo and the Sponsor against any and all costs, losses and damages arising out of any claims from third parties in relation to the Event.]

11. ASSIGNMENT

Neither party may assign any of its rights or obligations under this Agreement without the prior written consent of the other party, such consent not to be unreasonably withheld or delayed.

12. ANNOUNCEMENTS AND CONFIDENTIALITY

No announcement shall be made by either party in relation to this Agreement without the prior written consent of the other and neither party shall without the prior written consent of the other (save as required by law) disclose to any third party any information concerning the terms or subject matter hereof after the date hereof.

13. POINTS OF CONTACT

13.1 The principal point of contact for each party (unless the other party is notified otherwise in writing) shall be:

(a) EventCo: [   ]

(b) Sponsor: [   ]

13.2 The Sponsor acknowledges and agrees that it is not entitled to rely on any representation, authorisation or decision of EventCo unless made by the principal point of contact (or his designated replacement) set out at sub-clause 13.1 above.

14. NOTICES

14.1 The parties agree that all notices under this Agreement shall, unless otherwise notified, be served on the following addressees:

(a) EventCo: [   ]

(b) Sponsor: [   ]

14.2 All notices shall be in writing and may be delivered personally, by facsimile, by first class pre-paid post or by registered mail and shall be deemed to be properly given or served:

(a) [two] working days after being sent to the intended recipient by pre-paid post addressed as aforesaid; or

(b) if sent by facsimile on receipt of confirmation of transmission or if not a working day the first working day thereafter provided that a confirming copy is sent by first class pre-paid post to the address aforesaid within 24 hours of transmission.

15. GENERAL

15.1 The granting by any party of any time or indulgence in respect of any breach of any term of this Agreement by the other shall not be deemed a waiver of such breach and the waiver by any party of any breach of any term of this Agreement by the other shall not prevent the subsequent enforcement of that term and shall not be deemed a waiver of any subsequent breach.

15.2   This Agreement shall constitute the entire agreement between the parties with respect to the subject matter hereof, and shall supersede any and all prior agreements, representations or understanding between the parties, whether written or oral.

15.3   This Agreement may be executed in any number of counterparts, each of which when executed shall constitute an original, but all of which when taken together shall constitute one and the same Agreement.

15.4   All rights, remedies and powers conferred upon the parties are cumulative and shall not be deemed to be exclusive of any other rights, remedies or powers now or subsequently conferred upon them by law or otherwise.

15.5   Each party will do all things necessary including executing all documents necessary to give effect to the intention of the parties in relation to this Agreement.

15.6   Should any term of this Agreement be considered void or voidable under any applicable law, then such terms shall be severed or amended in such a manner as to render the remainder of this Agreement valid or enforceable, unless the whole commercial object is thereby frustrated.

15.7   This Agreement may only be modified or any provision waived if such modification or waiver is in writing and signed by a duly authorised representative of each party.

15.8   This Agreement shall be governed by and construed in accordance with [insert governing law] and the parties hereby submit to the non-exclusive jurisdiction of the [insert courts of jurisdiction] courts.

15.9   Any date or period mentioned in any clause of this Agreement may be extended by mutual agreement in writing between the parties but as regards any date or period (whether or not extended as aforesaid) time shall be of the essence in this Agreement.

15.10   Nothing in this Agreement shall be deemed to constitute a joint venture, partnership or relationship of agency or employment between the parties.

IN WITNESS WHEREOF, the parties have executed this Agreement as of the day and year first above written.

Signed by
a duly authorised representative
for and on behalf of
[INSERT PARTY]

Signed by
a duly authorised representative
for and on behalf of
[INSERT PARTY]

SCHEDULE 1

THE SPONSORSHIP RIGHTS

[1.   Naming, Advertising and Promotional Rights

1.1   EventCo shall use the Event Title with regard to all references made by it to the Event [and shall also communicate to its broadcast and media partners that the Event Title is the official name of the Event and should be used in all visual, written and verbal references.]

1.2   Subject to Clause 6.4, the Sponsor shall have the exclusive right [within the Brand Sector] to use the following Designation within the Territory on the Sponsor Materials to be used solely in connection with the Sponsor's products and/or services:

[insert appropriate Designation e.g. Official/Title Sponsor of XYZ Event]

1.3   The Sponsor shall have the right to use the Composite Mark within the Territory on the Sponsor Materials solely in connection with the Sponsor's products and services PROVIDED THAT the Sponsor shall comply with and only use the Composite Mark in accordance with Clause 6.4 of this Agreement.

2.   Signage, Advertising and Other Branding Rights

2.1   The Sponsor shall have the right, subject to Clause 6.4 and subject to the Sponsor meeting the cost of production of copy to be included in such advertising space, to display the following advertising in the Official Guide:
(i)   front cover: [insert details]
(ii)   back cover: [insert details]
(iii) inside programme: [insert details]
(iv)   Sponsor's credit page: [insert details]

2.2   The Sponsor shall have the right, subject to Clause 6.4 and subject to the Sponsor meeting the cost of production thereof, to the following signage boards at the Venue:
[insert details]

2.3   The Sponsor shall be entitled to have unrestricted access to the Venue on the day prior to the Event for the purposes of erecting any signage boards or other branding under this Agreement.

3.   Tickets and Hospitality

3.1   The Sponsor shall have the right to receive [insert number] tickets free of charge for the Event for use by Sponsor personnel and their guests (which shall be in the best available areas designated by EventCo), subject to compliance by such Sponsor personnel and their guests with the conditions of entry applicable to such ticket.

3.2   The Sponsor shall have the further right to purchase up to [insert number] additional tickets (which shall be in the best available areas designated by EventCo) for the Event together with hospitality packages, both tickets and hospitality to be subject to availability and to sufficient notice being received by EventCo.

3.3   Subject to availability and to the standard terms and conditions of use and to the Sponsor meeting the costs consequent on the provision of such hospitality, the Sponsor shall have the right to use the best available hospitality facilities as designated by EventCo or any reasonable alternative proposed by EventCo (which shall be for the exclusive use of the Sponsor) at or near the Venue.

3.4   Each individual enjoying a hospitality package at the Event shall receive, free of charge, a copy of the Official Guide.

3.5   EventCo shall procure up to [insert number] invitations for Sponsor personnel and guests to attend any suitable Event-related activities, at no further charge to the Sponsor.

4.   Internet, Database and Mobile Service Branding Rights

4.1   EventCo shall provide or facilitate the provision of:

(a)   a reciprocal hyper-text link between the Official Website home page and the Sponsor Website;

(b)   the Event Title to appear on the Official Website in a prominent position on each page and no less than:

(i)   one button of no less than 120 x 60 pixels (6K file) on each page;

(ii)   one banner ad of no less than 468 x 60 pixels (12K file) on each page;

(iii) up to two advertisements in the week preceding the Event;

4.2   EventCo and the Sponsor shall further work together in good faith to provide co-branded features for the Sponsor Website and the Official Website.

4.3   Subject to the provisions of all relevant data protection regulations, EventCo agrees to mail, at the Sponsor's cost, advertising and promotional materials for the Sponsor's products and services in a form approved by EventCo to those persons whose names and addresses are held on EventCo's database(s) PROVIDED THAT such persons have not objected to receiving information relating to EventCo's commercial partners and PROVIDED THAT such mailings shall be limited to one such mailing in [insert period of time].

5.   Further Rights

5.1   The Sponsor shall have the right to stage a press conference announcing the Sponsor's sponsorship of the Event, the time and location to be agreed between the parties and all costs in relation to such event to be borne by the Sponsor.

5.2   Subject to available space, all applicable regulations, and any contractual restrictions relating to the same, the Sponsor shall have the right to conduct advertising promotions at the Event subject in every case to the approval of EventCo.

5.3   The Sponsor shall have the right to present an award at the Event and the right to branding on the awards podium.

5.4   The Sponsor shall have such additional rights as EventCo may make available to the Sponsor on such terms as may be agreed between the parties from time to time.]

SCHEDULE 2

THE SPONSOR MARKS

[insert details]

SCHEDULE 3

EVENTCO MARKS

[insert details]

SCHEDULE 4

THE COMPOSITE MARK

1. The Sponsor shall have the right to design a Composite Mark which shall feature the EventCo Mark and Sponsor Mark, the final design of which shall be subject to the approval of EventCo, such approval to be exercised at EventCo's absolute discretion.

2. The Sponsor agrees that:

   2.1 title to any and all rights in the Composite Mark shall vest jointly in EventCo and the Sponsor;

   2.2 all use of the Composite Mark by the Sponsor shall be governed by the provisions of Clause 6.3 and 6.4;

   2.3 EventCo and the Sponsor shall apply jointly to register the Composite Mark as a trade mark provided that, on termination of this Agreement or expiry of the Term, the parties shall each consent to the withdrawal of any such application which is pending and to the surrender of any such trademark registration;

   2.4 neither party shall bring any action in respect of the Composite Mark without the prior written consent of the other party;

   2.5 the Sponsor shall procure that the designer of the Composite Mark enters into a deed of assignment of copyright and other intellectual property rights in favour of the Sponsor and EventCo in a form approved by both parties;

   2.6 [the costs of any trade mark registration of the Composite Mark shall be borne by the Sponsor.]

APPENDIX 2

VENUE HIRE CONTRACT

This Agreement is made the   day of

BETWEEN

(1)   [insert party] of [insert address] ("EventCo"); and

(2)   [insert party] of [insert address] ("the Company").

WHEREAS

(1)   EventCo owns or controls all rights in and to the Event;

(2)   EventCo wishes to hire and the Company has agreed to hire the Venue to EventCo for the Event Period in order to stage the Event on the terms and conditions set out in this Agreement.

IT IS AGREED

1.   DEFINITIONS

1.1   In this Agreement the words and expressions set out below shall, save where the context otherwise requires, have the following meanings:

Clean Venue   means the Venue, all areas of which, including, without limitation, building facades, reception areas, parking lots and any other facilities, shall be free from any sponsorship, advertising or other branding which may impair or inhibit the full exploitation by EventCo of the Commercial Rights;

Commercial Rights   means any and all rights of a commercial nature connected with the Event including, without limitation, broadcasting rights, so-called new media rights, interactive games rights, sponsorship rights, merchandising and licensing rights, ticketing rights, promotional rights and catering and hospitality rights;

Effective Date   means the date of signature of this Agreement;

Event   means [insert details] taking place on [insert details];

Event Period	means the period from [2] days prior to the Event to [2] days after the Event;
Event of Force Majeure	means any circumstance not foreseeable at the date of this Agreement and not within the reasonable control of the party in question, including but not limited to any strike, lock-out or other industrial action (not due to the acts of any party to this Agreement); any destruction (temporary or permanent), breakdown, malfunction or damage of or to any premises, plant, equipment (including computer systems) or materials; any civil commotion or disorder, riot, invasion, war or terrorist activity or threat of war or terrorist activity; any action taken by a governmental or public authority of any kind (including not granting a consent, exemption, approval or clearance); and any fire, explosion, storm, flood, earthquake, subsidence, epidemic or other natural physical disaster;
Fees	means the fees set out in Clause 3;
Term	means the period of [insert period] from the Effective Date, unless terminated earlier in accordance with Clause 7;
Venue	means the site known as [insert details], in particular that section detailed in Schedule 1 attached hereto.

1.2 Unless the context otherwise requires words denoting the singular shall include the plural and vice versa and words denoting any one gender shall include all genders and words denoting persons shall include bodies corporate, unincorporated associations and partnerships.

1.3 References in this Agreement to Schedules are to Schedules to this Agreement.

2. GRANT OF RIGHTS

2.1 In consideration of the Fee, the Company grants EventCo the sole and exclusive right to use the Venue during the Event Period for the staging of the Event, in accordance with the terms and conditions set out in this Agreement.

2.2 The Company shall ensure that EventCo, its employees, agents and representatives shall have unrestricted access to the Venue during the Event Period for the purposes of preparing for and staging the Event.

3. CONSIDERATION AND RIGHT OF REDUCTION

3.1   EventCo will pay the Company total Fees of [insert amount and whether or not inclusive/exclusive of any taxes] for the use of the Venue during the Event Period.

3.2   The Fees will be payable as follows:

[insert details]

3.3   In addition to the Fees, EventCo shall pay for the costs for the use of the utilities described in Clause 4.15 below.

3.4   All sums set out in Clauses 3.2 and 3.3 above shall be paid within [30 days] of receipt of an appropriate invoice.

4. THE COMPANY'S OBLIGATIONS

The Company represents, warrants and undertakes:

4.1   that it has full right, title and authority to enter into this Agreement and to perform its obligations under this Agreement;

4.2   that the Venue complies with any and all applicable laws, rules or regulations (including those relating to health and safety, planning, alcohol control and licensing, disability discrimination and fire certification) and that EventCo is entitled to apply for all relevant and necessary licences, clearances and consents to enable the Event to take place at the Venue;

4.3   that it has taken out and will maintain throughout the Event appropriate [general/public] liability insurance and will, if required, note EventCo's interest on any such policy;

4.4   that all space and advertising opportunities at the Venue shall be made available to EventCo for the exercise of the Commercial Rights;

4.5   to ensure a Clean Venue for the Event, including removal/covering of, without limitation, existing signage, advertising or sponsorship material or concessions;

4.6   that the Venue and other premises shall be fit for the purpose for which they are provided, namely [insert activities];

4.7   the Venue will be provided to a standard acceptable to EventCo;

4.8   that EventCo, its employees, agents and representatives shall have unrestricted access to the Venue during the Event Period for the purposes of preparing for and staging the Event;

4.9   that it shall not allow any [competing] events to take place at the Venue for a period of [three] weeks prior to the Event and [two] weeks thereafter;

4.10   that the Venue shall not be encumbered prior to or during the Event by any franchise, concession or other agreement which in the reasonable opinion of EventCo would conflict with any commercial agreement which EventCo has, or intends to, conclude or would hinder or prevent EventCo from exercising the Commercial Rights;

4.11   not to create any emblem, logo or motto connected with the Event nor to exploit any of the Commercial Rights or conduct any commercial activity associated with the Event other than with the prior written approval of EventCo;

4.12   to enable deliveries to the Venue of supplies necessary for the Event including, without limitation, beverages, equipment and materials throughout the [2] days preceding the Event and during the Event;

4.13   not to refuse entry, during the Event, to EventCo staff, sponsor personnel, camera crew, organisers, hospitality providers, security staff and guests;

4.14   to ensure that an identifiable and properly authorised representative will be present at all times during the duration of the Event to provide such on-site assistance as EventCo shall reasonably require;

4.15   that the Venue will be equipped with the following utilities, equipment and services:
       4.15.1 [Water, heating, and air conditioning;
       4.15.2 Lighting and electricity; and
       4.15.3 Toilet facilities]

4.16   that EventCo shall be entitled to [5] free car parking spaces in the main car-park during the Event;

4.17   to use its best endeavours to assist EventCo in preventing any ambush marketing activities in and around the Venue.

5   EVENTCO'S OBLIGATIONS

EventCo represents, warrants and undertakes:

5.1   that it shall pay the Fees in accordance with Clause 3.2;

5.2   that it shall not use the Venue for any purpose other than to stage the Event;

5.3   that it will undertake and manage all matters relating to the staging of the Event;

5.4   that it will secure, at its own cost, all necessary licences, permits, certificates, consents and approvals necessary to stage the Event, and will act in accordance with all regulations, conditions and by-laws related to such licences, permits, certificates, consents and approvals (including those relating to fire safety, entertainment, liquor, noise and waste);

5.5   that it shall be responsible for removing all litter, property and equipment brought into the Venue for the Event by [8 a.m. on the second day following the Event]. If EventCo fails to comply with this obligation, the Company will be entitled to remove such litter, equipment and property and EventCo shall meet the reasonable cost of such removal;

5.6   that it will comply with all reasonable health and safety requirements and take all reasonable precautions to ensure the safety of all those attending or working at the Event;

5.7   that it will provide sufficient security staff to ensure the safe running of the Event, including controlling access to certain areas at the Venue, controlling spectator movement before, during and after the Event and directing VIP's to certain areas at the Venue where necessary;

5.8   that it will pay to the Company the costs of making good all damage to the Venue suffered during the period of use which is not covered by insurance;

5.9   that it will provide a first-aid service with appropriately qualified personnel during the Event;

5.10   that it shall submit to the Company a plan of the intended layout for the Event;

5.11   that it will not obstruct or allow to be obstructed any exit, passageway or other access to or from the Venue;

5.12   that it shall not make any permanent structural alterations or additions to the Venue without the prior written consent of the Company;

5.13   that it will notify the Company immediately on becoming aware of any serious accident, injury or damage occurring within the Venue;

5.14   that it will nominate a point of contact to liaise with the Company prior to and during the Event;

5.15   that it shall not knowingly bring any unusually explosive, dangerous, flammable or noxious substances into the Venue buildings and that all materials brought into the Venue by EventCo shall comply with all reasonable safety requirements;

5.16   that it will not do anything which might invalidate any insurance maintained by the Company in respect of the Venue;

5.17   that it will ensure that the maximum number of persons attending at the Venue for the purposes of the Event does not exceed [insert number]; and

5.18   that it will ensure that all participants and attendees at the Event shall have left the Venue by no later than [insert time] on [insert date].

6   ACKNOWLEDGEMENT OF RIGHTS

6.1   The Company acknowledges that EventCo is owner of all the Commercial Rights and that all Commercial Rights which arise out of or are indirectly connected with the Event shall remain the property of EventCo.

6.2   The Company waives any of its rights in perpetuity and acknowledges the right of EventCo in perpetuity to:

6.2.1   all and any rights (including but not limited to the copyright) in any form of audio, visual and/or audio-visual or electronic coverage of any part of the Event at the Venue; and

6.2.2   all and any of the Commercial Rights.

6.3   The Company acknowledges that EventCo shall retain:

6.3.1   all rights to footage and photography shot at the Event, including that which features the Venue itself;

6.3.2   the right to fully exploit all Commercial Rights in relation to the Event, including the right to place advertisements or branding of event sponsors within and outside the Venue (provided that no such advertisement or branding shall be affixed to the Venue or parts thereof so as to cause damage to the Venue);

6.3.3   the right to all commercial revenues relating to or arising from the Event beyond the agreed Fees;

6.3.4   the right to allocate and sell retail trade stands at the Venue;

6.3.5   the right to allocate and sell food and beverage stands at the Venue;

6.3.6 the right to operate a stand for the purposes of marketing and selling a broad range of official event merchandise;

6.3.7 the right to prevent access to or remove from the Venue any person acting in a way which in the reasonable opinion of EventCo is regarded as offensive, harmful or undesirable, or who represents a security risk at the Event;

6.3.8 the right to erect temporary structures at the Venue for the purposes of staging the Event;

6.3.9 the right to promote and sample brands;

6.3.10 the right to promote, advertise and market associated event functions at the Venue;

6.3.11 [the right to obtain a liquor licence and operate an event bar at the Venue;]

6.3.12 the right to place promotional material at and around the Venue for a period of [3] weeks prior to the Event, subject to the Company's approval (not to be unreasonably withheld or delayed).

6.4 The Company shall have the right to:

6.4.1 remove from the Venue, and dispose of, all structures, goods, equipment, waste and other materials brought into the Venue by EventCo or its employees, sub-contractors and agents and left at the Venue after the Event Period;

6.4.2 free access at any time during the Event for officials and employees of the Company; and

6.4.3 prevent access or remove from the Venue any person acting in a manner which in the reasonable opinion of the Company is offensive, harmful or undesirable, or who represents a security risk.

7. TERMINATION

7.1 Either party shall have the right at any time to terminate this Agreement immediately by giving written notice to the other in the event that:

(a) the other party has committed a material breach of any obligation under this Agreement which breach is incapable of remedy or cannot be remedied in time for the Event;

(b) the other party has committed a material breach of any of its obligations under this Agreement and has not remedied such breach (if the same is capable of remedy) within fourteen days of being required by written notice so to do;

(c)   the other party goes into liquidation whether compulsory or voluntary or is declared insolvent or if an administrator or receiver is appointed over the whole or any part of that other party's assets or if that other party enters into any arrangement for the benefit of or compounds with its creditors generally or ceases to carry on business or threatens to do any of these things; or

(d)   either party undergoes a change of control or ownership.

7.2   EventCo shall have the right to terminate this Agreement by providing [3 month's] notice in writing to the Company in the event that it no longer wishes to stage the Event at the Venue or at all.

8.   CONSEQUENCES OF TERMINATION

8.1   The expiry or termination of this Agreement shall be without prejudice to any rights which have already accrued to either of the parties under this Agreement.

8.2   [Upon termination of this Agreement pursuant to Clause 7.2 or Clause 9 the Company shall immediately repay to EventCo such proportion of the Fees that have already been paid, and no further instalments (if any) shall be payable to the Company.]

9.   FORCE MAJEURE

9.1   Neither party to this Agreement shall be deemed to be in breach of this Agreement or otherwise liable to the other as a result of any delay or failure in the performance of its obligations under this Agreement if and to the extent that such delay or failure is caused by an Event of Force Majeure and the time for performance of the relevant obligation(s) shall be extended accordingly.

9.2   A party whose performance of its obligations under this Agreement is delayed or prevented by an Event of Force Majeure:

(a)   shall immediately notify the other party of the nature, extent, effect and likely duration of the circumstances constituting the Event of Force Majeure;

(b)   shall use all reasonable endeavours to minimise the effect of the Event of Force Majeure on the performance of its obligations under this Agreement; and

(c) shall (subject to Clause 9.3 below) immediately after the Event of Force Majeure has ended notify the other party and resume full performance of its obligations under this Agreement.

9.3 If any Event of Force Majeure delays or prevents the performance of the obligations of either party for a continuous period of [three months], the party not so affected shall then be entitled to give notice to the affected party to terminate this Agreement with immediate effect without penalty. Such a termination notice shall be irrevocable except with the consent of both parties and upon termination the provisions of Clause 8 shall apply.

10. LIABILITY

10.1 Under no circumstances shall either party be liable for any actual or alleged indirect loss or consequential loss howsoever arising suffered by the other, including, but not limited to, loss of profits, anticipated profits, savings, business or opportunity or loss of publicity or loss of reputation or opportunity to enhance reputation or any other sort of economic loss.

10.2 Each party undertakes and agrees that it will indemnify and hold the other harmless from and against all costs and expenses (including without limitation reasonable legal costs), actions, proceedings, claims, demands and damage arising from a breach of the other party's representations, warranties or undertakings contained herein or arising from the acts or omissions of the other party or its respective officers, employees or agents.

10.3 The Company shall have no responsibility for any loss of or damage to the property and effects brought into the Venue by EventCo, its officers, employees, agents and sub-contractors, or by the attendees and participants in the Event.

11. ASSIGNMENT

Neither party may assign any of its rights or obligations under this Agreement without the prior written consent of the other party, such consent not to be unreasonably withheld or delayed.

12. ANNOUNCEMENTS AND CONFIDENTIALITY

No announcement shall be made by either party in relation to this Agreement without the prior written consent of the other and neither party shall without the prior written consent of the other (save as required by law) disclose to any third party any information concerning the terms or subject matter hereof after the date hereof.

13. POINTS OF CONTACT

13.1 The principal point of contact for each party (unless the other party is notified otherwise in writing) shall be:

(a) EventCo: [   ]

(b) The Company: [   ]

13.2 The Company acknowledges and agrees that it is not entitled to rely on any representation, authorisation or decision of EventCo unless made by the principal point of contact (or his designated replacement) set out at sub-clause 13.1 above.

14. NOTICES

14.1 The parties agree that all notices under this Agreement shall, unless otherwise notified, be served on the following addressees:

(a) EventCo: [   ]

(b) The Company: [   ]

14.2 All notices shall be in writing and may be delivered personally, by facsimile, by first class pre-paid post or by registered mail and shall be deemed to be properly given or served:

(a) [two] working days after being sent to the intended recipient by pre-paid post addressed as aforesaid; or

(b) if sent by facsimile on receipt of confirmation of transmission or if not a working day the first working day thereafter provided that a confirming copy is sent by first class pre-paid post to the address aforesaid within 24 hours of transmission.

15. GENERAL

15.1 The granting by any party of any time or indulgence in respect of any breach of any term of this Agreement by the other shall not be deemed a waiver of such breach and the waiver by any party of any breach of any term of this Agreement by the other shall not prevent the subsequent enforcement of that term and shall not be deemed a waiver of any subsequent breach.

15.2 This Agreement shall constitute the entire agreement between the parties with respect to the subject matter hereof, and shall supersede any and all prior agreements, representations or understanding between the parties, whether written or oral.

15.3   This Agreement may be executed in any number of counterparts, each of which when executed shall constitute an original, but all of which when taken together shall constitute one and the same Agreement.

15.4   All rights, remedies and powers conferred upon the parties are cumulative and shall not be deemed to be exclusive of any other rights, remedies or powers now or subsequently conferred upon them by law or otherwise.

15.5   Each party will do all things necessary including executing all documents necessary to give effect to the intention of the parties in relation to this Agreement.

15.6   Should any term of this Agreement be considered void or voidable under any applicable law, then such terms shall be severed or amended in such a manner as to render the remainder of this Agreement valid or enforceable, unless the whole commercial object is thereby frustrated.

15.7   This Agreement may only be modified or any provision waived if such modification or waiver is in writing and signed by a duly authorised representative of each party.

15.8   This Agreement shall be governed by and construed in accordance with [insert governing law] and the parties hereby submit to the non-exclusive jurisdiction of the [insert courts of jurisdiction] courts.

15.9   Any date or period mentioned in any clause of this Agreement may be extended by mutual agreement in writing between the parties but as regards any date or period (whether or not extended as aforesaid) time shall be of the essence in this Agreement.

15.10   Nothing in this Agreement shall be deemed to constitute a joint venture, partnership or relationship of agency or employment between the parties.

IN WITNESS WHEREOF, the parties have executed this Agreement as of the day and year first above written.

Signed by
a duly authorised representative
for and on behalf of
[INSERT PARTY]

Signed by
a duly authorised representative
for and on behalf of
[INSERT PARTY]

SCHEDULE 1

VENUE PLAN

[insert plan]

APPENDIX 3

TICKET TERMS AND CONDITIONS OF SALE

1. This ticket is issued subject to the terms and conditions set out below ("the Terms and Conditions").

2. The purchase of this ticket constitutes acceptance of the Terms and Conditions.

3. This ticket cannot be exchanged or refunded after purchase, subject to Clause 14 below.

4. Entrance to the Venue may only be authorised upon presentation of a valid ticket [and, upon request, proof of identity with valid photograph and signature.]

5. EventCo reserves the right to refuse admission to any person in its absolute discretion, and EventCo also reserves the right to eject from the Venue any person who fails to comply with the Terms and Conditions or who in the opinion of EventCo represents a security risk, nuisance or annoyance to the staging of the Event or EventCo.

6. This ticket gives access only to the area indicated on the front of the ticket. The purchaser is not permitted to transfer between areas of the Venue.

7. There will be no pass-outs or re-admissions of any kind during the Event.

8. The ticket shall remain at all times the property of EventCo which has the right to recall the ticket at any time.

9. Unless otherwise authorised by EventCo, the ticket is issued for the purchaser's personal use only. The purchaser of the ticket shall act in his or her personal capacity and not as agent for any third party. It is not permitted for the purchaser to sell or otherwise transfer the ticket to others, to exploit the ticket commercially or non-commercially, to use it for promotional purposes, hospitality purposes, competitions or campaigns or to transfer and/or dispose of the ticket in any way.

10. Any ticket obtained in breach of Clause 9 shall be void and all rights conferred or evidenced by such ticket, including without limitation the right of entrance, shall be immediately nullified and withdrawn. EventCo shall have the right to confiscate such ticket, to deny access to the ticket-

holder, or to eject anyone who has used such ticket to gain access, all without any obligation to refund the purchase price to the purchaser.

11. No person may bring into the Venue or use within the Venue any equipment which is capable of recording or transmitting (by digital or other means) any audio, visual or audio-visual material or any information or data in relation to the Event or the Venue.

12. Mobile phones are permitted within the Venue provided that they are for personal and private use only. Any material, footage, information or data captured by mobile phone shall be for the personal use of the purchaser and the purchaser agrees not to distribute such material, footage, information or data for any commercial purpose whatsoever.

13. Entry will not be permitted if the purchaser is carrying in his or her possession prohibited items, which shall include but not be limited to food, drink, chemicals of any kind, containers, bottles, cans, recording equipment, laser pens, pets, cameras, video cameras, weapons, banners of any kind, flares, smoke bombs or flagsticks. Such prohibited items shall be confiscated by EventCo and kept by EventCo during the Event for return to the purchaser after the Event. EventCo shall not be responsible for any loss of or damage to such prohibited items during the Event.

14. If the Event is cancelled prior to the start of the Event, the purchaser shall be entitled to a refund in the amount of the face value of the ticket. If the Event is postponed the ticket will be valid for the re-arranged date. Refunds for cancellation or postponement will only be considered if the original ticket is returned to the point of purchase no later than [insert number] days after the original date of the Event. It is the responsibility of the purchaser to ascertain the date and time of the re-arranged Event.

15. EventCo will not be liable for any delay in performing its obligations as a result of fire, strikes, industrial disputes, abnormally inclement weather, acts of terrorism, governmental orders or decrees or any other cause beyond its reasonable control.

16. The purchaser consents to filming and sound recording of the Event as an attendee/member of the audience at the Event. The purchaser consents to the use of such recording in any broadcast in any territory in the world.

17. EventCo reserves the right to alter the advertised programme for the Event owing to any unforeseen or unavoidable circumstances and no refunds, exchanges or alternative use of tickets shall be offered or made available in such circumstances.

18. EventCo accepts no responsibility to replace lost, damaged or stolen tickets.

19. EventCo excludes to the maximum extent permitted by the law any liability for loss, injury or damage to persons or property in or around the Venue. Any liability on the part of EventCo shall be limited to the face value of the ticket and any relevant booking fee.

20. The purchaser shall comply with all relevant statutes, health and safety regulations and venue regulations when attending the Event. In addition, the purchaser shall comply with all reasonable instructions issued by EventCo during the Event.

21. Any ticket obtained in breach of these Terms and Conditions shall be void and all rights conferred or evidenced by such ticket shall be nullified and EventCo shall be entitled to deny right of access to the Venue and confiscate such ticket as a result.

22. Failure to observe any of these Terms and Conditions will constitute a breach of contract enforceable in law and may result in legal action by EventCo.

23. These Terms and Conditions are governed by [insert governing law] and the parties submit to the exclusive jurisdiction of the [insert courts of jurisdiction].

APPENDIX 4

RISK ANALYSIS

The following risks should be considered for an event such as a wedding:

- Where will the wedding take place? Is the venue easily accessible?
- Will parking problems delay the arrival of the guests?
- Is the venue sound? If the event is held in a marquee, is the tent of sound structure? Are there any risks of leaks?
- If the wedding is outdoors, are there any risks of adverse weather conditions, someone falling, trees or branches falling, surprise noise etc?
- Are there sufficient toilet facilities available? Is there any risk of sewage problems?
- Are there any risks of food poisoning?
- Will there be an open bar? If so, are there any risks of over-indulgence by the guests?
- Are there any special dietary requirements?
- What happens if there is a delay in proceedings?
- Is there a time by which the venue needs to be cleared?
- Is there sufficient security at the venue?
- Is there a safe place to hang up coats or leave valuables?
- Is there a safe place for presents?
- Does the venue have a custodian or manager? Will they be present during the event?
- Will you need a doctor on the premises?
- Is the florist reliable?
- Will the band have the access to the venue to set up their gear? How many power sources are required? Is there a risk of a power cut due to overload? Are there any noise restrictions at the venue?
- What types of people will be attending? What types of risks are inherent in their attendance? Who does and does not get along with whom? Will Aunty Joan be upset if she is seated at the same table as Uncle Jack? Does Aunt Maude traditionally faint just as the groom is about to kiss the bride? Will the bride's great-grandmother be able to have easy wheelchair access to the venue?
- Can the venue easily accommodate the number of guests attending?
- Is there a limit to the number of persons permitted in or at the venue?
- Will there be any fireworks? Are there any risks of accidents in this regard? What if someone gets burned? Is there a first-aid kit on the premises? If so, will someone have easy access to that kit?

APPENDIX 5

SUPPLIER/VENDOR CONTRACT

This Agreement is made the   day of

BETWEEN:

(1)   [insert party] of [insert address] ("EventCo"); and

(2)   [insert party] of [insert address] ("the Company").

WHEREAS:

1.   EventCo owns or controls all rights in and to the Event.

2.   The Company is in the business of providing [insert relevant Goods/ Services].

3.   EventCo wishes to engage the Company, and the Company has agreed to provide to EventCo the [Goods/Services] upon and subject to the provisions of this Agreement.

NOW IT IS HEREBY AGREED as follows:

1.   DEFINITIONS

1.1   In this Agreement the words and expressions set out below shall, save where the context otherwise requires, have the following meanings:

Commercial Rights   means any and all rights of a commercial nature connected with the Event including, without limitation, broadcasting rights, so-called new media rights, interactive games rights, sponsorship rights, merchandising and licensing rights, ticketing rights, promotional rights and catering and hospitality rights;

[Designation   means the wording ["Official Supplier to XYZ Event"] or such other designation as EventCo may approve in writing;]

Effective Date   means the [date of signature of this Agreement];

Event   means [insert details] taking place on [insert details];

Event Manager means the person appointed by EventCo whose identity shall be notified by EventCo to the Company from time to time;

Event Period means the period from [2] days prior to the Event to [2] days after the Event;

Event of Force Majeure means any circumstance not foreseeable at the date of this Agreement and not within the reasonable control of the party in question, including but not limited to any strike, lock-out or other industrial action (not due to the acts of any party to this Agreement); any destruction (temporary or permanent), breakdown, malfunction or damage of or to any premises, plant, equipment (including computer systems) or materials; any civil commotion or disorder, riot, invasion, war or terrorist activity or threat of war or terrorist activity; any action taken by a governmental or public authority of any kind (including not granting a consent, exemption, approval or clearance); and any fire, explosion, storm, flood, earthquake, subsidence, epidemic or other natural physical disaster;

EventCo Marks means the event titles, words and logo(s) which are owned or controlled by EventCo and which appear in Schedule 3;

Fees means the fees for the [Goods/Services] payable by EventCo to the Company in accordance with the provisions set out in Clause 4 of this Agreement;

[Goods means those goods set out in Schedule 2;]

[Official Guide means that full colour guide produced and/or published by or on behalf of EventCo which relates to the Event;]

[Rights means those rights granted to the Company in connection with the Event as set out in Schedule 1;]

[Services	means the Services set out in Schedule 2 which the Company provides or is to provide to EventCo pursuant to this Agreement;]
[Supplier Category	means [insert relevant industry e.g. telecommunications, food and beverage etc];]
Term	means the period described in Clause 2 below;
Territory	means [insert details];
Venue	means [insert details];

1.2   Unless the context otherwise requires words denoting the singular shall include the plural and vice versa and words denoting any one gender shall include all genders and words denoting persons shall include bodies corporate, unincorporated associations and partnerships.

1.3   References in this Agreement to Schedules are to Schedules to this Agreement.

2.   TERM

This Agreement is deemed to have taken effect on the Effective Date and shall continue until [insert date], unless terminated earlier in accordance with the provisions of Clause 7 (the "Term").

3.   APPOINTMENT AND GRANT OF RIGHTS

[3.1   In consideration of the Fees paid by the Company to EventCo in accordance with Clause 4, EventCo hereby appoints the Company as [the sole and exclusive] supplier of the [Goods/Services] to the Event within the Supplier Category in the Territory.]

[3.2   In consideration of the supply of the [Goods/Services] by the Company, EventCo grants to the Company the Rights as set out in Schedule 1 for use during the Event Period, which Rights shall be exclusive to the Company in the Territory within the Supplier Category.]

3.3   The Company acknowledges and agrees that EventCo is the owner of the Commercial Rights and that the Company shall not be entitled to exploit or enter into any commercial or other agreements to exploit any of the Commercial Rights other than as set out in this Agreement.

[3.4   For the avoidance of doubt, this Agreement shall not confer on the Company any right to use the name, likeness image and/or other characteristics of any individual or team participating in or attending any Event and the Company undertakes that it shall not use the same without prior authority.]

4.   CONSIDERATION

[4.1   In consideration of the proper and satisfactory provision by the Company of the Services, EventCo agrees to pay to the Company the Fees [(excluding relevant taxes)] as follows:]
[insert details]
[or]

[4.1   In consideration of the grant of the Rights, the Company agrees to provide to EventCo, free of charge, the [Goods/Services] set out in Schedule 2.

[4.2   All sums set out in Clause 4.1 above shall be paid within [30] days of receipt of an appropriate invoice.]

4.3   All costs and expenses incurred by the Company in providing the [Goods/Services] shall be borne by the Company.

5.   OBLIGATIONS OF EVENTCO

5.1   EventCo represents, warrants and undertakes:

    5.1.1   that it has and will continue to have throughout the Term full right and title and authority to enter into this Agreement and to accept and perform the obligations imposed on it under this Agreement;

    5.1.2   to organise and stage the Event in a professional manner [and to deliver or procure the delivery of the Rights to the Company];

    5.1.3   to provide unrestricted access to the Venue for the personnel of the Company during the Event Period for the purposes of providing the [Goods/Services];

    5.1.4   that it owns or controls the EventCo Marks and shall take all measures it considers reasonable during the Term to protect its rights in the EventCo Marks from infringement by any third party.

[5.2   In the event that, for whatever reason, EventCo is unable to provide any of the Rights precisely as described in Schedule 1, EventCo shall be entitled to substitute alternative rights in the nature of the Rights to an equivalent value without penalty.]

6.   OBLIGATIONS OF THE COMPANY

6.1   The Company hereby represents, warrants and undertakes that:

6.1.1   it shall provide the [Goods/Services] on such dates and times as indicated in Schedule 2 or as otherwise directed by EventCo, and it is acknowledged by the Company that time shall be of the essence in the delivery of such [Goods/Services];

6.1.2   it is a Company specialising in the provision of the [Goods/Services] and it has all the necessary experience, capability and personnel to deliver the [Goods/Services] to the highest industry standards;

6.1.3   in providing the [Goods/Services] under this Agreement, the Company and its personnel shall exercise all necessary professional judgement, technical skill and care;

[6.1.4   the Goods provided shall be fit for the purpose for which they are intended to be used;]

[6.1.5   in providing the [Goods/Services] under this Agreement, the Company shall ensure that the Company personnel:

6.1.5.1   wear suitable apparel, footwear and protective equipment;

6.1.5.2   have and display at all times during the Event Period proper identification in the form acceptable to EventCo;

6.1.5.3   comply at all times with all rules, regulations and policies of EventCo relating to health and safety, security and risk management at the Venue;]

6.1.6   it has, and will continue to have throughout the Term, full right and title and authority to enter into this Agreement and to accept and perform the obligations imposed on it hereunder;

6.1.7   it will not appoint or instruct any third party to provide any part of the [Goods/Services] without the prior written approval of EventCo. In the event that such approval is granted, the Company shall procure that such third party comply in every respect with the provisions of this Agreement as if such third party were contracting with EventCo as the party hereto and the Company shall be liable to EventCo for the acts and omissions of any such third party in providing the [Goods/Services];

[6.1.8   it shall exercise the Rights strictly in accordance with the terms of this Agreement. For the avoidance of doubt, the Company shall not be entitled to create any merchandise, premiums or other items which are either associated with the Event or EventCo or which bear the EventCo Marks;]

6.1.9   it shall not establish a separate Internet website relating to the Event;

[6.1.10 it shall not without the prior written approval of EventCo engage in any joint promotional activity or otherwise exploit any of the Rights with or in connection with any third party nor exercise the Rights in such a manner that a confusion may arise in the minds of the public as to the identity of the person to whom EventCo has granted the Rights;]

6.1.11   it shall not do anything or permit anything to be done which might adversely affect the Commercial Rights or the value of the Commercial Rights;

6.1.12   it shall be responsible for obtaining all licenses, consents, approvals and permission required for the purposes of providing the [Goods/Services] and shall be solely responsible for the costs of obtaining same;

6.1.13   it shall observe, and ensure that the Company's personnel observe, all relevant rules, regulations, directions, codes of practice or guidelines imposed by national law or any competent authority which are applicable to the provision of the [Goods/Services] for the Event;

6.1.14   it shall promptly observe and comply with all reasonable instructions, directions or regulations issued by or on behalf of EventCo including without limitation, those relating to the organisation, staging, safety and image of the Event and the exploitation of the [Goods/Services] related thereto;

[6.1.15 it shall ensure that its own invited personnel and guests are of a seniority appropriate to the nature of the Event and shall observe all reasonable directions of EventCo including, without limitation, in relation to safety matters, and acknowledges that EventCo shall have the right to remove any person from a hospitality area within the Venue whose behaviour is deemed by EventCo to be unacceptable in the circumstances;]

6.1.16 it shall ensure that neither it nor any of its directors, employees, or other members of staff make any defamatory or derogatory statements or take part in any activities which are or might be derogatory or detrimental to the reputation, image or goodwill of EventCo, the Event or any commercial partner of EventCo; and

[6.1.17 it acknowledges the importance of co-operating with the media to obtain maximum coverage and exposure for the benefit of the Event and agrees to co-operate with all reasonable requests of such a nature by EventCo and/or any broadcaster or other commercial partner of EventCo.]

7. TERMINATION

7.1 Either party shall have the right at any time to terminate this Agreement immediately by giving written notice to the other in the event that:

(a) the other party has committed a material breach of any obligation under this Agreement which breach is incapable of remedy or cannot be remedied in time for the Event;

(b) the other party has committed a material breach of any of its obligations under this Agreement and has not remedied such breach (if the same is capable of remedy) within fourteen days of being required by written notice so to do;

(c) the other party goes into liquidation whether compulsory or voluntary or is declared insolvent or if an administrator or receiver is appointed over the whole or any part of that other party's assets or if that other party enters into any arrangement for the benefit of or compounds with its creditors generally or ceases to carry on business or threatens to do any of these things; or

(d) either party undergoes a change of control or ownership.

7.2 EventCo shall have the right to terminate this Agreement by providing [3 month's] notice in writing to the Company in the event that it no longer wishes to stage the Event.

8. CONSEQUENCES OF TERMINATION

8.1 The expiry or termination of this Agreement shall be without prejudice to any rights which have already accrued to either of the parties under this Agreement.

[8.2   Upon termination of this Agreement pursuant to Clause 7.2 or Clause 9 the Company shall immediately repay to EventCo such proportion of the Fee that has been paid, and no further instalments (if any) shall be payable to the Company.]

[8.3   Upon expiry or termination of this Agreement:

    8.3.1   all of the Rights shall forthwith terminate and automatically revert to EventCo;

    8.3.2   the Company shall not use or exploit its previous connection with EventCo or the Event, whether directly or indirectly;

    8.3.3   EventCo shall be entitled to grant all or any of the Rights to any third party; and

    8.3.4   each party shall promptly return to the other all of the property of the other within its possession.]

9.   FORCE MAJEURE

9.1   Neither party to this Agreement shall be deemed to be in breach of this Agreement or otherwise liable to the other as a result of any delay or failure in the performance of its obligations under this Agreement if and to the extent that such delay or failure is caused by an Event of Force Majeure and the time for performance of the relevant obligation(s) shall be extended accordingly.

9.2   A party whose performance of its obligations under this Agreement is delayed or prevented by an Event of Force Majeure:

    (a)   shall immediately notify the other party of the nature, extent, effect and likely duration of the circumstances constituting the Event of Force Majeure;

    (b)   shall use all reasonable endeavours to minimise the effect of the Event of Force Majeure on the performance of its obligations under this Agreement; and

    (c)   shall (subject to Clause 9.3 below) immediately after the Event of Force Majeure has ended notify the other party and resume full performance of its obligations under this Agreement.

9.3   If any Event of Force Majeure delays or prevents the performance of the obligations of either party for a continuous period of [three months], the party not so affected shall then be entitled to give notice to the affected party to terminate this Agreement with immediate effect without penalty. Such a termination notice shall be irrevocable except with the consent of both parties and upon termination the provisions of Clause 8 shall apply.

10. LIABILITY

10.1 Under no circumstances shall either party be liable for any actual or alleged indirect loss or consequential loss howsoever arising suffered by the other, including, but not limited to, loss of profits, anticipated profits, savings, business or opportunity or loss of publicity or loss of reputation or opportunity to enhance reputation or any other sort of economic loss.

10.2 The Company undertakes and agrees that it will indemnify and hold EventCo harmless from and against all costs and expenses (including without limitation reasonable legal costs), actions, proceedings, claims, demands and damage arising from a breach of the Company's representations, warranties or undertakings contained herein or arising from the acts or omissions of the Company or its respective officers, employees, agents and sub-contractors.

10.3 EventCo shall have no responsibility for any loss of or damage to the property and effects brought into the Venue by the Company, its officers, employees, agents and sub-contractors.

10.4 The Company shall be responsible for all its personnel engaged in the provision of the [Goods/Services]. Such personnel shall remain employed or engaged by the Company and not by EventCo, and the Company will be fully responsible for paying all salaries, wages, commissions, bonuses, taxes, pensions, sick pay or all other amounts or benefits payable directly or indirectly in respect of their employment or engagement.

10.5 The Company shall maintain at its own expense comprehensive [general/public/professional indemnity/product] liability insurance in such amount as may be adequate to protect the Company and EventCo against any and all claims, actions, losses and damages arising out of the provision of the [Goods/Services], with a minimum cover under such policy per claim being not less than [insert amount]. A copy of such policy or policies shall be provided to EventCo for its records.

11. INTELLECTUAL PROPERTY

11.1 The Company acknowledges and agrees that the EventCo Marks shall belong exclusively and in their entirety to EventCo. Any goodwill generated in the EventCo Marks generated through the use of the

EventCo Marks in accordance with this Agreement shall belong entirely to EventCo.

11.2 The Company shall not commit, or authorise any third party to commit, any act or omission which would or might affect the validity of the EventCo Marks.

[11.3 The Company's right to use the EventCo Marks shall be limited to the extent provided in Schedule 1.]

12. ANNOUNCEMENTS AND CONFIDENTIALITY

No announcement shall be made by either party in relation to this Agreement without the prior written consent of the other and neither party shall without the prior written consent of the other (save as required by law) disclose to any third party any information concerning the terms or subject matter hereof after the date hereof.

13. POINTS OF CONTACT

13.1 The principal point of contact for each party (unless the other party is notified otherwise in writing) shall be:

(a) EventCo: [   ]

(b) The Company: [   ]

13.2 The Company acknowledges and agrees that it is not entitled to rely on any representation, authorisation or decision of EventCo unless made by the principal point of contact (or his designated replacement) set out at sub-clause 13.1 above.

14. NOTICES

14.1 The parties agree that all notices under this Agreement shall, unless otherwise notified, be served on the following addressees:

(a) EventCo: [   ]

(b) The Company: [   ]

14.2 All notices shall be in writing and may be delivered personally, by facsimile, by first class pre-paid post or by registered mail and shall be deemed to be properly given or served:

(a) [two] working days after being sent to the intended recipient by pre-paid post addressed as aforesaid; or

(b) if sent by facsimile on receipt of confirmation of transmission or if not a working day the first working day thereafter provided that a confirming copy is sent by first class pre-paid post to the address aforesaid within 24 hours of transmission.

15. GENERAL

15.1 The granting by any party of any time or indulgence in respect of any breach of any term of this Agreement by the other shall not be deemed a waiver of such breach and the waiver by any party of any breach of any term of this Agreement by the other shall not prevent the subsequent enforcement of that term and shall not be deemed a waiver of any subsequent breach.

15.2 This Agreement shall constitute the entire agreement between the parties with respect to the subject matter hereof, and shall supersede any and all prior agreements, representations or understanding between the parties, whether written or oral.

15.3 This Agreement may be executed in any number of counterparts, each of which when executed shall constitute an original, but all of which when taken together shall constitute one and the same Agreement.

15.4 All rights, remedies and powers conferred upon the parties are cumulative and shall not be deemed to be exclusive of any other rights, remedies or powers now or subsequently conferred upon them by law or otherwise.

15.5 Each party will do all things necessary including executing all documents necessary to give effect to the intention of the parties in relation to this Agreement.

15.6 Should any term of this Agreement be considered void or voidable under any applicable law, then such terms shall be severed or amended in such a manner as to render the remainder of this Agreement valid or enforceable, unless the whole commercial object is thereby frustrated.

15.7 Neither party may assign any of its rights or obligations under this Agreement without the prior written consent of the other party, such consent not to be unreasonably withheld or delayed.

15.8 This Agreement may only be modified or any provision waived if such modification or waiver is in writing and signed by a duly authorised representative of each party.

15.9   This Agreement shall be governed by and construed in accordance with [insert governing law] and the parties hereby submit to the non-exclusive jurisdiction of the [insert courts of jurisdiction] courts.

15.10 Any date or period mentioned in any clause of this Agreement may be extended by mutual agreement in writing between the parties but as regards any date or period (whether or not extended as aforesaid) time shall be of the essence in this Agreement.

15.11 Nothing in this Agreement shall be deemed to constitute a joint venture, partnership or relationship of agency or employment between the parties.

IN WITNESS WHEREOF, the parties have executed this Agreement as of the day and year first above written.

Signed by
a duly authorised representative
for and on behalf of
[INSERT PARTY]

Signed by
a duly authorised representative
for and on behalf of
[INSERT PARTY]

SCHEDULE 1

THE RIGHTS

[1.   The exclusive right within the Supplier Category to be designated the ["Official Supplier of/to XYZ Event"] during the Term.

2.   The right to use the Designation during the Term:

(i)   on the Company website;

(ii) in television advertising conducted by the Company;

(iii) in print advertising carried out by the Company; and

(iv) on the official Company letterhead;

3.   Subject to the prior written approval of EventCo, a non-exclusive royalty-free right during the Term to use the EventCo Marks in conjunction with the Designation.

4.   The right to one full page colour advertisement, together with the Designation, in the Official Guide, provided that such a guide is produced for the Event.

5.   The right to a mention in the credits of any television show produced for the Event.

6.   The right to the following hospitality benefits, free of charge and subject to the observance by guests of any applicable regulations relating to access:

6.1   [20] VIP tickets to the Event;

6.2   [20] VIP tickets to the Event After Party;

6.3   [10] Hotel rooms at one of the official hotels used by EventCo for the Event. Extras, including but not limited to telephone, room-service, mini-bar and laundry, shall be for the account of the Company and/or its personnel.|

SCHEDULE 2

[THE GOODS/SERVICES]

The Company shall provide the following [Goods/Services]:
[insert details]

SCHEDULE 3

THE EVENTCO MARKS

[insert details]

APPENDIX 6

CATERING CONTRACT

This Agreement is made the   day of

BETWEEN:

(1)   [insert party] of [insert address] ("EventCo"); and

(2)   [insert party] of [insert address] ("the Company").

WHEREAS:

1.   EventCo owns or controls all rights in and to the Event.

2.   The Company is in the business of providing catering services.

3.   EventCo wishes to engage the Company, and the Company has agreed to provide to EventCo the Services upon and subject to the provisions of this Agreement.

NOW IT IS HEREBY AGREED as follows:

1.   DEFINITIONS

1.1   In this Agreement the words and expressions set out below shall, save where the context otherwise requires, have the following meanings:

Commercial Rights   means any and all rights of a commercial nature connected with the Event including, without limitation, broadcasting rights, so-called new media rights, interactive games rights, sponsorship rights, merchandising and licensing rights, ticketing rights, promotional rights and catering and hospitality rights;

[Designation   means the wording ["Official Caterer to/for XYZ Event"] or such other designation as EventCo may approve in writing;]

Effective Date   means the [date of signature of this Agreement];

Equipment   means [insert details];

Event   means [insert details] taking place on [insert details];

Event Manager	means the person appointed by EventCo whose identity shall be notified by EventCo to the Company from time to time;
Event Period	means the period from [2] days prior to the Event to [2] days after the Event;
Event of Force Majeure	means any circumstance not foreseeable at the date of this Agreement and not within the reasonable control of the party in question, including but not limited to any strike, lock-out or other industrial action (not due to the acts of any party to this Agreement); any destruction (temporary or permanent), breakdown, malfunction or damage of or to any premises, plant, equipment (including computer systems) or materials; any civil commotion or disorder, riot, invasion, war or terrorist activity or threat of war or terrorist activity; any action taken by a governmental or public authority of any kind (including not granting a consent, exemption, approval or clearance); and any fire, explosion, storm, flood, earthquake, subsidence, epidemic or other natural physical disaster;
EventCo Marks	means the event titles, words and logo(s) which are owned or controlled by EventCo and which appear in Schedule 3;
Fees	means the fees for the Services payable by EventCo to the Company in accordance with the provisions set out in Clause 4 of this Agreement;
[Official Guide	means that full colour guide produced and/or published by or on behalf of EventCo which relates to the Event;]
Products	means the food and beverages and other consumables provided by the Company as set out in Schedule 2;
Representative	means the represented elected by the Company to liaise with EventCo and the Event Manager regarding the delivery of the Services;

[**Rights**	means those rights granted to the Company in connection with the Event as set out in Schedule 1;]
Services	means the Services set out in Schedule 2 which the Company provides or is to provide to EventCo pursuant to this Agreement;
[**Supplier Category**	means [the catering industry];]
Term	means the period described in Clause 2 below;
Territory	means [insert details];
Venue	means [insert details];

1.2   Unless the context otherwise requires words denoting the singular shall include the plural and vice versa and words denoting any one gender shall include all genders and words denoting persons shall include bodies corporate, unincorporated associations and partnerships.

1.3   References in this Agreement to Schedules are to Schedules to this Agreement.

2.   TERM

This Agreement is deemed to have taken effect on the Effective Date and shall continue until [insert date], unless terminated earlier in accordance with the provisions of Clause 7 (the "Term").

3.   APPOINTMENT

3.1   In consideration of the Fees paid by the Company to EventCo in accordance with Clause 4, EventCo hereby appoints the Company as the exclusive supplier of catering services to the Event.

[3.2   In consideration of the supply of the Services by the Company, EventCo grants to the Company the Rights as set out in Schedule 1 for use during the Event Period, which Rights shall be exclusive to the Company in the Territory within the Supplier Category.]

3.3   The Company acknowledges and agrees that EventCo is the owner of the Commercial Rights and that the Company shall not be entitled to exploit or enter into any commercial or other agreements to exploit any of the Commercial Rights other than as set out in this Agreement.

3.4 For the avoidance of doubt, this Agreement shall not confer on the Company any right to use the name, likeness image and/or other characteristics of any individual or team participating in or attending any Event and the Company undertakes that it shall not use the same without prior authority.

3.5 EventCo undertakes not to appoint any other party to, or to itself provide, Services at the Event unless the Company is unable to or incapable of providing the Services or a part thereof as requested by EventCo.

4. FEES

4.1 In consideration of the proper and satisfactory provision by the Company of the Services, EventCo agrees to pay to the Company the Fees [(excluding relevant taxes)] as follows:

[Insert details]

4.2 All sums set out in Clause 4.1 above shall be paid within [30] days of receipt of an appropriate invoice.

4.3 All costs and expenses incurred by the Company in providing the Services including, without limitation, all staffing and associated costs, costs of materials, the Equipment, Products, stock and all other overheads, will be borne by the Company, save where expressly stated otherwise in this Agreement.

5. EVENTCO'S OBLIGATIONS

5.1 EventCo represents, warrants and undertakes:

5.1.1 that it has and will continue to have throughout the Term full right and title and authority to enter into this Agreement and to accept and perform the obligations imposed on it under this Agreement;

5.1.2 to organise and stage the Event in a professional manner [and to deliver or procure the delivery of the Rights to the Company];

5.1.3 to provide unrestricted access to the Venue for the personnel of the Company during the Event Period for the purposes of providing the Services;

5.1.4 that it owns or controls the EventCo Marks and shall take all measures it considers reasonable during the Term to protect its rights in the EventCo Marks from infringement by any third party;

5.1.5 to notify the Company promptly of any queries or complaints made by any third parties relating to the Services with a copy of such query or complaint if the same is in writing.

[5.2 In the event that, for whatever reason, EventCo is unable to provide any of the Rights precisely as described in Schedule 1, EventCo shall be entitled to substitute alternative rights in the nature of the Rights to an equivalent value without penalty.]

6. COMPANY'S OBLIGATIONS

6.1 The Company hereby represents, warrants and undertakes that:

6.1.1 it shall provide the Services on such dates and times as indicated in Schedule 2 or as otherwise directed by EventCo, and it is acknowledged by the Company that time shall be of the essence in the delivery of such Services;

6.1.2 the Products shall be provided in accordance with the pricing set out in Schedule 4, unless otherwise agreed between the parties.

6.1.3 it is a Company specialising in the provision of Services and it has all the necessary experience, capability and personnel to deliver the Services to the highest industry standards;

6.1.4 in providing the Services under this Agreement, the Company and its personnel shall exercise all necessary professional judgement, technical skill and care;

6.1.5 the Company shall maintain adequate staffing levels and ensure that appropriately qualified and experienced staff are employed, and that all staff are trained for their particular tasks. In particular, the Company shall ensure that during the Event the Company's personnel:

6.1.5.1 wear suitable apparel, footwear and protective equipment;

6.1.5.2 have and display at all times during the Event Period proper identification in the form acceptable to EventCo;

6.1.5.3 comply at all times with all rules, regulations and policies of EventCo relating to health and safety, security and risk management at the Venue;

6.1.6   it has, and will continue to have throughout the Term, full right and title and authority to enter into this Agreement and to accept and perform the obligations imposed on it hereunder;

6.1.7   it will not appoint or instruct any third party to provide any part of the Services without the prior written approval of EventCo. In the event that such approval is granted, the Company shall procure that such third party comply in every respect with the provisions of this Agreement as if such third party were contracting with EventCo as the party hereto and the Company shall be liable to EventCo for the acts and omissions of any such third party in providing the Services;

[6.1.8   it shall exercise the Rights strictly in accordance with the terms of this Agreement;]

6.1.9   it shall not establish a separate Internet website relating to the Event;

6.1.10   it shall not do anything or permit anything to be done which might adversely affect the Commercial Rights or the value of the Commercial Rights;

6.1.11   it shall be responsible for obtaining all licenses, consents, approvals and permission required for the purposes of providing the Services and shall be solely responsible for the costs of obtaining same;

6.1.12   it shall promptly observe and comply with all reasonable instructions, directions or regulations issued by or on behalf of EventCo including without limitation, those relating to the organisation, staging, safety and image of the Event and the delivery of the Services related thereto;

6.1.13   it shall ensure that neither it nor any of its directors, employees, or other members of staff make any defamatory or derogatory statements or take part in any activities which are or might be derogatory or detrimental to the reputation, image or goodwill of EventCo, the Event or any commercial partner of EventCo;

6.1.14   it shall not claim or refer to itself as having any "official" status or any other association in connection with or relating to any participant or attendee at the Event without the prior written approval of EventCo and the individual concerned;

6.1.15 it shall ensure that the Products used as part of the Services are of the highest quality reasonably attainable given the nature of the Services being offered and the logistical constraints of the Venue;

6.1.16 it shall work with the Events Manager to address any complaints and to ensure that the reasonable expectations of EventCo are met;

6.1.17 it and those persons by whom the Services are provided pursuant to this Agreement shall comply in all respects with all relevant laws, legislation, health and safety regulations, governmental decrees, rules, regulations, registrations and court orders which relate in any way to the provision of the Services, including EventCo's prescribed hygiene standards and emergency procedures set out at Schedule 5;

6.1.18 it has, and shall maintain throughout the Term in full force and effect all licences [(including liquor licences)], registrations, permits, authorities, health and safety certificates, consents and other qualifications necessary or desirable for the provision of the Services and there has been no act, event or omission as a result of which such qualification will or may be withdrawn, not be renewed or otherwise cease to have effect. [The Company shall be responsible, in association with EventCo for all legal arrangements relating to the grant of a liquor licence. For the avoidance of doubt the costs associated with the grant of the liquor licence shall be borne by EventCo insofar as they relate to EventCo's business;]

6.1.19 in the event of a change in the legislation regulating the sale of alcohol at the Venue, it shall discuss immediately with EventCo the impact that such legislation may have on the Services and whether any changes need to be made to the Services provided by the Company or any other terms of this Agreement as a result of such change;

[6.1.20 it will nominate two designated representatives who shall be responsible for, and who shall be named as a party on, all relevant liquor licences and regulations pertaining to the provision of alcohol at the bar in the Venue;]

6.1.21 it shall, after the Effective Date, discharge and accept all responsibility for all liabilities, obligations, costs, claims, and demands arising from or in respect of any of the Assumed Workers (as defined in Clause 6.1.22 below) and shall indemnify EventCo against the same;

6.1.22   In relation to all of the Company's Assumed Workers and its staff, it shall comply in all material respects with all statutes, regulations, codes of conduct (whether produced by any relevant authority, by EventCo or otherwise) collective agreements, terms and conditions of engagement, orders and awards applicable to their conditions of engagement, their relationship with EventCo and their performance of the Services. For the purposes of this Agreement, "Assumed Workers" shall mean those individuals who are engaged whether in writing or through custom and practice by the Company to provide the Services and who are engaged by the Company after the Effective Date;

6.1.23   it, and those persons by whom the Services are provided pursuant to this Agreement, shall exercise all due care and diligence when using the Equipment available at the Venue. For the avoidance of doubt the Company shall indemnify EventCo against any loss, damages and any other costs sustained by EventCo and arising directly or indirectly as a result of the Company's misuse of or negligence in respect of the use of the Equipment.

7.   TERMINATION

7.1   Either party shall have the right at any time to terminate this Agreement immediately by giving written notice to the other in the event that:

7.1.1   the other party has committed a material breach of any obligation under this Agreement which breach is incapable of remedy or cannot be remedied in time for the Event;

7.1.2   the other party has committed a material breach of any of its obligations under this Agreement and has not remedied such breach (if the same is capable of remedy) within fourteen days of being required by written notice so to do;

7.1.3   the other party goes into liquidation whether compulsory or voluntary or is declared insolvent or if an administrator or receiver is appointed over the whole or any part of that other party's assets or if that other party enters into any arrangement for the benefit of or compounds with its creditors generally; or

7.1.4   the other party ceases or threatens to cease to carry on business.

7.2   EventCo shall have the right to terminate this Agreement by providing no less than [3 month's] notice in writing to the Company in the event that it no longer wishes to stage the Event.

8.   CONSEQUENCES OF TERMINATION

8.1   The expiry or termination of this Agreement shall be without prejudice to any rights which have already accrued to either of the parties under this Agreement.

[8.2   Upon termination of this Agreement pursuant to Clause 7.2 or Clause 9 the Company shall immediately repay to EventCo such proportion of the Fee that has been paid, and no further instalments (if any) shall be payable to the Company.]

[8.3   Upon expiry or termination of this Agreement:

8.3.1   all of the Rights shall forthwith terminate and automatically revert to EventCo;

8.3.2   the Company shall not use or exploit its previous connection with EventCo or the Event, whether directly or indirectly;

8.3.3   EventCo shall be entitled to grant all or any of the Rights to any third party; and

8.3.4   each party shall promptly return to the other all of the property of the other within its possession.]

9.   FORCE MAJEURE

9.1   Neither party to this Agreement shall be deemed to be in breach of this Agreement or otherwise liable to the other as a result of any delay or failure in the performance of its obligations under this Agreement if and to the extent that such delay or failure is caused by an Event of Force Majeure and the time for performance of the relevant obligation(s) shall be extended accordingly.

9.2   A party whose performance of its obligations under this Agreement is delayed or prevented by an Event of Force Majeure:

(a)   shall immediately notify the other party of the nature, extent, effect and likely duration of the circumstances constituting the Event of Force Majeure;

(b)   shall use all reasonable endeavours to minimise the effect of the Event of Force Majeure on the performance of its obligations under this Agreement; and

(c)   shall (subject to Clause 9.3 below) immediately after the Event of Force Majeure has ended notify the other party and resume full performance of its obligations under this Agreement.

9.3   If any Event of Force Majeure delays or prevents the performance of the obligations of either party for a continuous period of [three months], the party not so affected shall then be entitled to give notice to the affected party to terminate this Agreement with immediate effect without penalty. Such a termination notice shall be irrevocable except with the consent of both parties and upon termination the provisions of Clause 8 shall apply.

10.   LIABILITY

10.1   Under no circumstances shall either party be liable for any actual or alleged indirect loss or consequential loss howsoever arising suffered by the other, including, but not limited to, loss of profits, anticipated profits, savings, business or opportunity or loss of publicity or loss of reputation or opportunity to enhance reputation or any other sort of economic loss.

10.2   The Company undertakes and agrees that it will indemnify and hold EventCo harmless from and against all costs and expenses (including without limitation reasonable legal costs), actions, proceedings, claims, demands and damage arising from a breach of the Company's representations, warranties or undertakings contained herein or arising from the acts or omissions of the Company or its respective officers, employees, agents and sub-contractors.

10.3   EventCo shall have no responsibility for any loss of or damage to the property and effects brought into the Venue by the Company, its officers, employees, agents and sub-contractors.

10.4   The Company shall maintain at its own expense comprehensive [general/public/professional indemnity/product] liability insurance in such amount as may be adequate to protect the Company and EventCo against any and all claims, actions, losses and damages arising out of the provision of the Services, with a minimum cover under such policy per claim being not less than [insert amount]. A copy of such policy or policies shall be provided to EventCo for its records.

11. INTELLECTUAL PROPERTY

11.1 The Company acknowledges and agrees that the EventCo Marks shall belong exclusively and in their entirety to EventCo. Any goodwill generated in the EventCo Marks generated through the use of the EventCo Marks in accordance with this Agreement shall belong entirely to EventCo.

11.2 The Company shall not commit, or authorise any third party to commit, any act or omission which would or might affect the validity of the EventCo Marks.

12. ANNOUNCEMENTS AND CONFIDENTIALITY

No announcement shall be made by either party in relation to this Agreement without the prior written consent of the other and neither party shall without the prior written consent of the other (save as required by law) disclose to any third party any information concerning the terms or subject matter hereof after the date hereof.

13. POINTS OF CONTACT

13.1 The principal point of contact for each party (unless the other party is notified otherwise in writing) shall be:

(a) EventCo: [   ]

(b) The Company: [   ]

13.2 The Company acknowledges and agrees that it is not entitled to rely on any representation, authorisation or decision of EventCo unless made by the principal point of contact (or his designated replacement) set out at sub-clause 13.1 above.

14. NOTICES

14.1 The parties agree that all notices under this Agreement shall, unless otherwise notified, be served on the following addressees:

(a) EventCo: [   ]

(b) The Company: [   ]

14.2 All notices shall be in writing and may be delivered personally, by facsimile, by first class pre-paid post or by registered mail and shall be deemed to be properly given or served:

(a) [two] working days after being sent to the intended recipient by pre-paid post addressed as aforesaid; or

(b) if sent by facsimile on receipt of confirmation of transmission or if not a working day the first working day thereafter provided that a confirming copy is sent by first class pre-paid post to the address aforesaid within 24 hours of transmission.

15. GENERAL

15.1 The granting by any party of any time or indulgence in respect of any breach of any term of this Agreement by the other shall not be deemed a waiver of such breach and the waiver by any party of any breach of any term of this Agreement by the other shall not prevent the subsequent enforcement of that term and shall not be deemed a waiver of any subsequent breach.

15.2 This Agreement shall constitute the entire agreement between the parties with respect to the subject matter hereof, and shall supersede any and all prior agreements, representations or understanding between the parties, whether written or oral.

15.3 This Agreement may be executed in any number of counterparts, each of which when executed shall constitute an original, but all of which when taken together shall constitute one and the same Agreement.

15.4 All rights, remedies and powers conferred upon the parties are cumulative and shall not be deemed to be exclusive of any other rights, remedies or powers now or subsequently conferred upon them by law or otherwise.

15.5 Each party will do all things necessary including executing all documents necessary to give effect to the intention of the parties in relation to this Agreement.

15.6 Should any term of this Agreement be considered void or voidable under any applicable law, then such terms shall be severed or amended in such a manner as to render the remainder of this Agreement valid or enforceable, unless the whole commercial object is thereby frustrated.

15.7 This Agreement may only be modified or any provision waived if such modification or waiver is in writing and signed by a duly authorised representative of each party.

15.8 This Agreement shall be governed by and construed in accordance with [insert governing law] and the parties hereby submit to the non-exclusive jurisdiction of the [insert courts of jurisdiction] courts.

15.9   Any date or period mentioned in any clause of this Agreement may be extended by mutual agreement in writing between the parties but as regards any date or period (whether or not extended as aforesaid) time shall be of the essence in this Agreement.

15.10   Nothing in this Agreement shall be deemed to constitute a joint venture, partnership or relationship of agency or employment between the parties.

IN WITNESS WHEREOF, the parties have executed this Agreement as of the day and year first above written.

Signed by
a duly authorised representative
for and on behalf of
[INSERT PARTY]

Signed by
a duly authorised representative
for and on behalf of
[INSERT PARTY]

SCHEDULE 1

THE RIGHTS

[1.   In consideration of the provision of the Services, EventCo grants to the Company the following Rights:

(a)   The right to use the EventCo Marks and the Designation on all price lists and menus, subject to the prior approval of EventCo;

(b)   The right to use the EventCo Marks and the Designation on all the Company's own promotional materials and letterheads, subject to the prior approval of EventCo; and

(c)   The right to one full page of advertising in the Official Guide, provided such advertisement is provided to EventCo by no later than [insert date].

2.   EventCo grants to the Company a royalty-free, non-exclusive licence to use the EventCo Marks for the purposes of exercising the rights in paragraph 1 above, provided that the use of the EventCo Marks shall be consistent with the marks as set out in Schedule 3 hereto.]

SCHEDULE 2

SERVICES

[Products

1. The Company shall provide the following Products:

    [insert details]

2. The Products shall be provided for [insert number of people].

3. The Products shall be served at the Venue during the following times and in the following manner:

    [insert details]

Personnel

4. The Company shall maintain adequate staffing levels and ensure that appropriately qualified and experienced staff are engaged at all times to provide the Services, and that all staff are trained for their particular tasks.

5. The Company is responsible for all its staff, whether employed directly or sourced through other arrangements, and shall ensure that all staff:

    5.1 understand and comply with the legal requirements relevant to their area of work;

    5.2 have a thorough working knowledge of such of the Company's obligations to EventCo pursuant to this Agreement as it is in their province to know;

    5.3 are tidily dressed, clean and smart and that appropriate staff wear a uniform approved by the Company;

    5.4 are provided with and use at all times proper protective equipment supplied by the Company.

Management

6. The Event Manager will monitor the Services to ensure their delivery on time and to appropriate quality standards and shall be entitled for this purpose to carry out planned and random checks as are necessary throughout the Event Period.

7. The Company shall appoint a dedicated Representative to manage the relationship between EventCo and the Company and who shall be

responsible for the day to day delivery of the Services in accordance with the provisions of this Agreement. The Representative shall address all day-to-day management, compliance and operational issues arising under this Agreement to the Event Manager.

8. The Event Manager and the Representative shall hold meetings during the Event Period as and where necessary to discuss and review the provision of the Services.

9. The Company shall comply with all reasonable requests of EventCo in carrying out the monitoring of the Services, which may include Product tasting sessions and, for the avoidance of doubt, EventCo having access to all relevant information and documents held by/for or created by/for the Company in undertaking this Agreement.

[10. In addition to ongoing monitoring by EventCo of the Services, EventCo shall undertake performance reviews. These reviews shall include consideration of the following:

10.1 results of planned or random inspections;

10.2 finance procedures and security;

10.3 safety;

10.4 hygiene;

10.5 other relevant information.

If on completion of a review, or at any time during the Term, EventCo is dissatisfied with the performance of the Company, EventCo shall inform the Representative, indicating the areas of concern. If, after a period of [insert period], the Company still fails to satisfy EventCo in respect of the area(s) giving rise to concern, EventCo reserves the right to take such action as it deems appropriate, without prejudice to EventCo's remaining rights pursuant to Clause 7 of this Agreement or otherwise.]

Equipment

11. The Company shall, where necessary and at its own cost, supplement the catering areas at the Venue with portable catering points to ensure the adequate and satisfactory provision of the Services. The installation of these catering points and any modification thereof shall be subject to EventCo's prior written approval. The Company shall further ensure that, once installed, such catering points are at all times maintained to a standard satisfactory to EventCo, EventCo's Health & Safety executive and any other relevant authorities.

12. The Company may from time to time supply additional equipment unless EventCo has agreed to purchase such items.

13. The Company shall use its best endeavours to assist EventCo to set up and maintain in working order vending machines (dispensing drinks and food) in or around the Venue.

Other

14. The Company shall advise EventCo immediately of any accident or breach in health and safety regulations, regardless of whether any action is required by EventCo.

15. The Company shall supply immediately details of any complaints regarding the Services, including copies of correspondence and, at the request of and in the form approved by EventCo, such further information so that EventCo may respond to complaints about the provision of the Services.

16. In order to comply with health and safety regulations, the Company shall make all satisfactory arrangements for the removal of all waste from the catering areas and from the Venue immediately after the Event.

17. The Company shall procure all necessary goods, materials, equipment, and services for the provision of the Services, at the Company's cost (except where specified otherwise), including, without limitation, the following:-

    (a) maintenance of all equipment used by the Company in a clean and tidy condition;

    (b) maintenance of necessary stock levels of Products; and

    (c) provision of sample priced menus for all Products for approval by EventCo.]

SCHEDULE 3

THE EVENTCO MARKS

[insert details]

SCHEDULE 4

PRICE LIST

[insert details]

SCHEDULE 5

EMERGENCY PROCEDURES
AND HYGIENE STANDARDS

[insert details]

APPENDIX 7

HOSPITALITY CONTRACT

This Agreement is made the   day of

BETWEEN:

(1)   [insert party] of [insert address] ("EventCo"); and

(2)   [insert party] of [insert address] ("the Company").

WHEREAS:

1.   EventCo owns or controls all rights in and to the Event.

2.   The Company is in the business of providing hospitality for events.

3.   The Company wishes to provide Hospitality during the Event, and EventCo wishes to grant to the Company a concession allowing it to do so on the terms and conditions of this Agreement.

NOW IT IS HEREBY AGREED as follows:

1.   DEFINITIONS

1.1   In this Agreement the words and expressions set out below shall, save where the context otherwise requires, have the following meanings:

Box Hospitality   means the Hospitality to be provided by the Company in the Hospitality Boxes;

Commercial Rights   means any and all rights of a commercial nature connected with the Event including, without limitation, broadcasting rights, so-called new media rights, interactive games rights, sponsorship rights, merchandising and licensing rights, ticketing rights, promotional rights and catering and hospitality rights;

Designation   means the wording ["Official Hospitality Provider to XYZ Event"] or such other designation as EventCo may approve in writing;

Effective Date   means the [date of signature of this Agreement];

Event   means [insert details] taking place on [insert details];

Event Manager	means the person appointed by EventCo whose identity shall be notified by EventCo to the Company from time to time;
Event Period	means the period from [2] days prior to the Event to [2] days after the Event;
Event of Force Majeure	means any circumstance not foreseeable at the date of this Agreement and not within the reasonable control of the party in question, including but not limited to any strike, lock-out or other industrial action (not due to the acts of any party to this Agreement); any destruction (temporary or permanent), breakdown, malfunction or damage of or to any premises, plant, equipment (including computer systems) or materials; any civil commotion or disorder, riot, invasion, war or terrorist activity or threat of war or terrorist activity; any action taken by a governmental or public authority of any kind (including not granting a consent, exemption, approval or clearance); and any fire, explosion, storm, flood, earthquake, subsidence, epidemic or other natural physical disaster;
EventCo Marks	means the event titles, words and logo(s) which are owned or controlled by EventCo and which appear in Schedule 3;
Fees	means the fees for the Hospitality payable by EventCo to the Company in accordance with the provisions set out in Clause 4 of this Agreement;
Food and Drink	means [all types of food and drink that the Company may retail at the Venue and shall include, but not be limited to, varieties of fast food and restaurant products, confectionary, ice cream and alcoholic and non-alcoholic beverages;]
Hospitality	means the provision of catering, viewing and promotional facilities and packages as set out in Schedule 2 which are to be marketed and sold by the Company;

Hospitality Boxes means the temporary suites provided for Hospitality purposes at the Venue designated by EventCo in accordance with the terms of this Agreement;

Hospitality Packages means the packages to be offered for sale in respect of the Event by the Company for Marquee Hospitality and/or Box Hospitality as set out in Schedule 2;

Marquee Hospitality means the Hospitality to be provided by the Company in the Marquees;

Marquees means the temporary marquees provided for Hospitality purposes at the Venue designated by EventCo in accordance with the terms of this Agreement, the initial locations being as set out in Schedule 4;

Official Programme means that full colour guide produced and/or published by or on behalf of EventCo which relates to the Event;

Payment Date means [insert details];

Rights means those rights granted to the Company in connection with the Event, described in Clause 2.1 and Schedule 1;

Term means the period described in Clause 3 below;

Venue means [insert details];

Venue Manager means the person or persons notified to the Company from time to time by EventCo.

1.2   Unless the context otherwise requires words denoting the singular shall include the plural and vice versa and words denoting any one gender shall include all genders and words denoting persons shall include bodies corporate, unincorporated associations and partnerships.

1.3   References in this Agreement to Schedules are to Schedules to this Agreement.

2. LICENCE TO PROVIDE HOSPITALITY

2.1   In consideration of and subject to the payment by the Company of the Fees in accordance with Clause 4, EventCo grants to the Company the Rights, which shall include:

2.1.1   The exclusive right to provide Box Hospitality and Marquee Hospitality for the Event during the Term; and

2.1.2   The rights set out in Schedule 1 of this Agreement.

2.2   EventCo undertakes not to appoint any other party to, or to itself provide, Hospitality at the Event unless the Company is unable to or incapable of providing the Hospitality or a part thereof as requested by EventCo.

2.3   Nothing in this Agreement shall provide the right to the Company to provide Hospitality in any part of the Venue other than the Hospitality Boxes and/or Marquees.

2.4   The Company acknowledges and agrees that EventCo is the owner of the Commercial Rights and that the Company shall not be entitled to exploit or enter into any commercial or other agreements to exploit any of the Commercial Rights other than as set out in this Agreement.

3. TERM

This Agreement is deemed to have taken effect on the Effective Date and shall continue until [insert date], unless terminated earlier in accordance with the provisions of Clause 10 (the "Term").

4. FEES

4.1   In consideration of the grant of the Rights, the Company agrees to pay to EventCo Fees of [insert amount] in respect of each person to whom Marquee Hospitality is sold, and Fees of [insert amount] in respect of each person to whom Box Hospitality is sold. The Fees shall be paid in instalments in each year of the Term as follows:

4.1.1   [insert amount] on [insert date]; and

4.1.2   the balance of any Fees outstanding calculated in accordance with Clause 4.2 below on [insert date].

4.2   All other payments under this Agreement shall be made on [insert day and month] in each year of the Term and following the expiry or termination of this Agreement in respect of any further amounts due.

4.3   Neither party shall have the right to withhold any part of any amounts due to the other as a reserve against returns and/or credits.

4.4 The Company undertakes to make all payments required under this Agreement by cheque or bankers' draft in [insert currency] or by transfer to the account of EventCo as nominated by EventCo from time to time.

4.5 EventCo shall have the right to charge interest in respect of late payments of any sum due under this Agreement at a rate of [4%] per year above the base rate of [insert details] bank calculated on a daily basis from the date payment was due until the date payment was made.

4.6 All sums payable under this Agreement are exclusive of [insert relevant taxes] which shall be payable at the applicable rate at the time payment is made.

4.7 All costs and expenses incurred by the Company in providing the Hospitality including, without limitation, all staffing and associated costs, costs of materials, additional equipment provided by it, stock and all other overheads, will be borne by the Company, save where expressly stated otherwise in this Agreement.

5 EVENTCO'S OBLIGATIONS

5.1 EventCo represents, warrants and undertakes:

5.1.1 that it has and will continue to have throughout the Term full right and title and authority to enter into this Agreement and to accept and perform the obligations imposed on it under this Agreement;

5.1.2 to organise and stage the Event in a professional manner and to deliver or procure the delivery of the Rights to the Company;

5.1.3 to provide unrestricted access to the Venue for the personnel of the Company during the Event Period for the purposes of providing the Hospitality;

5.1.4 that it owns or controls the EventCo Marks and shall take all measures it considers reasonable during the Term to protect its rights in the EventCo Marks from infringement by any third party;

5.1.5 to notify the Company promptly of any queries or complaints made by any third parties relating to the Hospitality with a copy of such query or complaint if the same is in writing.

5.2   In the event that, for whatever reason, EventCo is unable to provide any of the Rights precisely as described in Schedule 1, EventCo shall be entitled to substitute alternative rights in the nature of the Rights to an equivalent value without penalty.

6.   COMPANY'S OBLIGATIONS

6.1   The Company hereby represents, warrants and undertakes that:

6.1.1   it shall provide the Hospitality on such dates and times as indicated in Schedule 2 or as otherwise directed by EventCo, and it is acknowledged by the Company that time shall be of the essence in the delivery of such Hospitality;

6.1.2   it is a company specialising in the provision of Hospitality and it has all the necessary experience, capability and personnel to deliver the Hospitality to the highest industry standards;

6.1.3   in providing the Hospitality under this Agreement, the Company and its personnel shall exercise all necessary professional judgement, technical skill and care;

6.1.4   the Company shall maintain adequate staffing levels and ensure that appropriately qualified and experienced staff are employed, and that all staff are trained for their particular tasks. In particular, the Company shall ensure that the Company's personnel:

6.1.4.1 wear suitable apparel, footwear and protective equipment;

6.1.4.2 have and display at all times during the Event Period proper identification in the form acceptable to EventCo;

6.1.4.3 comply at all times with all rules, regulations and policies of EventCo relating to health and safety, security and risk management at the Venue;

6.1.5   it has, and will continue to have throughout the Term, full right and title and authority to enter into this Agreement and to accept and perform the obligations imposed on it hereunder;

6.1.6   it will not appoint or instruct any third party to provide any part of the Hospitality without the prior written approval of EventCo. In the event that such approval is granted, the Company shall procure that such third party comply in every respect with the provisions of this Agreement as if such third party were contracting with EventCo as the party hereto and the Company shall be liable to EventCo for the acts and omissions of any such third party in providing the Hospitality;

6.1.7 it shall exercise the Rights strictly in accordance with the terms of this Agreement;

6.1.8 it shall not establish a separate Internet website relating to the Event;

6.1.9 it shall not do anything or permit anything to be done which might adversely affect the Commercial Rights or the value of the Commercial Rights;

6.1.10 it shall be responsible for obtaining all licenses, consents, approvals and permission required for the purposes of providing the Hospitality and shall be solely responsible for the costs of obtaining same;

6.1.11 it shall observe, and ensure that the Company's personnel observe, all relevant rules, regulations, directions, codes of practice or guidelines imposed by national law or any competent authority which are applicable to the provision of Hospitality for the Event;

6.1.12 it shall promptly observe and comply with all reasonable instructions, directions or regulations issued by or on behalf of EventCo including without limitation, those relating to the organisation, staging, safety and image of the Event and the exploitation of the Rights related thereto;

6.1.13 it shall ensure that neither it nor any of its directors, employees, or other members of staff make any defamatory or derogatory statements or take part in any activities which are or might be derogatory or detrimental to the reputation, image or goodwill of EventCo, the Event or any commercial partner of EventCo;

6.1.14 it shall not claim or refer to itself as having any "official" status or any other association in connection with or relating to any participant or attendee at the Event without the prior written approval of EventCo and the individual concerned;

6.1.15 it shall ensure that packages and products used or sold as part of all Hospitality Packages are of the highest quality reasonably attainable given the nature of the Event and the logistical constraints of the Venue;

6.1.16 it shall work with the Events Manager to address any complaints and to ensure that the reasonable expectations of EventCo are met;

6.1.17 it and those persons by whom the Hospitality are provided pursuant to this Agreement shall comply in all respects with all relevant laws, legislation, health and safety regulations, governmental decrees, rules, regulations, registrations and court orders which relate in any way to the provision of the Hospitality, including EventCo's prescribed hygiene standards and emergency procedures set out at Schedule 5;

6.1.18 it has, and shall maintain throughout the Term in full force and effect all licences [(including liquor licences)], registrations, permits, authorities, health and safety certificates, consents and other qualifications necessary or desirable for the provision of the Hospitality and there has been no act, event or omission as a result of which such qualification will or may be withdrawn, not be renewed or otherwise cease to have effect. [The Company shall be responsible, in association with EventCo for all legal arrangements relating to the grant of a liquor licence. For the avoidance of doubt the costs associated with the grant of the liquor licence shall be borne by [EventCo];]

6.1.19 in the event of a change in the legislation regulating the sale of alcohol at the Venue, it shall discuss immediately with EventCo the impact that such legislation may have on the Hospitality and whether any changes need to be made to the Hospitality provided by the Company or any other terms of this Agreement as a result of such change;

[6.1.20 it will nominate two designated representatives who shall be responsible for, and who shall be named as a party on, all relevant liquor licences and regulations pertaining to the provision of alcohol at the bar in the Venue;]

6.1.21 it shall, after the Effective Date, discharge and accept all responsibility for all liabilities, obligations, costs, claims, and demands arising from or in respect of any of the Assumed Workers (as defined in Clause 6.1.22 below) and shall indemnify EventCo against the same;

6.1.22 in relation to all of the Company's Assumed Workers and its staff, it shall comply in all material respects with all statutes, regulations, codes of conduct (whether produced by any relevant authority, by EventCo or otherwise) collective agreements, terms and conditions of engagement, orders and awards applicable to their conditions of engagement, their relationship with EventCo and their performance of the Hospitality. For the purposes of this Agreement, "Assumed Workers" shall mean those individuals who are engaged whether in writing or through custom and practice by the Company to provide Hospitality and who are engaged by the Company after the Effective Date;

6.1.23 it, and those persons by whom the Hospitality are provided pursuant to this Agreement, shall exercise all due care and diligence when using the Equipment available at the Venue. For the avoidance of doubt the Company shall indemnify EventCo against any loss, damages and any other costs sustained by EventCo and arising directly or indirectly as a result of the Company's misuse of or negligence in respect of the use of the Equipment;

6.1.24 It shall at its own cost maintain, repair and keep the Hospitality Boxes and Hospitality Marquees in good condition; and

6.1.25 It shall ensure that the Hospitality Boxes and the Marquees and the immediately adjacent areas surrounding each of them are kept clean and tidy and that all waste arising from the provision of the Hospitality is disposed of in appropriate containers. For the avoidance of doubt, the Company shall be fully responsible for the disposal in a suitable container of all liquid waste arising from the provision of Food and Drink by the Company, such containers to be provided by the Company.

6.2 The Company shall be responsible for the co-ordination of Hospitality sales and operations, but shall at all times consult with the relevant Venue Manager in this regard.

7. VENUE

7.1 The Company shall have the exclusive right to market and sell Hospitality Packages in the Hospitality Boxes for a capacity of not less than [insert number] and for a capacity of not less than [insert number] Hospitality Packages in Marquees at the sites designated in Schedule 4.

7.2 EventCo shall have the right to alter the location of the Hospitality Boxes or Marquees from time to time as it may reasonably require provided that the minimum capacities in Clause 7.1 shall not be reduced by EventCo and that the relocation of such Hospitality Boxes or Marquees shall be subject to the prior written consent of the Company, such consent not to be unreasonably withheld or delayed.

7.3   EventCo shall have absolute discretion and authority with regard to all matters relating to the operation of the Venue outside the Hospitality Boxes and the Marquees.

7.4   The Company undertakes and covenants with EventCo that during the Term it shall not use the Hospitality Boxes or Marquees except for the provision of Hospitality pursuant to this Agreement.

7.5   Both parties expressly acknowledge and declare that this Agreement shall not give rise to a tenancy relationship between the parties, nor will the Company have any rights whatsoever to possession or occupation of any, or any part of, the Hospitality Boxes or Marquees or any part of the Venue.

8.   HOSPITALITY

8.1   The Company shall purchase all Event hospitality tickets from EventCo or its licensed ticket agent in respect of all Hospitality Packages sold and shall not issue or sell any tickets other than as part of the Hospitality Packages.

8.2   The Company shall purchase a minimum number of [insert number] tickets from EventCo for sale as part of the Hospitality Packages.

8.3   The Company shall ensure that Hospitality Packages are sold under the name and logo of the Event or otherwise as may be agreed between the parties.

8.4   The Company shall only use EventCo's officially appointed caterers and EventCo undertakes to use all reasonable endeavours to achieve the delivery of the highest possible quality of products and services at market-related prices.

8.5   The Company shall purchase all Official Programmes exclusively from EventCo at face value. The Company shall purchase a minimum number of [insert number] of Official Programmes for the Event from EventCo.

8.6   The Company shall submit all promotional, sales and marketing material to EventCo for its prior written approval prior to distribution.

8.7   The parties shall use their best endeavours to discourage and prevent unofficial hospitality outside the Venue.

8.8   The parties agree to use their respective reasonable endeavours to facilitate parking and transportation for Hospitality guests around the site on the basis of a minimum of [1] car parking space per [4] Hospitality Packages.

9.   INTELLECTUAL PROPERTY

9.1   The Company acknowledges and agrees that the EventCo Marks shall belong exclusively and in their entirety to EventCo. The Company's right to use the EventCo Marks shall be limited to the extent provided in Schedule 9.

9.2   The Company shall not commit, or authorise any third party to commit, any act or omission which would or might affect the validity of the EventCo Marks.

9.3   The Company grants to EventCo a royalty-free, non-exclusive licence for the duration of this Agreement to use the Company's logos and trade marks for the purpose of promoting the provision of the Hospitality Packages by the Company although EventCo shall not be obliged to do so.

9.4   Nothing in this Agreement shall have the effect of transferring any proprietary rights between the parties and all goodwill generated from either party's use of the other's trade marks and logos shall vest in the other party.

10.   TERMINATION

10.1   Either party shall have the right at any time to terminate this Agreement immediately by giving written notice to the other in the event that:

(a)   the other party has committed a material breach of any obligation under this Agreement which breach is incapable of remedy or cannot be remedied in time for the Event;

(b)   the other party has committed a material breach of any of its obligations under this Agreement and has not remedied such breach (if the same is capable of remedy) within fourteen days of being required by written notice so to do;

(c)   the other party goes into liquidation whether compulsory or voluntary or is declared insolvent or if an administrator or receiver is appointed over the whole or any part of that other party's assets or if that other party enters into any arrangement for the benefit of or compounds with its creditors generally; or

(d)   the other party ceases or threatens to cease to carry on business.

10.2   EventCo shall have the right to terminate this Agreement by providing no less than [3 month's] notice in writing to the Company in the event that it no longer wishes to stage the Event.

11   CONSEQUENCES OF TERMINATION

11.1   The expiry or termination of this Agreement shall be without prejudice to any rights which have already accrued to either of the parties under this Agreement.

[11.2   Upon termination of this Agreement pursuant to Clause 10.2 or Clause 12 EventCo shall immediately repay to the Company such proportion of the Fee that has been paid to EventCo, and no further payments shall be payable to EventCo.]

11.3   Upon expiry or termination of this Agreement:

11.3.1   all of the Rights shall forthwith terminate and automatically revert to EventCo;

11.3.2   the Company shall not use or exploit its previous connection with EventCo or the Event, whether directly or indirectly;

11.3.3   EventCo shall be entitled to grant all or any of the Rights to any third party; and

11.3.4   each party shall promptly return to the other all of the property of the other within its possession.

12   FORCE MAJEURE

12.1   Neither party to this Agreement shall be deemed to be in breach of this Agreement or otherwise liable to the other as a result of any delay or failure in the performance of its obligations under this Agreement if and to the extent that such delay or failure is caused by an Event of Force Majeure and the time for performance of the relevant obligation(s) shall be extended accordingly.

12.2   A party whose performance of its obligations under this Agreement is delayed or prevented by an Event of Force Majeure:

12.2.1   shall immediately notify the other party of the nature, extent, effect and likely duration of the circumstances constituting the Event of Force Majeure;

12.2.2   shall use all reasonable endeavours to minimise the effect of the Event of Force Majeure on the performance of its obligations under this Agreement; and

12.2.3 shall (subject to Clause 12.3 below) immediately after the Event of Force Majeure has ended notify the other party and resume full performance of its obligations under this Agreement.

12.3 If any Event of Force Majeure delays or prevents the performance of the obligations of either party for a continuous period of [three months], the party not so affected shall then be entitled to give notice to the affected party to terminate this Agreement with immediate effect without penalty. Such a termination notice shall be irrevocable except with the consent of both parties and upon termination the provisions of Clause 11 shall apply.

13 LIABILITY

13.1 Under no circumstances shall either party be liable for any actual or alleged indirect loss or consequential loss howsoever arising suffered by the other, including, but not limited to, loss of profits, anticipated profits, savings, business or opportunity or loss of publicity or loss of reputation or opportunity to enhance reputation or any other sort of economic loss.

13.2 The Company shall indemnify and keep indemnified EventCo from and against all demands, claims, legal action, damages, costs (including, without limitation, legal costs and the fees of any expert witnesses incurred in connection with any actions or proceedings), loss, interest or expenses arising, directly or indirectly, out of any act or omission on the part of the Company in the delivery of the Hospitality or as a result of any breach of its obligations, representations, warranties or undertakings contained in this Agreement.

13.3 EventCo shall have no responsibility for any loss of or damage to the property and effects brought into the Venue by the Company, its officers, employees, agents and sub-contractors.

13.4 The Company shall maintain at its own expense comprehensive [third party/general/public/product] liability insurance in such amount as may be adequate to protect the Company and EventCo against any and all claims, actions, losses and damages arising out of the provision of the Hospitality, with a minimum cover under such policy per claim being not less than [insert amount]. A copy of such policy or policies shall be provided to EventCo for its records. The interest of EventCo shall be noted on any such policy.

14 ASSIGNMENT

Neither party may assign any of its rights or obligations under this Agreement without the prior written consent of the other party, such consent not to be unreasonably withheld or delayed.

15 ANNOUNCEMENTS AND CONFIDENTIALITY

15.1 No announcement shall be made by either party in relation to this Agreement without the prior written consent of the other.

15.2 Each party undertakes to each other that they shall at all times:

15.2.1 treat and safeguard as private, secret and confidential any and all information and data, howsoever recorded or preserved, relating to the Hospitality and/or EventCo or EventCo's business or the Company or the Company's business whether or not provided by EventCo or the Company ("Confidential Information");

15.2.2 use Confidential Information only in relation to the delivery of the Hospitality or in connection with the Agreement; and

15.2.3 not at any time disclose or reveal any Confidential Information to any person or party other than to persons or parties authorised to receive Confidential Information.

16 POINTS OF CONTACT

16.1 The principal point of contact for each party (unless the other party is notified otherwise in writing) shall be:

(a) EventCo: [   ]

(b) The Company: [   ]

16.2 The Company acknowledges and agrees that it is not entitled to rely on any representation, authorisation or decision of EventCo unless made by the principal point of contact (or his designated replacement) set out at sub-Clause 16.1 above.

17 NOTICES

17.1 The parties agree that all notices under this Agreement shall, unless otherwise notified, be served on the following addressees:

(a) EventCo: [   ]

(b) The Company: [   ]

17.2 All notices shall be in writing and may be delivered personally, by facsimile, by first class pre-paid post or by registered mail and shall be deemed to be properly given or served:

17.3 [two] working days after being sent to the intended recipient by pre-paid post addressed as aforesaid; or

17.4 if sent by facsimile on receipt of confirmation of transmission or if not a working day the first working day thereafter provided that a confirming copy is sent by first class pre-paid post to the address aforesaid within 24 hours of transmission.

18. GENERAL

18.1 The granting by any party of any time or indulgence in respect of any breach of any term of this Agreement by the other shall not be deemed a waiver of such breach and the waiver by any party of any breach of any term of this Agreement by the other shall not prevent the subsequent enforcement of that term and shall not be deemed a waiver of any subsequent breach.

18.2 This Agreement shall constitute the entire agreement between the parties with respect to the subject matter hereof, and shall supersede any and all prior agreements, representations or understanding between the parties, whether written or oral.

18.3 This Agreement may be executed in any number of counterparts, each of which when executed shall constitute an original, but all of which when taken together shall constitute one and the same Agreement.

18.4 All rights, remedies and powers conferred upon the parties are cumulative and shall not be deemed to be exclusive of any other rights, remedies or powers now or subsequently conferred upon them by law or otherwise.

18.5 Each party will do all things necessary including executing all documents necessary to give effect to the intention of the parties in relation to this Agreement.

18.6 Should any term of this Agreement be considered void or voidable under any applicable law, then such terms shall be severed or amended in such a manner as to render the remainder of this Agreement valid or enforceable, unless the whole commercial object is thereby frustrated.

18.7   This Agreement may only be modified or any provision waived if such modification or waiver is in writing and signed by a duly authorised representative of each party.

18.8   This Agreement shall be governed by and construed in accordance with [insert governing law] and the parties hereby submit to the non-exclusive jurisdiction of the [insert courts of jurisdiction] courts.

18.9   Any date or period mentioned in any clause of this Agreement may be extended by mutual agreement in writing between the parties but as regards any date or period (whether or not extended as aforesaid) time shall be of the essence in this Agreement.

18.10   Nothing in this Agreement shall be deemed to constitute a joint venture, partnership or relationship of agency or employment between the parties.

IN WITNESS WHEREOF, the parties have executed this Agreement as of the day and year first above written.

Signed by
a duly authorised representative
for and on behalf of
[INSERT PARTY]

Signed by
a duly authorised representative
for and on behalf of
[INSERT PARTY]

SCHEDULE 1

THE RIGHTS

[1.   In consideration of the provision of the Hospitality, EventCo grants to the Company the following Rights:

(a)   The right to use the EventCo Marks and the Designation on all materials that form part of the Hospitality Package, subject to the prior approval of EventCo;

(b)   The right to use the EventCo Marks and the Designation on all the Company's own promotional materials and letterheads, subject to the prior approval of EventCo; and

(c) The right to one half-page of advertising in the Official Programme, provided such advertisement is provided to EventCo by no later than [insert date].

2. EventCo grants to the Company a royalty-free, non-exclusive licence to use the EventCo Marks for the purposes of exercising the rights in paragraph 1 above, provided that the use of such marks shall be consistent with the marks as set out in Schedule 3 hereto.]

SCHEDULE 2

HOSPITALITY

Proposed structure of Hospitality Packages:
Box Hospitality

Package content: [insert details e.g. event tickets, meals, drinks, entertainment]
Package price: [insert details]

Marquee Hospitality

Package content: [insert details e.g. event tickets, meals, drinks, entertainment]

Package price: [insert details]

Dates and Times of Delivery of the Hospitality:
[insert details]

SCHEDULE 3

THE EVENTCO MARKS

[insert details]

SCHEDULE 4

MARQUEE SITES

[insert details]

SCHEDULE 5

EMERGENCY PROCEDURES
AND
HYGIENE STANDARDS

[insert details]

APPENDIX 8

PERFORMANCE CONTRACT

This Agreement is made the   day of

BETWEEN:

(1)   [insert party] of [insert address] ("EventCo"); and

(2)   [insert party] of [insert address] ("the Performer").

WHEREAS:

1.   EventCo owns or controls all rights in and to the Event.

2.   EventCo wishes to engage the Performer to provide the Performance at the Event, and the Performer has agreed to provide the Performance, on the terms and conditions of this Agreement.

NOW IT IS HEREBY AGREED as follows:

1.   DEFINITIONS

1.1   In this Agreement the words and expressions set out below shall, save where the context otherwise requires, have the following meanings:

Commercial Rights   means any and all rights of a commercial nature connected with the Event including, without limitation, broadcasting rights, so-called new media rights, interactive games rights, sponsorship rights, merchandising and licensing rights, ticketing rights, promotional rights and catering and hospitality rights;

Date   means [insert details];

Deposit   means the amount of [insert amount];

Effective Date   means the [date of signature of this Agreement];

Equipment   means the equipment of the Performer to be installed in or used at the Venue including those items set out in Schedule 4;

Event   means [insert details] taking place on [insert details];

Event Manager	means the person appointed by EventCo whose identity shall be notified by EventCo to the Performer from time to time;
Event of Force Majeure	means any circumstance not foreseeable at the date of this Agreement and not within the reasonable control of the party in question, including but not limited to any strike, lock-out or other industrial action (not due to the acts of any party to this Agreement); any destruction (temporary or permanent), breakdown, malfunction or damage of or to any premises, plant, equipment (including computer systems) or materials; any civil commotion or disorder, riot, invasion, war or terrorist activity or threat of war or terrorist activity; any action taken by a governmental or public authority of any kind (including not granting a consent, exemption, approval or clearance); and any fire, explosion, storm, flood, earthquake, subsidence, epidemic or other natural physical disaster;
Fees	means the fees for the Performance payable by EventCo to the Performer in accordance with the provisions set out in Clause 4 of this Agreement;
Performance	means the performance to be provided by the Performer on the Date, as described in Schedule 2;
Personnel	means the assistants and crew of the Performer as described in Schedule 3;
Venue	means [insert details].

1.2   Unless the context otherwise requires words denoting the singular shall include the plural and vice versa and words denoting any one gender shall include all genders and words denoting persons shall include bodies corporate, unincorporated associations and partnerships.

1.3   References in this Agreement to Schedules are to Schedules to this Agreement.

2. ENGAGEMENT

In consideration of the payment of the Fees by EventCo, the Performer agrees to provide the Performance on the Date at the Venue in accordance with the provisions of this Agreement.

3. TERM

This Agreement is deemed to have taken effect on the Effective Date and shall continue until the end of the Event, unless terminated earlier in accordance with the provisions of Clause 9.

4. PAYMENT AND PAYMENT PROCEDURES

4.1   In consideration of the Performer performing [his/her] obligations under this Agreement, EventCo agrees pay the Performer the Fees [(excluding relevant taxes)] as follows:

4.1.1   As to the Deposit, on the signing of this Agreement by the Performer; and

4.1.2   As to the balance thereof, on the day after completion of the Performance by certified cheque or bankers draft.

4.2   In addition to the Fees, EventCo shall provide the benefits described in Schedule 1 to the Performer free of charge.

4.3   All costs and expenses incurred by the Performer in providing, transporting and installing the Equipment will be borne by the Performer, save where expressly stated otherwise in this Agreement;

[4.4   In the event that EventCo is obliged by its Inland Revenue authority to deduct any withholding tax or any other tax on the Fees it shall be entitled to do so provided that:

4.4.1   The Inland Revenue is promptly and fully paid all such tax;

4.4.2   A tax deduction certificate is issued to the Performer without delay.]

5. EVENTCO'S OBLIGATIONS

5.1   EventCo represents, warrants and undertakes:

5.1.1   that it has and will continue to have throughout the Term full right and title and authority to enter into this Agreement and to accept and perform the obligations imposed on it under this Agreement;

5.1.2   to organise and stage the Event in a professional manner;

5.1.3   it shall provide a stage at the Venue of no less than [insert details] in size for the Performance;

5.1.4   to provide proper and adequate security both backstage and in the Venue at all times before and after the Performance;

5.1.5   to notify the Performer of any special requirements relating to the Venue or the Performance which are to be observed by the Performer or the Performer's Personnel;

5.1.6   to enable the Personnel to have unrestricted access to the Venue on the day prior to the Date to enable the Equipment to be installed [and a sound check to be undertaken];

5.1.7   to provide unrestricted access to all areas of the Venue for the Performer's Personnel during the Event;

5.1.8   to use its best endeavours to ensure that no unauthorised recording (whether audio or audio-visual) will be undertaken in the Venue during the Performance. If the Performer wishes to film or record the Performance EventCo shall be notified in writing and EventCo agrees that such recording may be undertaken provided that the filming or recording is conducted in accordance with all relevant local musician union rules or other appropriate regulations;

5.1.9   not to change the Venue without the prior written consent of the Performer;

5.1.10 that the Venue is fully licensed for entertainment and that all certificates or consents required from the local authorities in respect of the Venue and the Performance have been obtained and that all facilities at the Venue are in safe working order;

5.1.11 to add the Performer as additional insured on its [general/public liability] insurance for the Event.

5.2   In the event that, for whatever reason, EventCo is unable to provide any of the benefits precisely as described in Schedule 1, EventCo shall be entitled to substitute alternative benefits to an equivalent value without penalty.

5.3   EventCo agrees to consult and agree with the Performer as to the identity of any other performer engaged to perform as a support act prior to the Performance, including the timing, duration, status and billing of such other performer.

6. PERFORMER'S OBLIGATIONS

6.1 The Performer hereby represents, warrants and undertakes that:

6.1.1 [he/she] shall provide the Performance on the Date as directed by EventCo, and it is acknowledged by the Performer that time shall be of the essence in the delivery of the Performance;

6.1.2 the Performer shall render the Performance to the best of [his/her] ability;

6.1.3 the Performer will install its Equipment at the Venue on the day prior to the Date and at such times as shall be agreed with EventCo [and will conduct a satisfactory sound check upon completion of the installation];

6.1.4 all of its Equipment will be safe and in good working order and that the installation and use of the Equipment in the Venue will not cause any safety hazard;

6.1.5 if any of the Equipment is of an unusual nature, shape or size or requires a different or greater power supply than normal or if the construction of any stand or support of any of the Equipment requires unusual space or stability connection with the Venue structure or if the use of any special effects requires specific safety features or certificates or if there is any other matter in connection with the Equipment which should be notified to EventCo the Performer will advise the Event Manager thereof no less than [insert number] days prior to the Date.

6.1.6 The Performer shall provide to EventCo a list of all the Performer's Personnel who should have access to the Venue at any time so that security check-lists and back-stage, on-stage and general Venue passes can be produced as required for them;

6.1.7 in rendering the Performance, the Performer and its Personnel shall exercise all necessary professional judgement, technical skill and care;

6.1.8 the Performer shall ensure that the Personnel:

6.1.8.1 have and display at all times at the Venue proper identification in the form acceptable to EventCo;

6.1.8.2 comply at all times with all rules, regulations and policies of EventCo relating to health and safety, security and risk management at the Venue;

6.1.9   the Performer has full right and title and authority to enter into this Agreement and to accept and perform the obligations imposed on it hereunder, and it has no personal, touring, recording or other commitments which might interfere with the ability of the Performer to render the Performance at the Venue on the Date as set out herein;

6.1.10 the Performer shall not do anything or permit anything to be done which might adversely affect the Commercial Rights or the value of the Commercial Rights;

6.1.11 the Performer shall promptly observe and comply with all reasonable instructions, directions or regulations issued by or on behalf of EventCo including without limitation, those relating to the organisation, staging, safety and image of the Event and the nature and timing of the Performance;

6.1.12 neither the Performer nor any of the Personnel shall make any defamatory or derogatory statements or take part in any activities which are or might be derogatory or detrimental to the reputation, image or goodwill of EventCo, the Event or any commercial partner of EventCo.

7.   ACKNOWLEDGMENT

7.1   The Performer acknowledges that:

7.1.1   it will be the responsibility of the Performer to obtain in good time any travel visas and work permits required for the Performer and all Personnel accompanying the Performer; and

7.1.2   it will be the responsibility of the Performer to ensure that all Equipment is transported to the Venue in a timely fashion.

8.   INTELLECTUAL PROPERTY

8.1   The Performer hereby authorises EventCo to use the name, likeness, biographical details and approved photographs of the Performer in connection with the advertising and promotion of the Event and any television programme produced in relation to the Event.

8.2   The Performer grants to EventCo the right to record, film and photograph the Performance ("the Recordings") and agrees that the Recordings (or parts thereof) may be used by EventCo for the purposes of television broadcast (including live broadcast, recorded broadcast and broadcast on any in-flight entertainment on aeroplanes and ships) and in the production of DVDs and videos throughout the world for a period of [one year] after the Date. For the avoidance of doubt there shall be no use of the Recordings other than in accordance with this Clause 8.2.

8.3   The Performer agrees that the Recordings may be cut, edited or adapted for use in any television programme or the promotion of any television programme and the Performer hereby unconditionally, irrevocably and in perpetuity waives all intellectual property rights that the Performer may legally have now or in the future in relation to the Performance or the Recordings (including all performance rights, moral rights and any other rights under prevailing copyright legislation).

8.4   The Performer agrees to execute all and any documents to effect the license of the rights under this Clause if necessary.

9.   TERMINATION

9.1   Either party shall have the right at any time to terminate this Agreement immediately by giving written notice to the other in the event that:

(a)   the other party has committed a material breach of any obligation under this Agreement which breach is incapable of remedy or cannot be remedied in time for the Event;

(b)   the other party has committed a material breach of any of its obligations under this Agreement and has not remedied such breach (if the same is capable of remedy) within seven days of being required by written notice so to do.

[9.2   EventCo shall have the right to terminate this Agreement at any time prior to the Date in the event that it no longer wishes to stage the Event, in which case only the Deposit will be paid to the Performer together with any expenses necessarily incurred by the Performer up to the date of termination.]

9.3   In the event that the Performer cancels the Performance or fails to render the Performance in accordance with this Agreement EventCo shall be entitled to be reimbursed the Deposit within three days of the Date.

9.4   The Performer shall be entitled to terminate this Agreement if the Venue is wholly unsuitable for the staging of the Performance.

10.   FORCE MAJEURE

10.1   Neither party to this Agreement shall be deemed to be in breach of this Agreement or otherwise liable to the other as a result of any delay or failure in the performance of its obligations under this Agreement if and to the extent that such delay or failure is caused by an Event of Force Majeure and the time for performance of the relevant obligation(s) shall be extended accordingly.

10.2 A party whose performance of its obligations under this Agreement is delayed or prevented by an Event of Force Majeure:

(a) shall immediately notify the other party of the nature, extent, effect and likely duration of the circumstances constituting the Event of Force Majeure;

(b) shall use all reasonable endeavours to minimise the effect of the Event of Force Majeure on the performance of its obligations under this Agreement; and

(c) shall (subject to Clause 10.3 below) immediately after the Event of Force Majeure has ended notify the other party and resume full performance of its obligations under this Agreement.

10.3 If any Event of Force Majeure delays or prevents the performance of the obligations of either party for a continuous period of [one month], the party not so affected shall then be entitled to give notice to the affected party to terminate this Agreement with immediate effect without penalty. Such a termination notice shall be irrevocable except with the consent of both parties.

10.4 For the avoidance of doubt, sickness or ill-health of the Performer shall not be deemed to be an Event of Force Majeure unless the Performer shall have provided to EventCo a medical certificate from a suitably qualified medical practitioner verifying such sickness or ill-health.

11. LIABILITY

11.1 Under no circumstances shall either party be liable for any actual or alleged indirect loss or consequential loss howsoever arising suffered by the other, including, but not limited to, loss of profits, anticipated profits, savings, business or opportunity or loss of publicity or loss of reputation or opportunity to enhance reputation or any other sort of economic loss.

11.2 The Performer shall indemnify and keep indemnified EventCo from and against all demands, claims, legal action, damages, costs (including, without limitation, legal costs and the fees of any expert witnesses incurred in connection with any actions or proceedings), loss, interest or expenses arising, directly or indirectly, out of any defamatory, libellous or obscene material contained in the Performance or as a result of any breach of its obligations, representations, warranties or undertakings contained in this Agreement.

11.3   EventCo shall have no responsibility for any loss of or damage to the property and effects brought into the Venue by the Performer or the Performer's Personnel, including the Equipment.

11.4   The Performer shall be responsible for all its personnel engaged in the rendering of the Performance. Such personnel shall remain employed or engaged by the Performer and not by EventCo, and the Performer will be fully responsible for paying all salaries, wages, commissions, bonuses, taxes, pensions, sick pay or all other amounts or benefits payable directly or indirectly in respect of their employment or engagement.

11.5   The Performer and the Performer's Personnel shall exercise all due care and diligence when using the Equipment at the Venue. For the avoidance of doubt the Performer shall indemnify EventCo against any loss, damages and any other costs sustained by EventCo and arising directly or indirectly as a result of the misuse of or negligence in respect of the use of the Equipment by the Performer or the Personnel.

12.   ASSIGNMENT

Neither party may assign any of its rights or obligations under this Agreement without the prior written consent of the other party, such consent not to be unreasonably withheld or delayed.

13.   CONFIDENTIALITY

The parties agree that the terms of this Agreement shall remain confidential and shall not be disclosed to any third party (with the exception of the Performer's advisors) without the prior written consent of the other party.

14.   POINTS OF CONTACT

14.1   The principal point of contact for each party (unless the other party is notified otherwise in writing) shall be:

(a)   EventCo: [   ]

(b)   The Performer: [   ]

14.2   The Performer acknowledges and agrees that it is not entitled to rely on any representation, authorisation or decision of EventCo unless made by the principal point of contact (or his designated replacement) set out at sub-Clause 14.1 above.

15.   NOTICES

15.1   The parties agree that all notices under this Agreement shall, unless otherwise notified, be served on the following addressees:

(a)   EventCo: [   ]

(b)   The Performer: [   ]

15.2   All notices shall be in writing and may be delivered personally, by facsimile, by first class pre-paid post or by registered mail and shall be deemed to be properly given or served:

(a)   [two] working days after being sent to the intended recipient by pre-paid post addressed as aforesaid; or

(b)   if sent by facsimile on receipt of confirmation of transmission or if not a working day the first working day thereafter provided that a confirming copy is sent by first class pre-paid post to the address aforesaid within 24 hours of transmission.

16.   GENERAL

16.1   The granting by any party of any time or indulgence in respect of any breach of any term of this Agreement by the other shall not be deemed a waiver of such breach and the waiver by any party of any breach of any term of this Agreement by the other shall not prevent the subsequent enforcement of that term and shall not be deemed a waiver of any subsequent breach.

16.2   This Agreement shall constitute the entire agreement between the parties with respect to the subject matter hereof, and shall supersede any and all prior agreements, representations or understanding between the parties, whether written or oral.

16.3   This Agreement may be executed in any number of counterparts, each of which when executed shall constitute an original, but all of which when taken together shall constitute one and the same Agreement.

16.4   All rights, remedies and powers conferred upon the parties are cumulative and shall not be deemed to be exclusive of any other rights, remedies or powers now or subsequently conferred upon them by law or otherwise.

16.5   Each party will do all things necessary including executing all documents necessary to give effect to the intention of the parties in relation to this Agreement.

16.6   Should any term of this Agreement be considered void or voidable under any applicable law, then such terms shall be severed or amended in such a manner as to render the remainder of this Agreement valid or enforceable, unless the whole commercial object is thereby frustrated.

16.7   This Agreement may only be modified or any provision waived if such modification or waiver is in writing and signed by a duly authorised representative of each party.

16.8   This Agreement shall be governed by and construed in accordance with [insert governing law] and the parties hereby submit to the non-exclusive jurisdiction of the [insert courts of jurisdiction] courts.

16.9   Any date or period mentioned in any clause of this Agreement may be extended by mutual agreement in writing between the parties but as regards any date or period (whether or not extended as aforesaid) time shall be of the essence in this Agreement.

16.10   Nothing in this Agreement shall be deemed to constitute a joint venture, partnership or relationship of agency or employment between the parties.

IN WITNESS WHEREOF, the parties have executed this Agreement as of the day and year first above written.

Signed by
a duly authorised representative
for and on behalf of
[INSERT PARTY]

Signed by
a duly authorised representative
for and on behalf of
[INSERT PARTY]

SCHEDULE 1

THE BENEFITS

[EventCo shall provide the following free of charge to the Performer:

1.   First class flights for [insert number] people (including the Performer) to and from the nearest airport to the Venue;

2.   Transport from the airport to the hotel accommodation provided for the Performer and the Personnel;

3.   Hotel accommodation in a five star hotel for [insert number] people for [insert] days;

4.   Transport by limousine to and from the Venue on the day prior to the Date and for the purposes of rendering the Performance on the Date;

5.   [insert number] VIP tickets to the Event (including the best available seats);

6.   All-access passes for the Performer and the Personnel including on-stage and back-stage passes where necessary;

7.   2 personal security guards for the Performer when attending at the Venue;

8.   A dressing room with sofas and a full bar facility; and

9.   On-site technicians to assist with the installation of the Equipment, including an electrician, a sound mixer and a lighting director.]

SCHEDULE 2

THE PERFORMANCE

[The Performer shall provide no less than the following by way of the Performance:

1.   [insert number] songs;

2.   A performance of no less than [insert number] minutes;

3.   one encore;

4.   an appearance in the backstage lounge after the Performance for the purpose of signing autographs and conducting interviews; and

5.   an appearance at the official after-party.]

SCHEDULE 3

THE PERSONNEL

[The Personnel of the Performer shall include the following:

1.   1 hair and make-up assistant;

2.   1 stylist;

3.   1 personal assistant;

4.   3 supporting musicians; and

5.   1 manager]

SCHEDULE 4

THE EQUIPMENT

[insert details]

APPENDIX 9

PARTICIPATION CONTRACT

This Agreement is made the   day of

BETWEEN:

(1)   [insert party] of [insert address] ("EventCo");

(2)   [insert party] of [insert address] ("the Representative Body"); and

(3)   EACH MEMBER OF THE TEAM representing the relevant Representative Body whose name and address is to be supplied by each Representative Body, and who is also to enter into this Agreement by executing a formal Acceptance in terms of Schedule 6.

WHEREAS:

(A)   EventCo owns or controls all rights in and to the Event;

(B)   EventCo wishes to stage and manage the Event.

(C)   Each Representative Body has indicated its wish to participate in the Event on the terms and conditions of this Agreement (the "Terms of Participation") and has agreed that it and each Team Member shall adhere to the Terms of Participation by each executing this Agreement (in the case of the Representative Body) and a formal Acceptance in the form of Schedule 6 (in the case of each Team Member).

(D)   The Event has been approved by [insert sanctioning body] and will be played according to [the Rules of the Game] as adopted by [insert sanctioning body] and in accordance with the rules in respect of the Event contained in the Tournament Manual or as advised by EventCo from time to time.

IT IS AGREED:

1.   DEFINITIONS

1.1   The following terms shall have the meaning set out opposite them below, unless the context otherwise requires:

Commercial Partners means any third party with whom a contract is lawfully concluded for the exploitation of the Commercial Rights;

Commercial Rights means any and all rights of a commercial nature connected with the Event including, without limitation, broadcasting rights, so-called new media rights, interactive games rights, sponsorship rights, merchandising and licensing rights, ticketing rights, promotional rights and catering and hospitality rights;

Deviation means a route other than the most direct route taken on the Outward and/or Homeward Journeys;

Disciplinary and Anti-Doping Manual means that manual produced by EventCo dealing with disciplinary and anti-doping matters relating to the Event, attached at Schedule 2;

Effective Date means the [date of signature of this Agreement];

Event means [insert details] taking place on [insert details];

Event Period means the period from [the start of the Outward Journey to the end of the Homeward Journey as notified by EventCo];

Event of Force Majeure means any circumstance not foreseeable at the date of this Agreement and not within the reasonable control of the party in question, including but not limited to any strike, lock-out or other industrial action (not due to the acts of any party to this Agreement, including Team Members or their representatives); any destruction (temporary or permanent), breakdown, malfunction or damage of or to any premises, plant, equipment (including computer systems) or materials; any civil commotion or disorder, riot, invasion, war or terrorist activity or threat of war or terrorist activity; any action taken by a governmental or public authority of any kind (including not granting a consent, exemption, approval or clearance); and any fire, explosion, storm, flood, earthquake, subsidence, epidemic or other natural physical disaster;

EventCo Marks	means the event titles, words and logo(s) which are owned or controlled by EventCo and which appear in Schedule 3;
Event Technical Committee	means the committee established by EventCo to hear any disputes arising in relation to the Event;
Homeward Journey	means in respect of each Representative Body other than the Host Body, the air passage between a single international airport within the Host Country and a single international airport in the Home Country by a route selected by the Host Body or on its behalf;
Home Country	means the country from which the Representative Body is travelling to participate in the Event;
Host Body	means [insert hosting body];
Host Country	means [insert details];
Illness	means a medical disability arising during the Event Period;
Injury	means a physical disability arising during the Event Period;
Internal Travel	means internal air, coach, rail and other modes of transport within the Host Country;
Laws of the Game	means [insert official laws of the relevant game as recognised by the appropriate sanctioning body];
Liaison Officer	means the person appointed by the Host Body in respect of each Team and responsible for ensuring the legitimate requirements of the Team are met by the Host Body, looking after the general interests and welfare of the Team and making all necessary arrangements for training and for arrival of the Team at the Venue;
Match	means a match to be played as part of the Event at a Venue;

Match Official	means a representative appointed by [insert sanctioning body] to be responsible for the overall conduct of the Match;
Medical	means medical and/or dental (and "Medically" shall be construed accordingly);
Officials	means [the Directors of EventCo and other persons nominated by EventCo and the Match Officials];
Other Events	means those official events in relation to the Event as set out in Schedule 4 hereto;
Outward Journey	means in respect of each Representative Body other than the Host Body, the air passage between a single international airport in its Home Country and a single international airport in the Host Country, by a route or routes selected by the Host Body or on its behalf;
Press Officer	means the person appointed by EventCo to be responsible for media operations in relation to the Event;
Team	means the team of each Representative Body, which shall in each case include up to seven officials at its discretion, one of whom is to be the manager of the Team ("Team Manager"), a doctor, a physiotherapist, a coach, a baggage handler, a Team Media Liaison Officer and not more than [insert number] players;
Team Kit	means each Team's playing kit and any uniform to be worn on any Match occasion or Other Event;
Team Member	means any member of the Team;
Team Media Liaison Officer	means the Team Member responsible for liaison with the media and/or the Press Officer;
Term	means the period from [the date of signature of this Agreement] to [insert date];
Territory	means [insert territory];

Tournament Director means the person appointed by EventCo and the Host Body as being responsible for the administration and management of the Event;

Tournament Manual means the manual set out in Schedule 1;

Tournament Medical Officer means a representative of the Host Body who shall be the official doctor in attendance at each Match;

Training Areas means those areas designed for Team training by the Tournament Director and set out in the Tournament Manual;

Trophy means the trophy to be awarded to the winning Team as set out in the Tournament Manual;

Venue means any stadium, ground or place where any Match is to be played or any Other Event is to be held and includes all areas required by EventCo for the purpose of the Matches and related activities and all areas required by EventCo and/or the Commercial Partners for the exploitation of the Commercial Rights, including all playing areas, car parks in and around any stadium, ground or place, air space above it and other mobile or static objects outside such stadium, ground or place (to the extent that such objects are within the control of the Host Body) which may be visible by the public and/or the television cameras covering play within the Venue;

Venue Manager means the person appointed by the Host Body to be responsible for preparing and managing the Venue;

Venue Media Manager means the person appointed by the Host Body to be responsible for media operations at each Venue.

1.2 Unless the context otherwise requires words denoting the singular shall include the plural and vice versa and words denoting any one gender shall include all genders and words denoting persons shall include bodies corporate, unincorporated associations and partnerships.

1.3　　References in this Agreement to Schedules are to Schedules to this Agreement.

2.　　PARTICIPATION

2.1　　The parties agree that the Representative Body will participate in the Event in accordance with the Terms of Participation.

2.2　　The Representative Body on its own behalf and on behalf of each Team Member accepts the invitation to participate in the Event for the Trophy and upon the Terms of Participation. The Representative Body shall, and shall procure that each Team Member shall, observe and abide in every respect by the Terms of Participation and any decision of EventCo, or of the Host Body, the Event Technical Committee or any officer or body appointed by EventCo pursuant to the Disciplinary and Anti-Doping Manual. Such decisions shall be binding on the Representative Body and each Team Member and the Representative Body and its Team acknowledge that they shall not have the power to revoke or alter any such decisions.

2.3　　The Representative Body agrees that it shall ensure that each Team Member is made fully aware of and understands the Terms of Participation and that each Team Member will sign an Acceptance to that effect, an undertaking to be bound by this Agreement and a formal release of rights in the form of Schedule 6 as a condition of participation in the Event.

2.4　　The Representative Body acknowledges and agrees that during the Event Period, it may not be involved and it may not allow any Team Member to be involved in any match other than those matches set out in Schedule 5.

3.　　TITLE

3.1　　The Event shall be named [insert details] and the Teams competing therein shall play for the Trophy.

3.2　　The Representative Body and the Team Members shall use their best endeavours to refer to the Event with the title in Clause 3.1 above.

4.　　PARTICIPATION FEES

4.1　　In consideration of the acceptance of the Terms of Participation, the Representative Body shall receive the participation fees as set out in the Tournament Manual in Schedule 1 hereto.

4.2 Such participation fees shall be paid within seven days of the end of the Event Period into an account designated by the Representative Body.

5. OBLIGATIONS OF EVENTCO

5.1 EventCo represents, warrants and undertakes:

5.1.1 that it has and will continue to have throughout the Term full right and title and authority to enter into this Agreement and to accept and perform the obligations imposed on it under this Agreement;

5.1.2 to organise, manage and stage the Event in a professional manner;

5.1.3 that it owns or controls the EventCo Marks and shall take all measures it considers reasonable during the Term to protect its rights in the EventCo Marks from infringement by any third party.

6. OBLIGATIONS OF THE REPRESENTATIVE BODY

6.1 The Representative Body hereby represents, warrants and undertakes that:

6.1.1 it has, and will continue to have throughout the Term, full right and title and authority to enter into this Agreement and to accept and perform the obligations imposed on it hereunder;

6.1.2 it shall procure that its Team shall have arrived in the Host Country by no later than the start of the Event Period;

6.1.3 it shall not do anything or permit anything to be done which might adversely affect the Commercial Rights or the value of the Commercial Rights;

6.1.4 it shall observe, and ensure that the Team Members observe, all relevant rules, regulations, directions, codes of practice or guidelines imposed by national law or any competent authority which are applicable to the Event;

6.1.5 it shall promptly observe and comply with all reasonable instructions, directions or regulations issued by or on behalf of EventCo including without limitation, those relating to the organisation, staging, safety and image of the Event;

6.1.6 it shall ensure that neither it nor any of the Team Members make any defamatory or derogatory statements or take part in any activities which are or might be derogatory or detrimental to the reputation, image or goodwill of EventCo, the Event or any Commercial Partner; and

6.1.7 it acknowledges the importance of co-operating with the media to obtain maximum coverage and exposure for the benefit of the Event and agrees to co-operate with all reasonable requests of such a nature by EventCo and/or any broadcaster or other Commercial Partner of EventCo.

7. TERMINATION

7.1 EventCo shall have the right at any time to terminate this Agreement immediately by giving written notice to the Representative Body in the event that:

(a) the Representative Body has committed a material breach of any obligation under this Agreement which breach is incapable of remedy or cannot be remedied in time for the Event;

(b) the Representative Body has committed a material breach of any of its obligations under this Agreement and has not remedied such breach (if the same is capable of remedy) within fourteen days of being required by written notice so to do;

(c) the Representative Body goes into liquidation whether compulsory or voluntary or is declared insolvent or if an administrator or receiver is appointed over the whole or any part of that other party's assets or if that other party enters into any arrangement for the benefit of or compounds with its creditors generally, save in circumstances which are approved by EventCo; or

(d) the Representative Body ceases or threatens to cease to carry on business or to represent the Team.

7.2 EventCo shall have the right to terminate this Agreement by providing [3 month's] notice in writing to the Representative Body in the event that it no longer wishes, or is no longer able, to stage the Event.

[7.3 If this Agreement is terminated under the provisions of this clause, any participation fees that may have already been paid to the Representative Body under Clause 4 hereof shall be repaid to EventCo upon demand.]

8. DEFAULT

Without prejudice to any rights which EventCo may have whether pursuant to this Agreement (including Clause 7 hereof) or otherwise, if the Representative Body defaults on or is in breach of any of its obligations hereunder and fails to remedy such default or such breach forthwith upon notice from EventCo stipulating the same, EventCo may intervene (at the sole cost of the Representative Body) in the carrying out of any obligation of the Representative Body hereunder to ensure its proper and timely performance.

9. FORCE MAJEURE

9.1   No party to this Agreement shall be deemed to be in breach of this Agreement or otherwise liable to another party as a result of any delay or failure in the performance of its obligations under this Agreement if and to the extent that such delay or failure is caused by an Event of Force Majeure and the time for performance of the relevant obligation(s) shall be extended accordingly.

9.2   A party whose performance of its obligations under this Agreement is delayed or prevented by an Event of Force Majeure shall immediately notify the other parties of the nature, extent, effect and likely duration of the circumstances constituting the Event of Force Majeure.

9.3   In the event that EventCo is prevented from complying with any or all of its obligations under this Agreement by an Event of Force Majeure, the Representative Body shall use its best endeavours to provide such assistance as EventCo may request without delay to avoid and/or mitigate the consequences or likely consequences of the Event of Force Majeure.

9.4   Notwithstanding Clause 7.1 above, in the event that the Representative Body is prevented from complying with any or all of its obligations under this Agreement by an Event of Force Majeure, EventCo may, at is absolute discretion, without limitation, do one or more of the following:

9.4.1   Take itself or require the Representative Body to take such action as EventCo deems necessary to ensure that the Event takes place with the minimum disruption;

9.4.2   Terminate this Agreement forthwith and without penalty by giving notice to the Representative Body.

9.5   In the event that a Team fails or refuses to play a Match in accordance with Schedule 5, or abandons a Match before completion, for the reason of an Event of Force Majeure, the matter shall be referred to the Event Technical Committee for consideration. If, in the opinion of the Event Technical Committee, the reason for such failure and/or refusal and/or abandonment does not amount to an Event of Force Majeure, the Event Technical Committee shall be entitled to take such action as it deems fit, including but not limited to imposing a fine on the Representative Body, expelling the Team from the Event, deducting points held by the Team or rescheduling the Match. If, in the opinion of the Event Technical Committee such a failure and/or refusal and/or abandonment has arisen by virtue of an Event of Force Majeure, the provisions of Clause 9.4 above shall apply.

9.6   If any Event of Force Majeure delays or prevents the performance of the obligations of either party for a continuous period of [insert details], the party not so affected shall then be entitled to give notice to the affected party to terminate this Agreement with immediate effect without penalty. Such a termination notice shall be irrevocable except with the consent of all the parties.

10.   LIABILITY

10.1   Save in the event of any negligent or wilful act or omission on the part of the person or entity concerned, none of EventCo, the Host Body or the Tournament Director or any of their respective officers, agents or employees, shall be liable to any Team Member or member of any Representative Body for death or personal injury, damage to property or other loss or damage of any nature whatsoever suffered by any Team Member or member of any Representative Body whether on or off the playing enclosure.

10.2   Under no circumstances shall any party be liable for any actual or alleged indirect loss or consequential loss howsoever arising suffered by another party to this Agreement, including, but not limited to, loss of profits, anticipated profits, savings, business or opportunity or loss of publicity or loss of reputation or opportunity to enhance reputation or any other sort of economic loss.

10.3   Except where expressly provided in this Agreement, each Representative Body undertakes to EventCo and the Host Body to be liable for any death or personal injury to third parties, damage to property or any other claims, losses, costs (including, without limitation, all reasonable legal costs) or demands arising out of any negligent or wilful act or omission of the Representative Body or any Team Member on or off the playing enclosure during the Event Period.

10.4   The Representative Body undertakes and agrees that it will indemnify and hold EventCo harmless from and against all costs and expenses (including without limitation reasonable legal costs), actions, proceedings, claims, demands and damage arising from a breach of the Representative Body or Team Member's representations, warranties or undertakings contained herein or arising from the acts or omissions of the Representative Body or its respective officers, employees, agents, sub-contractors or Team Members.

10.5   Each Representative Body shall take out death, accident and health insurance for its Team and/or itself and a copy of such insurance policy shall be provided to the Tournament Director on or before the start of the Event Period.

10.6   EventCo shall take out [general/public liability and/or cancellation insurance] in respect of the Event and shall provide a copy of such insurance policy to the Representative Body if requested.

11.   POWER TO MAKE RULES AND OTHER PROVISIONS

11.1   The parties recognise that given the nature of the Event, issues may arise in relation to the Event that were not foreseen and therefore are not specifically addressed in this Agreement or that would have an unintended result if made subject to the Agreement without modification. The parties further recognise that it is in the best interests of the Event, and of all the participants in the Event, that such issues be addressed as quickly and effectively as possible. It is therefore agreed that EventCo shall have the right, exercisable unilaterally from time to time before and/or during the Event Period, (a) to supplement or amend the Terms of Participation; (b) to resolve any queries that arise in relation to the proper interpretation and application of the Terms of Participation; and (c) to issue directions as to the conduct of the Event or in respect of any other matters relating to the Event, including without limitation the conduct of the Representative Bodies and Team Members, the contents of the Tournament Manual and the preservation of the value of the Commercial Rights.

11.2   During the Event itself, EventCo may delegate the right conferred by Clause 11.1 above to one or more designees, including without limitation the Tournament Director, the Event Technical Committee and/or any official body established or person appointed by EventCo.

11.3   The Representative Body and the Team Members agree that any amended and supplemental Terms of Participation and any directions made pursuant to this Clause 11 shall become binding upon each Representative Body and the Team Members immediately upon communication to such Representative Body's Team Manager and shall be deemed to be included in the Terms of Participation for the purposes of this Agreement.

11.4   Decisions made pursuant to this clause to amend or supplement the Terms of Participation or to issue directions shall be final. No challenge shall be made by the Representative Body or any Team Member to any such decision.

12.   DISPUTE RESOLUTION

12.1   Each Match is controlled by the referee, who has full authority to enforce the Laws of the Game in relation to that Match. The referee shall be the sole judge of fact and of law during a Match. His or her decisions shall be final and not subject to challenge or review, save as expressly provided for in the Disciplinary and Anti-Doping Manual set out in Schedule 2. Neither the referee nor EventCo shall be held liable for any loss suffered by a Team Member that is or may be due to any decision that the referee makes in terms of the Laws of the Game or the normal procedures required to hold, play and control a Match.

12.2   Disciplinary issues arising out of the ordering off the playing enclosure and/or the temporary suspension of players and/or other misconduct matters arising out of or in connection with the playing of the Match and/or the Event shall be dealt with in accordance with the Disciplinary and Anti-Doping Manual set out in Schedule 2.

12.3   All matters relating to anti-doping shall be dealt with in accordance with the provisions of the Anti-Doping Programme set out in the Disciplinary and Anti-Doping Manual in Schedule 2.

12.4   If a Representative Body or the Team Members thereof do not conform to and/or are in breach of the Commercial Rules or Media Rules set out in the Tournament Manual, EventCo may refer the matter to the Event Technical Committee for consideration of what sanction, if any, should be imposed.

12.5   All other disputes, issues or complaints shall be referred in the first instance to the Tournament Director. The Tournament Director shall deal with any issues and/or complaints relating to the day to day administration and management of the Event as he or she sees fit.

12.6   In the event that a Representative Body and/or Team Member believes that any issue and/or complaint has not been dealt with adequately by the Tournament Director, such party may declare a dispute and refer the matter to the Event Technical Committee to be dealt with in accordance with the sub-clauses below.

12.7   The Event Technical Committee shall ordinarily comprise three (3) members, one of whom will be appointed by EventCo, one of whom will be appointed by the Host Body, and one whom (who will act as Chairman) will be appointed by the [insert sanctioning body] but shall be independent of EventCo, the Host Body, the [insert sanctioning body] and the Team Members.

12.8   The Host Body shall appoint a person to act as administrative secretary to the Event Technical Committee and shall provide and/or arrange such facilities as are necessary for the Event Technical Committee, including the use of a central office, fax machine and meeting room. The administrative secretary shall provide administrative support only and shall not take part in the decision-making of the Event Technical Committee.

12.9   The Event Technical Committee shall have the power to determine all issues of any nature arising in connection with the conduct of the Event, including but not limited to:

(a)   Matters referred to it pursuant to Clause 12.4;

(b)   Challenges referred to it pursuant to Clause 12.6 above;

(c)   Appeals under Clause 13.1(a);

(d)   Acting as an appeal committee on decisions taken pursuant to the Disciplinary Procedures or the Anti-Doping Programme set out in the Tournament Manual; and

(e)   Such other matters as EventCo may from time to time refer to the Event Technical Committee for adjudication.

12.10   Formal notice of the matter referred and all relevant documentation and materials relating thereto shall be delivered to the administrative secretary of the Event Technical Committee within [24 hours] after the declaration of the dispute.

12.11   The Event Technical Committee shall have full discretion as to its procedures and as to what evidence it may require. The Event Technical Committee will not be bound by judicial rules governing the procedure and/or admissibility of evidence provided that proceedings are conducted with reasonable notice and in a fair manner with a reasonable opportunity for relevant parties to present their case, always having due regard to the need to resolve disputes relating to the Event on an expedited basis. The Event Technical Committee shall be entitled to call on such experts (legal or otherwise) as it considers appropriate to assist in the matter under consideration.

12.12   Decisions of the Event Technical Committee shall be made by majority.

12.13   The following sanctions and powers shall be available to the Event Technical Committee:

(a)   To expel a Representative Body and its Team from the remainder of the Event; and/or

(b)   To expel any Team Member from the remainder of the Event;

(c)   To suspend and/or otherwise discipline a Representative Body and/or any Team Member thereof; and/or

(d)   To impose other Event-based sanctions; and/or

(e)   To impose restrictions on entry into official designated areas of the Event including Venues and Training Areas (without limitation); and/or

(f)   To require the payment or repayment of any sum by a Representative Body and/or Team and/or any Team Member thereof and to impose fines on the same; and/or

(g)   To cancel and/or vary the result of any Match and/or the points in relation thereto; and/or

(h)   To caution, reprimand and warn as to future conduct any Representative Body and/or Team and/or any Team Member; and/or

(i)   To impose such other punishment, penalty, restriction or other terms as it considers appropriate having regard to the circumstances; and/or

(j)   To take any other step which in the exercise of its powers the Event Technical Committee considers it would be appropriate to take in order to deal justly with the case in question; and/or

(k)   To make such cost order in relation to the matter as it considers appropriate; and/or

(l) To adjudicate on whether there has been a breach of the Commercial Rules or Media Rules set out in the Tournament Manual; and/or

(m) To adjudicate on whether an event constitutes an Event of Force Majeure, for the purposes of Clause 9.5; and/or

(n) Any combination of the above.

13. APPEAL PROCEDURE

13.1 A right of appeal shall exist from any ruling on a dispute by the Event Technical Committee, in accordance with the following procedure:

(a) In the first instance, a party may appeal to the Event Technical Committee to reverse and/or modify its decision, or to give reasons for its decision. The Event Technical Committee shall have absolute discretion as to how it deals with an appeal under this sub-paragraph;

(b) If a party remains dissatisfied with the decision after review by the Event Technical Committee, that party may make a further appeal to [the Ad Hoc Division of the Court of Arbitration for Sport ("CAS") situated at the Event];

(c) The appeal is to be made by filing a notice of appeal and statement of the full grounds on which the appeal is based with the office of the [Ad Hoc Division of the CAS], with a copy being served on EventCo, within [24 hours] from the time at which the decision of the Event Technical Committee was received;

(d) Such a party shall also be required to lodge a bond as security for costs in the event of failure of the appeal, for such amount as shall be directed by the Event Technical Committee;

(e) The procedures for the appeal shall be dealt with in accordance with [the Rules of the Ad Hoc Division of CAS for the Event];

(f) The decision of [the Ad Hoc Division of CAS] shall be in writing, including a brief statement of reasons for the decision; and

(g) [The Ad Hoc Division of CAS shall either make a final decision/award or refer the dispute to arbitration by CAS in accordance with the Code of Sports-related Arbitration. In the event of such a referral, the Ad Hoc Division may grant preliminary relief which remain in effect until the arbitrators decide otherwise by the application of the regular CAS procedure].

14. DISCIPLINARY AND ANTI-DOPING MANUAL

14.1   Prior to the commencement of the Event, EventCo shall provide to each Representative Body a copy of the Disciplinary and Anti-Doping Manual. The Representative Body shall ensure that each Team Member receives a copy of the Disciplinary and Anti-Doping Manual.

14.2   The Representative Body acknowledges, for itself and on behalf of each Team Member, that the provisions of the Disciplinary and Anti-Doping Manual, once communicated to the Representative Body, shall become binding upon each Representative Body and each Team Member and shall thereafter be included in the Terms of Participation.

14.3   The decisions of commissioners or committees (including the Event Technical Committee) appointed by EventCo pursuant to the Disciplinary and Anti-Doping Manual shall be binding on the Representative Body and the Team Members. The Representative Body and Team Members acknowledge that they shall not have the power to revoke or alter any such decisions.

15. PUBLICITY AND PRESS

15.1   Each Representative Body and Team Member acknowledges the importance of co-operating with the media to obtain maximum coverage and exposure for the Event. Subject to Clause 15.2 below, the Team Manager, subject to the Representative Body's approval, and the Team Members, subject to the Team Manager's approval, may communicate with the media and engage in radio and television broadcasts, provided always that their comments do not bring the game of [insert sport], EventCo, the Host Body or [the sanctioning body] into disrepute.

15.2   Any Team Member may be required by EventCo to attend and participate in the television and press conferences which may be held during the Event. If any Team Member is required by EventCo to attend and participate in any television and/or press conference or interviews, that Team Member will attend such television and/or press conference or interview in priority to any other television and/or press conference or interview. Any interviews which are given by a Team Member within a Venue shall only be given to a duly accredited media representative or broadcaster. The team captains and coaches of the two Teams participating in any Match shall attend an interview immediately after the end of each Match, and shall also be required to attend the post-match press conference.

15.3 A Team sheet containing the names and biographical details and statistics of each Team Member shall be provided to EventCo no later than [2 hours] prior to the start of each Match.

16. COMMERCIAL GUIDELINES

16.1 The Representative Body and each Team Member acknowledges that EventCo will be seeking to maximise the income from the exploitation of the Commercial Rights for the Event by entering into a number of agreements with Commercial Partners. The Representative Body and each Team Member undertake to co-operate with EventCo and the Commercial Partners in order to protect the Commercial Rights. In particular the Representative Body and each Team Member agrees that:

(a) The Representative Body shall not assert and shall procure that no Team Member asserts any claim to use, sell or exploit any of the Commercial Rights in connection with the Event and the Representative Body will not develop or acquire any rights in relations to the Event which are similar to or compete with the Commercial Rights;

(b) The Representative Body shall not and shall procure that each Team Member shall not, during the Event Period, directly or indirectly allow its or his or her name, image or likeness to be used in any advertising or endorsement or for any commercial purpose which involves a direct or indirect association with the Event and/or seeks to exploit (whether implicitly or explicitly) any connection therewith;

(c) The Representative Body will be entitled to place the logo of its authorised kit manufacturer on the front of any playing kit in accordance with the kit provisions set out in the Tournament Manual;

(d) No item of clothing or kit [or equipment] worn or used by any Team Member at any Match or Other Event or whilst boarding, on board or departing any coach or bus or other vehicle which transports the Team to or from any of the Venues or Other Events shall carry any visible logo, insignia, advertising or commercial identification save for the emblem of the Representative Body, the EventCo Marks or the kit manufacturers logo referred to in sub-clause (c) above, PROVIDED THAT this clause shall not apply to a manufacturer's logo on footwear used by a Team Member;

(e)   No use shall be made by the Representative Body or any Team Member of the description of a product or service as being the "Official" product or service of the Team's participation in the Event;

(f)   The Representative Body shall not create a mascot or other symbol for its Team's participation in the Event;

(g)   The Representative Body shall permit a designated member of its Team to make a single film on videotape of any Match in which its Team takes part provided that:

    (i)   No more than one video camera shall be used in making the film, and the cameraman observes all directions as to filming made by EventCo;

    (ii)   Not more than one additional copy is made of that film;

    (iii)   The film is made and used only in private sessions for the internal training purposes of the Team; and

    (iv)   The film, or any part thereof, is not exhibited or distributed or otherwise exploited in any format whatsoever to any public or private audience or for any other broadcast of whatever nature and any Team Member who makes such a film pursuant to this clause hereby assigns with full title guarantee to EventCo all rights of any nature whatsoever including but not limited to copyright in any such film.

16.2   The Representative Body shall, and shall procure that each Team Member shall, adhere to the Commercial Rules set out in the Tournament Manual.

17.   ASSIGNMENT

Neither party may assign any of its rights or obligations under this Agreement without the prior written consent of the other party, such consent not to be unreasonably withheld or delayed.

18.   ANNOUNCEMENTS AND CONFIDENTIALITY

No announcement shall be made by either party in relation to this Agreement without the prior written consent of the other and neither party shall without the prior written consent of the other (save as required by law) disclose to any third party any information concerning the terms or subject matter hereof after the date hereof.

19.   POINTS OF CONTACT

19.1   The principal point of contact for each party (unless the other party is notified otherwise in writing) shall be:

(a)   EventCo: [   ]

(b)   The Representative Body: [   ]

19.2   The Representative Body acknowledges and agrees that it is not entitled to rely on any representation, authorisation or decision of EventCo unless made by the principal point of contact (or his designated replacement) set out at sub-clause 19.1 above.

20.   NOTICES

20.1   The parties agree that all notices under this Agreement shall, unless otherwise notified, be served on the following addressees:

(a)   EventCo: [   ]

(b)   The Representative Body: [   ]

20.2   All notices shall be in writing and may be delivered personally, by facsimile, by first class pre-paid post or by registered mail and shall be deemed to be properly given or served:

(a)   [two] working days after being sent to the intended recipient by pre paid post addressed as aforesaid; or

(b)   if sent by facsimile on receipt of confirmation of transmission or if not a working day the first working day thereafter provided that a confirming copy is sent by first class pre-paid post to the address aforesaid within 24 hours of transmission.

21.   GENERAL

21.1   The granting by any party of any time or indulgence in respect of any breach of any term of this Agreement by the other shall not be deemed a waiver of such breach and the waiver by any party of any breach of any term of this Agreement by the other shall not prevent the subsequent enforcement of that term and shall not be deemed a waiver of any subsequent breach.

21.2   This Agreement shall constitute the entire agreement between the parties with respect to the subject matter hereof, and shall supersede any and all prior agreements, representations or understanding between the parties, whether written or oral.

21.3   This Agreement may be executed in any number of counterparts, each of which when executed shall constitute an original, but all of which when taken together shall constitute one and the same Agreement.

21.4   All rights, remedies and powers conferred upon the parties are cumulative and shall not be deemed to be exclusive of any other rights, remedies or powers now or subsequently conferred upon them by law or otherwise.

21.5   Each party will do all things necessary including executing all documents necessary to give effect to the intention of the parties in relation to this Agreement.

21.6   Should any term of this Agreement be considered void or voidable under any applicable law, then such terms shall be severed or amended in such a manner as to render the remainder of this Agreement valid or enforceable, unless the whole commercial object is thereby frustrated.

21.7   This Agreement may only be modified or any provision waived if such modification or waiver is in writing and signed by a duly authorised representative of each party.

21.8   This Agreement shall be governed by and construed in accordance with [insert governing law] and the parties hereby submit to the non-exclusive jurisdiction of the [insert courts of jurisdiction] courts.

21.9   Any date or period mentioned in any clause of this Agreement may be extended by mutual agreement in writing between the parties but as regards any date or period (whether or not extended as aforesaid) time shall be of the essence in this Agreement.

21.10 Nothing in this Agreement shall be deemed to constitute a joint venture, partnership or relationship of agency or employment between the parties.

IN WITNESS WHEREOF, the parties have executed this Agreement as of the day and year first above written.

Signed by
a duly authorised representative
for and on behalf of
[INSERT PARTY]

Signed by
a duly authorised representative
for and on behalf of
[INSERT PARTY]

SCHEDULE 1

TOURNAMENT MANUAL

[insert details]

SCHEDULE 2

DISCIPLINARY AND ANTI-DOPING MANUAL

[insert details]

SCHEDULE 3

EVENTCO MARKS

[insert details]

SCHEDULE 4

OTHER EVENTS

[insert details]

SCHEDULE 5

MATCH SCHEDULE

[insert details]

SCHEDULE 6

ACCEPTANCE

I, THE UNDERSIGNED

1. Accept the invitation to take part in the Event for the Trophy in accordance with the Terms of Participation for the Event, a copy of which has been provided to the Representative Body for which I will be competing and which I have had an opportunity to read, and have read and understood;

2. Agree to be bound by the Terms of Participation and the decisions of EventCo and the Event Technical Committee made under the Terms of Participation in relation to the Event;

3. Agree not to be involved in any other [insert sport] match during the Event Period;

4. Agree that I shall not have any claim against EventCo, the Host Body or the [insert sanctioning body] or any of their employees, officers or agents as a result of any liabilities which I may incur after the Event Period or during any period of absence from my official Team party during the

Event Period if EventCo permits me to prolong my stay in the Host Country beyond the duration of the Event Period or permits me to leave my official Team party at any time during the Event Period for whatever reason, either temporarily or permanently;

5.   Agree that my personal responsibilities will include, but will not be limited to, the arrangement and expense of homeward travel, accommodation and subsistence, medical treatment and insurance if I prolong my stay at or take leave of absence from the Event, whether temporarily or permanently;

6.   Agree that I will not make any representation to any third party which is likely to induce such third party to believe that EventCo, the Host Body or [insert sanctioning body] continues to be responsible for me during any such prolonged stay or leave of absence from the Event, whether temporary or permanent;

7.   Agree and consent to my performance or appearance as a sportsman on or off the field for a period from the execution of this acceptance up to and including 48 hours after the final Match has been played, being filmed and recorded in any audio, visual or and/or audio-visual or electronic form or coverage and that such audio, visual and/or audio-visual or electronic recording in sole or in part may at the absolute discretion of EventCo be incorporated without limitation in any television programme, film, video recording, DVD, broadcast or any other form of media or communication of whatever nature, including any computer game, on the internet or via mobile telephone;

8.   Agree to assign with full title guarantee in perpetuity to EventCo all and any rights of any nature whatsoever in any such audio, visual and/or audio-visual or electronic recording and consent to the exploitation of such recording by all and any means and in all and any media and formats now or hereafter invented throughout the world in perpetuity; and

9.   Consent to the use and reproduction of my name, likeness, signature, performance and appearance, and any audio, visual and/or audio-visual or electronic recordings of my performance or any part of it during the Event, by all and any means and in all and any form of media whether now known or hereafter to be invented (including, without limitation, in connection with any computer game or sticker collection or official website created by EventCo or one of its Commercial Partners) in relation to the Event throughout the world in perpetuity for the purposes of advertising, merchandising, publicity and otherwise in relation to the

exploitation of such audio, visual and/or audio-visual or electronic recording including any such computer game, sticker collection or web-site.

SIGNED:

DATED:

APPENDIX 10

MERCHANDISING CONTRACT

This Agreement is made the   day of

BETWEEN:

(1)   [insert party] of [insert address] ("EventCo"); and

(2)   [insert party] of [insert address] (the "Licensee")

WHEREAS:

(A)   EventCo owns or controls all rights in and to the Event(s); and

(B)   The Licensee wishes to acquire the exclusive licence to manufacture, package, market, sell and distribute the Licensed Products in the Territory during the Term.

IT IS AGREED as follows:

1.   DEFINITIONS

1.1   In this Agreement the words and expressions set out below shall, save where the context otherwise requires, have the following meanings:

"Advance"   means the non-refundable sum of [insert details] paid by the Licensee to EventCo in accordance with Clause 7;

"Commercial Partner"   means any third party with whom a contract is lawfully concluded for the exploitation of the Commercial Rights;

"Commercial Rights"   means any and all rights of a commercial nature connected with the Event(s) including, without limitation, broadcasting rights, so-called new media rights, interactive games rights, sponsorship rights, merchandising and licensing rights, ticketing rights, promotional rights and catering and hospitality rights;

"Contract Year"   means a 12-month period within the Term commencing with the first day of the Term or its anniversary date;

"Event[s]" means [insert details] taking place on [insert details];

"Event of Force Majeure" means any circumstance not foreseeable at the date of this Agreement and not within the reasonable control of the party in question, including but not limited to any strike, lock-out or other industrial action (not due to the acts of any party to this Agreement); any destruction (temporary or permanent), breakdown, malfunction or damage of or to any premises, plant, equipment (including computer systems) or materials; any civil commotion or disorder, riot, invasion, war or terrorist activity or threat of war or terrorist activity; any action taken by a governmental or public authority of any kind (including not granting a consent, exemption, approval or clearance); and any fire, explosion, storm, flood, earthquake, subsidence, epidemic or other natural physical disaster;

["Minimum Advertising Expenditure"] [means [insert amount];]

["Minimum Royalty"] [means [insert amount];]

'Licensed Product" means those Products specified in Schedule 1 which are manufactured, packaged, marketed, sold and distributed by the Licensee in conjunction with the Marks in the Territory together with any additions to such list of products which are agreed in writing between the parties;

"Marks" means the logos and trade marks related to the Event(s) which are owned or controlled by EventCo and which are set out in Schedule 4;

"Net Sales Revenue" means 100% of all income derived from the sale of the Licensed Products in the Territory during the Term [excluding sales taxes and value added taxes];

"Product" means the products specified in Schedule 1;

"Premiums"	means any item of Product offered to the public in connection with the sale or promotion of another product or service in such a way as to promote, publicise and/or sell such other products or services or their manufacturer or advertiser;
"Quarter"	means the period starting on a Quarter Date and ending on the day before the next Quarter Date;
"Quarter Date"	means 31st March, 30th June, 30th September and 31st December respectively in each calendar year during the Term;
"Royalty"	means [%] of Net Sales Revenue in respect of each item of Licensed Product sold during the Term [and in no event less than the Minimum Royalty in each Contract Year during the Term];
"Target Date"	means the date by which the Licensed Products shall be available for purchase by the public, which date shall be agreed between the parties;
"Term"	means [insert number] years commencing on [insert date];
"Territory"	means [insert territory];
"Venue(s)"	means [insert details of the venue(s) where Event is to be held].

1.2 Unless the context otherwise requires words denoting the singular shall include the plural and vice versa and words denoting any one gender shall include all genders and words denoting persons shall include bodies corporate, unincorporated associations and partnerships.

1.3 References in this Agreement to Schedules are to Schedules to this Agreement.

2   LICENSEE'S RIGHTS

2.1 In consideration of the Royalty and other payments to be made by the Licensee to EventCo and subject to and conditional upon the full and timely performance and observance by the Licensee of all of the obligations, warranties and undertakings of the Licensee contained herein, EventCo grants to the Licensee an exclusive licence to manufacture, package, market, sell and distribute the Licensed Products in the Territory during the Term.

2.2   [The Licensee acknowledges that the Commercial Partners shall be entitled to produce and distribute Premiums in the Territory for the purpose of promoting their products and services and their connection with the Event(s). For the avoidance of doubt, the parties agree that any promotion and distribution of such Premiums will not be a breach of the rights granted to the Licensee under this Agreement.]

2.3   The Company acknowledges and agrees that EventCo owns or controls the Commercial Rights and that the Company shall not be entitled to exploit or enter into any commercial or other agreements to exploit any of the Commercial Rights other than as set out in this Agreement.

3   QUALITY AND DESIGN OF LICENSED PRODUCT

The Licensee undertakes that:

3.1   The Licensee acknowledges that the reputation and goodwill of EventCo are likely to suffer damage if the Marks are reproduced, published or used otherwise than in connection with goods of high quality.

3.2   It shall submit the Licensed Products, their packaging, presentation and all matters relating thereto (including but not limited to all artwork and design) to EventCo for approval at all stages of development and production in accordance as far as reasonably practicable with the procedure set out in Schedule 2.

3.3   It shall not offer the Licensed Products for sale unless and until a sample of each of the Licensed Products together with all packaging and labels shall have been submitted to EventCo pursuant to sub-clause 3.2 and final approval thereof given in writing. Final approval may be withheld in the absolute discretion of EventCo but the Licensee shall be advised of the specific reasons in each case.

3.4   It shall carry out all artwork and design relating to the Licensed Products at its own cost.

3.5   The Licensed Products shall be manufactured, packaged, marketed, sold and distributed in accordance with all applicable laws in the Territory. The policy of sale, distribution and marketing by the Licensee shall be consistent with earning the highest possible royalties and making available the Licensed Products at the highest possible standard so as not to reflect in any adverse manner on the good name of EventCo or the Event(s).

3.6 Following approval of any sample or item pursuant to this Clause, the Licensee shall not depart in any material respect from the quality of such sample or item in manufacturing the same or the Licensed Products without the prior written consent of EventCo.

3.7 The Licensee shall from time to time as requested by EventCo provide EventCo at the expense of the Licensee with samples of the Licensed Products to enable EventCo to inspect and test the same.

3.8 It shall permit EventCo (through its authorised representative), upon giving the Licensee reasonable notice and at its own expense, to visit the premises of the Licensee during normal business hours to inspect the method of manufacture of the Licensed Products and the materials used and the packaging and storing of the Licensed Products.

4 APPROVAL OF ADVERTISING

4.1 The Licensee acknowledges and agrees that EventCo shall maintain control over the manner in which the Marks are used in advertising and promotion (including, without limitation, display, point of sale material and hangtags) and that EventCo must always be satisfied with the appearance of the Marks including the way the Marks appear on the Licensed Products.

4.2 Accordingly the Licensee shall submit to EventCo for prior approval in writing and in accordance with Schedule 2 all marketing plans and all advertising and promotional materials relating to the Licensed Products. Final approval may be withheld in the absolute discretion of EventCo but the Licensee shall be advised of the specific reasons in each case.

4.3 If during the Term any significantly unfavourable publicity or claim should arise or be made in relation to any particular item of advertising or promotional material EventCo shall have the right to withdraw approval of such item of material and thereafter the Licensee shall discontinue the use or publication of that disapproved item of advertising or promotional material.

5 PRODUCT LIABILITY

5.1 The Licensee warrants that Licensed Products will be free from defects in workmanship and materials and safe to all persons who may use or have contact with them and shall indemnify EventCo, its officers, employees and agents from and against all expenses, damages, losses and costs whatsoever arising out of or in any way connected with any claim or action for personal injury, death or other cause of action involving alleged defects in the Licensed Products, provided that the Licensee shall be given prompt notice of any such action or claim.

5.2 The Licensee shall at its own expense on behalf of itself and EventCo in all parts of the Territory where the same is permitted carry product liability insurance in an amount which is not less than [insert amount] and upon such other terms as EventCo shall reasonably require and approve and shall upon request supply EventCo with a copy of the relevant policy duly endorsed and with evidence that all premiums due have been paid. The Licensee shall do nothing which may in any way vitiate such policy. The Licensee shall notify EventCo of all claims made under the policy relating to the Licensed Products.

5.3 The Licensee further warrants that the Licensed Products, their packaging and get-up and all advertising and promotional material will comply with all relevant laws, regulations and codes of practice in the Territory and shall indemnify EventCo in respect of any liability, costs and expenses arising from any failure so to comply and in respect of any act or omission of the Licensee other than an act or omission which is expressly required of the Licensee by the terms of this Agreement.

6 MARKETING OF LICENSED PRODUCTS

The Licensee represents, warrants and undertakes that:

6.1 It shall use its best endeavours to ensure that the Licensed Products are well-known and readily available to the public at the Venues and through retail outlets throughout the Territory by no later than the Target Date;

6.2 It shall use its best endeavours to exploit the Marks and promote sales of the Licensed Products in all parts of the Territory and shall expend sums which shall at all times be sufficient to carry out its duties under this Agreement;

6.3 The Licensee shall refrain from seeking customers for the Licensed Products outside the Territory and from establishing any branch or maintaining any distribution depot in connection with the Licensed Products outside the Territory;

6.4 It shall maintain in the Territory such sales facilities as are adequate in order to ensure the most effective marketing of the Licensed Products and shall maintain a sufficiently representative and adequate stock of the Licensed Products to ensure a prompt response to customer demands;

6.5 [The Licensee shall keep EventCo informed of market conditions, competitive products and other factors material to the exploitation of the Marks and the marketing of the Licensed Products in the Territory;]

6.6 The Licensee shall not without the consent of EventCo in writing sell the Licensed Products as Premiums and shall not dispose of the Licensed Products otherwise than on arms' length commercial terms at the Venue(s) or by wholesale or retail sale through normal wholesale and retail outlets and in particular shall not dispose of any Licensed Products by way of gifts;

6.7 It has and will continue to have throughout the Term full right and title and authority to enter into this Agreement and to accept and perform the obligations imposed on it under this Agreement;

6.8 It shall not do or omit to do or permit there to be done any act which may denigrate the value of or render invalid any right of copyright or other rights licensed under this Agreement or in any way detract from the value of the Marks;

6.9 It shall not do anything or permit anything to be done which might adversely affect the Commercial Rights or the value of the Commercial Rights;

6.10 It shall ensure that neither it nor any of its directors, employees, or other members of staff make any defamatory or derogatory statements or take part in any activities which are or might be derogatory or detrimental to the reputation, image or goodwill of EventCo, the Event(s) or any Commercial Partner;

6.11 It shall at its own expense take all steps necessary to secure and protect the copyright and all other rights in the Marks and the Licensed Products in the Territory and during the Term in accordance with the directions (if any) of EventCo;

6.12 It shall give full particulars to EventCo on becoming aware of any actual or threatened claim by any third party in connection with the Licensed Products;

6.13 [It shall advertise the Licensed Products throughout the Territory during the Term and shall expend in each year not less than the Annual Minimum Advertising Expenditure;]

6.14 The Licensee shall ensure that the Licensed Products are given fair and equitable treatment and shall not unfairly discriminate in favour of any other product which the Licensee may have for distribution in the Territory;

6.15   No costs incurred in the manufacture, packaging, marketing, sale or distribution of the Licensed Products shall be deductible from any sums payable by the Licensee;

6.16   Nothing in this Agreement shall or shall be deemed to prevent EventCo from granting licences in respect of the Marks for products other than those in the Product Range;

6.17   EventCo reserves to itself absolutely the right to use and/or manufacture Premiums;

6.18   The Licensee shall not knowingly manufacture or distribute any defective or sub-standard items of Licensed Product and shall ensure that all items of Licensed Product are of the highest attainable quality;

6.19   The Licensee shall punctually pay to EventCo all sums owing to EventCo under this Agreement and in the event of any late payment all sums due shall bear interest in accordance with Clause 8.3.

7   ROYALTIES

7.1   The Licensee shall pay to EventCo:

7.1.1   the Advance on signature of this Agreement;

7.1.2   the Royalty within 30 days of each Quarter Date in accordance with the provisions of this Agreement.

7.2   The Advance is not refundable but may be recouped from the Royalty payable under Clause 7.1 in as far as this is sufficient.

[7.3   The Licensee shall pay to EventCo the Minimum Royalty in each Contract Year. If the Royalty payable in any Contract Year is less than the Minimum Royalty then (subject to the prior recoupment of the Advance) the Licensee shall pay the balance to EventCo within thirty days of the end of the Contract Year in question.]

7.4   Any sales or disposals of Licensed Products by the Licensee to its associates or by way of promotional or other use shall be deemed to be sales at full value and shall be taken into account for the purpose of calculation of the Royalty payable to EventCo.

7.5   The Licensee may not withhold any sums due to EventCo as a reserve against returns and/or credits. If the Licensee is required by law to make any withholding from sums to be remitted to EventCo the Licensee shall prior to withholding such payment furnish EventCo with evidence satisfactory to EventCo as to the Licensee's obligation to make such withholding of payment.

7.6   If exchange control or other restrictions prevent or threaten to prevent the remittance to EventCo of any money payable under this Agreement the Licensee shall immediately advise EventCo in writing and follow EventCo's instructions in respect of the money to be remitted, including if required depositing the same with any bank or other person designated by EventCo at such location as may be designated by EventCo.

7.7   If any withholding or other taxes are required to be deducted from any monies provided to be remitted to EventCo pursuant to this Agreement the Licensee must ensure that no improper deductions are made and that EventCo is provided with all necessary receipts, certificates and other documents and all information required in order to avail EventCo of any tax credit or other fiscal advantage.

8   PAYMENT

8.1   The Licensee shall pay the Royalty due in respect of the Quarter ending on the Quarter Date within thirty days of the end of each Quarter Date in accordance with the royalty report required under Clause 9.1 and accompanied by such report in all cases.

8.2   All payments shall be made in the relevant currency which shall be [insert currency] unless otherwise stated.

8.3   Interest at [%] per annum above the base lending rate of [insert details] Bank shall accrue from day to day before as well as after judgment on all payments from time to time outstanding under this Agreement and the Licensee shall pay such interest to EventCo at the same time as the payment in respect of which it has accrued.

8.4   All payments due hereunder are exclusive of [insert relevant taxes].

8.5   The Licensee shall in no circumstances be entitled to make any deduction from the payments due hereunder by way of set-off or otherwise in respect of any claim or counterclaim which it may have against EventCo.

9   ROYALTY REPORTS AND ACCOUNTING RECORDS

9.1   The Licensee shall send to EventCo a royalty report in the form set out in Schedule 3 within thirty days of the end of each Quarter Date.

9.2 The Licensee shall keep full, proper and up-to-date records relating to the manufacture and sales of the Licensed Products and shall allow EventCo on no more than once in each Contract Year to carry out a full audit of the Licensee's accounts and records and a stock-take of Licensed Products on reasonable notice. Such audit and stock-take shall be carried out at the cost of EventCo unless it discloses under-reporting by the Licensee resulting in underpayment in excess of [3%] in any Contract Year and in such event the costs shall be paid by the Licensee.

9.3 The Licensee shall co-operate fully in any inspections, audits and stock-takes carried out under sub-clause 9.2.

9.4 The Licensee shall inform EventCo forthwith of any event or circumstances which may materially affect its ability to perform its obligations under this Agreement.

10 COPYRIGHT AND TRADEMARKS PROTECTION

10.1 The Licensee shall cause to be imprinted irremovably and legibly on each Licensed Product manufactured, packaged, marketed, sold or distributed under this Agreement (included but not limited to advertising, promotional packaging and wrapping material and any other such material wherein the Marks shall appear) the copyright notice: [Insert details] together with any additional notices which may be required by law within the Territory in order to protect the Licensed Products and the Marks and in particular but without limitation all rights of copyright and trade mark in the Licensed Products and the Marks. EventCo may stipulate from time to time any other notices or credits which are to be so affixed, incorporated or represented and the Licensee shall comply with all such stipulations reasonably made.

10.2 The Licensee shall promptly bring to the attention of EventCo any unauthorised representation or imitation of any part of the Marks or any improper or wrongful use or other infringement in the Territory of the copyright or other rights connected with the Marks (including but not limited to the goodwill attached to the reputation connected with the Marks) or any threat to do any of those things which may come to its notice and shall assist EventCo in taking all steps (if any) which EventCo may consider necessary to protect and defend such rights. The Licensee shall not take any action in respect of the same unless it shall have first sought and obtained the written consent of EventCo.

10.3 At the termination or expiry of this Agreement the ownership of all rights licensed pursuant to this Agreement shall automatically revert to EventCo and the Licensee shall execute any instruments required by EventCo to confirm the foregoing.

11 INTELLECTUAL PROPERTY RIGHTS

11.1 No trade mark, commercial description, manufacturing symbol, copyright, slogan, design or other property authorised hereby to be used in connection with the Licensed Products or goodwill connected therewith shall be or become the Licensee's property. The Licensee shall not be entitled to claim any rights or ownership in any of the above during or at any time after the Licence Period and will not register or arrange or seek to have registered in the Territory or elsewhere any trade mark, trade description, manufacturing symbol, copyright, slogan or design which is similar to or the same as or an imitation thereof.

11.2 The Licensee agrees that on termination or expiry of this Agreement the Licensee shall be deemed to have assigned, transferred and conveyed to EventCo any and all rights of copyright, trade mark, trade rights, equity, goodwill, title, design or other right in and to the Marks and the Licensed Products which may have been obtained by the Licensee or vested in the Licensee and the Licensee undertakes to execute any instruments requested by EventCo to accomplish or confirm the foregoing.

11.3 The Licensee transfers to EventCo by way of future assignment all such copyright and other rights referred to in Clause 11.2 together with any rights of EventCo of whatever nature which may for whatever reason become vested in the Licensee so that EventCo has the right to licence such rights for gain or otherwise and the Licensee agrees to do all things which may become necessary to perfect such assignment.

11.4 The cost of all artwork to be used by the Licensee in connection with the Licensed Products shall be borne by the Licensee.

11.5 EventCo shall have the non-exclusive and irrevocable licence in respect of all artwork produced by the Licensee to use such artwork in any Territory reserved by EventCo or to licence the use of such artwork to other third party licensees of EventCo and the Licensee acknowledges that it shall have no right in respect of the use of such artwork in any territories other than the Territory and EventCo shall not be required to make any payments to the Licensee in respect of its use or the use by any third party of such artwork.

11.6 EventCo shall have the right but not the obligation to use the name of the Licensee in any publicity or advertising relating to the Marks or the Licensed Products.

11.7   The Licensee undertakes that it shall not during the Licence Period manufacture, package, market, sell or distribute any item or product of the description of the Licensed Product or any other product which may be similar to the Licensed Product.

11.8   If the Licensee commissions, engages or employs any third party to create any materials or work in connection with this Agreement in relation to which intellectual property rights may be created, the Licensee shall procure that such third party will execute and deliver to EventCo prior to any such works or materials being created a properly executed assignment from such third party in respect of such intellectual property rights.

12   DURATION AND TERMINATION BY NOTICE

12.1   Without prejudice to any other remedy for the breach or non-performance or observance of any of the Licensee's obligations hereunder EventCo may terminate this Agreement forthwith by notice to the Licensee if:

12.1.1   the Licensee fails to make any payment hereunder in full on the date when it shall become due;

12.1.2   the Licensee has committed a material breach of any obligation under this Agreement which breach is incapable of remedy or cannot be remedied in time for the Events;

12.1.3   the Licensee has committed a material breach of any obligation under this Agreement and has not remedied such breach (if the same is capable of remedy) within 14 days of being required by notice to do so;

12.1.4   the Licensee is found on any inspection or audit materially to have under-reported sales on [three] or more occasions;

12.1.5   the Licensee is guilty of fraud or misconduct (whether or not in connection with this Agreement);

12.1.6   the Licensee convenes a meeting of its creditors or makes any arrangements or composition with or any assignment for the benefit of its creditors or a petition is presented or a meeting is convened for the purpose of considering a resolution or other steps are taken for the winding up of the Licensee or its estate (save for the purpose of a voluntary reconstruction or amalgamation previously approved in writing by EventCo) or if an encumbrancer takes possession of or a trustee, receiver, liquidator, administrator or similar officer is appointed in respect of all or any part of its business or assets or any distress, execution or other legal process is levied, threatened, enforced upon or sued out against any of such assets;

12.1.7 the Licensee disposes of all or a substantial part of its business or abandons or announces that it intends to abandon the business of exploiting merchandising rights;

12.1.8 the Licensee fails to manufacture and sell a minimum of [insert number] of items of the full range of the Licensed Products within [12 months] of the date of signature of this Agreement; or

12.1.9 the Licensee allows or permits its insurance cover in accordance with Clause 5 to lapse or not be renewed.

12.2   EventCo shall have the right to terminate this Agreement by providing [3 month's] notice in writing to the Licensee in the event that it no longer wishes to stage the Event(s).

13   CONSEQUENCES OF TERMINATION

13.1   Upon termination or expiry of this Agreement the Licensee shall pay to EventCo immediately all outstanding amounts due in relation to this Agreement and shall submit an additional account in respect of those payments and shall inform EventCo of its stocks of the Licensed Products on hand at the termination date.

13.2   In the case of termination as a result of the Licensee's breach of this Agreement, all stocks of the Licensed Products then on hand shall, at the option of EventCo, be surrendered and delivered up to EventCo on the termination date or be destroyed. Within 3 days of such destruction the Licensee shall supply EventCo with written confirmation of the same in such form as EventCo may require.

13.3   In all other cases (but not otherwise) if the Licensee has complied fully with its obligations under this Agreement then the Licensee may continue to sell, market and distribute such stocks for [six months] after the termination date and thereafter shall account to EventCo and pay Royalties in respect of all sales and at the option of EventCo deliver up or destroy all remaining stock PROVIDED THAT the Licensee will not manufacture or cause to be manufactured in the last [six months] of the Term a number of Licensed Products greater than it has manufactured or caused to be manufactured in the previous [six-month] period of the Term. Within three days of such destruction the Licensee shall supply EventCo with written confirmation of the same in such form as EventCo may require.

13.4   Upon the expiry or termination of this Agreement, unless EventCo instructs the Licensee otherwise, the Licensee shall ensure that all artwork, print sets, moulds, casts, dies, reproduction processes and all other items and processes used by or on behalf of the Licensee or any manufacturer in connection with the Licensed Products are destroyed or altered to the extent that they may no longer be used to manufacture or reproduce the Licensed Products. Within three days of such destruction or alteration the Licensee shall supply EventCo with written confirmation of the same in such form as EventCo may require and, in addition, EventCo shall be entitled to inspect the premises where the Licensed Products are manufactured or reproduced in order to verify the accuracy of such written confirmation.

14.   FORCE MAJEURE

14.1   Neither party to this Agreement shall be deemed to be in breach of this Agreement or otherwise liable to the other as a result of any delay or failure in the performance of its obligations under this Agreement if and to the extent that such delay or failure is caused by an Event of Force Majeure and the time for performance of the relevant obligation(s) shall be extended accordingly.

14.2   A party whose performance of its obligations under this Agreement is delayed or prevented by an Event of Force Majeure:

(a)   shall immediately notify the other party of the nature, extent, effect and likely duration of the circumstances constituting the Event of Force Majeure;

(b)   shall use all reasonable endeavours to minimise the effect of the Event of Force Majeure on the performance of its obligations under this Agreement; and

(c)   shall (subject to Clause 14.3 below) immediately after the Event of Force Majeure has ended notify the other party and resume full performance of its obligations under this Agreement.

14.3   If any Event of Force Majeure delays or prevents the performance of the obligations of either party for a continuous period of [three months], the party not so affected shall then be entitled to give notice to the affected party to terminate this Agreement with immediate effect without penalty. Such a termination notice shall be irrevocable except with the consent of both parties and upon termination the provisions of Clause 13 shall apply.

15. LIABILITY

15.1 Under no circumstances shall either party be liable for any actual or alleged indirect loss or consequential loss howsoever arising suffered by the other, including, but not limited to, loss of profits, anticipated profits, savings, business or opportunity or loss of publicity or loss of reputation or opportunity to enhance reputation or any other sort of economic loss.

15.2 The Licensee shall indemnify and keep indemnified EventCo from and against all demands, claims, legal action, damages, costs (including, without limitation, legal costs and the fees of any expert witnesses incurred in connection with any actions or proceedings), loss, interest or expenses arising, directly or indirectly, out of any act or omission on the part of the Licensee or as a result of any breach of its obligations, representations, warranties or undertakings contained in this Agreement.

16. ASSIGNMENT

Neither party may assign any of its rights or obligations under this Agreement without the prior written consent of the other party, such consent not to be unreasonably withheld or delayed.

17. ANNOUNCEMENTS AND CONFIDENTIALITY

17.1 No announcement shall be made by either party in relation to this Agreement without the prior written consent of the other.

17.2 Each party undertakes to each other that they shall at all times:

17.2.1 treat and safeguard as private, secret and confidential any and all information and data, howsoever recorded or preserved, relating to EventCo or the Event(s) or the Licensee or the Licensee's business whether or not provided by EventCo or the Licensee ("Confidential Information");

17.2.2 use Confidential Information only in relation to the Agreement; and

17.2.3 not at any time disclose or reveal any Confidential Information to any person or party other than to persons or parties authorised to receive Confidential Information.

18.   POINTS OF CONTACT

18.1   The principal point of contact for each party (unless the other party is notified otherwise in writing) shall be:

(a)   EventCo: [   ]

(b)   The Licensee: [   ]

18.2   The Licensee acknowledges and agrees that it is not entitled to rely on any representation, authorisation or decision of EventCo unless made by the principal point of contact (or his or her designated replacement) set out at sub-Clause 18.1 above.

19.   NOTICES

19.1   The parties agree that all notices under this Agreement shall, unless otherwise notified, be served on the following addressees:

(a)   EventCo: [   ]

(b)   The Licensee: [   ]

19.2   All notices shall be in writing and may be delivered personally, by facsimile, by first class pre-paid post or by registered mail and shall be deemed to be properly given or served:

(a)   [two] working days after being sent to the intended recipient by pre-paid post addressed as aforesaid; or

(b)   if sent by facsimile on receipt of confirmation of transmission or if not a working day the first working day thereafter provided that a confirming copy is sent by first class pre-paid post to the address aforesaid within 24 hours of transmission.

20.   GENERAL

20.1   The granting by any party of any time or indulgence in respect of any breach of any term of this Agreement by the other shall not be deemed a waiver of such breach and the waiver by any party of any breach of any term of this Agreement by the other shall not prevent the subsequent enforcement of that term and shall not be deemed a waiver of any subsequent breach.

20.2   This Agreement shall constitute the entire agreement between the parties with respect to the subject matter hereof, and shall supersede any and all prior agreements, representations or understanding between the parties, whether written or oral.

20.3 This Agreement may be executed in any number of counterparts, each of which when executed shall constitute an original, but all of which when taken together shall constitute one and the same Agreement.

20.4 All rights, remedies and powers conferred upon the parties are cumulative and shall not be deemed to be exclusive of any other rights, remedies or powers now or subsequently conferred upon them by law or otherwise.

20.5 Each party will do all things necessary including executing all documents necessary to give effect to the intention of the parties in relation to this Agreement.

20.6 Should any term of this Agreement be considered void or voidable under any applicable law, then such terms shall be severed or amended in such a manner as to render the remainder of this Agreement valid or enforceable, unless the whole commercial object is thereby frustrated.

20.7 This Agreement may only be modified or any provision waived if such modification or waiver is in writing and signed by a duly authorised representative of each party.

20.8 This Agreement shall be governed by and construed in accordance with [insert governing law] and the parties hereby submit to the non-exclusive jurisdiction of the [insert courts of jurisdiction] courts.

20.9 Any date or period mentioned in any clause of this Agreement may be extended by mutual agreement in writing between the parties but as regards any date or period (whether or not extended as aforesaid) time shall be of the essence in this Agreement.

20.10 Nothing in this Agreement shall be deemed to constitute a joint venture, partnership or relationship of agency or employment between the parties.

IN WITNESS WHEREOF, the parties have executed this Agreement as of the day and year first above written.

Signed by
a duly authorised representative
for and on behalf of
[INSERT PARTY]

Signed by
a duly authorised representative
for and on behalf of
[INSERT PARTY]

SCHEDULE 1

LICENSED PRODUCTS

[insert details]

SCHEDULE 2

APPROVAL OF LICENSED PRODUCTS

[insert details]

SCHEDULE 3

ROYALTY REPORT

[insert details]

SCHEDULE 4

THE MARKS

[insert details]

APPENDIX 11

BROADCASTING CONTRACT

This Agreement is made the   day of

BETWEEN:

(1)   [insert party] of [insert address] ("EventCo"); and

(2)   [insert party] of [insert address] ("the Broadcaster").

WHEREAS:

(A)   EventCo owns or controls all the rights in and to the Event.

(B)   EventCo wishes to grant the Broadcaster certain rights in connection with the [live and delayed broadcast] of the Event, on the terms and conditions of this Agreement.

IT IS AGREED:

1.   DEFINITIONS

1.1   In this Agreement the words and expressions set out below shall, save where the context otherwise requires, have the following meanings:

Broadcast Substitution means the ability to super-impose an electronic image on any surface whether real or imaginary or the ability to alter any image, whether by electronic or other means;

Commercial Partners means any third party with whom a contract is lawfully concluded for the exploitation of the Commercial Rights;

Commercial Rights means any and all rights of a commercial nature connected with the Event including, without limitation, broadcasting rights, so-called new media rights, interactive games rights, sponsorship rights, merchandising and licensing rights, ticketing rights, promotional rights and catering and hospitality rights;

Effective Date means the [date of signature of this Agreement];

Event	means [insert details] taking place on [insert details];
Event Feed	means the live signal of the Event produced by the Producer with audio track of natural sound and commentary;
Event Period	means the period from [2] days prior to the Event to [2] days after the Event;
Event of Force Majeure	means any circumstance not foreseeable at the date of this Agreement and not within the reasonable control of the party in question, including but not limited to any strike, lock-out or other industrial action (not due to the acts of any party to this Agreement); any destruction (temporary or permanent), breakdown, malfunction or damage of or to any premises, plant, equipment (including computer systems) or materials; any civil commotion or disorder, riot, invasion, war or terrorist activity or threat of war or terrorist activity; any action taken by a governmental or public authority of any kind (including not granting a consent, exemption, approval or clearance); and any fire, explosion, storm, flood, earthquake, subsidence, epidemic or other natural physical disaster;
EventCo Marks	means the event titles, words and logo(s) which are owned or controlled by EventCo and which appear in Schedule 2;
Fees	means the fees paid by the Broadcaster to EventCo in accordance with the provisions set out in Clause 4 of this Agreement;
Minimum Commitment	means the minimum commitment of broadcast coverage of the Event by the Broadcaster as follows: [insert details]
[Official Guide	means that full colour guide produced and/or published by or on behalf of EventCo which relates to the Event;]

Producer	means [insert details] or such other person as the Broadcaster appoints in consultation with EventCo to produce the Event Feed;
Programme	means the audio-visual programme produced by the Broadcaster for the Event using the Event Feed;
Rights	means those rights granted to the Broadcaster as set out in Schedule 1;
Term	means the period from the Effective Date up to and including [3] days after the Event, including the Event Period;
Territory	means [insert details];
Venue	means [insert details].

1.2   Unless the context otherwise requires words denoting the singular shall include the plural and vice versa and words denoting any one gender shall include all genders and words denoting persons shall include bodies corporate, unincorporated associations and partnerships.

1.3   References in this Agreement to Schedules are to Schedules to this Agreement.

2.   GRANT OF RIGHTS

2.1   In consideration of the obligations to be undertaken by the Broadcaster pursuant to this Agreement, EventCo hereby grants to the Broadcaster exclusively the Rights in the Territory during the Term.

[2.2   EventCo acknowledges that any unintentional overspill into those areas beyond the Territory will not amount to a breach of this Agreement.]

2.3   The Broadcaster acknowledges and agrees that EventCo is the owner of the Commercial Rights and that the Broadcaster shall not be entitled to exploit or enter into any commercial or other agreements to exploit any of the Commercial Rights other than as set out in this Agreement.

3. TERM

This Agreement is deemed to have taken effect on the Effective Date and shall continue until the end of the Term, unless terminated earlier in accordance with the provisions of Clause 9.

4. PAYMENT AND PAYMENT PROCEDURES

4.1 In consideration of the grant of the Rights, the Broadcaster shall pay to EventCo the Fees [(excluding relevant taxes)] as follows:

[insert details]

[4.2 All sums set out in Clause 4.1 above shall be paid within [insert number] days of receipt of an appropriate invoice.]

4.3 In addition to the above, the Broadcaster agrees to pay any collecting society royalties or fees in connection with the use of any music contained within the Feed.

5. EVENTCO'S OBLIGATIONS

5.1 EventCo represents, warrants and undertakes:

5.1.1 that it has and will continue to have throughout the Term full right and title and authority to enter into this Agreement and to accept and perform the obligations imposed on it under this Agreement;

5.1.2 to organise and stage the Event in a professional manner and to deliver or procure the delivery of the Rights to the Broadcaster;

5.1.3 to provide unrestricted and free access to the Venue for the personnel and equipment of the Broadcaster during the Event Period for the purposes of exercising the Rights, including access to:

5.1.3.1 [sufficient car parking facilities in the parking lot at the Venue;

5.1.3.2 a power supply;

5.1.3.3 the team sheets, statistics and biographical information on the participants in the Event;

5.1.3.4 the participants before, during and after the Event for the purposes of conducting interviews; and

5.1.3.5 the changing rooms and other restricted areas for the purposes of conducting interviews.]

5.1.4 that it owns or controls the EventCo Marks and shall take all measures it considers reasonable during the Term to protect its rights in the EventCo Marks from infringement by any third party;

5.1.5 that it will provide or shall procure that the Broadcaster is provided with such information as the Broadcaster may reasonably request in relation to the Event; and

5.1.6 that it will provide sufficient facilities for the proper and full exercise of the Rights, including the provision of suitable gantries, camera platforms and commentary booths.

6. BROADCASTER'S OBLIGATIONS

6.1 The Broadcaster hereby represents, warrants and undertakes that:

6.1.1 it shall produce the Programme to a standard of at least the same quality as other sports programming currently being produced by the Broadcaster;

6.1.2 it is a company specialising in broadcasting and it has all the necessary experience, capability and personnel to perform its obligations under this Agreement to the highest industry standards;

6.1.3 it shall use its best endeavours to exploit the Rights by procuring the transmission of the Programme in the Territory simultaneously with the Event or at the times, dates and from the locations set out in Schedule 3. If the Broadcaster is unable to transmit the Programme in such a manner, it shall do so as soon as reasonably practicable thereafter;

6.1.4 it shall pay for the costs of production of the Programme;

6.1.5 it shall not appoint a broadcast sponsor or grant any sponsorship rights in respect of the Event or the Programme without the prior written consent of EventCo;

6.1.6 it shall not accept any advertising intended for transmission during, immediately before or immediately after the Programme that is, in the reasonable opinion of EventCo, in direct competition with EventCo or any of the Commercial Partners;

6.1.7   it shall ensure that its personnel:

      6.1.7.1   have and display at all times during the Event Period proper identification in the form acceptable to EventCo;

      6.1.7.2   comply at all times with all rules, regulations and policies of EventCo relating to health and safety, security and risk management at the Venue;

6.1.8   it has, and will continue to have throughout the Term, full right and title and authority to enter into this Agreement and to accept and perform the obligations imposed on it hereunder;

6.1.9   it shall exercise the Rights strictly in accordance with the terms of this Agreement;

6.1.10   it shall not interfere with the running of the Event or do or permit anything to be done which might adversely affect the Commercial Rights or the value of the Commercial Rights;

6.1.11   it shall be responsible for obtaining all licenses, consents, approvals and permissions required for the purposes of exercising the Rights and shall be solely responsible for the costs of obtaining same;

6.1.12   it shall observe, and ensure that the Broadcaster's personnel observe, all relevant rules, regulations, directions, codes of practice or guidelines imposed by national law or any competent authority which are applicable to the exploitation of the Rights for the Event;

6.1.13   it shall promptly observe and comply with all reasonable instructions, directions or regulations issued by or on behalf of EventCo including without limitation, those relating to the organisation, staging, safety and image of the Event and the positioning of its personnel and equipment at the Venue;

6.1.14   it shall ensure that neither it nor any of its directors, employees, or other members of staff make any defamatory or derogatory statements or take part in any activities which are or might be derogatory or detrimental to the reputation, image or goodwill of EventCo, the Event or any of the Commercial Partners;

6.1.15   it shall not effect any Broadcast Substitution on any signal transmitting the Programme unless specifically requested in writing by EventCo;

6.1.16 it shall use its best endeavours to support EventCo's agreements with the Commercial Partners, provided that such agreements do not contravene current broadcasting regulations;

6.1.17 it shall select and provide at its own cost announcers, commentators, technical and other personnel sufficient to produce the Programme;

6.1.18 it shall provide the Minimum Commitment in respect of broadcast coverage of the Event and use its best endeavours to provide no less than [insert number] hours broadcast coverage [(whether live or delayed)] [during the Event];

6.1.19 it shall promote the Event at its own cost during the period from the Effective Date up until the Event as follows:

[insert details]

6.1.20 the camera locations will not unnecessarily exclude, obscure or restrict coverage of any advertising boards, signage and logos placed at the venue; and

6.1.21 it shall provide EventCo with copies of all broadcast coverage for its own viewing purposes.

7. OWNERSHIP OF THE RIGHTS

7.1 The Broadcaster shall be the first owner of the copyright in the Programme.

7.2 The Broadcaster shall not exploit its copyright in the Programme other than in the exploitation of the Rights in accordance with this Agreement.

[7.3 At the end of the Term and in consideration of the sum of [insert nominal amount] (receipt of which is acknowledged) the Broadcaster shall assign to EventCo all of its copyright in the Programme for the remaining unexpired period of copyright and all rights of the Broadcaster shall cease.]

8. INTELLECTUAL PROPERTY

8.1 The Broadcaster shall promptly notify EventCo of any actual, threatened or suspected infringement in the Territory of the EventCo Marks which comes to the Broadcaster's notice and the Broadcaster shall at the request and expense of EventCo do all such things as may be reasonably necessary to assist EventCo in protecting the EventCo Marks or taking or resisting any proceedings in relation to any such infringement.

8.2　The Broadcaster acknowledges and agrees that the EventCo Marks shall belong exclusively and in their entirety to EventCo. Nothing in this Agreement shall give the Broadcaster any rights in respect of EventCo's Marks or the goodwill associated therewith. The Broadcaster acknowledges that any additional goodwill generated by the Broadcaster from the use of the Marks shall accrue for the sole benefit of EventCo. The Broadcaster's right to use the EventCo Marks shall be limited to the extent provided in Schedule 1.

8.3　The Broadcaster shall not authorise any third party to use the EventCo Marks. If any third party requires the use of the EventCo Marks the Broadcaster shall inform EventCo of such requirement and EventCo may, in its absolute discretion, grant the use of the EventCo Marks to that third party.

8.4　The Broadcaster shall not commit, or authorise any third party to commit, any act or omission which would or might affect the validity of the EventCo Marks.

9.　TERMINATION

9.1　Either party shall have the right at any time to terminate this Agreement immediately by giving written notice to the other in the event that:

(a)　the other party has committed a material breach of any obligation under this Agreement which breach is incapable of remedy or cannot be remedied in time for the Event;

(b)　the other party has committed a material breach of any of its obligations under this Agreement and has not remedied such breach (if the same is capable of remedy) within fourteen days of being required by written notice so to do;

(c)　the other party goes into liquidation whether compulsory or voluntary or is declared insolvent or if an administrator or receiver is appointed over the whole or any part of that other party's assets or if that other party enters into any arrangement for the benefit of or compounds with its creditors generally or ceases to carry on business or threatens to do any of these things; or

(d)　either party undergoes a change of control or ownership.

9.2　EventCo shall have the right to terminate this Agreement by providing [3 month's] notice in writing to the Broadcaster in the event that it no longer wishes to stage the Event.

10.   CONSEQUENCES OF TERMINATION

10.1   The expiry or termination of this Agreement shall be without prejudice to any rights which have already accrued to either of the parties under this Agreement.

[10.2   Upon termination of this Agreement pursuant to Clause 9.2 or 11 EventCo shall immediately repay to the Broadcaster such proportion of the Fee that has been paid, and no further instalments (if any) shall be payable by the Broadcaster.]

10.3   Upon expiry or termination of this Agreement:

10.3.1 all of the Rights shall forthwith terminate and automatically revert to EventCo;

10.3.2 the Broadcaster shall not use or exploit its previous connection with EventCo or the Event, whether directly or indirectly;

10.3.3 EventCo shall be entitled to grant all or any of the Rights to any third party; and

10.3.4 each party shall promptly return to the other all of the property of the other within its possession.

10.4   If EventCo terminates this Agreement under Clause 9 then it will be taken to have received the assignment from the Broadcaster of all rights including any unexpired copyright in the Programme under Clause 7.3.

10.5   If the Broadcaster terminates this Agreement under Clause 9 during or immediately after the Event has been held that termination will not affect the assignment of all rights in the Programme to EventCo at the expiration of the Term under Clause 7.3.

11.   FORCE MAJEURE

11.1   Neither party to this Agreement shall be deemed to be in breach of this Agreement or otherwise liable to the other as a result of any delay or failure in the performance of its obligations under this Agreement if and to the extent that such delay or failure is caused by an Event of Force Majeure and the time for performance of the relevant obligation(s) shall be extended accordingly.

11.2   A party whose performance of its obligations under this Agreement is delayed or prevented by an Event of Force Majeure:

(a)   shall immediately notify the other party of the nature, extent, effect and likely duration of the circumstances constituting the Event of Force Majeure;

(b)   shall use all reasonable endeavours to minimise the effect of the Event of Force Majeure on the performance of its obligations under this Agreement; and

(c)   shall (subject to Clause 11.3 below) immediately after the Event of Force Majeure has ended notify the other party and resume full performance of its obligations under this Agreement.

11.3   If any Event of Force Majeure delays or prevents the performance of the obligations of either party for a continuous period of [three months], the party not so affected shall then be entitled to give notice to the affected party to terminate this Agreement with immediate effect without penalty. Such a termination notice shall be irrevocable except with the consent of both parties and upon termination the provisions of Clause 10 shall apply.

12.   LIABILITY

12.1   Under no circumstances shall either party be liable for any actual or alleged indirect loss or consequential loss howsoever arising suffered by the other, including, but not limited to, loss of profits, anticipated profits, savings, business or opportunity or loss of publicity or loss of reputation or opportunity to enhance reputation or any other sort of economic loss.

12.2   EventCo shall not be liable to the Broadcaster for breach of any of the terms of this Agreement for an amount of money that is greater than [the amount of the Fees together with the direct costs to the Broadcaster of producing the Programme.]

12.3   The Broadcaster undertakes and agrees that it will indemnify and hold EventCo harmless from and against all costs and expenses (including without limitation reasonable legal costs), actions, proceedings, claims, demands and damage arising from a breach of the Broadcaster's representations, warranties or undertakings contained herein or arising from the acts or omissions of the Broadcaster or its respective officers, employees, agents and sub-contractors, including any damage to the Venue caused by the Broadcaster or its respective officers, employees, agents or sub-contractors.

12.4   EventCo shall have no responsibility for any loss of or damage to the property and equipment brought into the Venue by the Broadcaster, its officers, employees, agents and sub-contractors.

12.5   The Broadcaster shall be responsible for all its personnel engaged in the provision of the Services. Such personnel shall remain employed or engaged by the Broadcaster and not by EventCo, and the Broadcaster will be fully responsible for paying all salaries, wages, commissions, bonuses, taxes, pensions, sick pay or all other amounts or benefits payable directly or indirectly in respect of their employment or engagement.

13.   ASSIGNMENT

Neither party may assign any of its rights or obligations under this Agreement without the prior written consent of the other party, such consent not to be unreasonably withheld or delayed.

14.   ANNOUNCEMENTS AND CONFIDENTIALITY

14.1   No announcement shall be made by either party in relation to this Agreement without the prior written consent of the other.

14.2   Each party undertakes to each other that they shall at all times:

14.2.1 treat and safeguard as private, secret and confidential any and all information and data, howsoever recorded or preserved, relating to the Event and/or EventCo or EventCo's business or the Broadcaster or the Broadcaster's business whether or not provided by EventCo or the Broadcaster ("Confidential Information");

14.2.2 use Confidential Information only in relation to the exploitation of the Rights or in connection with the Agreement; and

14.2.3 not at any time disclose or reveal any Confidential Information to any person or party other than to persons or parties authorised to receive Confidential Information.

15.   POINTS OF CONTACT

15.1   The principal point of contact for each party (unless the other party is notified otherwise in writing) shall be:

(a)   EventCo: [   ]

(b)   The Broadcaster: [   ]

15.2   The Broadcaster acknowledges and agrees that it is not entitled to rely on any representation, authorisation or decision of EventCo unless made by the principal point of contact (or his designated replacement) set out at sub-Clause 15.1 above.

16.   NOTICES

16.1   The parties agree that all notices under this Agreement shall, unless otherwise notified, be served on the following addressees:

(a)   EventCo: [   ]

(b)   The Broadcaster: [   ]

16.2   All notices shall be in writing and may be delivered personally, by facsimile, by first class pre-paid post or by registered mail and shall be deemed to be properly given or served:

(a)   [two] working days after being sent to the intended recipient by pre-paid post addressed as aforesaid; or

(b)   if sent by facsimile on receipt of confirmation of transmission or if not a working day the first working day thereafter provided that a confirming copy is sent by first class pre-paid post to the address aforesaid within 24 hours of transmission.

17.   GENERAL

17.1   The granting by any party of any time or indulgence in respect of any breach of any term of this Agreement by the other shall not be deemed a waiver of such breach and the waiver by any party of any breach of any term of this Agreement by the other shall not prevent the subsequent enforcement of that term and shall not be deemed a waiver of any subsequent breach.

17.2   This Agreement shall constitute the entire agreement between the parties with respect to the subject matter hereof, and shall supersede any and all prior agreements, representations or understanding between the parties, whether written or oral.

17.3   This Agreement may be executed in any number of counterparts, each of which when executed shall constitute an original, but all of which when taken together shall constitute one and the same Agreement.

17.4   All rights, remedies and powers conferred upon the parties are cumulative and shall not be deemed to be exclusive of any other rights, remedies or powers now or subsequently conferred upon them by law or otherwise.

17.5   Each party will do all things necessary including executing all documents necessary to give effect to the intention of the parties in relation to this Agreement.

17.6   Should any term of this Agreement be considered void or voidable under any applicable law, then such terms shall be severed or amended in such a manner as to render the remainder of this Agreement valid or enforceable, unless the whole commercial object is thereby frustrated.

17.7   This Agreement may only be modified or any provision waived if such modification or waiver is in writing and signed by a duly authorised representative of each party.

17.8   This Agreement shall be governed by and construed in accordance with [insert governing law] and the parties hereby submit to the non-exclusive jurisdiction of the [insert courts of jurisdiction] courts.

17.9   Any date or period mentioned in any clause of this Agreement may be extended by mutual agreement in writing between the parties but as regards any date or period (whether or not extended as aforesaid) time shall be of the essence in this Agreement.

17.10   Nothing in this Agreement shall be deemed to constitute a joint venture, partnership or relationship of agency or employment between the parties.

IN WITNESS WHEREOF, the parties have executed this Agreement as of the day and year first above written.

Signed by
a duly authorised representative
for and on behalf of
[INSERT PARTY]

Signed by
a duly authorised representative
for and on behalf of
[INSERT PARTY]

SCHEDULE 1

THE RIGHTS

The Broadcaster shall have the right at its own cost to:

[1.   Produce the Programme and broadcast it by means of live or delayed recorded, encrypted or unencrypted transmissions to persons by [a satellite direct to domestic reception equipment/terrestrial free-to-air television/cable];

2.   Advertise, promote or publicise the Programme by transmission to its audience;

3.   Include instant replays as part of the Programme;

4.   Include a highlights package as part of the Programme;

5.   Insert commercial and promotional announcements during the Programme, subject to Clause 6.1.6;

6.   Insert on-screen graphics and information;

7.   A full page advertisement in the Official Guide, provided that such advertisement is provided to EventCo by no later than [insert date];

8.   Use the EventCo Marks in the production of the Programme in the form set out in Schedule 2, subject to the provisions of Clause 8.

9.   Add commentary and sound to the Event Feed in producing the Programme.]

SCHEDULE 2

EVENTCO MARKS

[insert details]

SCHEDULE 3

SCHEDULE OF DATES, TIMES AND LOCATIONS

[insert details]

APPENDIX 12A

EVENT MANAGEMENT CONTRACT

This Agreement is made the   day of

BETWEEN:

(1)   [insert party] of [insert address] ("the Company"); and

(2)   [insert party] of [insert address] ("EventCo").

WHEREAS:

(1)   The Company owns or controls all the rights in and to the Event;

(2)   EventCo has experience in event management and promotion; and

(3)   The Company wishes to engage EventCo to perform various event management and promotional services in relation to the Event on the terms and conditions set out in this Agreement.

IT IS AGREED:

1.   DEFINITIONS AND INTERPRETATION

1.1   In this Agreement the words and expressions set out below shall, save where the context otherwise requires, have the following meanings:

Budget   means the budget for the Event set by the Company and agreed with EventCo or as varied in accordance with this Agreement;

Commercial Partners means any third party with whom a contract is lawfully concluded for the exploitation of the Commercial Rights;

Commercial Rights means any and all rights of a commercial nature connected with the Event including, without limitation, broadcasting rights, so-called new media rights, interactive games rights, sponsorship rights, merchandising and licensing rights, ticketing rights, promotional rights and catering and hospitality rights;

Effective Date   means [the date of signature of this Agreement];

Event	means [insert details] taking place on [insert details];
Event of Force Majeure	means any circumstance not foreseeable at the date of this Agreement and not within the reasonable control of the party in question, including but not limited to any strike, lock-out or other industrial action (not due to the acts of any party to this Agreement); any destruction (temporary or permanent), breakdown, malfunction or damage of or to any premises, plant, equipment (including computer systems) or materials; any civil commotion or disorder, riot, invasion, war or terrorist activity or threat of war or terrorist activity; any action taken by a governmental or public authority of any kind (including not granting a consent, exemption, approval or clearance); and any fire, explosion, storm, flood, earthquake, subsidence, epidemic or other natural physical disaster;
Fees	means the consideration set out in Clause 4;
Marks	means the event titles, words and logo(s) which are owned or controlled by the Company and which appear in Schedule 2;
Services	means those event management and promotion services described at Schedule 1;
Term	means the term of this Agreement described in Clause 2;
Territory	means [insert territory];
Venue	means [insert details].

1.2 Unless the context otherwise requires words denoting the singular shall include the plural and vice versa and words denoting any one gender shall include all genders and words denoting persons shall include bodies corporate, unincorporated associations and partnerships.

1.3 References in this Agreement to Schedules are to Schedules to this Agreement.

2. TERM

This Agreement shall have effect from the Effective Date and shall subsist until [thirty days] after the Event, subject to the provisions of Clause 11 below.

3. APPOINTMENT

3.1 The Company appoints EventCo to provide the Services for the Event during the Term in the Territory in accordance with the terms and conditions of this Agreement.

3.2 EventCo agrees to provide the Services in the Territory for the Event during the Term.

3.3 The Company agrees not to appoint any other third party to provide the Services in the Territory during the Term.

4. CONSIDERATION

4.1 In consideration of the provision of the Services provided by EventCo pursuant to the provisions of this Agreement, the Company agrees to pay to EventCo the Fees [(excluding relevant taxes)] as follows:

[insert details]

4.2 All sums set out in Clause 4.1 above shall be paid within [30] days of receipt of an appropriate invoice.

5. BUDGET AND ACCOUNTING

5.1 EventCo shall perform the Services in accordance with the Budget.

5.2 The Company shall provide such monies and pay all invoices and bills and enter into such contracts in indicated in the Budget and as necessary for EventCo to provide the Services as soon as practicable after receipt of such invoices, bills and contracts from EventCo.

5.3 EventCo shall forward immediately after receipt all invoices, bills and contracts entered into in accordance with the Budget directly to the Company for payment.

5.4 Subject to Clause 5.5 and unless otherwise agreed in writing by the Company, EventCo shall not be entitled to receive or hold any income or refunds of expenditure arising from the provision of the Services for the Event. If EventCo does receive or hold such monies it shall immediately inform the Company and transfer such monies to the Company in accordance with the Company's instructions.

5.5   The parties shall agree the most practicable method of payment for necessary expenses and costs incurred during the Term.

5.6   The Company may, in consultation with EventCo, vary the amount of the Budget and the allocation of funds therein. EventCo may request that the Budget be varied but the Company is under no obligation to approve such variation.

5.7   EventCo shall be responsible for the Budget and shall not incur any expenditure in excess of the amount allocated in terms of the Budget without the prior consent of the Company in accordance with Clause 5.6 above.

5.8   EventCo shall submit to the Company during the Term such information regarding the progress of the Event organisation, an analysis of current expenditure, estimates of any likely variation to the Budget, copies of all invoices, receipts, contracts and other relevant documentation relating to the Services or the Event as the Company may reasonably request.

5.9   EventCo shall keep and maintain full, accurate and proper records and books of account relating to the Event with copies of all invoices, vouchers and other records evidencing all receipts, expenses, charges and taxes incurred in providing the Services for the Event.

5.10   The Company shall be entitled, upon reasonable notice, to attend at the offices of EventCo and inspect such books of account, or appoint an auditor to inspect such books of account. The costs of any audit shall be borne by the Company, except where the audit reveals a deviation of more than [3%] of the value of the Budget, in which case the costs of such audit shall be borne by EventCo.

5.11   Any savings against the Budget shall be re-allocated to other items in the Budget under the direction and approval of the Company.

6.   EVENTCO'S WARRANTIES

EventCo represents, warrants and undertakes that:

6.1   it has and will continue to have throughout the Term full right and title and authority to enter into this Agreement and to accept and perform the obligations imposed on it under this Agreement;

6.2   it is a company specialising in the provision of Services and it has all the necessary experience, capability and personnel to deliver the Services in a professional and timely manner and according to the highest industry standards;

6.3   it will not appoint or instruct any third party to provide any part of the Services without the prior written approval of the Company. In the event that such approval is granted, EventCo shall procure that such third party comply in every respect with the provisions of this Agreement as if such third party were contracting with the Company as the party hereto and EventCo shall be liable to the Company for the acts and omissions of any such third party;

6.4   all Commercial Rights are the property of and reserved exclusively to the Company and EventCo shall not be entitled to exploit any of the same save as set out in this Agreement. EventCo shall not do anything or permit anything to be done which might adversely affect the Commercial Rights or the value of the Commercial Rights;

6.5   it shall ensure that neither it nor any of its directors, employees or other members of staff make any defamatory or derogatory statements or take part in any activities which are or might be derogatory or detrimental to the reputation, image or goodwill of the Company or the Event;

6.6   it shall ensure that sufficient personnel of a suitably senior or junior level are available at all reasonable times to carry out the Services along with such other personnel as EventCo may decide (in consultation with the Company) to use in providing the Services;

6.7   it shall make its personnel available at all reasonable times and upon reasonable notice to the Company for the purposes of consultation and advice relating to this Agreement and the Event;

6.8   it shall not hold itself out or permit any person to hold themselves out as being authorized to bind the Company in any way;

6.9   it shall not engage in any assignment or undertaking which would conflict with or prejudice its ability to carry out its duties and obligations under this Agreement;

6.10   it shall observe, and ensure that EventCo's personnel observe, all relevant rules, regulations, directions or codes of practice imposed by national law or any competent authority in relation to the Event;

6.11   it shall promptly observe and comply with all reasonable instructions issued by the Company in relation to the Event;

6.12   it shall not issue any press release on or relating to the Event without the prior written approval of the Company.

7.   THE COMPANY'S WARRANTIES

The Company represents, warrants and undertakes that:

7.1   it owns or controls the Commercial Rights in and to the Event;

7.2   that it has and will continue to have throughout the Term full right and title and authority to enter into this Agreement and to accept and perform the obligations imposed on it under this Agreement;

7.3   it shall obtain at its own cost all necessary consents, approvals and licences required to stage the Event during the Term;

7.4   it shall not engage any third party other than EventCo to provide the Services during the Term;

7.5   it shall use all reasonable endeavours to ensure that neither it nor any of its directors, employees or other members of staff make any defamatory or derogatory statements or take part in any activities which are or might be derogatory or detrimental to the reputation, image or goodwill of EventCo;

7.6   it shall keep EventCo fully informed of all relevant matters relating to the Event; and

7.7   that it owns or controls the Marks and shall take all measures it considers reasonable during the Term to protect its rights in the Marks from infringement by any third party.

8.   APPOINTMENT OF COMMERCIAL PARTNERS

The Company shall appoint such Commercial Partners in relation to the Event as the Company shall in its absolute discretion determine from time to time. EventCo shall not unless otherwise agreed make any statements, promises, guarantees or representations concerning the Event and shall use all reasonable endeavours to ensure full delivery of the Company's commitments and obligations to the Commercial Partners.

9.   APPROVAL OF PROMOTIONAL MATERIALS

9.1   EventCo shall send to the Company for its approval all promotional materials in respect of the Event, where such materials use the Marks.

9.2   Where EventCo has not received a response from the Company in respect of such promotional materials within [insert number of days], such materials will be deemed to have been approved by the Company.

10. INTELLECTUAL PROPERTY

10.1 The Company hereby grants to EventCo a royalty-free, non-exclusive license for the Term to use the Marks in relation to the Event and the promotion thereof.

10.2 EventCo acknowledges that the Marks shall be the sole property of the Company and undertakes not to do or permit to be done any act which would or might jeopardize or invalidate any registration of the Marks or any application for registration nor to do any act which might assist or give rise to an application to remove any of the registered Marks from the register or which might prejudice the right or title of the Company to any of the Marks.

10.3 EventCo will not make any representation or do any act which may be taken to indicate that it has any right, title or interest in or to the ownership or use of any of the Marks and acknowledges that nothing contained in this Agreement shall give EventCo any right, title or interest in or to the Marks.

10.4 EventCo shall give particulars to the Company as soon as reasonably practicable after becoming aware of any potential or actual infringement of the intellectual property rights in the Commercial Rights or Marks and the Company shall take such action as it deems appropriate in relation to any such potential or actual infringement.

11. TERMINATION

11.1 Either party shall have the right at any time to terminate this Agreement immediately by giving written notice to the other in the event that:

(a) the other party has committed a material breach of any obligation under this Agreement which breach is incapable of remedy or cannot be remedied in time for the Event;

(b) the other party has committed a material breach of any of its obligations under this Agreement and has not remedied such breach (if the same is capable of remedy) within fourteen days of being required by written notice so to do;

(c) the other party goes into liquidation whether compulsory or voluntary or is declared insolvent or if an administrator or receiver is appointed over the whole or any part of that other party's assets or if that other party enters into any arrangement for the benefit of or compounds with its creditors generally or ceases to carry on business or threatens to do any of these things; or

(d)   either party undergoes a change of control or ownership.

11.2   The Company shall have the right to terminate this Agreement by providing [3 month's] notice in writing to EventCo in the event that it no longer wishes to stage the Event.

12.   CONSEQUENCES OF TERMINATION

12.1   The expiry or termination of this Agreement shall be without prejudice to any rights which have already accrued to either of the parties under this Agreement.

[12.2   Upon termination of this Agreement pursuant to Clause 11.2 or Clause 13 EventCo shall immediately repay to the Company such proportion of the Fee that has been paid, and no further instalments (if any) shall be payable to the EventCo.]

[12.3   Upon expiry or termination of this Agreement:

12.3.1   EventCo shall not use or exploit its previous connection with the Company or the Event, whether directly or indirectly;

12.3.2   each party shall promptly return to the other all of the property of the other within its possession.]

13.   FORCE MAJEURE

13.1   Neither party to this Agreement shall be deemed to be in breach of this Agreement or otherwise liable to the other as a result of any delay or failure in the performance of its obligations under this Agreement if and to the extent that such delay or failure is caused by an Event of Force Majeure and the time for performance of the relevant obligation(s) shall be extended accordingly.

13.2   A party whose performance of its obligations under this Agreement is delayed or prevented by an Event of Force Majeure:

(a)   shall immediately notify the other party of the nature, extent, effect and likely duration of the circumstances constituting the Event of Force Majeure;

(b)   shall use all reasonable endeavours to minimise the effect of the Event of Force Majeure on the performance of its obligations under this Agreement; and

(c) shall (subject to Clause 13.3 below) immediately after the Event of Force Majeure has ended notify the other party and resume full performance of its obligations under this Agreement.

13.3 If any Event of Force Majeure delays or prevents the performance of the obligations of either party for a continuous period of [three months], the party not so affected shall then be entitled to give notice to the affected party to terminate this Agreement with immediate effect without penalty. Such a termination notice shall be irrevocable except with the consent of both parties and upon termination the provisions of Clause 12 shall apply.

14. LIABILITY

14.1 Under no circumstances shall either party be liable for any actual or alleged indirect loss or consequential loss howsoever arising suffered by the other, including, but not limited to, loss of profits, anticipated profits, savings, business or opportunity or loss of publicity or loss of reputation or opportunity to enhance reputation or any other sort of economic loss.

14.2 EventCo undertakes and agrees that it will indemnify and hold harmless the Company from and against all costs and expenses (including without limitation reasonable legal costs), actions, proceedings, claims, demands and damage arising from a breach of the EventCo's representations, warranties or undertakings contained herein or arising from the acts or omissions of the EventCo or its respective officers, employees, agents and sub-contractors.

14.3 EventCo shall be responsible for all its personnel engaged in the provision of the Services. Such personnel shall remain employed or engaged by EventCo and not by the Company and EventCo will be fully responsible for paying all salaries, wages, commissions, bonuses, taxes, pensions, sick pay or all other amounts or benefits payable directly or indirectly in respect of their employment or engagement.

14.4 EventCo shall maintain at its own expense comprehensive [general/ public/] liability insurance in such amount as may be adequate to protect the Company and EventCo against any and all claims, actions, losses and damages arising out of the Event or the provision of the Services, with a minimum cover under such policy per claim being not less than [insert amount]. A copy of such policy or policies shall be provided to the Company for its records prior to the Event.

15. ASSIGNMENT

Neither party may assign any of its rights or obligations under this Agreement without the prior written consent of the other party, such consent not to be unreasonably withheld or delayed.

16. ANNOUNCEMENTS AND CONFIDENTIALITY

No announcement shall be made by either party in relation to this Agreement without the prior written consent of the other and neither party shall without the prior written consent of the other (save as required by law) disclose to any third party any information concerning the terms or subject matter hereof after the date hereof.

17. POINTS OF CONTACT

17.1 The principal point of contact for each party (unless the other party is notified otherwise in writing) shall be:

(a) EventCo: [   ]

(b) The Company: [   ]

17.2 The Company acknowledges and agrees that it is not entitled to rely on any representation, authorisation or decision of EventCo unless made by the principal point of contact (or his designated replacement) set out at sub-clause 17.1 above.

18. NOTICES

18.1 The parties agree that all notices under this Agreement shall, unless otherwise notified, be served on the following addressees:

(a) EventCo: [   ]

(b) The Company: [   ]

18.2 All notices shall be in writing and may be delivered personally, by facsimile, by first class pre-paid post or by registered mail and shall be deemed to be properly given or served:

(a) [two] working days after being sent to the intended recipient by pre-paid post addressed as aforesaid; or

(b) if sent by facsimile on receipt of confirmation of transmission or if not a working day the first working day thereafter provided that a confirming copy is sent by first class pre-paid post to the address aforesaid within 24 hours of transmission.

19. GENERAL

19.1 The granting by any party of any time or indulgence in respect of any breach of any term of this Agreement by the other shall not be deemed a waiver of such breach and the waiver by any party of any breach of any term of this Agreement by the other shall not prevent the subsequent enforcement of that term and shall not be deemed a waiver of any subsequent breach.

19.2 This Agreement shall constitute the entire agreement between the parties with respect to the subject matter hereof, and shall supersede any and all prior agreements, representations or understanding between the parties, whether written or oral.

19.3 This Agreement may be executed in any number of counterparts, each of which when executed shall constitute an original, but all of which when taken together shall constitute one and the same Agreement.

19.4 All rights, remedies and powers conferred upon the parties are cumulative and shall not be deemed to be exclusive of any other rights, remedies or powers now or subsequently conferred upon them by law or otherwise.

19.5 Each party will do all things necessary including executing all documents necessary to give effect to the intention of the parties in relation to this Agreement.

19.6 Should any term of this Agreement be considered void or voidable under any applicable law, then such terms shall be severed or amended in such a manner as to render the remainder of this Agreement valid or enforceable, unless the whole commercial object is thereby frustrated.

19.7 This Agreement may only be modified or any provision waived if such modification or waiver is in writing and signed by a duly authorised representative of each party.

19.8 This Agreement shall be governed by and construed in accordance with [insert governing law] and the parties hereby submit to the non-exclusive jurisdiction of the [insert courts of jurisdiction] courts.

19.9 Any date or period mentioned in any clause of this Agreement may be extended by mutual agreement in writing between the parties but as regards any date or period (whether or not extended as aforesaid) time shall be of the essence in this Agreement.

19.10 Nothing in this Agreement shall be deemed to constitute a joint venture, partnership or relationship of agency or employment between the parties.

IN WITNESS WHEREOF, the parties have executed this Agreement as of the day and year first above written.

Signed by
a duly authorised representative
for and on behalf of
[INSERT PARTY]

Signed by
a duly authorised representative
for and on behalf of
[INSERT PARTY]

SCHEDULE 1

THE SERVICES

[EventCo shall provide the following Services to the Company in respect of the Event:

1.   Managing all aspects of the Event, including the following:

1.1   Arranging all necessary travel and accommodation for participating athletes, officials and event staff as provided in the Budget;

1.2   Arranging all aspects of venue preparation and management, including venue hire, branding and signage, communications, security, stewards, turnstile operators, event staff and all necessary equipment;

1.3   Ensuring the provision of necessary medical officers and equipment (including doctors, physiotherapists and paramedics);

1.4   Arranging the provision and management of drug testing facilities and officers;

1.5   Overseeing all aspects of hospitality and catering in relation to the Event, such as civic hospitality, VIP hospitality and catering, participant catering, event and support staff catering, official catering, media catering, press conference facilities, medals, gifts and goodie bags;

1.6   Managing all aspects in relation to external event staff, such as venue announcers, floor managers, production manager, support staff, participant management, ambassadors and official photographers;

    1.7   Ensuring the provision of a results service, including an accurate results and timing services operation;

    1.8   Arranging travel, accommodation and subsistence for relevant EventCo representatives;

    1.9   Arranging for the production of all necessary printed materials for the Event, such as athlete bibs, photographer bibs, event stationery, accreditation passes, ticket printing and distribution, box office management and programme production and distribution.

    1.10 Arranging all necessary production facilities, such as sound, lighting, electricity and scoreboard facilities;

    1.11 Co-ordinating all aspects relating to competitor entries and participation in the Event.

2.   Managing the promotion and marketing of the Event, including liaison with the press and media, PR, direct advertising and all promotional materials, such as the design, artwork and printing thereof;

3.   Arranging insurance, in accordance with Clause 14.4;

4.   Arranging and managing the provision of specialist legal advice in respect of the Event, including all necessary agreements;

5.   Arranging all necessary accounting advice in relation to the management and auditing of the books of account in relation to the Event;

6.   Liaising with the Company regarding the delivery and management of the Commercial Rights to the Commercial Partners;

7.   Ensuring insofar as it is reasonably able to do so that no products or services which are competitive with those of any Commercial Partners are advertised and that no such competitor products or services are sampled, sold, demonstrated or advertised at the Event venue;

8.   Submitting to the Company a full report of the Event operations and how the same can be improved, detailing issues relating to venue, officials and format;

9.   Managing Commercial Partners' concessions, franchises, displays, sampling activities and demonstrations at the venue;

10.   Preparing the Budget and arranging for the Budget to be approved by the parties;

11.   Liaising with all relevant governing bodies regarding the Event and participation in it.]

SCHEDULE 2

THE MARKS

[insert detail]

APPENDIX 12B

EVENT MANAGEMENT TERMS AND CONDITIONS

1. Definitions

1.1 "Administration Fee" means the sum paid in respect of the initial meeting and the administration and organisation of the Client's details and requirements.

1.2 "Client" means any person, firm or company placing an order for Services whether for that person, firm or company or on behalf of another firm, person or company.

1.3 "Equipment" means the tools, machinery and other equipment used at, or in connection with the Event which (for the avoidance of doubt) shall remain owned by EventCo or its sub-contractors (as appropriate).

1.4 "Estimate" means the estimate provided to the Client, recording the details and requirements of the Client, a description of the Services, the proposed Event Budget and the Price, and enclosing these Terms and Conditions.

1.5 "Event" means the function, party, reception or other event in respect of which the Services are to be provided.

1.6 "EventCo" means [insert details of the company].

1.7 "Event Budget" means the budget for the Event as agreed between EventCo and the Client and as amended from time to time by agreement between the same parties.

1.8 "Personnel" means any individual (including employees, sub-contractors and volunteers) engaged and provided by EventCo to perform the Services.

1.9 "Price" means the cost of the Services, other charges, expenses and [insert relevant taxes, if applicable] payable by the Client in accordance with the Estimate and these Terms and Conditions.

1.10 "Services" means any services to be supplied to or for the Client in accordance with the Estimate.

1.11 "Terms and Conditions" means these standard terms and conditions.

2.   Applicability

2.1   Upon enquiry by the Client for the provision of the Services, an Estimate will be provided to the Client by EventCo.

2.2   The provision of an Estimate by EventCo shall constitute an invitation to the Client to make an offer on these Terms and Conditions, to the exclusion of any other terms and conditions (including any which the Client may purport to apply under any order confirmation or similar document).

2.3   The Client's subsequent order (either in writing or verbally) shall be deemed an offer to purchase the Services on these Terms and Conditions. No contract shall come into existence unless the Client's order is accepted by EventCo in writing [or by proceeding with the order].

2.4   Any variation of these Terms and Conditions (including any special terms and conditions agreed between the parties) shall be inapplicable unless specifically agreed in writing by EventCo.

3.   Administration Fee

3.1   When making an offer, the Client shall pay to EventCo the Administration Fee which shall be non-refundable.

4.   Price and Payment

4.1   The Client will pay EventCo the Price.

4.2   EventCo reserves the right to vary the Price immediately and/or recover any and all further costs, charges, expenses and [insert relevant taxes, if applicable] if it incurs such additional costs either due to factors occurring after the making of the contract which are beyond the reasonable control of EventCo, or which arise due to the Client's variation of the Services or the Client's default (including without limitation the Client's failure to comply with its obligations under these Terms and Conditions). Such variations of the Price or further costs shall be notified to the Client as soon as reasonably practicable. EventCo shall obtain the Client's consent (such consent not to be unreasonably withheld) to any increase in excess of [15%] over the Price specified in the Estimate.

4.3   Unless specified otherwise in the Estimate, invoices for Services will be issued from time to time for Services performed and (if applicable) expenses incurred in that period. A final invoice will be issued between 7 and 14 days before the Event. Such an invoice may include provision for a reasonable deposit to be paid by the Client for particular items or

Services where the full charge will only be determinable after the Event (including, but not limited to, the provision of drinks and extra cleaning-up services after the Event). A supplementary invoice will be issued after the Event in respect of any such outstanding charges.

4.4   In respect of each invoice issued before the Event, cleared funds shall be due before the date of the Event or 28 days from the date of that invoice, whichever is sooner. In respect of any supplementary invoice issued after the Event, cleared funds shall be due within 28 days from the date of the invoice. However, if any invoice shall remain unpaid on its due date, EventCo may (without prejudice to its other rights and remedies) cease to provide the Services without liability. The balance of the Price for Services performed and expenses incurred up to that date (to the extent not previously invoiced) together with all unpaid invoices already issued shall then upon written demand by EventCo accompanied by such further invoices as necessary, become immediately due and payable (with interest).

4.5   Interest on overdue payments shall accrue on a daily basis at the rate of [%] per calendar month from the date of invoice until payment in full and shall accrue at that rate after as well as before any judgement.

5.   Third Parties

5.1   EventCo, in making arrangements on behalf of its Clients, may contract with third parties for provision of any of the Services in accordance with the Event Budget. In doing so it is expressly agreed that EventCo acts only as agent of the Client and that no liability of any kind howsoever caused shall attach to EventCo in connection with or arising out of such arrangements. In the event that such Services shall not be available, for whatever reason, any liability of EventCo shall be limited to the return of all sums paid by the Client for such Services.

5.2   Any contracts for the Services or expenditure incurred outside of the Event Budget shall be approved in advance by the Client.

5.3   When the arrangements and/or facilities for any Event are changed or cancelled by a third party, EventCo will use its best endeavours to provide a suitable alternative and/or secure a refund for the Client only of monies paid to a third party, but is not obliged and cannot guarantee to do so.

6. Personnel and Services

6.1 The Client will provide EventCo with such information as it may reasonably need concerning the Client's requirements and/or operations and answers to queries, decisions and approvals which may be reasonably necessary for EventCo to perform the Services. The Client is responsible for ensuring such information and answers are accurate and complete. EventCo shall treat all such information as strictly confidential except to the extent it is within the public domain or EventCo is required to disclose it by law or government authority.

6.2 If EventCo shall have given an estimate of time, the right is nevertheless reserved to vary such estimate to take account of intervening events and factors of which EventCo was not previously aware and could not have foreseen, or which arise because of the Client's failure to comply with its obligations under these Terms and Conditions.

7. Cancellation

7.1 The Client may, by giving not less than [14 days] written notice to EventCo, cancel the order. In such an event, EventCo will issue an invoice as soon as is reasonably practicable for all expenses incurred by it up until the moment of cancellation, together with charges for all Services performed up to that date. Such an invoice shall be payable in accordance with Clause 4. Any Administration Fee paid as well as any sums and disbursements paid by EventCo to third parties will not be refunded to the Client.

7.2 EventCo may, by giving not less than [14 days] notice to the Client, cancel the order. In such an event, EventCo shall refund all deposits paid to it by the Client, with the exception of the Administration Fee.

8. Limitations and Exclusions

8.1 The Client acknowledges that the Estimate (together with any amendments thereto agreed between the Client and EventCo in writing) constitutes the entire agreement and understanding between the parties and supersedes all prior agreements, and that it has not relied upon or been induced to enter into the contract by any oral representation made by EventCo or its servants or agents. To the extent permitted by law and unless otherwise as set out in this Agreement, all other warranties relating to the provision and performance of the Services or the supply of any materials by EventCo are excluded.

8.2   EventCo shall not be liable for any default due to an event beyond its reasonable control ("a Force Majeure Event") including (but not limited to) any act of God, war, act of terrorism, strike, lock out, industrial action, fire, flood, drought, storm or non- availability of Personnel. On the occurrence of a Force Majeure Event rendering performance of its obligations impossible EventCo shall be released from such obligations whereupon the Client shall immediately pay to EventCo all monies due for Services performed and expenses incurred up to that date.

8.3   Under no circumstances shall either party be liable for any actual or alleged indirect loss or consequential loss howsoever arising suffered by the other, including, but not limited to, loss of profits, anticipated profits, savings, business or opportunity or loss of publicity or loss of reputation or opportunity to enhance reputation or any other sort of economic loss.

8.4   EventCo shall not be liable for any loss, damage, expenses or costs incurred by the Client as a result of the Event or the Services except where such loss, damage, expenses or costs arises from the negligence of EventCo or its employees or from a material breach of these Conditions by EventCo or its employees. Nothing in these Terms and Conditions shall affect the statutory rights of any consumer.

8.5   The Client shall be responsible for, and will indemnify EventCo in respect of any damage to or loss of furnishings, utensils, equipment or other property ("Property") (including any Property owned by EventCo) caused by any act, omission or default of the Client or the guests thereof (whether negligent or otherwise) and shall pay on demand the amount required to make good or remedy any such damage or loss.

8.6   EventCo shall be responsible for all its personnel engaged in the provision of the Services. Such personnel shall remain employed or engaged by EventCo and not by the Company and EventCo will be fully responsible for paying all salaries, wages, commissions, bonuses, taxes, pensions, sick pay or all other amounts or benefits payable directly or indirectly in respect of their employment or engagement.

9.   Further Obligations of Client

9.1   The Client shall maintain at its own expense comprehensive [general/ public] liability insurance in such amount as may be adequate to protect the Client and EventCo against any and all claims, actions, losses and damages arising out of the Event or the provision of the Services, with a minimum cover under such policy per claim being not less than [insert amount]. A copy of such policy or policies shall be provided to EventCo for its records prior to the Event.

9.2   If necessary, the Client will, at its own expense, make an application for any licence, permission or consent from the local authority, the courts, the police or any other relevant authority which shall be necessary for the Event.

10.   General Provisions

10.1   The granting by any party of any time or indulgence in respect of any breach of any term of this Agreement by the other shall not be deemed a waiver of such breach and the waiver by any party of any breach of any term of this Agreement by the other shall not prevent the subsequent enforcement of that term and shall not be deemed a waiver of any subsequent breach.

10.2   If any part of these Terms and Conditions is found by a Court of competent jurisdiction or other competent authority to be invalid, unlawful or unenforceable then such part will be severed from the remainder of the Terms and Conditions which will continue to be valid and enforceable to the fullest extent permitted by law.

10.3   Neither party shall assign, sub-contract, license or otherwise dispose of all or any part of its rights or obligations under this contract without the prior written consent of the other.

10.4   Any notice to be served on either party by the other shall be hand delivered to the recipients address or sent by ordinary first class post to that address, or sent by facsimile transmission. The Notice shall be deemed received by the addressee within 48 hours of posting or 24 hours if hand delivered or upon receipt of confirmation of transmission if sent by facsimile.

10.5   This Agreement may only be modified or any provision waived if such modification or waiver is in writing and signed by a duly authorised representative of each party.

10.6   This Agreement shall be governed by and construed in accordance with [insert governing law] and the parties hereby submit to the non-exclusive jurisdiction of the [insert courts of jurisdiction] courts.

APPENDIX 13

SOUVENIR PROGRAMME PRODUCTION CONTRACT

This Agreement is made the   day of

BETWEEN:

(1)   [insert party] of [insert address] ("EventCo"); and

(2)   [insert party] of [insert address] ("the Company").

WHEREAS:

1.   EventCo owns or controls all rights in and to the Event.

2.   The Company is in the business of producing, marketing and selling souvenir programmes for events.

3.   EventCo wishes to engage the Company, and the Company has agreed to provide to EventCo the Services (as defined below) upon, and subject to, the provisions of this Agreement.

NOW IT IS HEREBY AGREED as follows:

1.   DEFINITIONS

1.1   In this Agreement the words and expressions set out below shall, save where the context otherwise requires, have the following meanings:

Commercial Partner means any third party with whom a contract is lawfully concluded for the exploitation of the Commercial Rights;

Commercial Rights means any and all rights of a commercial nature connected with the Event including, without limitation, broadcasting rights, so-called new media rights, interactive games rights, sponsorship rights, merchandising and licensing rights, ticketing rights, promotional rights and catering and hospitality rights;

Effective Date means the [date of signature of this Agreement];

Event means [insert details] taking place on [insert details];

Event Manager	means the person appointed by EventCo whose identity shall be notified by EventCo to the Company from time to time;
Event Period	means the period from [2] days prior to the Event to [2] days after the Event;
Event of Force Majeure	means any circumstance not foreseeable at the date of this Agreement and not within the reasonable control of the party in question, including but not limited to any strike, lock-out or other industrial action (not due to the acts of any party to this Agreement); any destruction (temporary or permanent), breakdown, malfunction or damage of or to any premises, plant, equipment (including computer systems) or materials; any civil commotion or disorder, riot, invasion, war or terrorist activity or threat of war or terrorist activity; any action taken by a governmental or public authority of any kind (including not granting a consent, exemption, approval or clearance); and any fire, explosion, storm, flood, earthquake, subsidence, epidemic or other natural physical disaster;
EventCo Marks	means the event titles, words and logo(s) which are owned or controlled by EventCo and which appear in Schedule 3;
Fees	means the fees for the Services payable by EventCo to the Company in accordance with the provisions set out in Clause 4 of this Agreement;
Official Programme	means a full colour souvenir programme which relates to the Event, the details of which are set out in Schedule 2;
Rights	means those rights granted to the Company in connection with the Event as set out in Schedule 1;
Services	means the Services set out in Schedule 2 which the Company provides or is to provide to EventCo pursuant to this Agreement;

Term	means the period described in Clause 2 below;
Venue	means [insert details].

1.2 Unless the context otherwise requires words denoting the singular shall include the plural and vice versa and words denoting any one gender shall include all genders and words denoting persons shall include bodies corporate, unincorporated associations and partnerships.

1.3 References in this Agreement to Schedules are to Schedules to this Agreement.

2. TERM

This Agreement is deemed to have taken effect on the Effective Date and shall continue until [insert date], unless terminated earlier in accordance with the provisions of Clause 7 (the "Term").

3. APPOINTMENT AND GRANT OF RIGHTS

3.1 In consideration of the Fees paid by the Company to EventCo in accordance with Clause 4, EventCo hereby appoints the Company provide the Services to the Event.

3.2 In consideration of the supply of the Services by the Company, EventCo grants to the Company the Rights as set out in Schedule 1 for use during the Event Period.

3.3 The Company acknowledges and agrees that EventCo is the owner of the Commercial Rights and that the Company shall not be entitled to exploit or enter into any commercial or other agreements to exploit any of the Commercial Rights other than as set out in this Agreement.

3.4 EventCo shall have the right to approve prior to production of the Official Programme all editorial copy, layout, advertising and use of the EventCo Marks in the Official Programme. Such approval shall be deemed to have been provided if not withheld in writing within 7 business days following submission to EventCo. Such approval may be withheld in the absolute discretion of EventCo.

4. CONSIDERATION

4.1 The Company agrees to pay to EventCo the Fees [(excluding relevant taxes)] as follows:

[4.1.1 [%] of the net revenues from the sale of the Official Programmes and advertising therein, after deduction of vendor commission (not to exceed [%]), taxes, shipping or transportation charges, printing costs, writer/photo fees, advertising commissions (not to exceed [%]) and other reasonable, documented out-of-pocket expenses. Expenses, exclusive of commissions and applicable taxes, will not exceed [insert amount] without EventCo's prior written approval.] or

[4.1.1 [%] of the gross revenues from the sale of the Official Programmes and advertising therein, without deduction for any commissions, expenses or taxes.]

4.2 The Company shall issue a statement and payment to EventCo [30 days] following the Event, with a final reconciliation no later than [120 days] after the Event.

4.3 The Company will pay to EventCo a guarantee against the percentage stated in Clause 4.1.1 above of [insert amount] on the Effective Date ("the Guarantee").

4.4 The Company shall maintain separate books of account in respect of the revenue arising from the Official Programme. EventCo shall have the right to inspect such books of account upon reasonable notice to the Company and shall, in addition, have the right to appoint an auditor for the purposes of conducting an audit in respect of such books of account. Such audit shall be carried out at the cost of EventCo, unless it discloses under-reporting by the Company resulting in underpayment in excess of [3%]. In such event the costs shall be paid by the Company.

5. OBLIGATIONS OF EVENTCO

5.1 EventCo represents, warrants and undertakes:

5.1.1 that it has and will continue to have throughout the Term full right and title and authority to enter into this Agreement and to accept and perform the obligations imposed on it under this Agreement;

5.1.2 to organise and stage the Event in a professional manner and to deliver or procure the delivery of the Rights to the Company;

5.1.3 to provide unrestricted access to the Venue for the personnel of the Company during the Event Period for the purposes of providing the Services;

5.1.4   that it owns or controls the EventCo Marks and shall take all measures it considers reasonable during the Term to protect its rights in the EventCo Marks from infringement by any third party;

5.1.5   that it shall not appoint any other party to provide the Services, nor will it co-operate with any other person in the production of an "official" programme or souvenir book for the Event.

[5.2   In the event that, for whatever reason, EventCo is unable to provide any of the Rights precisely as described in Schedule 1, EventCo shall be entitled to substitute alternative rights in the nature of the Rights to an equivalent value without penalty.]

6.   OBLIGATIONS OF THE COMPANY

6.1   The Company hereby represents, warrants and undertakes that:

6.1.1   it shall provide the Services on such dates and times as indicated in Schedule 2 or as otherwise directed by EventCo, and it is acknowledged by the Company that time shall be of the essence in the delivery of such Services;

6.1.2   it is a Company specialising in the provision of the Services and it has all the necessary experience, capability and personnel to deliver the Services to the highest industry standards [in particular to produce a publication of a quality commensurate with that of similar events staged by EventCo];

6.1.3   in providing the Services under this Agreement, the Company and its personnel shall exercise all necessary professional judgement, technical skill and care;

6.1.4   in providing the Services under this Agreement, the Company shall ensure that the Company personnel:

6.1.4.1   have and display at all times during the Event Period proper identification in the form acceptable to EventCo;

6.1.4.2   comply at all times with all rules, regulations and policies of EventCo relating to health and safety, security and risk management at the Venue;

6.1.5   it has, and will continue to have throughout the Term, full right and title and authority to enter into this Agreement and to accept and perform the obligations imposed on it hereunder;

6.1.6   it shall exercise the Rights strictly in accordance with the terms of this Agreement. For the avoidance of doubt, the Company shall not be entitled to create any merchandise, premiums or other items which are either associated with the Event or EventCo or which bear the EventCo Marks other than as provided in this Agreement;

6.1.7   it shall not do anything or permit anything to be done which might adversely affect the Commercial Rights or the value of the Commercial Rights;

6.1.8   it shall observe, and ensure that the Company's personnel observe, all relevant rules, regulations, directions, codes of practice or guidelines imposed by national law or any competent authority which are applicable both to the provision of the Services and the advertising contained in the Official Programme;

6.1.9   it shall promptly observe and comply with all reasonable instructions, directions or regulations issued by or on behalf of EventCo or the Event Manager including without limitation, those relating to the organisation, staging, safety and image of the Event and the provision of the Services related thereto;

6.1.10 it shall ensure that neither it nor any of its directors, employees, or other members of staff make any defamatory or derogatory statements (either in the Official Programme or otherwise) or take part in any activities which are or might be derogatory or detrimental to the reputation, image or goodwill of EventCo, the Event or any Commercial Partner;

6.1.11 the content or images contained in the Event Programme shall not infringe the copyright, privacy or other right of any person;

6.1.12 it shall not sell advertising space to sellers of products or services which are competitive to the Commercial Partners without the prior written consent of EventCo;

6.1.13 all advertising in the Official Programme except as specifically set out herein shall be paid for by third parties, except with EventCo's prior written approval; and

6.1.14 [It shall deliver to EventCo one-half of any unsold Official Programmes within 60 days following the Event, and thereafter the Company shall have no right to further reprint the Official Programme. Both parties may sell their remaining Official Programmes for their own account.]

7. TERMINATION

7.1   Either party shall have the right at any time to terminate this Agreement immediately by giving written notice to the other in the event that:

(a)   the other party has committed a material breach of any obligation under this Agreement which breach is incapable of remedy or cannot be remedied in time for the Event;

(b)   the other party has committed a material breach of any of its obligations under this Agreement and has not remedied such breach (if the same is capable of remedy) within fourteen days of being required by written notice so to do;

(c)   the other party goes into liquidation whether compulsory or voluntary or is declared insolvent or if an administrator or receiver is appointed over the whole or any part of that other party's assets or if that other party enters into any arrangement for the benefit of or compounds with its creditors generally or ceases to carry on business or threatens to do any of these things; or

(d)   either party undergoes a change of control or ownership.

7.2   EventCo shall have the right to terminate this Agreement by providing [3 month's] notice in writing to the Company in the event that it no longer wishes to stage the Event.

[7.3   Without prejudice to the rights in Clause 7.1 and 7.2 above, EventCo shall have the right to terminate this Agreement without liability of any kind by written notice to the Company in the event that the Official Programme is not produced in a form satisfactory to EventCo by [insert date]. Upon termination in accordance with this sub-clause, EventCo shall have the right to appoint any other third party to provide the Services with immediate effect.]

8. CONSEQUENCES OF TERMINATION

8.1   The expiry or termination of this Agreement shall be without prejudice to any rights which have already accrued to either of the parties under this Agreement.

[8.2   Upon termination of this Agreement pursuant to Clause 7.2 or Clause 9 EventCo shall immediately repay to the Company the Guarantee, and no further instalments (if any) shall be payable to EventCo.]

8.3   Upon expiry or termination of this Agreement:

8.3.1 all of the Rights shall forthwith terminate and automatically revert to EventCo;

8.3.2 the Company shall not use or exploit its previous connection with EventCo or the Event, whether directly or indirectly;

8.3.3 EventCo shall be entitled to grant all or any of the Rights to any third party; and procure the Services from any third party;

8.3.4 each party shall promptly return to the other all of the property of the other within its possession.

9. FORCE MAJEURE

9.1 Neither party to this Agreement shall be deemed to be in breach of this Agreement or otherwise liable to the other as a result of any delay or failure in the performance of its obligations under this Agreement if and to the extent that such delay or failure is caused by an Event of Force Majeure and the time for performance of the relevant obligation(s) shall be extended accordingly.

9.2 A party whose performance of its obligations under this Agreement is delayed or prevented by an Event of Force Majeure:

(a) shall immediately notify the other party of the nature, extent, effect and likely duration of the circumstances constituting the Event of Force Majeure;

(b) shall use all reasonable endeavours to minimise the effect of the Event of Force Majeure on the performance of its obligations under this Agreement; and

(c) shall (subject to Clause 9.3 below) immediately after the Event of Force Majeure has ended notify the other party and resume full performance of its obligations under this Agreement.

9.3 If any Event of Force Majeure delays or prevents the performance of the obligations of either party for a continuous period of [three months], the party not so affected shall then be entitled to give notice to the affected party to terminate this Agreement with immediate effect without penalty. Such a termination notice shall be irrevocable except with the consent of both parties and upon termination the provisions of Clause 8 shall apply.

10.   LIABILITY

10.1   Under no circumstances shall either party be liable for any actual or alleged indirect loss or consequential loss howsoever arising suffered by the other, including, but not limited to, loss of profits, anticipated profits, savings, business or opportunity or loss of publicity or loss of reputation or opportunity to enhance reputation or any other sort of economic loss.

10.2   The Company undertakes and agrees that it will indemnify and hold EventCo harmless from and against all costs and expenses (including without limitation reasonable legal costs), actions, proceedings, claims, demands and damage arising from a breach of the Company's representations, warranties or undertakings contained herein or arising from the acts or omissions of the Company or its respective officers, employees, agents and sub-contractors in providing the Services under this Agreement.

10.3   The Company agrees that it will publish a disclaimer in the Official Programme in the following terms: ["Although every effort has been used to ensure the accuracy of the information contained in this publication, neither the Company nor EventCo shall accept any liability for errors or omissions contained therein. Reference to products or the inclusion of articles or advertisements in the Official Programme does not constitute an endorsement by the Company or EventCo of such products, articles or advertisements".]

10.4   EventCo shall have no responsibility for any loss of or damage to the property and effects brought into the Venue by the Company, its officers, employees, agents and sub-contractors.

10.5   The Company shall be responsible for all its personnel engaged in the provision of the Services. Such personnel shall remain employed or engaged by the Company and not by EventCo, and the Company will be fully responsible for paying all salaries, wages, commissions, bonuses, taxes, pensions, sick pay or all other amounts or benefits payable directly or indirectly in respect of their employment or engagement.

10.6   The Company shall maintain at its own expense comprehensive [general/public/product] liability insurance in such amount as may be adequate to protect the Company and EventCo against any and all claims, actions, losses and damages arising out of the provision of the Services, with a minimum cover under such policy per claim being not less than [insert amount]. Such insurance shall also cover the loss or destruction of the

Official Programmes before their sale. A copy of such policy or policies shall be provided to EventCo for its records.

11. INTELLECTUAL PROPERTY

11.1 The Company acknowledges and agrees that the EventCo Marks shall belong exclusively and in their entirety to EventCo. Any goodwill generated in the EventCo Marks generated through the use of the EventCo Marks in accordance with this Agreement shall belong entirely to EventCo.

11.2 The Company shall not commit, or authorise any third party to commit, any act or omission which would or might affect the validity of the EventCo Marks.

11.3 The Company's right to use the EventCo Marks shall be limited to the extent provided in Schedule 1.

11.4 EventCo acknowledges that, with the exception of any copy or images provided by EventCo to the Company, all copyright in the Official Programme shall vest in the Company and the Company agrees to grant to EventCo an exclusive royalty-free licence to use any content or images contained in the Official Programme for its own purposes in perpetuity.

12. ANNOUNCEMENTS AND CONFIDENTIALITY

No announcement shall be made by either party in relation to this Agreement without the prior written consent of the other and neither party shall without the prior written consent of the other (save as required by law) disclose to any third party any information concerning the terms or subject matter hereof after the date hereof.

13. POINTS OF CONTACT

13.1 The principal point of contact for each party (unless the other party is notified otherwise in writing) shall be:

(a) EventCo: [   ]

(b) The Company: [   ]

13.2 The Company acknowledges and agrees that it is not entitled to rely on any representation, authorisation or decision of EventCo unless made by the principal point of contact (or his designated replacement) set out at sub-clause 13.1 above.

14.   NOTICES

14.1   The parties agree that all notices under this Agreement shall, unless otherwise notified, be served on the following addressees:

(a)   EventCo: [   ]

(b)   The Company: [   ]

14.2   All notices shall be in writing and may be delivered personally, by facsimile, by first class pre-paid post or by registered mail and shall be deemed to be properly given or served:

(a)   [two] working days after being sent to the intended recipient by pre-paid post addressed as aforesaid; or

(b)   if sent by facsimile on receipt of confirmation of transmission or if not a working day the first working day thereafter provided that a confirming copy is sent by first class pre-paid post to the address aforesaid within 24 hours of transmission.

15.   GENERAL

15.1   The granting by any party of any time or indulgence in respect of any breach of any term of this Agreement by the other shall not be deemed a waiver of such breach and the waiver by any party of any breach of any term of this Agreement by the other shall not prevent the subsequent enforcement of that term and shall not be deemed a waiver of any subsequent breach.

15.2   This Agreement shall constitute the entire agreement between the parties with respect to the subject matter hereof, and shall supersede any and all prior agreements, representations or understanding between the parties, whether written or oral.

15.3   This Agreement may be executed in any number of counterparts, each of which when executed shall constitute an original, but all of which when taken together shall constitute one and the same Agreement.

15.4   All rights, remedies and powers conferred upon the parties are cumulative and shall not be deemed to be exclusive of any other rights, remedies or powers now or subsequently conferred upon them by law or otherwise.

15.5   Each party will do all things necessary including executing all documents necessary to give effect to the intention of the parties in relation to this Agreement.

15.6 Should any term of this Agreement be considered void or voidable under any applicable law, then such terms shall be severed or amended in such a manner as to render the remainder of this Agreement valid or enforceable, unless the whole commercial object is thereby frustrated.

15.7 Neither party may assign any of its rights or obligations under this Agreement without the prior written consent of the other party, such consent not to be unreasonably withheld or delayed.

15.8 This Agreement may only be modified or any provision waived if such modification or waiver is in writing and signed by a duly authorised representative of each party.

15.9 This Agreement shall be governed by and construed in accordance with [insert governing law] and the parties hereby submit to the non-exclusive jurisdiction of the [insert courts of jurisdiction] courts.

15.10 Any date or period mentioned in any clause of this Agreement may be extended by mutual agreement in writing between the parties but as regards any date or period (whether or not extended as aforesaid) time shall be of the essence in this Agreement.

15.11 Nothing in this Agreement shall be deemed to constitute a joint venture, partnership or relationship of agency or employment between the parties.

IN WITNESS WHEREOF, the parties have executed this Agreement as of the day and year first above written.

Signed by
a duly authorised representative
for and on behalf of
[INSERT PARTY]

Signed by
a duly authorised representative
for and on behalf of
[INSERT PARTY]

SCHEDULE 1

THE RIGHTS

[The Company shall have the following rights:

1. The right to one full page colour advertisement in the Official Programme, in order to promote the business of the Company or its prior programmes.

2. A non-exclusive royalty-free right during the Term to use the EventCo Marks in producing the Official Programme.

3. The right to use the name, likeness image and/or other characteristics of any individual or team participating in or attending the Event, with the prior consent of the EventCo.

4. [insert number] free tickets to the Event.

5. The right to use the term 'Official Publisher' in relation to the Event.]

SCHEDULE 2

THE SERVICES

[The Company shall:

(a) produce and deliver to EventCo no less than [insert number] full colour souvenir Official Programmes of the following specifications:

(i) size: [insert dimensions];

(ii) [insert number] pages;

(iii) [hard/soft cover/glossy cover];

(iv) [insert details of binding];

(v) [insert quality of paper];

(vi) [The editorial content shall include specific issues, feature interviews and articles directly relating to the Event's audience];

(vii) [insert pricing information]; and

(viii) [other]

(b) produce and deliver the Official Programme by no later than [insert date];

(c) handle all design, layout and production functions for the Official Programme, including the commissioning and arranging of all editorial features, editorial design, pre-press, pictures and artwork [subject to (m) below] at its own cost;

(d)   negotiate and be responsible for paying all printing charges for the Official Programme;

(e)   be solely responsible for collecting all funds due for advertisements which appear in the Official Programme, and shall provide EventCo with a copy of all invoices sent to advertisers in relation to advertisements placed in the Official Programme;

(f)   market and sell the Official Programme at no less than [insert number] of locations in and around the Venue during the Event;

(g)   provide sufficient (and sufficiently trained) personnel for the purposes of (f) above, at its own cost;

(h)   be responsible for obtaining any necessary permission to sell the Official Programme at locations outside the Venue;

(i)   be responsible for the distribution of the Official Programmes to the Venue and the locations where the Official Programmes are to be marketed and sold;

(j)   provide a free whole page advertisement on the inside front cover of the Official Programme for the title sponsor of the Event or any other official sponsor designated by EventCo;

(k)   provide one free editorial page of promotional copy for the Event title sponsor or any other official sponsor designated by EventCo;

(l)   provide a free one-half editorial page of promotional copy for each official supplier designated by EventCo;

(m)   provide a free one page editorial of promotional copy for EventCo.]

SCHEDULE 3

THE EVENTCO MARKS

[insert details]

References

Allen, Judy *The Business of Event Planning: Behind-the-Scenes Secrets of Successful Special Events.* Ontario, Canada, John Wiley & Sons Canada Ltd, 2002.

Foster, John S *The Law of Meetings, Conventions and Trade Shows: Selected Articles on Meetings & Liability.* Georgia, USA. John S. Foster, 1990.

Friedmann, Susan *Meeting and Event Planning for Dummies*, Wiley Publishing Inc, 2003.

Graham, Stedman; Goldblatt, Joe Jeff; Delpy, Lisa *The Ultimate Guide to Sport Event Management and Marketing.* USA. McGraw-Hill, 1995.

Goldberg, James M *The Meeting Planner's Legal Handbook.* Washington DC, USA Goldberg & Associates, 1996.

Goldblatt, Dr Joe *Special Events*, John Wiley & Sons, 2002.

Gordon-Davis, Lisa; Cumberledge, Peter *Legal Requirements for South African Students and Practitioners.* Lansdowne, South Africa. Juta & Co. Ltd, 2004.

Health & Safety Executive's *The Event Safety Guide: A Guide to Health, Safety and Welfare at Music and Similar Events.* Norgate, UK. Her Majesty's Stationery Office, 1999.

Lewis, Adam; Taylor, Jonathan *Sport: Law and Practice.* UK. Butterworths LexisNexis, 2003.

Lutzker, Arnold *Copyrights and Trademarks for Media Professionals* (Broadcast and Cable Series), Focal Press.

Macdonald, Iain; Hulme, Amanda *Food Standards Regulation: the New Law*, Jordans, 2000.

Manchester, Colin; Popplestone, Susanna; Allen, Jeremy *Alcohol and Entertainment Licensing Law*, Cavendish Publishing, 2005.

O'Rourke, Raymond *Food Standards and Product Liability* Palladium Law Publications Limited, 2000.

Roysner, Mark *Convention Centre Facilities Contracts: Making Sense of Your Agreements and Current Conventional Wisdom.* TX, USA. International Association for Exhibition Management, 2003.

Sorin, David *The Special Events Advisor: A Business and Legal Guide for Event Professionals.* New Jersey, USA. John Wiley & Sons Inc, 2003.

Tarlow, Peter E *Event Risk Management and Safety.* New York, USA. John Wiley & Sons Inc, New York, 2002.

Verow, Richard; Lawrence, Clive; McCormick, Peter *Sport, Business & The Law.* Bristol, UK. Jordon Publishing Ltd, 1999, and revised (2005)

Index